Torn Between Two Lands:
Armenians in America,
1890 to World War I

Harvard Armenian Texts and Studies, 7

Torn Between Two Lands

Armenians in America, 1890 to World War I

Robert Mirak

Distributed for
The Department of Near Eastern
Languages and Civilizations,
Harvard University
by
Harvard University Press
Cambridge, Massachusetts
1983

Parts of Chapter 4 were previously published as "Armenian Emigration to the United States to 1915 (I): Leaving the Old Country," in *Journal of Armenian Studies*, Autumn, 1975. A shorter form of Chapter 10 appeared as "On New Soil: The Armenian Orthodox and Armenian Protestant Churches in the New World to 1915," in Randall M. Miller and Thomas D. Marzik, eds., *Immigrants and Religion in Urban America* (Philadelphia: Temple University Press, 1977). Both are reprinted with permission.

Photo Credits

First Grouping   *Young Armenian graduate:* Courtesy of Mrs. Parsegh B. Kanlian; *Kharpert:* Melikian Studio; *Village Near Marash:* Armenian Library and Museum of America; *Primary school children:* Courtesy of John Mirak; *Silk mill workers:* Library of Congress; *Foundry laborers:* Armenian Revolutionary Federation; *Bogigian's store:* Courtesy of Dr. Martin Deranian; *Market in Jamaica Plain:* Courtesy of Ruth Thomasian's Project SAVE, donor, Hasmig Aroian; *Varaztad Kazanjian:* Armenian Revolutionary Federation; *Hagop Bogigian:* Courtesy of Dr. Martin Deranian; *William Saroyan:* William Saroyan Foundation; *Stephen P. Mugar:* Courtesy of Mrs. Stephen P. Mugar.

Second Grouping   *Picnickers:* Melikian Studio; *Backgammon players:* Photo World; *Boghos Nubar Pasha:* Armenian Revolutionary Federation; *Diocesan Assembly:* Courtesy of Dr. Martin Deranian; *Rev. Bedikian:* Courtesy of Ruth Thomasian's Project SAVE, donor, Marie Bedikian; *Karekin Chitjian:* Melikian Studio; *Raffi, E. Agnooni, S. Bartevian, A. Vramian,* and *Armenian fedayees:* Armenian Revolutionary Federation; *Young Armenian Americans training:* Church of Our Saviour, Worcester, Massachusetts; *Gulesian Family, 1892 and 1902:* Courtesy of Ruth Thomasian's Project SAVE, donor, Decran Gulesian.

To
Alice
With Love

Crane

Where do you come from, crane?
I ache to hear your call,
to know you come from home.
Have you any news at all?

I bless your wings, your eyes,
My heart is torn in two.
The exile's soul, all sighs
waiting for bits of news.

— *Excerpt from an Armenian folk song
attributed to Nahabed Kuchag.
Translated by Diana Der Hovanessian.*

Preface

The field of Armenian American history has been largely neglected. The only important study of the community — *The Armenians in America* (Boston, 1919) — was written over sixty years ago by M. Vartan Malcom. The neglect in the field is surprising in view of the extraordinary burst of scholarly activity in Armenian studies over the past two decades, especially in the United States, and in view of the enormous interest in American ethnic history since about 1970. I must share in the responsibility for the neglect. In 1965 I completed a dissertation on the Armenian community in the United States to 1915, and perhaps because of my interest, others assumed that I would soon produce a book on the subject. Since 1965 I have in fact endeavored to complete that book, but the call of other scholarly obligations, and the demands of family and a nonacademic career made me postpone that task more than once. At last the work — a thorough rewriting and expansion of the dissertation — is completed. I hope it fills some of the void in the field of Armenian American history.

In the three and one-half decades before World War I, powerful upheavals destroyed the foundations of Armenian society in the Ottoman Empire. The Russo-Turkish War of 1877–1878, the cholera epidemics and famine of the 1880s, the Hamidean massacres of the mid-1890s, and the ensuing prolonged economic and political crisis spelled the end of the populous Armenian towns and villages of Eastern Anatolia. The systematic massacre and deportation of one million Armenians during World War I completed that devastation.

During the same period Armenian refugees found new homes in the Middle East, the Caucasus, Greece, and Western Europe. By 1920 more than one hundred thousand immigrants had also established an important community in the United States, which in time became the largest Armenian community in the diaspora. The purpose of this work is to examine the origins and development of that community from 1890 to World War I.

Part One of the study surveys the Armenian communities in the Ottoman Empire. After examining the traditional roots and structure of the society, it depicts the explosive historical forces that transformed and then destroyed that society in the course of the late nineteenth and early twentieth centuries. Part Two examines the origins and character of the migration to the United States. Since the movement of the Armenians occurred at the same time as did the great Southern and Eastern European and Middle Eastern migration to the New World, and indeed formed a part of that exodus, attention is paid to the similar and dissimilar features of the movements. The character of the Armenian immigrants' economic, physical, and social adjustments to urban America is discussed in Part Three; their struggle to assist their countrymen against the oppressive regimes in Turkey and Russia makes up Part Four. A concluding section traces the steps by which the community·became acculturated to the New World.

The most important sources for the study were the words of the immigrants themselves, in the columns of the immigrant newspapers. No other documentation so richly revealed the immigrants' thoughts and aspirations and the realities of immigrant life in the United States; the press also reflected the incredible diversity within the community itself. Important, too, was the enormous outpouring of local, state, and federal English language studies of the "immigrant problem," which shed light on virtually all aspects of the immigrants' social and economic adjustments to the new environment. The local press in the larger Armenian communities of Worcester, Massachusetts, and Fresno, California, was also of considerable help. Oral histories and interviews were extremely helpful, even though many of the historical figures were no longer living and the memories of the survivors had grown dim.

A brief note will help explain the system of transliteration used. Modern Armenian has two dialects: Turkish Armenians use a western variant, Russian and Iranian Armenians an eastern one. Since the vast majority of Armenians in the United States trace their roots to Turkey, I have employed the Western Armenian system of transliteration, devised by the Library of Congress. Diacritical marks have been omitted. Place names are those which were in use during the period; thus, Constantinople instead of Istanbul, Smyrna instead of Izmir. In some cases I have used personal and place names which violate even the Western Armenian system of transliteration because a strict adherence to the system would be awkward.

Much of the modern history of the Armenians is highly controversial, especially that of the church and politics. Some readers may feel that I have displayed partisanship or enmity toward one group or another. Others may feel that topics that reflect badly on the Armenian community should have been omitted. However, I have sought throughout to be objective and to tell the truth as I saw it, relying on the Armenian American community to understand that a history which ignores controversial or unattractive topics demeans and debases the past and the achievements of those whose story it is.

A work that has taken so many years to complete obviously rests on the encouragement, good will, and patience of many people. I sincerely thank each one of them.

My chief intellectual debt is to Professor Oscar Handlin, who directed the original dissertation, kept after me to "bring out the book," and was unstinting in his support of its final publication. Like so many others, I was spurred on by the example of his remarkable scholarship and by his insistence on the seriousness and importance of the historian's calling.

I also appreciate the assistance of Robert Thomson, Mashtots Professor of Armenian Studies at Harvard, who read the manuscript and was extremely helpful in having it published. The Department of Near Eastern Languages and Civilizations at Harvard University, under whose auspices the Harvard Armenian Texts and Studies series is produced, and the President and Fellows of Harvard College graciously supported the publication of the work.

Many other individuals helped in many ways. Manoog Young of the National Association for Armenian Studies and Research first suggested the topic. I am particularly obligated to James Tashjian and the late James Mandalian, both of the *Armenian Weekly* and *Armenian Review*, for their stimulating presence and encouragement during my research at the Armenian Revolutionary Federation headquarters in Boston. There, too, Dr. Kevork Donabedian, editor-in-chief of Hairenik Publications, kindly permitted me access to the ARF's priceless manuscripts. In Watertown, Massachusetts, the staff of the Armenian Democratic Liberal Organization kindly allowed me to read *Azk*. The late Vahan Topalian of the Armenian Cultural Foundation in Arlington, Massachusetts, opened the foundation's rich resources to me. In Fresno, California, the late Andre Amourian, editor of *Asbarez*, and George Mason, editor of the *California Courier*, extended courtesies far beyond the usual.

I was also helped by Foster Palmer of Widener Library and Carolyn Jakeman of Harvard University's Houghton Library; by the staffs of the State House Library, Boston; the Watertown and Worcester Public Libraries; the National Archives in Washington, D.C.; the Fresno Public Library; and the University of California Library at Berkeley.

The following individuals critically read sections of the manuscript: Professors Saul Engelbourg and Robert Smart of Boston University; Professor Krikor Maksoudian of Columbia University; and

Dr. Barbara Merguerian, editor of the *Armenian Mirror-Spectator*. Thomas J. Davis, III, senior editor of the Book Club Division of Doubleday, carefully edited much of an early draft. Professor Richard Hovannisian of UCLA kindly permitted me access to his graduate students' manuscript schedules, which were useful for Chapters 4 and 5. Professor Kevork Bardakjian of Harvard University and Hagop Atamian of the Armenian Cultural Foundation assisted me with specific language problems.

The task of editing and preparing the text for production was ably handled by Denise Thompson-Smith. Her keen eye for style, consistency, and accuracy immeasurably improved the work and saved me from countless errors. The map of Armenia was ably prepared by Mardiros Minasian. The photographs for the book were compiled through the generous assistance of the following people: Ruth Thomasian, Director of Project SAVE; Jirair Libaridian, Director, Archives of the Armenian Revolutionary Foundation; Mary Melikian, Melikian Studios, Worcester, Massachusetts; Dr. Martin Deranian; and Rev. Vartan Hartunian of the Armenian Library and Museum of America.

The most important moral support came from my family. My parents, Artemis Yeramian Mirak and John Mirak, whose biographies are part of the story, continue to inspire me by word and by their courage and strength. Jill and Jennifer, our daughters, grew up with the research and writing and cheerfully shared too much time with the book. My greatest debt is to my wife, Alice Kanlian Mirak, who assisted in every phase of the project and whose wise counsel, constant companionship, and unfailing encouragement made the long journey a happy and successful one.

Contents

Illustrations

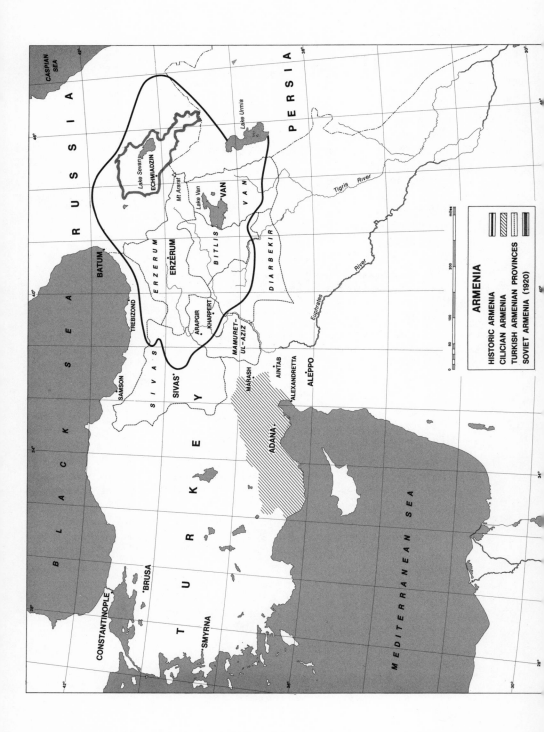

PART ONE

The Old World

1.

Antecedents

Until the early twentieth century Armenian civilization had existed on the Armenian Plateau for two millenia. During much of this long history, the Armenian people had lived in relative security as an ethnic minority within the Ottoman Empire. But in the nineteenth century, the Armenians of Turkey underwent a political, social, and intellectual awakening that introduced them to the main currents of western ideas; their world was shaken by the forces of political reform, modern education, and nationalism.

The cost of this awakening was dear. It ruptured permanently the centuries-old relationship with the Turks that had ensured the survival of the Armenians. Indeed, the new ideas so threatened and infuriated the ruling Turks that between 1894 and World War I they indiscriminately massacred thousands of Armenians, and hundreds of thousands more Armenians fled the atrocities and shattered economy of Turkey for Russia, western Europe, and the United States.

Historic Armenia

Historic Armenia lies in the mountainous northeast corner of Asia Minor. Its center is the Armenian Plateau, a westerly expanse of the Iranian massif. The northern frontier of the upland area is formed by the Pontus Mountains and the Kur and Rioni Rivers; this line separates the territory from both the Black Sea and the Caucasus. On the east, Armenia runs into the Plateau of Azerbaijan and the Caspian Sea. The southern extremity of the country stretches to the Taurus Mountains, which separate it from Kurdistan and the edge of the Mesopotamian Plain; the Euphrates River marks the westernmost reaches of the plateau.

These highlands comprised "Greater Armenia." Then to the west of the Euphrates lay a smaller, lowland region known as "Lesser Armenia." Together the two regions, which lie between 37 and 47.5 degrees east longitude and 37 and 41.5 degrees north latitude, make up an area of between 120,000 and 140,000 square miles.[1] A third

3

region, Cilicia, to the southwest, which was occupied by the Armenians in the medieval period, comprised over 250 miles of Mediterranean littoral from the Gulf of Alexandretta west to the town of Satalia.

All of this land, except Cilicia, is very mountainous, averaging 5,000 feet above sea level. The towering mountain chains cut across the Armenian Plateau in an east-west direction, and the valleys are cut by deep, rapid flowing river courses. Because of the rugged terrain, Armenia was referred to as the "Switzerland of Asia Minor." The winters are long and hard but they are followed by a "brief but very warm summer during which the whole country bursts into life."[2] And the countryside is rich in natural beauty. The plateau is capped by Mt. Ararat (elevation 16,946 feet), the national symbol of the Armenians, and the countryside boasts abundant deep blue lakes. An American visitor described its rich river valleys as being "of unsurpassed fertility, equal, in the natural richness of its soil, to the far-famed prairies of the Mississippi Valley."[3] The mountains were filled with flocks of sheep and cattle and wild fowl, and the soil was rich in iron, copper, bauxite, coal, alum, and sulphur.[4]

Cilicia, on the other hand, in the fertile lowland triangle formed by the Taurus and Amanus ranges, has a near tropical climate, approximating that of the neighboring Syrian plain. It was and is a very richly endowed land producing plentiful harvests of fruits, wines, wheat, and cotton under the hot Mediterranean sun. In the nineteenth century poetic travelers termed Cilicia the "Lombardy of the Turk" after the fertile plain in Northern Italy.

The strategic location of the Armenian Plateau between East and West, as well as its rich agricultural lands and natural resources, rendered the territory prey to its hostile neighbors. The history of the Armenians on the plateau is a chronology of long sieges, subjugation, vassalship and martyrdom interspersed with brief but brilliant periods of political independence and cultural efflorescence.

The origins of the Armenians are still subject to historians' debates, although it is generally agreed that the proto-Armenians, an Indo-European people, appeared in history sometime in the eighth century before Christ as emigrants from Thrace who settled on the plateau, conquered the native population, and gradually assimilated them into their culture.[5] There followed long periods of foreign rule over the Armenians, first by the Medes, then by the Persian Achemenid dynasty, and the Seleucid Greeks following the conquest of Alexander the Great. Then the Armenians, under the Artaxiad dynasty, regained their autonomy for a period of two-hundred years before the birth of Christ. Under the vigorous leadership of King Tigranes II (95–55 B.C.), supremely important in Armenian history, Armenia became a united kingdom "powerful enough to preserve its unity and independence for nearly five hundred years."[6] Under Tigranes II, the Armenian imperium stretched from the Caucasus to the Mediterranean and from the Caspian Sea to Cappadocia.

During the half millenium after the birth of Christ the Armenians forged their distinct cultural identity. Though technically a vassal kingdom in the Roman Empire, the Armenians in this period remained autonomous. In the early fourth century A.D. through the evangelist Gregory, the ecclesiastical hero of Armenia, the nation adopted Christianity (and, according to tradition, before Constantine espoused the religion for the whole Roman Empire). A century later Saints Sahag and Mesrob invented an Armenian alphabet, a development which ushered in the "Golden Age of Armenian literature." The country had inherited the political stability created under Tigranes II, providing the "chrysalis [for] the interaction of religion and language [that] produced the new germ of modern Armenian nationality; and when the chrysalis was rent at last, the nation emerged so strongly grown that it could brave the buffets of the outer world."[7] Thereafter, the Armenian character and consciousness were so deeply infused with the heady mixture of Christianity and the native literature, language, and culture that the Armenian national identity could survive the turbulence of the Middle Eastern arena.

Subjected once again the the fifth century to foreign rule, Armenia successively endured the suzerainty of Persians, Byzantines, and Arabs until the country emerged in 886, under the Bagradit dynasty, as an independent power once again. In this new period of independence, Armenian sculpture, arts, and literature flowered. The brilliant cultural display was capped by the regal, ecclesiastical splendor of the 1,001 churches in the capital of Ani.

But the next half millenium, from the tenth to the fifteenth centuries, was to that point the "most disastrous period in the whole political history" of the people. Early in the eleventh century another new power appeared out of Central Asia. The Seljuk Turks, who, usurping the Muslim mantle of the decaying Arab power, "brutalized and at the same time stimulated the Islamic world"; and Armenia felt the brunt of the conquest.[8] Then, in quick succession, followed invasions of Turkmen and Tatars. These disasters were but a prelude to the invasions of the Mongols and the "barbarities of the bloody Tamerlane who on the eve of the fifteenth century reduced Armenia to one vast charnal-house from Van to Kars."[9] Few nations have ever endured such a sequence of turmoil, massacre, and humiliation.

This succession of foreign invaders, who laid waste the countryside and ruined the economy, forced great numbers of the indigenous population to flee from the Armenian Plateau. Many Armenians "crossed the Anti-Taurus ranges into Asia Minor — 400,000 in one year (1021) alone," and they founded the Cilician Kingdom, which existed more or less independently from 1080 to 1375.[10] At various times other Armenians moved eastward into Persia, or north and west across the Black Sea and the Aegean to the Crimea, Moldavia, Poland, and Italy. Other Armenians found their way to Smyrna and Constantinople, or east to India, China, and the islands of the Pacific and Indian Oceans.[11]

Ironically, it was the rise of yet another warlike horde, the Ottoman Turks, which ended four hundred years of conflict and chaos in the Middle East.[12] In 1453 the Ottoman Turks conquered Constantinople, until then the capital of the Byzantine Empire, and in 1514 their legions drove into the last large unconquered regions of Armenia, thereby reducing the Armenian nation to the status of a Turkish principality.

The Armenian Millet

With the occupation of Constantinople in 1453, Sultan Mehmet II, in accordance with "the centuries-old division of Near Eastern society into religious rather than national and racial units," organized his non-Muslim subjects into separate and virtually autonomous communities called *millets*.[13] Like the communities of the Jews and Orthodox Greeks which were run by their own religious leaders, the Armenian community was entrusted in 1461 to the control of its newly appointed patriarch, the Bishop of Brusa.

It was the patriarch's responsibility to collect the community's annual taxes and to be the community's sole contact with the Turkish government; through him the church, her officers, and co-religionists communicated with the government in case of injustice, to secure a privilege, or to obtain legal rights.[14] The patriarch personally controlled not only religious affairs, but also the direction of such communal matters as education, the administration of hospitals, marriage and baptism, and even the granting of passports for travel in Turkey and abroad. Until 1839 the patriarch had the authority to inflict ecclesiastical and civil penalties on his people, and he maintained a small police force and his own jail at Constantinople. Above all, as sovereign head of the Armenian millet he represented his co-religionists at the Sublime Porte as a recognized official of the Ottoman ruling institution with the rank of vizier.

The establishment of the millet system reflected Ottoman and Koranic precepts in that the Muslim Turk, instead of seeking to amalgamate his own flock with the *rayah* or unwashed infidel (sheep), preferred to keep the conquered segregated. The Turks granted autonomy to their subjects, but they expected the infidels to recognize their own inferiority in Turkish eyes and to pay special tribute to their masters. With the millet system the militaristic Turks also solved the vexing administrative problems of governing the empire's populous and heterogeneous communities.[15] But for subject peoples, the millet system ensured religious and national homogeneity, the Armenians in Turkey were protected from intermarriage, conversion, and assimilation, and the Armenian church's historic role as the foremost aspect of Armenian nationality was fortified.

Socially, the "unclean" rayahs were viewed with "inexpressible contempt" by Turks of all ranks — from the Imperial Divan to the lowliest peasant.[16] In general, the Ottomans regarded contact with the infidel as a "sort of defilement," The Turkish Armenians were prohibited from ringing the bells in their churches, except for one stroke to be sounded as a call to prayer, and Armenian testimony was frequently rejected in Turkish courts. Armenians were raped and there were sudden conversions on occasion. Sporadic pogroms against the wealthy Armenians were common. Thus the condition of the Armenians in Turkey closely resembled that "of the Jews in the Christian states of Europe" during the same centuries.[17]

Yet, on the broad political level, the Armenians lived in relative tranquility and security in Turkey until the nineteenth century. The Ottoman conquest itself brought peace and order to the centuries-old turmoil of the Armenian Plateau. Ottoman armies guarded the frontiers from attack. Abdolonyme Ubicini, the distinguished Italian traveler of the mid-nineteenth century, remarked of the Armenians in the Ottoman Empire:

Peaceable, industrious, and contented, connected by interest with the Turks, whose language, costume, and habits they adopted without sacrificing their faith — losing more and more all memory of their former country — they might have appeared almost unconscious of their own national existence, had they not been from time to time roused from their lethargy ... by convulsions arising from the rivalry of parties or the violence of persecutions.[18]

2.

In the Nineteenth-Century Ottoman Empire

Concentrated in the cities of Western Turkey, especially Constantinople, and in the provinces of eastern Anatolia, the Armenians comprised the largest non-Muslim minority in Turkey in the nineteenth century. They were vital cogs in the Ottoman economy and bureaucracy. Physically, their upper classes, both lay and clerical, lived relatively well; the Armenians artisans made a living; but even in the nineteenth century "Armenian peasants lived as most of the peasants of Europe during the Middle Ages — slightly better than their domestic animals" — under the pall of the Ottoman cloak.[1]

Constantinople and the West

Finance. For the Armenians in Turkey, the city of Constantinople was the political, social, and economic hub of their world. No one knows exactly how many Armenians there were in Constantinople, but Ubicini in the mid-nineteenth century estimated 205,000. Certainly they were the largest and most important non-Muslim minority in the city, far outstripping the Greeks (132,000), and the Jews (37,000).[2] At the head of the community were the *amiras* (bankers and moneylenders), whose great power resided in their financial usefulness to the Sublime Porte. For example, well-placed Turks who coveted high governmental posts like pashaliks, but who lacked the cash to bribe their way to power, in the corruption-ridden empire of the eighteenth and nineteenth centuries, often borrowed funds from Armenian moneylenders. Thereafter, the Turks became the amiras' mortgagees and because of the large debts, lived in virtual financial bondage to them. In addition to their usefulness as moneylenders to improvident pashas, the amiras were important even to the sultans themselves. For, the sultans regarded the rich Armenians' wealth "with no unfriendly eye, as their riches are not squandered by extravagant habits, nor expended in rebellious enterprises, but remain carefully hoarded in their coffers till some pretext or some necessity brings it into the *Miri* (treasury)."[3]

The amira class constituted an oligarchy in Armenian society, and they exercised power even over the extremely powerful patriarch. Although initially an independent entity, the patriarchate during the seventeenth century had come to be controlled by a moneyed aristocracy, who bought the office for favorites and manipulated the affairs of the community to advance their own interests. Scandals over elections to the patriarch's chair were extremely common: during a fifty-year period in the seventeenth century, fourteen persons were made patriarch, one of whom was elected and deposed nine times. The sordid and debased character of election to the highest religious and political office in the Armenian community now copied Ottoman government practice, for if rival candidates were proposed, cash made the choice: "the highest office of a Christian church is virtually set up at auction, a moslem holds the hammer, and takes the offer of the highest bidder."[4] There was little protest against the buying and selling of the office of patriarch. Quite the contrary: "All the influential and more wealthy part of the Christian population, as the Bishops, *Vartabeds* (Doctors of Divinity), bankers, merchants, land-holders, are combined with the Turks to uphold the system. By it they also get their gains, and oppress the poor."[5]

Still, these corrupt but rich aristocrats were admired. To be an amira was the highest ambition of the humble folk of the interior. A passage in the nineteenth-century travel literature describes provincial Armenian migrants en route to the Imperial City: "Thousands, which migrate every year voluntarily from their native mountains . . . practice for years the humble occupation as porters and water-carriers; but almost invariably do they . . . , or . . . their children, work . . . into trade; beginning with the . . . grade of mechanic, ascending gradually to that of merchant, and finally, the more able or fortunate, reaching that of banker, the acme of their ambition."[6]

Commerce and the Professions. Although everyone wanted to be a banker, the amira class could be only a small segment of the Armenian community of Constantinople. In addition there were numerous professional people, businessmen, and government officials, some of whom rendered valuable service to the sultans themselves. For example, Casas Aratoon headed the imperial mint.[7] Harutiun Bezjian (1771–1834), son of an emigrant from Kars, with a rudimentary education from the patriarchal academy in Constantinople, "by dint of personal worth and native talent and with the help of the Duzians whom he first served and later (1819) succeeded in the imperial mint, . . . climbed up in the social and civic scale until he attained to the highest place ever given by an Ottoman ruler to one of Christian birth."[8] Mahmud II commissioned the architect Kri-

kor Balyantz to design several palaces and the Selimi garrison. In the
late nineteenth century Sultan Abdul Hamid II employed Portukalian
Pasha, an extremely influential, able, and learned Armenian as his
personal treasurer and in the foreign office of the Sublime Porte.
Another key figure of the mid-nineteenth century was Gabriel Nora-
dounghian — scholar, lawyer, and diplomat — who served the sultan's grand vizier.[9]

The merchants of Constantinople were known as great travelers,
and "almost every important fair or mart, from Leipsic and London
to Bombay and Calcutta, is visited by them."[10] In the late eighteenth
and early nineteenth centuries they extended their influence when
European goods began to penetrate Turkey's markets on a large scale;
by the time of the Crimean War, the markets were flooded with cheap
European goods. A native Armenian middle class of buyers, agents,
importers, distributors, and the financial and commercial representatives of foreign interests grew up.[11] Business matters were shunned
by the Muslim Turks, and the Greeks and Armenians seized the
opportunity to grow rich.[12]

Crafts and Labor.   Armenian craftsmen in Constantinople were
divided into *esnafs* (corporations) according to their trades — architects, goldsmiths, watchmakers, locksmiths, painters, silkweavers,
tanners, and the like. The degree of Armenian control in these fields
was considerable, as the skilled trades were conducted primarily in
Armenian quarters by Armenian workmen. The Armenians who
emigrated to the Imperial City in the sixteenth century from other
cities in Anatolia such as Sivas, Angora, and Konia, tended to be
either tradesmen or artisans and lesser workmen. Well before the
middle of the eighteenth century, carpentry, blacksmithing, tailoring,
and work in iron and gold had fallen into the hands of Armenians.
They held the bakery contracts for the government, and "a large
proportion of the employees in the luxurious establishments of
Turkish pashas were Armenians."[13] In the nineteenth-century city,
the printers, restauranteurs, and the fine craftsmen were mainly
Armenian.

On the lowest rungs of the Armenian social structure were the
day laborers, who were in fact part of an urban proletariat. The
number of these *hamals* (porters), navvies, water carriers, and peddlers is not known, but the estimates vary from 16,000 (Ubicini) to
80,000 (Lynch).[14] Towns of the interior like Chemisgazak sent all
their men to Constantinople, at least temporarily, as hamals.[15] Hamals spent from three to ten years at a time in back-breaking work.
Then they would return with full purses to the provinces for a few
years, only to go back to the ports for another period of migrant labor
when the money ran out. Although the pressure of a large labor

supply made the jobs pay badly, the Armenian hamals were always welcome for their physical strength, diligence, and honesty. Even the lowliest Armenian labor was indispensable to the Turkish economy.

Other cities of western Turkey — Smyrna and Brusa, for example — and the Black Sea towns of Samson and Trebizond, as well as interior towns such as Angora and Caesaria, were centers of Armenian employment just like Constantinople but on a smaller scale. Smyrna was the empire's second most important commercial center, with an Armenian population in the nineteenth century estimated between 17,000 and 50,000.[16] The prominence of Smyrna's Armenians in the nineteenth century appeared "in their dress, in the elegance of their houses, in splendid churches, in public charities, and schools."[17] On a slightly smaller scale Brusa, to the east of Constantinople, on the rail line to Angora, boasted a late nineteenth-century population of 60,000 of whom the Armenians composed one-sixth.[18]

Armenian dominance in banking, commerce, and the crafts meant that the influence of the Armenians in the Western Turkish economy was thus out of all proportion to their relatively limited numbers. Indeed, the presence of the 250,000 Armenians in Western Turkey helped protect their vastly more numerous compatriots in the Turkish interior. Constantinople, which was the seat of the Armenian patriarchate, and after 1860 the seat of the Armenian National Assembly as well, was the political, economic, and social linchpin of Armenian life in the Ottoman Empire.

Towns in the Provinces and Cilicia

Yet if only one in eight of the empire's Armenians lived in Constantinople and the western urban centers — where were the Armenian people to be found? All nineteenth-century authorities concur that the bulk of the population lay in the eastern provinces of Van, Erzerum, Sivas, Bitlis, Diarbekir, and Mamuret-ul-Aziz, and in the southern provinces of Adana and Aleppo. Population figures varied. Ubicini, writing in the 1840s, estimated that 2,000,000 Armenians dwelled in Asiatic Turkey, 83 percent of the total of 2,400,000.[19] Half a century later, Kevork Mesrob estimated the empire's Armenian population at 2,660,000 of whom 2,000,000 (75 per cent) were in the interior.[20]

Although they were relatively more numerous in the interior so-called Armenian provinces, Armenians were not the majority population even here. The centuries of Asiatic invasions had decimated the Armenian population and hundreds of thousands had fled to Cilicia or to the Mediterranean, Russia, and Eastern Europe. Then, the lands formerly occupied by the Armenians were colonized by the Seljuk and Ottoman Turks and by Muslim Kurdish tribesmen from the southeast who, some said, were deliberately encouraged by the Ottoman regime to settle in Armenia in order to dilute the indigenous Christian population.[21] So by the nineteenth-century, in the plateau which bore their name the Armenians were no more than a substantial minority.

The Economic and Bureaucratic Structure. The economy of the provinces in the nineteenth century was backward, archaic, and circumscribed. Had the Turkish government encouraged the production of economic goods, or had it neglected to disrupt life, or even if it had supplied elementary security and transportation for the region, Turkish Armenia would have been the garden of the Middle East. Though the area was mountainous, the combination of rich alluvial valleys, the abundant resources of coal, salt, sulphur, iron, alum, and copper, along with the hardworking Armenian population, gave interior Turkey important advantages over neighboring areas. But there was widespread corruption in the imperial government, and the sultans were desultory in subduing the nomadic Kurds; both factors made economic progress very difficult.

Within the provinces, and despite their small numbers, the provincial Armenians, as in the West, constituted a most important productive force in the economic and bureaucratic life of the provinces. Certainly the ethnic distribution of merchants indicates that they controlled commerce in Kharpert, Marsovan, and other centers.[22]

	Armenian merchants	Turkish merchants	Other merchants
Marsovan	111	23	4
Kharpert	50	2	0

Furthermore, in the town of Arapgir, the manufacture of striped cotton goods, which employed from 500 to 600 families working from their homes, was controlled by 8 to 10 rich Armenians.[23] In fact, one survey of the entire Armenian Plateau stated that

through hard work, thrift, native intelligence, and a cultural level generally higher than that of the Turks, they [the Armenians] had become a prosperous and important community. In the eastern vilayets (provinces) they were the predominant economic force. In these vilayets more than half of all the merchants (58 percent), physicians and pharmacists (60 percent), and three-quarters of all persons engaged in mining (75 percent) were Armenians. In the same vilayets the Turks accounted for only one quarter of all merchants, doctors, and so on.[24]

Armenian merchants were responsible for the few attempts at large scale economic production in the Turkish interior. By the 1880s, Krikor Fabricatorian, who had traveled to Damascus, Aleppo, and Lyon, France, to learn about the production of woven goods, imported European machinery in Kharpert, where he started a textile factory. At the same time, the Paragian family, in the neighboring village of Husenig, returned from the United States with lathes and other machines for a newly established foundry. And in Sivas, Armenians laid the foundation for a very successful native rug manufacturing industry.[25]

Yet, during this period, Armenians who attempted to import modern tools and equipment were looked upon with suspicion. One family in Aintab which imported harnesses and plows from the West were driven from their equipment by local Turks frightened by the new machines, and when the equipment was destroyed or stolen, the Turkish government did nothing. Modern coal mining operations around Erzerum were halted because of the Turks' resistance to industrial development. Often Armenian industry and initiative were thwarted by Turkish suspicions or bribes, or as one European expert concluded, native manufacturing and commerce was "killed by the ignorance and stupidity of the Turkish Government."[26]

Though fewer in number than the business people, Armenian civil servants were significant in turning the wheels of the Turkish provincial government. Their heightened participation came about because the Ottoman government had decreed greater equality for the empire's non-Muslim minorities in recent laws (Hatti-Sherif, 1839, reaffirmed in the Hatti-Humayum, 1856), and because the government reorganized the provincial administrative structure in 1864, thus requiring a larger number of public officials. The chart below shows the Turkish bureaus or departments staffed by Armenians.[27]

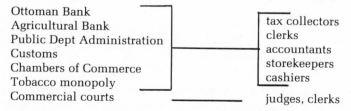

Ottoman Bank
Agricultural Bank
Public Dept Administration
Customs   tax collectors
Chambers of Commerce   clerks
Tobacco monopoly   accountants
                                 storekeepers
                                 cashiers
Commercial courts   judges, clerks

For political reasons, the lowest percentages of Armenians holding responsible governmental posts occurred in the province of Erzerum, near the Russian frontier, where the Turks were very sensitive about security, while the highest percentage of participation was in the south, especially in Diarbekir, which was "politically safe."[28]

At a significantly lower level in the social and economic hierarchy than that of the bureaucrats and business people were the large
numbers of Armenian artisans and laborers who had dominated the
manufacture in the provinces at least since the seventeenth century.[29]
The Armenian-dominated trades in Kharpert and Marash were typical examples of their important roles:[30]

Baking	Fulling	Saddling
Carpentry	Furniture making	Shoemaking
Coppersmithing	Goldsmithing	Soapmaking
Cottonweaving	Masonry	Stonecutting
Dyeing	Milling	Tailoring
Feltmaking	Pottery	Weaving

The Armenians were so vital in this area that in Erzerum, a missionary reported that during the Russo-Turkish War of 1828, "the emigration of the Christians [Armenians] who were its mechanics and
tradesmen, had almost entirely stopped all local business."[31]

These small tradesmen, who usually worked in a shop below
their dwellings, were not prosperous except by the standards of rural
Turkey; contemporary Westerners considered them on the edge of
poverty. Lynch, the nineteenth-century British traveler, lumped
Armenians with Turks in noting that the poor economy of the country
as a whole necessarily limited the native industries.[32] And a missionary lamented: "What compensation do men obtain for their services in . . . manual labor? From twenty-five to fifty dollars a year!
. . . And with this pittance he must support not only himself, but his
family. . . ."[33]

After the Crimean War when the empire tried in vain to mod-
ernize its military forces, the Ottoman rulers granted trading conces-
sions to the European powers in return for badly needed capital. The
growing volume of imported English textiles, French silks, hard-
wares, and the like brought about a calamitous disruption in the
hand labor of many interior towns in Turkey and inflicted hardship
on their people. One commentator noted that even the famous Brusa
("Turkish") towels were being imitated in Europe and sold much
cheaper on being brought back to Turkey, and that combs, cutlery,
and silks from Sheffield, Manchester, and Lyons were causing havoc
for the local handicraft manufactures.[34] Thus, the provincial poverty
of the first half of the century was worsened in the second half by
indiscriminate importing.

By western standards, life for this poorer class was unenviable
even in normal times, and many of the larger towns and provincial
capitals were regarded with distaste by tourists. Even the city of
Erzerum, which boasted one of the finest school systems in the whole

Turkish interior, was cited by an English journalist as having low, ugly houses crowded together and dogs abounding in the streets. And he lamented that, except for the wealthy, the natives lived with their "horses, cattle, sheep, and poultry, . . . so the atmosphere inside an Armenian house is simply indescribable."[35] Since modern sanitation was lacking everywhere, there were frequent epidemics of small pox and typhus, and a fearfully high mortality rate. "It is not uncommon for a man to have had a . . . dozen children, but it would be . . . remarkable . . . if he had not lost from six to ten of them."[36] It was therefore understandable that most travelers who crossed from Turkish to Russian territory in the nineteenth century remarked with relief that the transition was "a rapid change from barbarism to civilisation."[37]

The Peasantry

Like the small tradesmen of the provincial towns, the Armenian farmers were extremely poor, and this peasant class formed the majority of the Armenian population. According to Mesrob, 85 percent of the Armenians of the provinces, or 1,000,000 persons, were villagers.[38] Marcel Leart, the distinguished nineteenth-century French demographer, reckoned that the heaviest concentrations of Armenian peasants were in the easternmost provinces of Van and Bitlis.[39] Similarly, in the Cilician provinces of Adana and Aleppo most of the Armenians were peasants.

Husbandry. Like their counterparts in the towns, the Armenian husbandmen were highly esteemed for their industry and thrift. An American consul in the nineteenth century termed them "sober, hardworking, and frugal," and Ubicini commented that they were more "advanced in agriculture than the Musulmans."[40] Indeed, with government assistance, the Armenian peasantry might have turned the marvelously rich provinces into a productive oasis. But the government neglected and exploited its indigenous rural populations, both Christian and Muslim, with the result that farming was backward and primitive. On the Armenian Plateau, the peasants knew nothing of artificial fertilizers or modern machinery and tools. In the customary method of breaking up new ground, "a wooden plow is used, . . . Each furrow is turned so slowly that the amount turned per day would not equal a few hours' plowing with an up-to-date plow and a strong team of horses. . . ."[41] This backwardness made farm work so very difficult that very little land was cultivated at all.

The lack of transportation and communication also caused land to lie fallow. Even in the nineteenth century the chief means of transport were the camel and the horse- or mule-drawn wagon, traveling in heavily armed caravans. Because of the cost of protection, transportation was so expensive and difficult that it was uneconomical to ship goods any great distance. The 205-mile trip from Erzerum to Trebizond, on the Black Sea, required 12 to 15 days, and as a result native grain shipped over the route was bound to be prohibitively expensive on European markets. (A British official remarked that a railroad connecting Kharpert, Sivas, and Diarbekir to Samson on the Black Sea would have developed a "second Odessa," — a rich port like the famous Russian city near the Crimea. Yet, as late as 1914, when the narrow guage railroad had made inroads into Western Turkey and Syria, there was still no rail transport in the provinces.[42])

Kurdish Predators. In spite of all their other hardships, the heaviest yoke borne by the Armenians of the plateau was imposed by the Kurds. This fierce, ruthless, and wild mountain people entered the plateau in the fifteenth or sixteenth century to fill the vacuum left when the sedentary Armenian population fled earlier Asiatic invaders. By the nineteenth century there were sharp differences between the two cultures — the Armenians were sedentary farmers and the Kurds were nomadic mountain dwellers. Moreover, the antagonisms between the two peoples were exacerbated by the Kurds being nominal Muslims who looked down upon the Christians and felt "perfectly justified in exploiting them."[43]

In the early nineteenth century, Turkish reformers took steps to curb the power of the Kurdish beys — who were most powerful in the provinces of Bitlis, Van, and Erzerum — and attempts were made to settle their nomadic followers in villages. By 1853, a missionary reported that "most of the Koordish tribes were conquered; and their beys were seized and sent into exile, their fire-arms having been taken from them." The missionary added, however, that the Kurds were "exceedingly restive," and he lamented that they were obliged to work at "cultivating the earth."[44] For political and military reasons, however, the Turks found it increasingly difficult to control the Kurds, and the Turkish *valis* (governors) allowed the Kurds to exploit the Armenians. Kurdish outrages against Armenian settlements became commonplace. James Bryce, the distinguished English diplomat and historian, noted that there were "instances of murder, robbery, and plunder [which] reach my ears almost daily. . . . The police are few and unorganized . . . [but] a sort of traditional awe still surrounds the government in the eyes of all but the Kurds, who are practically independent and wander about as far west as Sivas, plundering and murdering to their hearts' content."[45]

In addition, throughout the nineteenth century, the Ottoman government sanctioned Kurdish depredations of Armenian villagers through the *kishlak* (right to quarter). In return for taxes to the government, the nomadic Muslim Kurds were permitted by the author-ities to fall upon unarmed villagers and demand winter quarters, for sometimes up to six months, for themselves and their animals. Con-ditions under the system grew intolerable for the Armenians. Because it was lucrative for the government, however, the authorities did not "interfere when Kurds molested and mistreated and even murdered the Armenians."[46]

Because the Ottomans prohibited Armenians from possessing firearms, they in effect encouraged the Kurds to attack the Christians. "This question of the possession of arms is vital in a country like Asiatic Turkey," for "without a rifle, you are as a woman."[47] Only in the mountainous regions of Dersim and Sasun were the Armenians able to keep their weapons and hold their own against the Kurds. Dersim, south of Kharpert, was a "no-man's land of winding valleys and tiny upland plateaus," populated by rugged Armenian moun-taineers, and the Sasunlis had long been known for their independ-ence and ferocity against both Kurdish and Turkish enemies.

Taxation. The final affliction visited on the harassed Armenian peasantry was taxation, most onerous in the form of the hated tithe. Traditionally a heavy 10 percent, this tax on agricultural produce was sometimes raised to 12, 15, or even 18 percent.[48] Furthermore, the form of tax collection was as oppressive as the taxes themselves. The Porte, from time immemorial, had used the *ultizam* system of tax farming — auctioning the right to collect taxes to the highest bidder. Before the harvest, wealthy Armenian and Turkish notables would bid for the right to collect taxes and, once in the provinces, the tax farmer or his agents often collected from the hapless peasants far more than the amount due to the government. In Adana, for example, the Armenians were even more oppressed by their own tax collectors than by the Turkish governor, for the Armenian chiefs would pocket three piastres for themselves each time they collected one for the governor. Or, if a peasant raised 200 bushels of wheat, the tax gatherer would declare that there were 250 bushels, and the tax on the extra 50 bushels would go into his own pocket.[49]

Associated with tax farming was a hospitality tax, which obliged villagers to feed and house the hordes of tax-collecting officials and soldiers as well as their animals.[50] And finally, there was an annual military exemption tax (the *bedel*) levied by the Turkish government on the Christian Armenian minority. An individual often paid the bedel from birth to death.

In the worst plight were the Armenian tenant farmers or share-croppers. For example the Armenian peasantry of the Charsanjak region of the province of Mamuret-ul-Aziz who leased land from Armenian, Turkish, and Kurdish landlords paid one-half of their

crops annually to the landowners as rent, and in addition they paid
20 percent to others, including the church, as a convent tax. As a
result many tenant farmers and sharecroppers were chronically in
debt to moneylenders to pay taxes or rent, or to buy seed. The most
desperate tenants paid 8 percent interest permonth on loans.[51]

Hunger and Disease. Life for the Armenian peasants, then,
especially in the provinces with large Kurdish populations, was
backward, gaunt, and necessitous. Across the mountains from Sivas
to Van, the Armenian tillers of the soil inhabited rude one-story
buildings. The family and the cattle shared the same quarters in the
winter, and everyone slept on dirt floors. Even in bountiful times,
the poorer peasants subsisted on a meagre diet of millet, lamb, and
goat's milk. Said one Yankee traveler, the "very paupers [of America]
live better than the respectable farmers of Armenia."[52] And when
famine, crop failure, and locusts were added to the grinding taxes,
many peasants went to bed hungry. People subsisted whole days "on
cucumbers because they cannot procure a sufficiency of bread."[53]

Indeed, famine was a frequent visitor to Central Turkey. During
the tragic famine of the mid-1870s, emaciated villagers with blackened skin were said to have died in the streets of Yozgat "crying
piteously for something to appease the raging of terrible hunger."[54]
A "fearful famine" came in 1887, along with drought and locusts.
There was a severe famine near Marash and Adana in 1888 and in
Eastern Turkey as well. Disease was an ever present threat in these
wretched circumstances. There were outbreaks of cholera in the
Armenian provinces after 1887, and at "almost every point" in Central Turkey in 1890. The scourge moved to Bitlis in 1891, to Aintab
in 1892, to Trebizond, Erzerum, and Van in 1893, and it was found in
Trebizond and throughout Eastern Turkey in 1894.[55] The bitter cry
of all the provinces was of "poverty, *poverty*, misrule, and hunger."[56]

How did the Armenians endure their tragic circumstances?
Many resorted to Armenian or Turkish moneylenders and usurers
and prayed for good harvests the following season. Others more
adventurous, and perhaps more realistic, sought to relieve their poverty by migrating to the coastal ports — to Constantinople, Smyrna,
or Batum — an immemorial custom among the male Armenians in
Eastern Turkey.[57] But many Armenians were rooted to the soil by the
unending chain of poverty, misrule, and hopelessness. Even though
they were ambitious and hardworking, these Armenians were caught
in the vicious cycle of depredations and tax exactions. Lynch wrote
of the small Armenian village of Sach, near Van, where the natives
subsisted on cakes of millet seed and had little corn or barley despite
their being surrounded by fertile soil: "When I upbraided them with
their indolence, I received the answer that their labour was useless

so long as the peasant was not permitted to enjoy the fruits of his toil."[58]

The Religious Culture

The Armenian people, once known for their rugged independence, were reduced by the Ottoman conquest and rule to helpless servility. Why did they continue to accept defeat over the centuries? "They are charged," wrote the famous historian, William Ramsay, "by the voice of almost every traveler, with timidity and even with cowardice; but for centuries they had the choice offered them between submission and death."[59] The great Russian-Armenian writer Hagop Melik-Hagopian ("Raffi") speculated about the lack of vigorous action in Armenia during the Russo-Turkish War of 1877–1878. He was outraged when his fellow Armenians in Turkey failed to react to the sufferings of their kinsmen in the border villages between Russia and Turkey; and he bewailed their supine willingness to endure the repeated outrages inflicted on them by Kurds and Turks alike. Trying to understand the Armenians, Raffi noted that they were without the protection of the law or the sword, and they waited with "hebraic patience" during the atrocities. But in addition, Raffi thought that the Armenian typically believed he must be "subservient in the face of tyranny, and allow them [Turks and Kurds] to rob him, in order to remain alive." According to Raffi, the traditional Armenian believed that his present plight and the oppression he suffered were not caused by Turkish misrule but were the punishment of God on the Armenians for their transgressions against Him: "God has given a sword to the Turk and the Kurd in order that he might rob the Armenians, . . . and it is for the people's sin that the Almighty punishes them."[60]

Indeed this feeling of self-contempt did exist, and it was deeply engrained. Probably their stoic acceptance of oppression went back to the time for the first invasions and depredations against the Christian Armenians. As John the Catholicos wrote in the tenth century:

Who can foretell our future?
Spare me the attempt
We are like a harvest reaped by bad husbandmen
Amidst encircling gloom and cloud.[61]

But if their religion encouraged them to accept oppression silently, the Christianity of the Armenians was also the major anchor of their pride in themselves, and it was a vital aspect of their culture in Turkey. Missionaries were astonished that the Armenians had clung to their church over the centuries despite "pecuniary oppressions, civil disabilities, and systematic contempt."[62] Although the Armenian people were neither theologically oriented nor particularly devout, their church was an immovable symbol of their existence as a people and nation; the church represented an historic compact between the institution and its flock. A modern theologian remarked that even if the younger generation were less inclined to follow the guidance of their clergy, no one considered breaking "the covenant which the nation has entered into with the Church." The Armenian who might lose his formal faith never ceased to be loyal to the Church. He instinctively felt that if the church "becomes undermined, all will crumble."[63] (The Armenian Church maintained that a communicant who left the Church to join the Protestant or Catholic faith had renounced his historic nationality.)

The Church was also entrusted with the nation's education, chiefly through monastic institutions, which under the stifling Ottoman influence had badly lapsed from their previous important role. The clergy used the hoary classical language, *Krapar*, and not the vernacular, *Ashkharapar*, along with methods which were centuries behind those of the West. Until the mid-nineteenth century, the provincial Armenians lived in illiteracy except where boys were taught by half-educated priests, or learned a few rudiments of writing and reading from the master of their trade. Education for females was forbidden.

Despite the Church's educational backwardness, the day-to-day existence of the Armenians was shaped by its rituals, commandments, and precepts. The Armenian peasant considered the act of seeding as a form of religious observance. "He distributes the seeds on four sides in the form of a cross: one handful for God, another for the poor, the third for the birds, and the fourth for himself."[64] Religious festivals were an indelible part of provincial life, as Armenians expressed joy or sought solace in the celebration of the hundred saints' days, fast days, and special celebrations of Christmas and Easter. Easter Week was the high point of religious observance, and the women in the towns and villages spent weeks preparing feasts for houses full of guests. "Easter in Trebizond! What a holiday that was! The schools closed for two weeks, and there was goodness and happiness on the faces of people as they prepared to rejoice in the resurrection of Christ." Holy Week was the busiest week of the year. The festival began on Maunday Thursday or before, and on Saturday "we went home and had our traditional meal of fish, with colored eggs and paschal cake."[65] Armenians faithfully observed saints' days, and they were particularly careful of the rites connected with St. Sahag and St. Mesrob, and St. Gregory the Illuminator, and the days devoted to the Mother of God.[66]

It was as part of their adherence to Christianity that the Turkish Armenians followed the solemn injunctions to be charitable in caring for their own. Fearing the spectacle of their compatriots begging from strangers, the Armenians had for centuries maintained quarters for the elderly and orphaned connected with their homes and churches. For proud Armenians, begging or idleness were unforgiveable sins. "My parents taught me that begging is an evil thing," said one young Armenian victim of a pogrom, and he said that even in the most anguished times, "I should try to earn my bread with the labor of my own hands."[67]

Religious pilgrimages, especially to the holy places in Jerusalem and to Echmiadzin in Russia were considered supreme acts of devotion. The pilgrimage was called "doing haji," and it was an article of faith that every Armenian at least once during his lifetime should attempt to "perform the sacred duty of visiting the dominical sanctuaries" at Jerusalem, and "of atoning there for his sins." Furthermore, it was believed that a pilgrim who died in the Holy City itself "would be assured of inheriting eternal life." Before the pilgrim returned, he tatooed a cross on the skin of his wrist, thereby attesting for the rest of his life that he had seen the Holy City.[68]

3.

The Armenian Awakening

In the half century after 1860 the traditional society of the Armenians was transformed and then destroyed. An intellectual and social renaissance, brought to Turkey by westernized intellectuals and American missionaries, began the transformation. Part of the much broader impact of westernization on the long slumbering societies of the Middle East, the movement included the founding of schools, hospitals, self-help organizations, presses, libraries and colleges. The political awakening, stirred by Ottoman reformist elements and Armenian liberals in Constantinople, included the adoption of a separate Armenian constitution in 1860 which greatly broadened the base of political power in the Armenian millet.

The rebirth brought to thousands of Armenians the rudiments of modern secular education, giving them a considerable advantage over other Middle Eastern groups. The new outlook opened opportunities to long-stifled youth to emigrate to and study in the West, especially in the New World. The reform assisted Armenian self-organizational efforts in political, social, and cultural life, and it finally stirred their long dormant sense of national self-consciousness. The impact of the West broke the chains of poverty, misrule, and degradation which had bound many to a backward level of existence. And the effects of this awakening were felt by Armenians as far away from Turkey as America.

The sacrifices incurred by the national revival were costly, for the political and intellectual yearnings of the Armenians and their attempt to create a national state in Eastern Turkey undermined the centuries-old relationship with the Turkish government which had assured their survival. The Turks cynically exploited the self-assertions of the Armenians, and in 1894–1896, 1904, and 1909 hundreds of thousands paid the high price of forced exile, economic ruin, and sudden death for their resistance to Ottoman rule.

Stage One: Revivalism and Reform

The Missionaries and Education. The first stage of the awakening began in the middle decades of the nineteenth century when Protestant American missionaries initiated far reaching religious and educational changes in the Armenian provinces in Turkey.[1]

The Protestant mission to the Armenians began in 1831. Prior to that the American Board of Commissioners for Foreign Missions had sought to propagate Christianity among the Muslim Turks, but found that very dangerous to do. Also the missionaries believed that the "corrupt" Christianity of the Eastern churches, especially the Armenian Church — "wholly given to superstitution and to idolatrous worship of saints" — was the "chief obstacle" to spreading the gospel among the heathen.[2] Thus, the Protestants wanted to "reform" the Armenian Church and thereby furnish to the Turks a living example of "pure Christianity."[3]

The early years of the mission were checkered. Although the evangelicals resolved "not to subvert ... not to pull down," they quickly criticized the ancient Armenian rites as no more than "scriptural perversion" and "external ceremonies" (the Armenian clergy were termed "hirelings" and their behavior was called "immoral or vicious)."[4] Resenting the intrusive and unwanted criticism of the Americans, the Apostolic clergy thwarted the missionaries' attempts to establish schools and had their native helpers thrown into the patriarchal jail and their native helpers thrown into the patriarchal jail and then exiled from the capital.[5]

Because of the death of the sultan who sanctioned the persecutions and because of foreign problems which diverted the Turks' attention, tensions eased, and this permitted missionaries to expand their preaching and publishing activities. Missionary scripture reprints in Armenian and Armeno-Turkish, published in Smyrna, reached a distribution level of over 6,000,000 pages annually, and missionaries extended their preaching efforts into the interior, along the Black Sea, and along the Mediterranean.[6]

In the mid-1840s, however, amid growing missionary strength and the flowering of doctrinal differences, the Armenian patriarch began systematic persecution of his Protestant foes. Armenian converts to Protestantism were forced to recant their new affiliations or else face excommunication. A bull of 1846 included economic sanctions, such that "whosoever has a son that is such a one [Protestant] ... and gives him bread, or assists him in making money ... let such persons know that they are nourishing a venomous serpent. . . . Such persons give bread to Judas ... and are destroyers of the holy orthodox Armenian church, and a disgrace to the whole nation."[7] As a result of the decree, men were driven from their homes and were refused shelter or food; even the dead were denied a place for burial.[8]

The reaction came in early 1847, when the Ottoman authorities, prompted by English pressures, eased the Patriarch's sanctions on the dissenters and forced him to recant his anathema, declaring that religion was free in Turkey. Then in November 1847 an imperial decree, stimulated by strong English influence at the Porte, recognized the Protestants in Turkey as a separate religious community (millet) with freedom of conscience and worship.[9]

From 1850 to World War I, Protestant missionary work rapidly expanded. In 1860, the mission field was so large that it was subdivided into three separate missions: Western Turkey, Central Turkey, and Eastern Turkey. All this was the prelude to a truly massive educational and religious movement, for by 1908, after two generations' effort, the American Board reported the following achievements: Twenty stations and 269 outstations employed 195 missionaries and their wives and 852 teachers. There were 130 organized churches with 15,748 communicants and 41,802 "adherents," along with 5 theological schools, 49 colleges, and many boarding and high schools with 4,600 students — an impressive enterprise by any reckoning.[10]

Still, the Protestants formed a separate community; it took them two generations to build up their schools and churches; and for many intervening years they were subjected to "petty persecutions" not only in the more primitive provinces but even in Constantinople itself. In 1860 in the Balat quarter of the imperial city, a "mob kept possession of the Armenian cemetery for four days and nights, and ultimately succeeded in preventing the interment of the remains of . . . a charter member of the First Evangelical Church of Constantinople, in consecrated grounds," (The deceased was finally buried by the Turks in a public highway.)[11] In 1883 a missionary's newly rented lodging in the interior village of Erzingan was invaded and sacked by a mob of local Apostolic Armenians acting out of religious intolerance.[12] The missionaries also suffered verbal abuse, since a corruption of the word for Protestant in Armenian (*pohokagan*) is *porod* or leper. Thus a missionary in 1853 complained that "scarcely ever can we walk the streets but the cry of 'prote,' 'prote,' . . . is raised, and the words [are] accompanied with stones." Jealous natives accused the missionaries of winning converts through brazen offers of cash or of Singer sewing machines.[13]

On their side the missionaries continued their narrow-minded criticism of the Apostolic Church for containing "the worst errors of Rome," and they maintained that the Armenians lived in ignorance, immorality, superstition, and ecclesiastical bondage. On occasion missionaries were personally condescending to natives. In 1881 an

Armenian reported that one preacher said, "'Your nation is ignoble, ignorent [sic] mean and beggar'd' and many other words that grevously wounded our hearts."[14]

Yet, for all the divisiveness generated by the Protestants, in the long run the missionary movement effected monolithic changes in the Armenian millet. In the first place the recognition in 1847 of the Protestants as a separate religious body in Turkey broke down the age old monopoly of the Armenian Apostolic Church in Christian religious matters, and the new situation, in conjunction with the great Turkish reform edict, the Hatti-Humayum of 1856, helped pave the way for a series of political and religious reforms which included the epoch making liberal Armenian Constitution of 1860. It was the recognition of the Protestants that weakened the tie between civil and religious authority. No longer was a member of the civil community *de facto* a member of the Apostolic Church, which hitherto had defined the community.[15]

Also the Protestant mission facilitated the awakening of the Armenians in education. The earliest important schools in Constantinople stressed a modern curriculum, based on mathematics, physics, and chemistry and thorough instruction in English. Bible study, history, and geography were also taught exclusively in the modern Armenian language. And these schools, for the first time also for females, and taught by American educated instructors, soon spread to every sizeable Armenian town and village in Turkey. In addition, the missionaries established printing presses and newspapers, among which *Avedaper* (The Awakener) was the most important, while the missionary "colleges" — Robert College in Constantinople, Anatolia College in Marsovan, Central Turkey College in Aintab, and Yeprad College in Kharpert, as well as the International College at Smyrna and St. Paul's Institute at Tarsus — which, in effect, were college preparatory schools, rivalled the best Armenian institutions in the empire.[16]

Through the schools and their preaching, the missionaries opened the eyes of many Armenians to the opportunities and freedom of the New World. Cyrus Hamlin, for many decades president of Robert College, noted just after his arrival in Constantinople in the 1840s that a young Armenian who had just witnessed Turkish troops beating an elderly countryman, cherished the "idea of escaping, at some future day, to America," and that there were hundreds of young men who, longing for "liberty, with neither sultan, patriarch, nor bankers to fear," might well follow to the promised land.[17] Even before missionary schools were numerous, Armenians were fascinated by America and its distance from Turkey. America had the "honor of giving name to whatever is curious or particularly good."

Thus water-carriers distributed among their customers " 'American water,' meaning good fresh water," or else advertised "an American bird."[18] As time passed and as the number of schools mushroomed, ever increasing numbers of missionary-educated Armenians left their native land for further education, adventure, or freedom in the New World.

Pressured by the presence of the missionary schools, the Apostolics opened many new educational institutions of their own. The American Board of Commissioners for Foreign Missions in 1866 noted that the Kharpert mission maintained fifty-four schools. This example forced the Apostolics to emulate them by opening perhaps twice that number.[19] A field report from Marash in 1890 stated that the opening of free schools among the Armenians was a direct response to the missionaries' inroads. The traveler Lynch, writing near the end of the century, commented that the Armenian schools were "greatly benefited" by competition "with the less fashionable American institutions."[20]

A final by-product of the missionary movement was its stimulus to the growth of Armenian national consciousness. This development occurred despite the missionaries' studious desire to avoid entanglements with rising nationalist currents among the Armenians of the late nineteenth century. The missionaries thought that a nationalist movement such as had erupted among the Greeks, Bulgarians, and Macedonians, coming in the heartland of Turkish Armenia, would be extremely bloody and would threaten their half century of effort and their property, valued at $4,000,000. Missionaries sought therefore to inculcate a sentiment of loyalty to the Ottoman regime among their Armenian pupils and church adherents.[21] In one school, a missionary preached that Christ was a patriot and savior, but not a rebel. "I pictured Him weeping over Jerusalem because He foresaw that, in place of repenting & turning to God, they w'd rejec [sic] & crucify His Son, put their trust in man and rebel against the Roman govt, & thus bring ruin on their city & nation."[22] Students were expelled for preaching revolutionary dogmas, considered "contrary to morality, viz. the justificability of falsehood, theft, murder, etc. if used in the cause of patriotism."[23]

Despite their professed efforts, the missionaries' depiction of Western ideas and institutions promoted the desire among Armenians to emulate conditions in western Europe and in America. Students who learned about liberal constitutions, gradually and inevitably were stirred to a "yearning for security, some feeling of equality, a sense of justice," and a desire for freedom from degradation.[24] It was impossible to expose young men to history and to the West and still keep them chained to Turkish despotism. Thus, the missionaries were properly termed the midwives of the birth of nationalism among the Armenians in Turkey.

The Middle Class and Politics.   While the Protestant missionaries were promoting a renaissance in Turkey, a second reforming source — the Armenian middle class in western Turkey, especially in Constantinople — was making its own powerful contribution to the awakening. Throughout the nineteenth century the Armenian community of Constantinople had expanded its contacts with western Europe through the growth of trade and the creation of a class of agents, importers, distributors, and financial representatives of the foreign interests in Turkey. Then, too, the Armenians of Constantinople and Smyrna had had contacts with Europe since the seventeenth century: many Armenians had been educated in Italian universities and thus were "prepared, both linguistically and intellectually, to receive the new Western ideas of the time."[25]

The western Turkish Armenians had been enjoying a minor cultural renaissance of their own for some time, stimulated principally by the revival of classical Armenian learning at the Catholic Armenian Mekhitarist Monastery in Venice, and classical learning gradually made way for the codification of the vernacular tongue.[26] In the 1840s, the beginnings of an Armenian press in Turkey furthered this trend. *Massis*, the most important journal of Constantinople, was founded in the 1850s by Garabed Utijian. The example of the Protestant movement and the spirit of the western-inspired Turkish *tanzimat* (reform) tradition, expressed in the edicts of Hatti-Sherif of 1839 and the Hatti-Humayum of 1856, strengthened reformist feelings.[27]

One powerful expression of reform was the Armenian Constitution of 1860. Stimulated by the Ottoman Hatti-Humayum of 1856, which required the reorganization of all Turkey's religious millets, the Armenian national constitution, drafted in 1860 and approved by the Ottoman regime in 1863, laid out the powers and responsibilities of the clergy and the laity in the governing of the millet in a new, heavily secularized formula. Although the patriarch remained the chief executive of the millet, he was elected by a general assembly mainly composed of popularly elected, nonclerical members. A lay council was authorized to determine matters in each province, and a council of clerical officals controlled and administered matters of religion and social law. Although the church's control remained in some areas, and although the Ottoman regime retained a veto power over major decisions, the new constitution dealt a heavy blow to the amira class of Constantinople and the clerical control of the millet.[28]

The establishment of the constitution released forces eager for the reform of the social, educational, and ecclesiastical life of the Armenian community. First, although the Ottoman regime did not intend it, the constitution reaffirmed the autonomy in Turkey of the Armenian minority *qua* Armenians, and it heightened the distinctions between Turks and Armenians in the empire. This, of course, was an important foundation for the nationalist movement of the latter part of the nineteenth century.[29] Second, the increased lay participation in the millet and particularly the growing emphasis on secular education gave a new élan to ethnic and national feelings. Between 1860 and 1914, a series of Armenian societies originating in Constantinople, in Russia, and the diaspora, promoted the establishment of secular education on a massive scale. The national societies, supplementing the missionary and Apostolic schools, succeeded by World War I in providing every Armenian child, male and female, with a "good common-school education."[30]

By the 1880s, for example, provincial communities of 100 families or more were receiving schools and teachers, whose expenses were borne largely by the societies in Constantinople and by donations from Armenians from the diaspora. Before the outbreak of World War I, the Armenian patriarchate had established 2,000 church-affiliated schools and 52 upper-level schools; the United Society, one of the important benevolent groups, had founded 143 schools; the Armenian General Benevolent Union, 40 schools; and the Society of Armenian women, 40 schools. By 1912, the 9 Armenian provinces boasted 3,000 Armenian-sponsored elementary and secondary schools, with a student enrollment of 150,000, and these figures do not include the important efforts of the Protestant community.[31]

The direct connection between secular education and nationalism is clear, but it is important to notice too that the schools were vital for disseminating the literature of the vernacular and re-establishing the ancestral tongue as the primary mode of written expression for Armenians. Further, the growth of the school system promoted the rebirth of the Armenian language among the Turkish-speaking Armenians, principally on the Cilician Plain. For the first time in generations, young Armenians, in exultation, were learning to speak their historic language and learning about their national heroes and myths. In their own language, they heard the clarion call for a resurgent Armenia.

Stage Two: The Revolution

If the middle decades of the century were characterized by movements for religious and educational revival, the period after 1880 was characterized by political rebirth. Indeed, the decade of the 1880s is the turning point, the time of irreversible change for the Armenian awakening. It was then that a radical minority of Armenians turned from reform of education and the millet to more strident demands — for political autonomy and liberation from their Turkish overlords.

The Influence of Russian Armenians. The seeds of the movement for political independence were sown in part by the Armenian communities in Transcaucasia, then socially and culturally more advanced than the Armenian centers in Turkey proper. The number of Armenian settlements north of the Russo-Turkish border had been increasing during the eighteenth and nineteenth centuries, partly because the czars conquered Turkish territory in 1778, 1822, and 1878. And each time Russian armies marched onto Turkish soil, thousands of hopeful Armenians greeted their Christian neighbors as deliverers and migrated to Russia. By 1896 the Armenian population of Transcaucasia had grown to over 800,000.[32]

Within the Caucasus, the Armenians, under the peaceful and relatively beneficent Russian rule, prospered in entrepreneurial roles in Tiflis, Batum, Baku, and Erevan. Armenian benefactors sponsored such famous educational centers as the Lazarian Institute in Moscow and the Janasarian Academy in Tiflis; the more prosperous enrolled their sons in Russian universities, and the student generation in turn adopted the nationalist-socialist currents of western and eastern Europe. A vigorous Armenian national revival in the press, literature, and pulpit in Russia far surpassed the awakening in Turkey. Russian-Armenian journalism came to the fore through the pen of Krikor Ardzrouni, and his paper *Mshag* (The Laborer) of Tiflis was termed the most important Armenian newspaper in the Caucasus, if not in the world. The new aspirations found expressions in the literary works of Gabriel Soundoukian. Teacher and historian Raffi (Hagop Melik-Hagopian), author of a torrent of romantic, nationalistic novels and essays, fired the imagination of the Armenian reading public. Poets — Kamar Katiba, Bedros Tourian, and Mikael Nalbandian — echoed the nationalist impulses, calling for a revival of ancient Armenian traditions and the birth of a new Armenia.[33] By the 1880s the nationalistic groundswell among Russian Armenians urged political independence for their hapless co-religionists in Turkey.

The Russo-Turkish War. The Russo-Turkish War of 1877–1878 was a catalyst in the mixture of issues and sentiment moving Armenian nationalists toward a bid for independence. At the end of that conflict Armenians pinned their hopes on Western assistance in alleviating their plight in the Turkish-ruled provinces. And, at the deliberations for a peace treaty between Russia and Turkey (Treaty of San Stefano, January 1878), the signatories decreed that reforms were to be implemented immediately thoughout the Ottoman Empire and that Russian armies were to remain on Turkish soil as guarantors

of the treaty. However, because the western powers, especially Great
Britain, feared Russian advances in Asia Minor, the Concert of
Europe, in the more comprehensive Treaty of Berlin (July 1878)
swept away the guarantees of San Stefano and placed the responsibility for compelling the sultan to carry out reforms upon all the
signatories — France, Great Britain, Italy, Austria-Hungary, and Germany, as well as Russia. "What was everybody's business," it was
ruefully remarked, "was nobody's business."[34] For a decade utter
misrule continued in the provinces; the West failed to assist the
Armenians: unmitigated Kurdish and Circassian attacks on the
unprotected Armenian minority continued throughout the 1880s;
and Turkish governors looked on with indifference. Was there to be
no end to this travail?

Nationalist Organizations in Turkey.   In the late 1880s activitist
Armenians finally took matters into their own hands, and by 1890
important socialist paramilitary organizations had formed to press
Armenian nationalist demands for security and liberation.[35] Of these
groups, the most important was the Armenian Revolutionary Federation. The federation, formed in 1890, grew out of a group of older
socialist, Marxist, and nationalist revolutionary organizations, and
its purpose was to secure the administrative and economic autonomy
— but not political independence — of Turkish Armenia. To effect
these ends, the federation planned to "organize fighting units, arm
the populace, operate an espionage network, propagandize to raise
the revolutionary spirit of Armenians, and in particular, resort to the
terrorization of corrupt officials, traitors, and exploiters" — methods
akin to the Russian nihilist organization — Narodnia Volia — "which
maintained close contact and ideological bonds with the Armenian
leaders."[36]

Eventually, the Armenian Revolutionary Federation was to be
the chief source of revolutionary activity, but in the early years —
1890 to 1895 — the impetus of the movement came from an older,
rival group, the Social Democratic Hnchagian Party. Founded in 1887
in Geneva by a tiny band of Russian-Armenia intellectuals, this was
the only revolutionary group to call for the complete independence
of the Armenians throughout its history. Like the Armenian Revolutionary Federation, the Hnchagists advocated the use of intimida-
tion, terror, and assassination to coerce wealthy Turkish- and
Russian-Armenians to contribute to their holy cause and to "force
Turkish and Kurdish officials to comply with requests."[37]

In 1887 the Hnchag Party began publishing *Hnchag* (The Clarion)
in Geneva. Soon after, the Hnchags began setting up cells in Turkish
territory — in Erzerum, Trebizond, Kharpert, Smyrna, Aleppo, and
Aintab, with headquarters in Marsovan.[38] By 1890 revolutionary

placards were brandished during demonstrations in the cities: the Armenian Awakening had become the Armenian Revolution.

In response to the demonstrations beginning in 1890, and insurrectionary agitation shortly thereafter, the Turks reacted with unparalleled violence against the Armenian population throughout Turkey, without reference to age or sex or political afflilation. From 1894 to 1896 the Turks perpetrated the worst atrocities in the whole history of Armeno-Turkish relations. Over 100,000 men, women, and children were slain, and perhaps 500,000 were orphaned and made homeless. This was a new and frightening aspect of the awakening.

Thus, the efforts of two generations of dedicated Armenians and westerners in revitalizing and energizing the Armenian awakening ended in violence. Education, the advancement of secular learning, the opening of horizons to the West, the rise of a long suppressed nationalism — all at last broke the shackles of an oppressive and stifling past. But advancement was swiflty followed by the untold suffering and pain of the mass atrocities inflicted on the helpless subjects of Ottoman Turkey.

For generations, the endemic poverty of the harrassed Armenian Plateau had compelled many thousands of hopeful Armenians to trek across the mountain passes to the bustling ports on the Mediterranean or the Black Sea or to the Cilician fields. But with the massacres of the 1890s and 1900s, the stream became a flood of emigrants to the West. Emigration became a way of life for vast numbers of Armenians.

PART TWO

The Migration

4.

Leaving the Old Country

It was a source of pride to late nineteenth-century immigrants that Armenians had arrived in the New World long before the 1800s. The story was told in the first English-language history of the Armenians in the United States, written in 1919 by a young lawyer, M. Vartan Malcom. According to Malcom's research, the British State Colonial Papers, the Court Book of the Virginia Company of London, and Peter Force's Historical Tracts confirmed that Armenians were among the first families in Virginia.[1] The first such colonist was one "Martin the Armenian," "Martin Armenean," or "Martin an Armeanean," — also referred to as "John Martin the Persian." Very little is known of his origins or why he came to the Virginia wilderness, but he arrived very early in Virginia history — 1618 or 1619 — probably as colonial governor George Yeardley's servant. In Virginia he became an English subject — and that, boasted Malcom, entitled him to the distinction of being the "first naturalized person on the American continent."[2]

Martin spent four years in Virginia. When he returned to England with a parcel of tobacco he had grown in the colony, customs officials levied double the usual duties because of his foreign birth. Martin thereupon petitioned the London Company for relief and promptly received it. References to Martin continue in the records of the Virginia Company in London until 1624.[3] Nothing is heard of him after that.

Armenians next arrived in Virginia in 1653 to grow silk. The Virginia colonists had tried for a decade to promote sericulture to vary their exports, but their experiments with silkworms and mulberry trees were dismal failures. Edward Diggs — a prominent Virginia planter who had heard through his father, then the English Ambassador to Russia, that Armenians were expert silkworm cultivators — engaged two Armenians, perhaps from Smyrna, who were reputed in their native land to have experience in silk production, to come to Virginia. John Ferrer, an "earnest supporter" of the fledgling colony, eulogized the sponsor of the Armenians in his monumental epic "To the most Noble deserving Esquire Diggs: upon the Arrival of his two Armenians out of turky into Virginia":

His two *Armenians* from Turky sent
Are now most busy on his brave attempt
And had he stock sufficient for next yeare
Ten thousand pound of Silk would then appeare
And to the skies his worthy deeds upreare.

Two years later the Virginia General Assembly resolved in favor of one of Diggs's men: "That George the Armenian for his encouragement in the trade of silk and to stay in the country to follow the same have four thousand pounds of tobacco allowed him by the Assembly."[4]

The arrival of Martin the Armenian and Diggs's two silkgrowers is historically unimportant; their significance lies in their mythological role for a later generation of immigrant Armenians. That Armenians had come to America at the time of the Virginia Cavaliers or the *Mayflower* permitted the late nineteenth-century newcomers to feel a part of American history; like Yankee bluebloods, they too possessed deep roots in America. And accordingly, M. Vartan Malcom devoted many pages to their early history.

Armenian writers were not alone in exaggerating the importance of their early settlers; every new immigrant group in the United States eulogized its earliest colonists, expostulated on their "contributions" to the discovery of America, the winning of the Revolution, and so forth. Establishing a history in America was a necessary step in adjusting to an alien environment. But the Armenians of the colonial period were not the true pioneers; they did not start an exodus of Armenians to America; they were strays, removed from the main currents of the migration.

Phase One: The Pioneers, to 1890

The actual chronicle of the origins of the Armenian migration belongs instead to the nineteenth century. The first phase of the movement is composed of three separate but interconnected stages. Initially, a group of Armenian students and clergymen came to the United States in the period after 1834 to further their education. Then young business people from Constantinople, Smyrna, and the interior ventured to New York City and Chicago to expand their commercial operations. Finally, in the period after the 1870s began a rural exodus of the poorer laboring and artisan class, which heralded the mass migration of the 1890s.

For Education. The first stage was directly connected with American missionary endeavor in Turkey. In 1831 the American

Board of Commissioners for Foreign Missions had established a mission to the Armenians in Turkey (Chapter 3). Having failed in attempts to proselytize among the Muslim Turks, the Protestant missionaries, who were convinced that the "corrupt Christianity" of the Eastern Christian churches was impeding the spread of the gospel among the "heathen" Turks, began to preach among the Armenians.

The Protestant mission stimulated interest in the New World in a variety of ways. First, emigration to America was a natural and direct outgrowth of missionary endeavor, since the missionaries in the early decades of the mission encouraged promising young Protestant Armenians to seek higher religious education in the United States so that they would return to Turkey as Protestant ministers. The most important institution for such training was the Andover Theological Seminary in Massachusetts. Further, many Armenian graduates of missionary schools sought to complete their higher education in science, medicine, or dentistry at American colleges and universities. At the same time Cyrus Hamlin, American missionary and first president of Robert College in Constantinople, encouraged many young men to seek education in the modern methods of industry at his institution and in American technical schools.[5] One Armenian who had been incarcerated by the Armenian Apostolic Church authorities, apparently for befriending Protestants, confided to a missionary in 1840 that "as soon as my boys become old enough, I am going to send them to America for an education."[6] A few adventurous Armenians emigrated to the United States as the servants of American missionaries.

American missionaries were not entirely sympathetic to the migration of promising young "natives" to the New World under their auspices, for they soon discovered that many young, intelligent Armenians failed to return to Turkey to take up the religious or educational tasks for which they were originally intended. As early as 1842 the Reverend H. O. Dwight discouraged two young Armenians in Constantinople from emigrating to America.[7] Years later, the embittered missionary Knapp, reporting from the provinces, said that he entirely opposed the migration because only one emigrant in forty returned, and he complained to his superiors in Boston that the "stampede" included many Protestant students who in his opinion had received their education "under false intentions."[8] Indeed, in the middle decades of the century some missionaries refused to teach English to their students in order to thwart their migration. Missionaries also objected to the migration on the grounds that an American education unfitted the more zealous graduates for "reforming work" in Armenia; that is, the young graduates of Andover Theological Seminary, Yale, and Columbia found it hard, upon returning to Turkey, to serve in the menial roles often assigned them by American missionaries.[9] But in fact, many young Protestant Armenian graduates of Andover Theological Seminary, Yale, Princeton, Amherst, and Clark returned to teach at missionary schools and colleges in Turkey.[10] The most prominent returnee, however, was not a Protestant; he was the Reverend Harutiun Vehebedian, who later became Armenian Apostolic Patriarch of Constantinople and then of Jerusalem — the highest religious posts of the Armenians in the empire.

The precise numbers of these "pioneers" will never be known, since emigrants to the United States from the Ottoman Empire were categorized not by ethnic group but by geographical origin. That is, until 1899, they were classified as coming from "European Turkey," "Asiatic Turkey," or "Armenia." These first two categories included Jews, Syrians, Greeks, and a few Turks as well as Armenians. The most reliable estimates place the number of students emigrating to America in all the years before 1890 at no more than sixty to seventy-five.[11]

These ambitious, well-educated pioneers, who often were able to speak English before they came, built remarkable careers in America. The "pathfinder" of the group was Khachadur Osganian, a pupil of the missionaries at the Bebek school near Constantinople, who sailed for the New World in 1834. Within some years of arriving in the United States, Osganian graduated from New York University, founded a newspaper in Constantinople, and returned to America as a correspondent for Bennett's *New York Herald*. Osganian presided over the New York Press Club, at one time served as consul in New York City for the Turkish government, wrote *The Sultan and His People* (1857), and acted as correspondent for the influential Armenian-language daily of Constantinople, *Massis*. Among his projects was a plan, publicized through *Massis*, to set up an Armenian colony in the United States. The *Cincinnati Inquirer* reported in September 1868 that he (perhaps along with another Armenian) planned to purchase land in Richmond, Virginia, on which to colonize two hundred Armenians. According to one source, Osganian intended to name his colony New Ani (after the medieval Armenian capital of Ani), and to name the boulevards after Armenian cities and heroes.[12]

Christopher Der Seropian, who arrived in the United States in 1848, inaugurated the Class Book custom while enrolled at Yale University, and later discovered "the black and green colors now used on all United States paper currency."[13] Then, during the American Civil War, three Armenian medical students — Bornig Mataosian, Calousdian, and Simon Minasian — served in Northern hospitals, while Dr. Garabed Vartanian, a graduate of New York University Medical School, received a Silver Medal for service in the

18th Regular Infantry in the Army of Tennessee commanded by General William Rosecrans. After the war Vartanian returned to practice as a prominent surgeon in his native Constantinople.[14] So, too, did most other medical students.

For Commerce. The establishment of the American missionary movement in Turkey after 1834 obviously produced a stream of students traveling to the New World, but it also indirectly fostered the expansion of Armenian business interests from Turkey to America in the 1860s and 1870s. Hagop Bogigian of Kharpert first emigrated to the United States in 1876 as the manservant of an American missionary, and he worked for a few years in a Woburn, Massachusetts, tannery. He returned to Turkey soon after, apparently to serve as a native Protestant preacher but quarreled with his immediate superiors and left again for the United States. Bogigian settled in the Bay State where he opened a lucrative oriental rug business in Cambridge and Boston.[15] Jacob Arakelyan, who became prosperous as the owner of the Pilgrim Press in Boston, arrived in 1867 as the servant of an American missionary family.[16] Similarly, many oriental rug firms in the United States were opened in the 1870s and 1880s by young Armenian businessmen who had been educated at a missionary school or college. The Pushman family of Diarbekir sent a son to Yeprad College while another son opened a business in Constantinople. In 1887 the family emigrated to Chicago to become the largest oriental rug firm in the Midwest. Hagop Isganian, a graduate of Marsovan College, emigrated in 1865 to enter the trade in rugs in New York City, as did Samuel Donchian in 1884.[17]

Significantly, these men were not the nabobs of Constantinople or Smyrna. To be sure, the House of Gulbenkian had established a branch of their enterprise in New York City by 1890, but the largest Armenian merchants in Turkey did not generally venture to the New World; if they expanded, it was to the more accessible and traditional markets of London, Manchester, Paris, Athens, Marseilles, Leghorn, or Cairo. Most Armenian businessmen in New York City, Chicago, or Boston who emigrated through contacts with American missionaries in the 1880s or before were of the "middling sort."[18]

Students and business people did not exhaust the list of early "pioneers," for there were tradesmen, scientists, and various others. Some emigrants were eccentrics like "Lucky Rupe" Minasian, who, arriving in 1867, lived among American Indian tribes, learned farming from the Mormons, prospected for gold and silver in Idaho, and became a cowboy.[19] Also, there was "Joe the Turk" (!) Garabedian, who left Turkey in 1880 or 1881 and who, as a reformed drunk, joined the Salvation Army and was reputed to have been jailed fifty-six times for "public disturbances" in the process of saving God's children from perdition through drink.[20]

For Jobs and for Freedom. Business people, students, professionals — all were important members of the fledgling Armenian colony in the United States. This educated group rapidly adapted to American ways and provided important leadership for the immigrants. In the 1880s, however, another group of Armenians began to join them, this time coming from the poorer villages and towns of the Turkish interior. After the mid-1880s it was these abstemious and alert, but poorer artisans and laborers who comprised the overwhelming majority of Armenian immigrants.

The flow of the artisan and peasant class of Armenians from the interior began principally in the Kharpert Plain in the late 1870s. The reasons for this movement were many: first, the Kharpert Plain had remained the focus of intense missionary effort in Eastern Turkey since 1852 when the Reverend George W. Dunmore, on a tour of the Armenian provinces on behalf of the American Board of Commissioners for Foreign Missions, exclaimed that it was "the richest country and the most inviting and promising missionary field I have seen in Turkey."[21] (The "vast, rich plain [was] studded with three hundred and sixty-six villages, of from one hundred to five thousand inhabitants each, nearly all Armenians, and all within a few hours' ride of the city [Kharpert]."[22] The substantial Armenian population of Kharpert itself in midcentury was about 25,000.) In 1852 the American evangelicals established their mission in Kharpert, and seven years later they founded Yeprad College, for training Armenian Protestant clergy. In 1880 Yeprad College expanded greatly to promote secular education; by this time the populous plain boasted over 62 mission outstations and 21 churches.[23] Second, as noted earlier, emigration from Kharpert and other provincial towns was no novelty; for generations provincial Armenians had migrated to Smyrna, Constantinople, and Adana and lately to Baku and Tiflis, where they took on the menial, backbreaking tasks of *hamals* (porters), navvies, and watercarriers until they had amassed sufficient savings to return to their native villages and pay their taxes and interest on loans and to purchase land. Finally, conditions on the plain in the 1880s had deteriorated a great deal. One missionary wrote of "increasing exactions . . . [by] the government in the face of failing crops, industries completely prostrate, lack of business, work, food, of almost everything except swarms of tax-collecting soldiers."[24] Another reported that large numbers of men "who, a few years ago, were considered well off but are today in absolute need"; another "the drainage of money, the stagnation of business, the increase of taxes and their relentless collection, are reducing the common people to an extreme of poverty that threatens, very soon, to become appalling."[25]

The first Armenian emigrant from Kharpert to the United States may have been one "Garo," who accompanied the Reverend George Knapp on a home leave to Worcester, Massachusetts, about the year 1867. There he served Knapp in his home until an "Irish laundress," employed in the Knapp home, opened Garo's eyes to the opportunities for better pay in Worcester's wire mills. Garo, who had been paid on the Turkish scale of 75 cents per week, was informed that he could exceed that amount in one day in a Worcester factory. He thereupon left his domestic labor and went to work in a Worcester mill. Like many hundreds of immigrants to follow, Garo wrote home to his friends and relatives in Kharpert and his "enthusiastic letters" stimulated movement to the United States.[26]

Thus by the 1880s men from the poorer classes, already well accustomed to periodic emigration to Constantinople or Batum, were lured by the spreading word of overnight fortunes and limitless opportunities to shift their sights to the more ambitious journey to America. "America promises everything. . . . Fabulous stories are related here of the rapidity with which wealth is obtained there."[27] This impression was constantly reiterated. A typical missionary field report from a Kharpert station in 1885 stated, "large numbers of young men are starting for America in search of work. . . . The impulse of those who are ambitious is to leave the country altogether."[28] The emigration naturally claimed a large proportion of the young, well-educated, and aggressive teachers and students of the missionary schools on the plain, to the deep dissatisfaction of their American teachers.

The "American fever" in Kharpert became so intense that in late 1888 the Reverend James Barton, President of Yeprad College, informed Oscar Straus, American Minister to the Sublime Porte, of the situation:

From this immediate ward of . . . [Kharpert], which constitutes less than one sixth of the whole city, 105 persons are at present either on their way to or in the U. S. I have not the figures for the whole city, but judge the above to be a fair proportion. From Husenik, a good sized village one half mile away over 200 are now in the U. S. and fully as many more are ready to start as soon as this (the Ottoman) government gives full liberty of emigration.[29]

Barton also reported that over 100 men stood ready to start for the United States from Keserig and that if those departed in 1888, "twice that number will go in 1889." Barton warned that his information concerned only two out of about "one hundred villages in this plain, from nearly every one of which have already gone from one to twenty or more, and in which large numbers are ready to start, or are talking of going in the near future."

Recognition by State Department officials of the emigration's broadening scope, evidenced by Barton's letter, prompted diplomatic policy interchange between Washington and Constantinople. Pendleton King, the American *chargé d' affaires ad interim* at Constantinople, on September 25, 1888, while forwarding Barton's letter to Secretary of State Thomas Bayard, requested directives on two pressing concerns: first, how to inform the people in the Kharpert area of the conditions on which they would be permitted to land and remain in the United States, and second "of the limitations of their rights after naturalization, if they should return to Turkey."[30]

Washington's response, based on the precedent set earlier the same year regarding Greek emigration to the United States, was sparse in providing guidelines but by no means obstructive. G. L. Rives, Acting Secretary of State, on October 23, simply called attention to the U. S. Statute of 1882 which debarred from entry "any convict, lunatic, idiot, or any person unable to take care of himself or herself without becoming a public charge," but stated that with these exceptions this "Government's attitude is passive with respect to such immigration." As to the second query, no response was forthcoming.[31]

In the same period emigration from the provinces of Erzerum, Sivas, and Bitlis was taking place on a smaller scale. C. B. Norman, the distinguished British war correspondent, noted that thousands of Armenians were enduring terrible suffering along the Russian frontier, and that "many of the wealthier families . . . have determined on emigrating; and more than one already . . . has gone to America." The first large settlement of Armenians in Fresno, California, arrived in 1883 when forty immigrants came to the San Joaquin Valley directly from Marsovan.[32] A missionary noted that a rivulet of emigration out of mountainous Bitlis province was perceptible from 1867 on.[33] The province was more mountainous than Kharpert and lacked its dense population, but a vigorous missionary effort had established missions at Mush and Bitlis in 1864. In the 1880s missionaries there were bitterly lamenting that students and preachers were leaving to "cash in on the present 'Boom' in Southern California; and in the estimation of our poor, down trodden people here, have amassed fortunes, or are obtaining incredibly large wages. Glowing reports encourage emigration among the young, and teaching the young men English only abets this 'unfortunate movement.' "[34]

In the late 1880s yet another discrete band of Armenians joined the exodus — political refugees. By 1887, it will be remembered, Russian Armenian revolutionaries and terrorists, modeled on Russian insurrectionary groups, had begun issuing propaganda for an independent Armenian Socialist state among the Turkish Armenian population. The Turkish government retaliated with a wave of arrests, beatings, and jail sentences. Between 1887 and 1890 probably a handful of the nationalists emigrated to, or were exiled to the United States where they began to establish cells, raise funds, or pursue a livelihood in exile. The most important of these early publicists of the Armenian nationalist movement was Dr. M. Smpad Kaprielian, who was arrested and exiled from Turkey in 1886 for possessing revolutionary materials. Settling in New York City, he edited an early revolutionary journal, *Haik* (Armenia), and wrote a number of works on the Armenian question.[35] On the whole, however, political exiles did not emigrate to the United States in this early period because America was so far from Turkey; most revolutionaries went to Greece, Switzerland, the Caucasus, or London.

The Turkish Reaction. The Turkish government had no fixed policy toward Armenian emigration to the United States, but it often placed obstacles in the way, sometimes forcibly stopping emigrants or temporarily banning emigration. The first such incident occurred in the spring of 1888 when the Turks interdicted all Armenian emigration to the United States on the grounds that the American government would not permit Armenians to enter the country. The more probable reason was to thwart the flight — and return as naturalized citizens with important immunities thereof — of suspected Armenian nationalists and revolutionaries.[36] The ban was lifted shortly thereafter, but by September, Frank Calvert, consular agent in the Dardanelles, complained to the United States consular general at the Turkish capital that Armenian families en route to the United States were forced to debark from their (French) steamer and return to their homes, at their own expense; Calvert reported on the painful separation of families, especially one woman traveling with three small children, who was prevented from joining her husband in America.[37]

Turkish officials in the United States as well expressed a curious solicitude for the welfare of entering "Turkish" immigrants. In June 1889 the Turkish minister in Washington, Mavroyeni Bey, addressed a letter to Secretary of State Blaine requesting attention to the hardships of these newcomers at New York, because of their ignorance of English and the alleged failure of American authorities to assist them from the perils of fraud on "their arrival in a strange land." The Turkish minister's request for permission for the Ottoman consul general in New York City to be present when Turkish immigrants landed was granted; his further plea that Turkish immigrants be prevented from landing *except* in the presence of the Ottoman consul general was summarily denied, probably as an intrusion on the rights of immigrants.[38]

Meanwhile, in late 1888 or early 1889, some 150 Armenians in the United States petitioned the Turkish legation in Washington to prevent the further emigration of Armenians to Worcester because "hundreds of them were idle and without any prospect of getting work." On January 12, 1889, the *Worcester Daily Telegram* reported that 30 Armenians en route to America were turned back at Constantinople because of the Worcester request; this ban was also shortlived.[39]

The numerical volume of emigration of Armenians to the United States through the 1880s cannot be determined owing to the absence of compilations on the basis of ethnic groups. United States Treasury Department statistics for emigration from "Armenia," "Turkey in Asia," and "Turkey in Europe" indicate a small but rising immigrant tide. In the 1880s there were 971 immigrants from "Armenia," virtually all of whom were Armenians, and a total of 4,242 from "Asiatic" and "European" Turkey, of whom perhaps 450 were also Armenians.[40] The American consul in Marseilles, the primary port of call en route to the United States, reported in 1889 a "decided increase in the Oriental movement — Syrians and Armenians."[41] The tabulations of the Treasury Department confirm that this was overwhelmingly a movement of males, for 92 per cent of those entering the country from "Armenia" were males, and 85 percent of those enumerated as originating from "Turkish in Asia" were also male.[42] The total volume of Armenian emigration to the United States through the 1880s may have amounted to about 1,500.[43]

By the late 1880s, then, a small stream — chiefly men of the artisan and laboring classes from Kharpert province, with scattered numbers of political refugees, business people, and students — was making its way to the United States. The initial impetus came from the presence of American missionaries, but the chief cause was the desire of the poverty stricken to find jobs. "The thought of the people," reported an observer in Kharpert in 1888 is "to thus better their condition. They hope to escape in this way some of the oppressive taxations of this Government."[44] Grinding poverty and governmental exactions — not political repression — drove most Armenians to the United States before 1890.

Phase Two: Flight, 1890–1899

After 1890 the emigration moved into its second phase, characterized by a nearly exponential increase in the volume of emigration, a wider distribution of the emigrants, and sheer panic. The

American fever spread from Kharpert to Sivas, Van, Erzerum, Trebizond, Bitlis, and Cilicia. In 1891 alone over 800 immigrants from
"Armenia" arrived in the United States; in 1892 the number exceeded 1,000.[45] These two years exceeded the total emigration of the
entire preceding half century.

The Revolution.   The rapid spurt in emigration in the early
1890s was triggered by the beginnings of the Armenian revolutionary
movement. In 1890 Russian Armenian revolutionaries (Hnchags)
organized protest demonstrations against Turkish misrule in the
streets of Erzerum and Constantinople. The Hnchags, as noted earlier,
were developing insurrectionary cells in all the major Turkish-
Armenian centers, and their followers were beginning to distribute
revolutionary propaganda and placards everywhere.[46]

The response of Sultan Abdul Hamid II's regime to the demonstrations was brutal, exploiting psychological fears and historic
socio-economic hatreds between Armenians and Turks. The sultan
organized his irregular Kurdish troops into uniformed Hamidié regiments, modeled on the czar's cossacks, and unleashed them on
strategic Armenian villages along the Russian frontier. The provinces
of Van and Erzerum thereafter became a nightmare of looting and
destruction; cattle were stolen, sheep and goats driven off, wheat
fields set on fire, and Armenians, including women and children,
were killed or held for ransom.[47]

In 1891 British diplomats also reported increased revolutionary
activity and rising Muslim-Christian tensions on the Kharpert Plain,
the principal source of the American emigration, though conditions
there were less troubled than in Van and Erzerum.[48] Turkish troops
and police conducted exacting searches for weapons, suspected
Armenian revolutionaries were thrown into jail by the hundreds on
the slightest pretext. "The Armenians . . . are in constant apprehension, either with or without cause, of suddenly having their houses,
books, and papers searched, and of being on some trifling pretext
imprisoned, and perhaps condemned as political exiles."[49] Professors at Anatolia College in Marsovan were summarily arrested and
thrown into prison; in Mush an estimated twenty "scholars and
teachers have been sent off into exile, while four are sentenced for
life in such miserable prisons as only such a land can produce."[50]

After 1890 flight out of Turkey to safer lands became a headlong
rush. In 1892–1893, 3,500 Armenians obtained visas from the Russian Consulate in Erzerum to flee to Russia, and an equal number
crossed the Russian frontier without passports; in all, an estimated
20,000 men, women, and children sought the protection of the
Romanovs.[51] In 1894 the Armenian Archbishop of Erzerum and the

Russian authorities both cut the flow of Armenians to Russia by granting permits only to those crossing for temporary visits.[52]

Meanwhile, flight from Kharpert to America sharply increased. Thus in 1890 "The native [Protestant] pastorate has . . . diminished . . . the exodus to America during this year being greater than ever"; In 1891 "the Armenian emigration to America is nowhere more pronounced than from this station"; in 1893: "A very large number of Armenians from the Kharpert region have emigrated within the last few years."[53]

Then abruptly, in mid-1892, the Turkish government interdicted all movement of Armenians, especially from Kharpert, to America by curtailing the issuance of teskeres (travel permits to the coast). The authorities also compelled Armenians at the coast to take Turkish steamers through the Black Sea to Constantinople. Prospective Armenian immigrants who had been smuggled on board European vessels were arrested, imprisoned, and beaten. Consequently, emigration to America plummeted in 1893 and 1894.[54]

The Massacres.   All of this activity was merely a prelude to the devastating pogroms that ripped through the Turkish interior from 1894 to 1896.[55] These outrages began in the rugged mountains of Sasun in August 1894 when Kurdish and Turkish troops with artillery were mustered to quell a Hnchagist insurrection. The Turks destroyed the surrounding villages as well as the uprising, and in short order they massacred 10,000 Armenians in retaliation.[56] Thereupon, beginning in August 1895, the Turks instituted premeditated massacres in every major Armenian town and city in Turkey — from the Bosphorus to the Caspian Sea. At Trebizond in October 1895 a missionary reported that "500 to 800 Armenians were shot in broad daylight without provocation and in utter cold blood by the Muslim populace whom the Governor did nothing to restrain."[57] In 1895 and again in 1896, in the very capital of Constantinople, over 6,000 innocent Armenians were butchered in the streets. New massacres took place in succession at Erzinga, Baiburt, Bitlis, Erzerum, Arabgir, Diarbekir, Malatia, Kharpert, Sivas, Amasia, Marsovan, Aintab, Marash, Caesaria, Urfa and their surrounding villages to "the number of 2,500" villages. Armenians from Constantinople to Van reeled from the blows.[58] In all, by late 1896, when the last bugle calling for Jihad (Holy War) had sounded, about 100,000 Turkish Armenians had been slain and upwards of half a million had been made homeless and "robbed of all their worldly goods."[59]

As before, Russia became the great receiving station of the survivors from the northern provinces. Some 60,000 Armenians fled across the frontier, often on foot during the dead of winter, to escape "further massacres or arrest."[60] Major ports like Smyrna, untouched by the bloodshed, became sanctuaries for the stricken, maimed, and frightened Armenians. Many thousands fled Cilicia for Syria, Palestine, and Egypt. After three days of riots in Constantinople in 1896, thousands of Armenians fled in terror to Bulgaria, Greece, and Egypt. The numbers escaping from Turkey to the far off United States rose to the new peaks of about 2,500 annually in 1896 and 1897 and to 1,900 in 1898.[61]

The situation in Aintab was typical: "The Armenians are now wholly disarmed, broken in spirit & impoverished; their leading men are in prison or in exile, their business annihilated & even the tools of the common workman plundered or destroyed." In addition the "great mass of Moslems have been brought to look upon them as traitors to the Turkish government & enemies to the Moslem faith — a standing menace to the supremacy of Islam. By disseminating such ideas . . . the Moslem leaders have been able to rouse the 'Old Turkish' party . . . for a supreme effort to solve all these perplexing questions once for all by wholly ridding themselves" of the Armenians. "Many of our youth are fleeing to America," wrote A. G. Fuller, president of Central Turkey College in Aintab, "Who wonders?"[62]

Survivors. The fortunate survivors who escaped to America were but a fraction of those longing to flee. Westerners like Professor J. Rendel Harris of Oxford University, one of the first Europeans permitted to tour the devastated Turkish interior in 1896, were beseeched by refugees, some of whom were subsisting on grass or seeds alone, to help them emigrate. "Almost the entire population of Diarbekir would emigrate if the way were made, for otherwise they will die of starvation next winter," Harris was told. "We hear that from several provinces the Armenians have petitioned the Sultan either to give them the means of re-tilling their fields, or to let them leave the country, or to send his soldiers back again to put them out of their misery." Harris sought to convince a "rich American railroad king" passing through Smyrna to take thousands of Armenian refugees to the United States and settle them in the West. "Is it any wonder," concluded Harris, that "they talk of leaving the country, and eagerly discuss any and every possible scheme of emigration?"[63]

Meanwhile, the American Minister in Constantinople and American officials and missionaries in the interior were besieged by Armenians in the United States for information about the fate of their families caught in the massacres. Were they still alive? Were they in need? How soon could they be rescued and brought to the United States? Three such inquiries, addressed through the State Department to Minister Terrell in Constantinople in early 1896, follow; their formal language masking the depth of anxiety of the writer: "I enclose a copy of a . . . petition from the uncle of Armenak G. Iskiyan,

praying that he be protected, if living, and assisted to return to the
United States. . . . The young man was living at Marash at the time
of the recent massacres." Another: "The Department has received a
petition . . . signed by a large number of residents of Jackson, Michigan, praying it to ascertain the correctness of a report which has
reached Garabed Asadoorian, said to be a naturalized citizen of the
United States, that his wife, children, and mother were killed during
the disturbances at Echema, Harpoot." And "Baghdasar Avedisian
. . . desires the intervention of this Government to secure the freedom
of his mother and sisters who, he states, were carried away in cap-
tivity during the riots at Khokh, Harpoot."[64]

In most cases, money for relief and passage to America was sent
to Minister Terrell, or to the treasurer of the American Bible House
in Constantinople (one Mr. Peet), and then to missionaries in the
field. Thus in 1897 Stephen Caraglamaian of Boston sent a fifty pound
note to Peet who forwarded it to Rev. Barnum of Kharpert to pay the
expenses of four children of Caraglamaian's deceased brother to
emigrate to America.[65] Not surprisingly, the Turkish *valis* (local governors) and *kaymakams* (mayors) evaded or delayed requests from
the American Minister through the Sublime Porte for permission for
wives and minor children of naturalized Armenian Americans to
emigrate. In one instance, after Minister Terrell sought to obtain
permission to emigrate for 26 wives and children of naturalized
Armenian Americans who survived the Kharpert massacres, the
unfortunate families were stranded in the city for months because
the Turkish vali obstructed the Porte's orders. To ensure the safe
passage of the Armenians in these disturbed times, the frustrated
minister sent them under escort of his *cavasses* (guards) to the sea-
shore and then onto a western ship bound for America.[66]

The flight to America in the 1890s peaked in 1897 and then
slowly declined therafter. By 1899 the numbers reached a new low
for the period. Well over 12,000 Armenians had fled Turkey for
America during the decade. The massacres were over and times
slowly returned to normal.[67] During the same years, from across the
Russian frontier, refugee families slowly returned to their shattered
ancestral towns and villages in Turkish Armenia to shoulder the task
of rebuilding. The year 1899 marked the end of the flight begun in
1891 and the close of the second phase of the migration.

Phase Three: Mass Migration, 1900–1914

At the turn of the century a third and climactic phase of the
migration to America began. For in 1900 emigration to the New

World became a gradually increasing spiral. The urge to emigrate expanded into every part of Turkish Armenia and was especially strong in the communities of Aintab and Marash. According to one authority, four fifths of the "recent migration" (1901) was from the provinces of Kharpert and Diarbekir.[68] After 1903 the fever spread into Russian Armenia, and some thousands left the czar's regime for the New World. Smaller contingents left Egypt, Greece, and Bulgaria. By 1907 nearly 3,000 Armenians were arriving annually in America and in 1913 nearly 10,000 Armenians entered the promised land. For the first time spokesmen in Turkey in 1913 bewailed the exodus as a "white massacre" draining Armenia of its lifeblood — its young and able-bodied hands. Old people complained that towns and villages were deserted by the young; town squares were empty, as if it were wartime. Even the authorities in Constantinople began to investigate the "bleeding sore" of emigration

Economic Ills. At the heart of the movement after 1900 was the desire to escape the economic and political ills of the Ottoman Empire, even though economic life seemed to be recovering from the ravages of the massacres. Massive relief efforts of American, European, and Armenian welfare and relief agencies along with the International Red Cross had begun to assist the homeless and orphaned refugees of the 1894–1896 massacres in scattered locales. As early as 1897 the city of Marsovan, with missionary help, had begun rebuilding its shattered weaving industry: "The favorite form of relief has been that of . . . employment, principally the weaving of native ginghams. The capital invested in this way has already done service four times over, as the product of the looms, already over 100,000 yards, has mainly been sold on the ordinary market. Those who have helped in this way are not pauperized, and the weaving industry, completely wrecked by the massacres, has been revived and is now flourishing."[69] In 1898 in Marsovan, business was better than it had been for the past 20 years, and relief even to the sick and aged, as well as industrial assistance, ceased.[70] Reports from the Cilician Plain after 1900 also spoke of favorable economic conditions: "Marked progress has been made in agriculture and in the use of agricultural implements, new lines of work are opening, there has been a great increase in the population as well as the prosperity of many cities in this plain."[71] Others reported that by 1900 the Armenians of Sivas had "recovered wonderfully" from the "great disaster."[72]

Nevertheless, large numbers of Armenians continued to leave Turkey because of fear, oppression, and the lasting paralysis of trade and commerce in areas that had not received aid. The American consul in Kharpert in early 1901 saw near the Euphrates "a party of twenty men, from this vicinity, trudging along merrily bound for

Samsoun, en route for the 'promised land,' " and he warned his superiors in Washington to expect a large outflow of emigrants that coming spring because of the "growing conviction of hopelessness in the effort to resist continued injustice, oppression, and persecution on the part of the dominant class and local officials. Details of persecutions, of exactions, and of accompanying bodily torture come frequently to my ears. Such cases are unknown in Mezreh, are rare in Harput, but are . . . frequent . . . in outlying villages.[73]

What were the realities of the situation? First, business remained sluggish because Turkish officials imposed rigorous controls that prevented the Armenian traders from traveling into the interior. In fact, travel to Constantinople, the chief supply and exchange center, was sporadically outlawed from 1895 until 1903.[74] After that date the controls were relaxed slightly, but they still weighed heavily on the commerce of the region. All travel was forbidden in the Erzerum region in 1903 due to Turkish fears of Armenian revolutionary agitation there.[75] Second, taxation continued to be oppressive. Turkish tax collectors remorselessly collected both present and past taxes from the new impoverished Armenian population. Thus, Consul Thomas Norton reported from Kharpert that, "Unusual oppression is being exerted to force Armenians to pay military taxes for their male relatives in America, covering many years, and also to extort double payment of back taxes, when receipts were lost in the robberies and conflagrations of 1895. Payment of taxes is being required likewise for the years subsequent to 1895, when by Imperial order, taxes were to be remitted. In some cases when . . . receipts are shown, [they] . . . are forcibly destroyed."[76] About 300 Armenians in the Kharpert region, including many women, were thrown into prison in connection with tax collections. In Aintab in 1900 the government was reported "pressing the exaction of taxes with great vigor, in some cases almost to the impoverishment of the whole community."[77]

Third, Armenians continued to fear the outbreak of new massacres. Stephen Mugar, who emigrated with his parents and sisters to Boston in 1906, recalled that his father took his family to America then because he "could never trust a Turk."[78] Indeed, political crises came up periodically, and rumors of impending massacres were endemic. Thus, a missionary reported in 1900 that "while there have been no general massacres in the mission during the year, there has been much fear on the part of the Christians, which has been kept alive by repeated clashes from the Turks and Koords . . . The condition of great poverty, and the . . . continuous fear . . . is not conducive to vigorous, aggressive, Christian work. . . . Young men who are trained, and well able to hold positions of leadership . . . far too frequently drop the work and start for America."[79]

In 1903, troubles in Macedonia reverberated throughout Turkey, and local Turks openly displayed their firearms and took a "malicious pleasure in aggravating" the Armenians "by more or less open threats of an approaching massacre. The natural result," reported an eyewitness, "has been a widespread dread and anxiety among the Christian population. Such panics are . . . frequent . . . here, and there are usually one or two in the course of each year."[80]

Even wealthy Armenians who were "comparatively free" from oppressive officials, manifested an intense desire to place their children in a "healthful environment" and give them the "opportunity to make their way in the world subject only to the natural laws of competition." One Armenian, reputed to be the wealthiest man in the Kharpert region, and a member of its provincial council, said he would sacrifice half his property if he could "quietly sell out, and settle in the United States." Another Armenian elaborated on the feelings of the wealthy: "Here, I am surrounded by friends and relatives and old associations; I am a man of means, enjoying good social position, and am respected by all classes and creeds." In America he would count for no more than a beggar in Turkey. Yet, in America his children "and their children will have the blessings of liberty and a free opportunity to lead useful and happy lives." The Armenian vowed to "sacrifice all" for their sake.[81] To the American Consul Norton, these words recalled the brave utterances of the Pilgrim fathers of 1620, before embarking for the "inhospitable shores of the New World."[82]

Help from Armenians in America.   Then, too "American fever" became self-generating as many newly established Armenians in America brought relatives and friends into their homes in chains of migration. The system usually worked like this: first, a young male family member would be smuggled out of Turkey to America. Upon arriving, he would write his family of his intentions to bring them over, too, and within weeks or months he would begin to send back bank orders or American Express checks to Turkey for his family's savings. His letters would provide information about the New World, routes to travel, the preferred ship lines. In a year, the young immigrant would send a prepaid ticket for his brother, sister, or wife, and after whole families discussed the event, poured over the strange looking documents, and said their farewells, another Armenian would set off en route to America.

Statistically, in the fifteen years from 1899 to the outbreak of World War I, prepaid tickets accounted for approximately 25 percent of all Armenians emigrating to the United States (the other 75 percent purchased their own tickets in Turkish ports or en route to the United States). This percentage rose in the years after 1900: in 1900, only 12 percent of the tickets of entering Armenians were of the prepaid category; by 1913 this figure had almost tripled to over one-third of all entering Armenian immigrants.[83]

The "nativists" in the United States opposed the immigration of all Southern and Eastern European nationalities; they accused steamship companies with routes from England to Turkey of luring "undesirable types" to the New World through blatant advertising, enticing posters, and active salesmanship in European and Middle Eastern villages. This accusation did not apply to the Ottoman Empire, however, since free emigration from Turkey was strictly proscribed by the government, except with special permission of the Sublime Porte. This policy was absolute until 1908 and it manifestly kept steamship agents from establishing agencies and offices for promoting the emigration of Turkish subjects to the United States. As the American chargé d' affaires in Constantinople testified in 1889: "The emigration [from Turkey] is free and voluntary, and is not stimulated or encouraged by any transportation companies."[84] The ports of Samson and Alexandretta had one or two commission agents, and after 1908, when the Ottoman regime liberalized emigration restrictions, the large European transportation companies established offices at the major Black Sea and Mediterranean ports. It is true, however, that the Armenian immigrant press, from its inception in the late 1890s, carried weekly advertisements of such European steamship lines as the Compagnie General Transatlantique, the Austro-American Line, and the British Lloyd Lines, with printings of sailing dates and passage costs.[85]

It became easier to leave Turkey when the cost of steerage passage from the Black Sea and the Mediterranean to New York City began to decline. In 1900, for example, a one-way passage in steerage from Constantinople to New York cost about $34. By 1913 this price had declined to about $24, because of increasing immigration, the rising number of commercial contacts for shipping firms, and the new, more spacious vessels.[86]

Influences on Emigration.   It is curious that depressed economic conditions in the United States did not dampen enthusiasm for emigration. When the news reached Turkey of the 1907 depression, there were reports that "the emigration . . . was . . . stopped by the news of 'hard times' in America." Statistically, however, this impression was inaccurate; the fiscal year 1908 saw a net gain of Armenian emigrants over 1907 — from 2,644 (1907) to 3,299 (1908), or nearly the proportionate increase that would be expected in a "normal" year of this period.[87] The lamentations and dire warnings of Armenian newspapers in the United States of "immigrants walking the streets," and "no work, no jobs," in 1908 and again in 1913–1914, made no appreciable impact on the number of Armenian emigrants coming to America.[88] Perhaps the Armenians in their backward, poverty-stricken, and oppressed villages refused to believe pessimistic or negative reports about their idealized America.

Events in Turkey had a more significant effect on the actions of the Armenians. In particular, *Ittihad ve Terakki* (The Committee of Union and Progress), a fusion of Young Turk reformers and officers of the Third Ottoman Macedonian Army, in 1908 electrified Turkey and indeed the entire Middle East by overthrowing the hated regime of Abdul Hamid II. The committee promulgated a Turkish constitution with guarantees of individual liberties, freedom of speech and of the press and of travel, as well as amnesty for thousands of political prisoners. The new liberal leadership appeared to herald a new day in Armeno-Turkish relations. Armenians and Turks rejoiced in the streets at the bright new era of accord and progress.[89]

The luminous prospects of economic and political rejuvenation under Young Turk rule, along with the prominence of the Armenian Revolutionary Federation in the new government, convinced many prospective emigrants to remain in Turkey for a while. However, observers in the interior noted a different reaction: for some "people not knowing how long this sudden freedom would last . . . took advantage of the privilege in great numbers" and emigrated to America. So, the number of emigrants entering the United States in the twelve months ending June 30, 1909 was reduced only to 3,108, down from the previous twelve months' total of 3,299.[90] But even this small reduction in numbers is impressive in view of the Young Turks' wiping out of previous restrictions on Armenian emigration, lowering the high costs of passports, and removing other impediments. Thus, the Young Turk revolt promised to make the ancestral home politically secure for the restive Armenians.

Within the Ottoman Empire optimists called the Young Turk revolt "Daybreak in Turkey," while pessimists warned that "the habits of vicious and corrupt government will be too strong to reform." Tragic events confirmed the pessimistic view; in early 1909 there was a wanton massacre in Cilicia, and again Armenians were impelled to flee Turkey. The Young Turk regime had faced a counterrevolution mounted by the conservative forces of Abdul Hamid. The new regime promptly crushed the fitfully organized insurgency, and exiled and dethroned the figurehead Sultan Hamid. But the hapless Armenians became the uprising's true victims, for during the insurrection, conservative elements, in league with the duplicitous, local Young Turks who had been stirred up by the prosperity and revolutionary exuberance of the Armenians, instigated massacres against the Cilician Armenians.[91]

Hardest hit were the major urban centers of Adana, Marash, Aintab, Urfa, and Antioch. During Easter Week 1909, Turkish rabble, supported by their religious leaders and protected by local militia and police, raped and murdered thousands of defenseless men, women, and children. In the large village of Kessab, 530 houses were burned, many with their inhabitants trapped inside. In Antioch, numerous Armenian shops were "gouged" within less than an hour, and their owners were shot at point blank range or were knifed before they could escape.[92] In the Yenemaballe suburb of Adana, "Soldiers entered the house and badly wounded both children [age 4 and 5] in arms and legs by Martini bullets. A third, age 3, was sitting in the same house playing on the floor when the soldiers entered and they shot her through the abdomen." One Armenian, who climbed up a chimney to hide, was discovered by Turkish troops. They shot up the chimney at him, and when one bullet tore through his foot, he incredibly stiffled his pain and managed to feign death.[93] Such incidents were common throughout the Cilician Plain, and by the end of April 1909 between 15,000 and 20,000 Armenians had been killed, as many more orphaned, and many thousands made homeless; property damage was in the the millions of dollars.[94]

The Armenian Revolutionary Federation, which had championed Armeno-Turkish amity after the 1908 coup, sought to exonerate the Young Turk regime from the bloodletting by assigning blame to the reactionary Hamidean forces. The federation, like many other Armenian political groups, was deeply committed to the building of a new, vibrant Turkey, and it discerned no alternative to Young Turk rule. All this reasoning, however, was useless to survivors of the massacres — the homeless, widowed, orphaned, and starving, who now sought any means to flee Turkey forever for America.

In June 1909 S. R. Trowbridge, president of Central Turkey College in Aintab, addressed a plea to American Consul G. Bie Ravndal in Beirut: "About 500 families in the city of Aintab wish to emigrate to America. Their representatives have begged me to write to the State Department or to influential friends in New York . . . to secure an offer of free land and if possible assistance in transportation. These people are from the middle and lower classes, chiefly weavers and other wage earners. On the whole I think they would make respectable and desirable citizens." Consul Ravndal flatly refused: "It is not in the best interest of our country (yours and mine), nor, under the circumstances, permissible." The consul suggested, rather that the survivors of the massacres stay and "join enlightened Turks, Greeks, etc., in working for the realization of the reforms made possible under the Ottoman Constitution," since

I am convinced that a brighter day is dawning upon Turkey and that while great sacrifices will be required, the future holds out such promises that it would be e [sic] fearful mistake and misfortune if, at the first serious reverse under the new order of things, an important, nay necessary element of the population should emigrate instead of keeping the faith and finishing the course.[95]

Ravndal's position, though substantially the same as that of the Armenian Revolutionary Federation, was arrogant and presumptuous in view of his position of enormous power and his total lack of intellectual commitment to a nascent Turkey or Armenia; it was applauded by the State Department in Washington, because "assisted emigration would . . . be unlawful."[96]

After 1909 Armenians everywhere wanted to flee. The Reverend F. W. Macallum of Marash predicted in June 1909 that "it is only a question of time before another massacre takes place," and he suggested that relief funds for the surviviors would be better used by transporting them to the United States, Canada, or Brazil, instead of keeping them alive in misery in Turkey "with every prospect of a massacre" in fifteen years.[97] Although the 1909 massacres had been restricted to Cilicia, the stream of emigration overflowed everywhere, because of the "great fear among the people [at Kharpert] of another massacre breaking out at any time." Observers in Marseilles, the first port of call en route to America, witnessed a larger number of women and children fleeing in distress from Adana. From Kharpert, Malatia, and Caesaria, from Van and Arabgir, a widening stream of Armenians was fleeing Turkey in search of safety and jobs. The numbers of Armenians entering the United States in the year after Adana represented the single largest total (5,508) in the history of the exodus, almost double that of the preceding year (3,108).[98]

Then in September 1909 the Young Turk government began to induct Christian subjects of the empire into the Turkish Army. Historically, non-Muslim subjects, including the Armenians, had been exempt from military service because devout Muslim Turks loathed military contact and dealings with the despised *giavours* (Christians). In 1855 Turkish reformers had opened military service to the non-Muslim minorities, but Christians were permitted to commute their military duty by paying the *bedel* (exemption fee). In 1909, however, this policy was reversed, because the Young Turks looked upon the non-Muslim subjects' military service as a vital facet of their new policy of forced Ottomanization.[99] The only legal way an able-bodied subject could secure exemption from the dreaded service was to pay a prohibitive fee of 50 Turkish pounds ($220).[100]

As would be surmised, most Turkish Armenian males of military age refused to serve. To be sure, some joined the Ottoman military to serve with valor and distinction in the Ottoman wars commencing in 1911. There exists ample proof of the courage and military zeal of the Armenians in their heroic defense of their own countrymen during World War I; but throwing one's life away in the uniform of the Turkish oppressors was a wholly different matter. Armenians certainly asked whether, after the duplicity of Adana, they could expect to return alive from service, even in peacetime. Would Armenian regiments be earmarked for slaughter on the Balkan front, or would they perish in the Arabian deserts?

Thus, after 1909 Armenians of military age commonly evaded the military draft and fled to America. Despite the Young Turk edicts, government officials at the ports, as well as political and military officers, were persuaded — by heavy bribes — to turn their backs on the flight of young male Armenians to America. Many corrupt Turkish officials were also probably anxious to rid Turkey of the potentially traitorous, despised Armenians. This feeling would explain why the Turkish *gendarmerie* so frequently closed their eyes and issued passports to young Armenian men for America. Jesse Jackson, American Consul in Aleppo, reported in October 1912 that the amount required for legal exemption had been raised to 60 Turkish pounds ($264), which, by rendering legal exemption more expensive, gave an added impetus to emigration to the "poorer classes of Christians who seek, above all, to avoid this forced military service."[101]

After 1911 there were ominous rumblings of Balkan and pan-European wars, and these rumors further exacerbated Armeno-Turkish relations, while Eastern Turkey's continuing economic paralysis added motives for leaving. In September 1911 Italy attacked the Ottoman possession of Tripolitania; and thirteen months later, in October 1912, the Balkan states mounted a combined attack on European Turkey. Each military defeat which the Ottoman armies suffered at the hands of the Europeans created skirmishes between Turks and the Armenians whom they regarded as potentially disloyal. Thus, in the Turkish interior in 1912 there were kidnappings and tortures and robberies. Armenians grew fearful of the rising brigandage, especially in Kurdistan and Eastern Turkey, to which the Ottoman regime was wholly indifferent and probably powerless to curb.[102]

In January 1913 the Armenian patriarch laid before Turkish authorities repeated complaints of Kurdish depredations. The complaints also recalled the Turks' refusal to surrender Armenian lands seized since the mid-1890s' massacres — all to no avail.[103] In May 1913 a delegation composed of the Armenian patriarch, two Armenian bishops, and the president and vice president of the Armenian lay council, presented a *démarche* on behalf of the Armenian National Assembly:

The constitutional regime . . . has thus far been a disappointment to the Armenian community. While the vexatious oppression suffered by the Armenians has continued uninterruptedly and has even increased in the past four or five years, "disquieting symptoms, precursors of a massacre, of a catastrophe capable of overshadowing, in its horror, the most fearful tragedies of the past" have become manifest more recently. . . . The opinion is fostered among the Moslem masses that "it will not be possible to preserve from European encroachments what still remains of Ottoman Territory, except by annihilating the Armenian element."[104]

All of these frightening signs increased the pressure on Armenians and led to an unusual exodus. An Armenian from Dicranagert reported in early 1913 that the uncertain political circumstances and the disastrous economic situation were increasing the emigration by way of Aleppo, Beirut, and Alexandretta. Homes and farms in Kharpert were sold in a minute at half price by prospective emigrants to America.[105] Despite a promising harvest in 1913 in Kharpert, the able-bodied youth continued to emigrate, leaving houses and schools deserted and churches and associations peopled by only the elderly. Because of the unending numbers of caravans moving to the Black Sea and the Mediterranean, Turkey was growing "thin like a consumptive." In 1913 9,355 Armenians, the single largest annual total — almost double the high reached in 1910, immediately after the Adana massacres — entered the United States.[106]

Emigration from Russia. Russian Armenians also emigrated in the early years of the twentieth century although only fifteen had gone to the United States before 1898.[107] The movement of the Russian Armenians was the indirect result of the czarist persecution of the Russian Dukhobors and Molokans. The Dukhobors, who resembled and drew the sympathy of English and American Quakers, had been persecuted intermittently since 1792. In 1895 the Dukhobors in the Caucasus were again savagely persecuted, this time by Czar Nicholas II's cossacks for their refusal to serve in the czar's armies; some were brutally whipped, others were killed or exiled or imprisoned, and some 4,000 were forcibly resettled in Armenian and Georgian villages. In 1898 the Dukhobors, who had secured the financial and political support of Count Tolstoy and other humanitarians, were granted government permission to emigrate from Russia, and after a disastrous false start in Cyprus, a large contingent sailed for Winnepeg, Canada.[108] Letters to fellow Dukhobors and neighboring Russian Armenians in the Caucasus began a flow of Armenian emigrants to Canada.

Once in Canada the first Russian Armenians fell to quarreling among themselves over financial matters, and one group pushed on to Los Angeles, where Dukhobors had settled earlier. The Russian Armenian "pioneers" wrote glowing letters from Los Angeles to friends and relatives, and these inspired migrants chiefly from the villages south of Alexandropol (Shirag), Khazarabad, Sivanirli, and Aghzolou.[109]

Also, under Nicholas II in Russia, the evangelical, pacifist Molokan sect was being persecuted by the czar's archconservative Orthodox procurator Count Pobedonostsev. Because of the Molokans' alleged refusal to recognize the sacrament of baptism, the government forcibly took children from their parents and had them dispatched to religious institutions to be raised. Like the Dukhobors, the Molokans, who lived mainly in the Shirag region, determined to leave Russia for Canada and the United States. Their letters to neighbors in the village of Karakala began a trickle of Russian Armenians from that region to the New World.[110]

A deep economic depression in the Caucasus enlarged the movement of Russian Armenians to the United States after 1900. The petroleum industry at Baku and on the Black Sea went through a market slump, and similar problems afflicted mining at a time when large contingents of migrant Turks and Russian laborers were competing for jobs already held by Armenians. The Russian Revolution of 1905 and the Russo-Tatar Wars of 1905–1907 worsened the plight of the inhabitants of the Caucasus.

Chiefly, then, the Russian Armenian emigrants were young males, often married, who left their homes hoping to earn money and return after a few years with their purses full. They were hardworking and sturdy, but very poor, peasants. In order to migrate many had to sell their "cattle or household furniture, or jewelry, and some [of them] borrowed money." Only a few possessed funds for the expenses of the long journey. The largest migration occurred between 1908 and 1914, and as with the Turkish Armenians, the movement was cut off by the coming of World War I.[111]

The volume of Russian Armenian migration to the United States never achieved major proportions. According to a census published in the Fresno, California, Armenian-language paper *Asbarez* (The Arena), 50 Russian Armenians emigrated to the United States between 1900 and 1905, some 300 emigrated between 1905 and 1910, and 1,200 arrived between 1910 and 1913. The total number of Russian Armenians emigrating to the United States prior to World War I was not more than 2,500 persons.[112]

The number of Russian Armenians was so much smaller probably because political persecution had taken less violent forms; there were no Protestant missionaries to encourage education and inspire emigration as there had been in the Ottoman Empire; and Russian Armenia's level of economic development, while low, was still higher than Turkey's. Also, because the migration started later, it was soon cut off by the war.

Thus ended the flight from Turkey and Russia to the New World. By the eve of World War I over 60,000 hopeful sons and daughters of *Hayastan* (Armenia) had forsaken their ancestral homes in the quest for a new life in far off America. Shouldering their few precious possessions, they set their sights and dreams westward.

5.

Routes and Reactions

Leaving Russia or Turkey was just the first step of what could be a long and hazardous journey to America. The immigrant press was full of the perils and trials of the unfortunate travelers en route to the New World, and consular officials, investigators, and diplomats corroborated these stories. Yet the tide of emigrants surged on. At the same time, Armenians in both the Old World and the New began increasingly to see another side of the emigration and to speak out against the continuing exodus from Turkey to America.

Enroute to America

Reaching the Sea. Until 1911 Samson, on the Black Sea, was the major port of embarkation for emigrants from the Armenian Plateau, while emigrants from Cilicia trekked to Alexandretta and Beirut on the Mediterranean. After 1911, however, the Mediterranean ports were more frequently chosen, especially by men fleeing the Turkish draft, because there were fewer police and officials to detain them if they had no proof of any army discharge. Russian Armenians generally traveled by rail to Batum, although a few journeyed half way across Russia to Riga and Libau on the Baltic to make their departure.[1]

The most common mode of transport to either the Black Sea or the Mediterranean was the time-honored wagon caravan. Forty to eighty emigrants in eight to ten wagons, plus a few Kurdish or Turkish guides, would make up such a group. Within the caravan's protection, the poorest emigrants traveled much of the way on foot. Parents carried infants on their backs or strapped them, in wooden baskets, on both sides of donkeys or mules. The more affluent rode in the "Circassian" wagons.

The day of departure from the village was a special event. Work ceased to permit all the villagers' thoughts to be with the travelers. The women sewed jewelry, money, and good omens such as blue beads or pieces of blue cloth into the voyagers' clothes. Children were blessed, embraced, and given silver crosses by saddened kin.

One immigrant vividly remembered seeing his grandmother running after the wagons, weeping that she would never see her children again.[2]

In addition to their sorrow as they saw their familiar village pass from view, the travelers felt some apprehensions because the trip to the coast, which took several weeks and wound through the rugged mountains, was known to be dangerous. Furthermore, the Armenian emigrants were unarmed and at the mercy of their Kurdish or Turkish guides, who were often in league with the omnipresent Kurdish brigands. In 1903, for example, a caravan en route from Hoolou to Samson was held up by forty Kurdish brigands; the travelers were stripped of their money and worldly possessions and forced to return home. Consular officials in Kharpert and Diarbekir frequently reported robbed caravans between the interior and the coast; and children later remembered pitched gun battles between loyal guides and Kurdish outlaws.[3] During war time, all travel was strictly forbidden to Armenians, and those who happened to be en route during pogroms risked instant massacre if they were caught. A party of emigrants en route to the Mediterranean during the Adana massacres in April 1909 had a particularly horrible experience:

There were forty-one [sic] emigrants that left this neighborhood some weeks ago, thirty-eight men and two women, all Armenians, for Adana ostensibly, altho several of the number intended ultimately to sail for America, four of the number being youn [sic] men who had been raised and educated at the American mission at Harput. These people being all poor and without much baggage engaged a little caravan of mules and horses to carry their few effects, the emigrants themselves walking and along with them they took a little flock of sheep and goats. The *Katiajis* (guides) in charge of the transport animals were Turks and there were also some fifty Turkish emigrants along with the party. Some six hours out from Marash the whole party stopped for the night at a khan [inn], and it seems they were most hospitably received in fact a party of Turks and Kurds went out to meet them upon the road. At daybreak the next morning the khan was surrounded by armed Turks and Kurds and thirty-five of these poor unfortunate Armenians were overpowered and let out one at a time and shot, the executioners finishing up the bloody work with an axe. Three of the men were sleeping out with the sheep and thus they escaped and the two women after being repeatedly assaulted were permitted to return here and it was from these women that these facts have been ascertained. The Turkish emigrants accompanying this party were unmolested and continued on their way.[4]

Until 1908, when the Young Turk government liberalized restrictions, it was extremely difficult to obtain permission to emigrate from Turkey.[5] Teskeres (passports) permitting travel from the interior to the coast were not always available, since local officials held them back to raise the price or because they feared that issuing teskeres would cost a province its largest taxpayers.[6] Accordingly, bribes were always required for the teskere. (Forged teskeres were also available at a premium.) The bribes usually amounted to between $20 and $30, or ten to fifteen times the $2 legal fee for a travel permit.

In fact it was as expensive to obtain permission to leave Turkey as it was to sail from Turkey to America.[7] The average combined expense for a visa and steamship ticket ($50 to $60) amounted to a year's wages for a journeyman in Turkey, or the accumulated savings of an artisan for no less than three full years. Because the ticket was so expensive, some emigrants bribed boatsmen to smuggle them on board European vessels; some stowed away in the ships' coal bins. Others made the trip in two or three stages, earning money on the way. "The journey from Bitlis to New York took almost two years," recounted William Saroyan, "for it was necessary for my grandmother Lucy, who was in charge of the journey, to halt several times while she and her daughters . . . and her son . . . worked to earn money for further passage." "They spent three or four months in Erzeroum, a month or two in Marseilles, and almost six months in Havre. My uncle, . . . then eleven or so, learned French and acted as interpreter for many Armenians on their way to America. The women knitted stockings which . . . [he] sold to small shopkeepers."[8]

Exploitation.   At the ports en route, sadly, Armenians exploited their own newly arrived countrymen. The abuses began at Samson. "These emigrants, . . . as soon as they reach in the han [inn], [a] crowd composed of inn-keepers . . . Commission Agents, brokers and their fellow citizens, fall like crowd upon them insisting and forcing them to attend to their business; this is made with the sole intention to exploit them and get illegal profits. Terrible abuses and deformities are taking place by these exploiters."[9] At Marseilles, the Armenians who knew no French, were herded by Armenian-speaking guides (or "runners") to "comfortable, reasonable" accommodations at an "Armenian Hotel." Once arrived the immigrants found themselves in dilapidated, vermin-infested boardinghouses where they were overcharged and forced to room with a large number of other unfortunate victims of the Armenian *smsars* (agents). One of the most notorious was the Hotel D'Armenie, 40 Rue Belsune, Marseilles.

The travellers' rooms are upstairs. One room, which has low ceilings, and small windows, is generally dark while others are darker and less ventilated. The room has twenty persons, increases to thirty in the traveling season. There are no beds, bedspreads or bedding. Some with blankets sit cross legged on them; those without blankets get worn out, infested sacks. In the summer the emigrants sit on the steps outside to avoid the miserable smell and the heat of the place. The place is filthy, and festering from top to bottom. . . . There is rubbish up to one's knees, and excrement, like a stable.[10]

The range of exploitative devices that the smsars used from Turkish ports to Marseilles and Liverpool was astonishing even to hardened travelers. Immigrants who had paid hard-earned money to buy decent second-class accommodations on America-bound ships were given cramped steerage quarters; travelers from Samson, arriving at Naples, found that their expensive "through tickets to America" were valid only from Samson to Naples; immigrants were regularly shortchanged on their American Express checks and money orders; smsars detained and fleeced unwary travelers, using the ruse that ships traveling to America lacked space; women were abused and assaulted.[11]

In time American and European authorities sought to eradicate the worst abuses of the smsars; in Samson, the American consuls posted schedules of rates for room charges at the khans, the wharf tax, transportation charges, and information regarding steamers, ticket prices, and cashing checks. Consul Norton in 1904 also urged emigrants to purchase through tickets from Turkey to the United States since "the disadvantages of such a broken journey for women and children, ignorant of European languages and of the outside world, are obvious."[12] In Marseilles by about 1910 the "chief offenders were driven out of the district," and French authorities established strict regulations governing room and board rates. They informed steerage passengers prior to debarking at Marseilles of their liberty to stay at any boardinghouse and of their tariffs.[13] However, since many emigrants lacked the funds to pay for the "through" trip to the United States from Turkey, and because they were ignorant of French and of the "world," they were forced to rely on the Armenian-speaking agents.

Trachoma. Even more foul than the gouging of emigrants for accommodations and tickets was the smsars' brisk trade in promising cures for trachoma victims. Trachoma, a pernicious, contagious disease, characterized by granulation and inflammation at the eyelids, could lead to blindness in acute cases. The disease was very common in the Middle East; an American consul estimated that 40 percent of all Turkish Armenians were trachoma victims. In 1897 the United States Congress termed trachoma a "dangerous contagious disease" and required all immigrants to be examined for its presence; those infected were not permitted to enter the country and were compelled to return to their native lands. It was no wonder then that immigrants in New York Harbor were terrified of being "sick in the eyes," since the family would be split up at Ellis Island, and the "no bono" (diseased) family member would be condemned to return to Turkey.[14]

The legislation of 1897 imposed a fine of $100 for each time a steamship line carried a trachoma victim to the United States. This policy led eventually to the establishment of medical inspection stations at European ports for prospective emigrants prior to embarkation for the United States. In Naples, inspection was carried out by physicians of the United States Public Health Service; at Liverpool it was done by medical officials of the British Board of Trade; elsewhere, resident physicians of the steamship companies performed the task. According to the American consul in Kharpert, a total cure of trachoma could be attained with a few week's treatment by a licensed physician, or occasionally by an operation.[15]

It is truly lamentable that at Marseilles and Liverpool the Armenian hotel and innkeepers, in league with quack doctors and charlatans, plied such a lucrative, inhuman trade in the sufferings of the trachoma victims. Although a large majority of Armenians passed the examinations, those who failed were lured by the hotel keepers into one of a number of traps. For example, hotel keepers regularly arranged "low cost" treatments with "doctors." The immigrant, perhaps a woman with two children, one of whom had not passed the examination, would unwittingly take her child to the charlatan for a treatment; she would then be told to return in a week for a second treatment. After this came a third and fourth treatment; by this time a month had passed, her child was not cured and the woman's savings would be exhausted. All the fees for the treatments, of course, would be divided between the hotel keeper and the "physician."

Other immigrants were inveigled into paying bribes to the hotel keeper and to the "French authorities," who could secure a "bono" certificate for the emigrant; this proved useless, however, when the still diseased emigrant was debarred at Ellis Island. And emigrants whose "treatments" in France effected a partial remission, passing the French inspection, often failed the American examination.[16] The most diabolical slant of all was the invention of the smsars who would convince an *unafflicted* voyager that he was in fact, diseased, and, that he had to undergo treatment.[17] Other trachoma victims were persuaded to purchase expensive tickets to St. Johns, New Brunswick, where trachoma examinations purportedly were less rigorous, and still others, reported the United States Immigration Commission, "who doubtless would be admitted at United States ports are deluded into going via Mexico [usually Vera Cruz] by the spoilers who prey upon ignorant emigrants at Marseilles and eastern Mediterranean ports."[18]

One nefarious scheme, unconnected with the smsars, involved smuggling debarred trachoma victims into the United States as members of ships' crews because these men normally did not undergo medical examinations upon debarking at New York. In 1909 the American Consul General at Antwerp uncovered a smuggling ring, connected to the Northwest Transportation Company, that had offices at Marseilles, Liverpool, Rotterdam, Antwerp, and Constantinople. The company signed on many of the unfortunate "no bono" Armenians, some of whom were "so anxious to try again to get into our country" that they paid Northwest as much as 50 British pounds to sail as crew members. The State Department alerted Immigration Department authorities at Ellis Island, and one group of 60 afflicted men, mostly Armenians, was turned back at Rotterdam. The would-be immigrants were so desperate to enter the United States that, despite their second debarment, a number of them waited at Antwerp, then traveled to Liverpool, where they no doubt tried again.

Other Abuses. The Northwest Transportation Company, according to the Consul in Antwerp, also flagrantly violated the federal contract labor laws by hiring Armenians at Constantinople for $200 a year and farming them out at New York City for $500 a year to American employers.[19]

Other emigrants, for a variety of causes, were stranded often for weeks at a time without funds at the European ports. One group of eighty or ninety Armenians was delayed at Batum in early 1906 because of hostilities between Armenians and Tatars in the Caucasus, and they appeared "ragged" and "unkempt" after staying there some weeks. Another band, in 1907, having funds only for passage, was quarantined due to a cholera epidemic and as a result became destitute and faced starvation.[20] An unfortunate group of Russian Armenians was detained at Ellis Island in 1911 pending an investigation of contract labor law violations. According to the Commissioner General of Immigration, one "Krikeroff" and 16 companions had arrived in New York from Russian Armenia en route to Riverside, California. An Armenian had been to their native village and had told them how to enter the country and how "to obtain employment in a cement works at Riverside." Most of the fellows, who had no inkling that such "contracts" were illegal, had borrowed money for the passage, often at usurious rates; in some cases homes were mortgaged as security to pay for passage. Because their migration had been induced and encouraged by promises of work, all but four were ordered deported. Indeed passage to America frequently caused both physical and mental suffering.

It was not surprising that the rates for Armenians debarred from entry into the United States prior to World War I generally exceeded those of most other contemporary emigrant groups. Between 1899 and 1915 a total of 2,356 Armenians, or approximately 4 percent of the total, were debarred from entry. Of these 577 were debarred for trachoma or other diseases, 929 for being "paupers or persons likely to become public charges" (without the minimum $25 in their possession), and 257 as "undesirable persons." The total average rate of debarment of all emigrant groups in the same years was approximately 1 percent.[21]

The New World Responds

Concern for the Historic Homeland. Both in the New World and the Old, some Armenians began to see in the rising number of emigrants a danger to the continuing existence of the Old Country. Shrill warnings of the peril were published on both sides of the Atlantic.

In the United States the Armenian Revolutionary Federation (Tashnagtsutiun, or the Tashnags) used its journal and party gatherings to urge the stateside families of prospective emigrants to thwart further migration to America. The Tashnags were politically and intellectually committed to the success of the Turkish Constitutional regime of 1908 and especially to nurturing Armeno-Turkish amity under Young Turk rule. Accordingly, when the Young Turks began drafting non-Muslim minorities, the Tashnags supported the move and urged Armenians to volunteer in the empire's regiments. In a Providence, Rhode Island, meeting in 1911, for example, the federation resolved that "Draft fleeing is disrespectful and wrong. . . . Such flight is . . . a severe blow to self-preservation, self-protection and the new [Young Turk] regime."[22] Second, the Tashnags supported the principle of Armenian self-defense — the arming of men in Turkey as self-protective bodies against Kurdish aggression in the villages. All the young, able-bodied men who comprised the bulk of the emigrants constituted a critical loss for the potential fighting force in Armenia.[23] Finally, the more socialist-oriented writers in the federation, as well as in the Hnchag Party, condemned the capitalist economy of the United States where the emigrants formed the proletarian class.

Such intellectual and political views appealed only to a small minority of patriotic followers; they meant little to the hungry and oppressed mass of the Armenian population in Turkey or to their families in America. As a result, the editors of *Hairenik*, a Tashnag journal in Boston, appealed instead to "bread and butter" issues to thwart the migration. Witness the June 17, 1913, headline of *Hairenik*: "DO NOT MIGRATE — AMERICAN JOBS ARE SLACK — especially for new immigrants." In 1912, *Hairenik* had urged prospective young emigrants in Turkey to consider the 70,000 unemployed workers in San Francisco and the 200,000 unemployed in Chicago, pointing out that mass unemployment spelled suffering for the newcomers. Tashnag writers pictured America as vastly different from the glowing reports of "gold in the streets" so fervently believed in the Old Country. Hence, patriotic Armenians in the United States were counseled by the federation not to write encouraging letters to Armenia or to send snapshots of themselves in "high fashion," but rather to tell the truth of the "insufferable" factory toil in order to stave off the migration that was depleting Turkey.[24] One Armenian in Fresno criticized another immigrant's alluring letters for failing to mention the weeks he hunted for a job in the vineyards; said he, don't write home about just "the rose and the lily."[25]

Not all Tashnag writers concurred in this policy of discouraging emigration, either for nationalistic or for economic reasons. For example, one Armenian in Fresno stated baldly that "the only solution to the Armenian Question is emigration, to where we can be free, . . . there we make our fatherland." M. K. Ferrahian, in Asbarez, in Fresno, sharply criticized the extreme Tashnag views, because "the life in the old country is a perfect hell, and everyone who can, will attempt to escape it, as we have escaped it." Ferrahian, one of the more outspoken writers of the period, dismissed the party policy of repatriation as unrealistic. "If emigration is wrong, if repatriation is the correct solution, why don't we repatriate? If we do not return because of the insecurity [in Turkey] how can we urge others to remain [in Turkey]?" Querried Ferrahian, "How can a well fed man understand a starving man's condition?" So too, when others criticized the emigration as a "white massacre," bleeding Armenia of her able-bodied men, critics argued that as long as the Turkish interior was unsafe for Armenians, no one should have the presumption to argue against the emigration.[26]

Until 1913 the most prominent political and religious bodies in Turkey and Russia were silent about the emigration, both because very few of the intellectual leaders and other visible elements of the population were emigrating and because tumultuous problems were occupying Armenian officials during the Young Turk period. After 1913, however, the year of the single largest exodus, various bodies deliberated on the issue. In July the Armenian National Assembly, in Constantinople, the largest deliberative body of Armenians in Turkey, unanimously recommended a program to halt the ever growing flood of emigrants to America. The assembly planned to dispatch lay and clerical representatives to the provinces to speak about the issue and to appeal to the Armenians in Constantinople and the diaspora for financial contributions to aid the country's reconstruction. The assembly also resolved that for the supreme "interest of

Armenia," it was urgent to halt the exodus from the fatherland and to defend the nation's existence.[27]

Another concerned body was the Armenian General Benevolent Union, founded in Cairo in 1908. Largest of the Armenian philanthropic and educational organizations, with branches throughout the world, the AGBU appropriated 25,000 francs to assist the efforts directed against emigration and to aid former emigrants in repatriating to Turkey. The Tashnag party in 1913 approved the AGBU's stance, and they also looked with satisfaction on the Turkish government's announcement that the gendarmerie wouuld be dispatched, along with valis from the province of Rumelia to Armenia, to restore order and stem the migration. Everywhere, groups of Armenian leaders strove to contain the movement.[28]

But the nationalists' was not the only Old World point of view. The conservative daily journal *Puzantion* (Byzantium), published in Constantinople, perceived benefits from the "white massacre." According to this journal, Armenia's salvation would come from the West, by the hands of the emigrants who, through education, "learning industries, and by becoming rich in new enterprises, will remember the fatherland." Conceding that some of the hundred Armenians with higher degrees in the United States would remain in their new land, *Puzantion* was sure that others would return home, that they indeed were "even under oath to work for a certain period in the fatherland." Moreover, the new colony was full of promise, for "Armenians in America have their churches and schools, and do not forget the Armenian language and history. Armenian students in America who enter universities . . . will work for their nation, and become leaders in the future civilized life of the Armenian fatherland; . . . many also have in the fatherland parents and relatives to whom they send money, and the money sent by Armenian colonies in Europe, America, and Egypt is a large sum."[29] But for most Armenians in official capacities the emigration was a source of profound and increasing disquiet on the eve of World War I.

Help in Present Trouble.   While most spokesmen were inveighing against the migration, the private charities sought to alleviate the worst sufferings of the emigrants en route to the New World.

The first and most celebrated outpouring of charity occurred in 1896, in the wake of the Constantinople massacre. Between August 28 and 30, over 6,000 Armenians were slain in the streets of Constantinople — chiefly by the sultan's club-wielding Kurdish rabble. Some Armenians caught in the open escaped to European ships in the harbor, but the sultan's regime mandated that no Armenians on European vessels could return to Turkish soil — alive. The vessels then took their passengers to Marseilles where, without funds for food, clothing, or passage, they were marooned. There were "heart-rending scenes" of men "tramping the streets in misery . . . with nothing to eat, and no steps were being taken to help them."[30]

Anglo-American humanitarians, hearing of the plight of the Armenians in Marseilles, began to organize a practical relief effort. Lady Henry Somerset, an English philanthropist, and Emma Willard, President of the American Women's Christian Temperance Union, rushed to Marseilles where they distributed clothing and coal and cooked meals for the refugees,[31] Simultaneously, they began looking for permanent homes for the Armenians. A few were sent off to England for shelter, but the women planned to help two or three hundred refugees go to the United States. The restrictions against "paupers" and persons "liable to be public charges" notwithstanding, the humanitarians learned from a ship's agent that "he would have no trouble getting them in." Transportation was chartered for the refugees, and in late October 1896 the steamer *Obdam* and the *California* arrived in New York Harbor.[32]

Hardly had the Armenian refugees set foot on American soil when opposition arose to their entry. The *Boston Evening Transcript* quoted Immigration Commissioner Delahanty's objection to bringing "large numbers to Boston on largely sentimental grounds." The commissioner promised that the refugees would be "sent back to Turkey, even if chances were they might fall into the hands of Turkish cruelty," if they were declared public charges. A rumor that the refugees might settle in Hokokus, New Jersey, prompted an angry petition from residents and taxpayers, as follows: "For some time past men and women dressed in the uniforms of the Salvation Army have been engaged in systematic begging for the support and maintenance of a horde of Armenians, the same being aliens and paupers, and we protest against the said aliens and paupers being sent into the community."[33] Hagop Bogigian, a well-to-do Armenian businessman in Boston, retorted: "It seems almost incredible that these Armenians who have escaped death in Turkey should now be held at the very threshold of this free country with the prospect of being returned staring them in the face."[34] The Armenians were detained at Ellis Island pending resolution of the problem.

Even before the refugees arrived, Lady Henry Somerset wired the immigration authorities that she was willing to post personal bond should any of her people become public charges. Bogigian; Moses Gulesian, another prominent Armenian American businessman; Moorfield Storey; Mrs. Susan B. Fessenden of the Massachusetts State Board of the W.C.T.U., Emma Willard; Alice Stone Blackwell; and others posted personal bonds and used contributions from Sunday church appeals up to $65,000 to secure the refugees' release. On November 1, 1896, the first of the much-publicized newcomers finally crossed the threshold of the United States, thanks to the efforts of this gallant assembly of humanitarians.[35]

At the same time, hurried steps were taken for the refugees' board and housing. The single largest group of them were temporarily housed in the third floor of Moses Gulesian's cornice factory in Boston, and their immediate needs met by contributions from the Friends of Armenia, Julia Ward Howe, and the WCTU. Soon, through the efforts of Alice Stone Blackwell, Gulesian, and Bogigian, the refugees had places as "farmers, carpenters, barbers, tailors, drivers, and as servants."[36] The 1896 episode was the first and most noteworthy joint English, Armenian, and American effort to aid immigrants and refugees. After that, as emigrants moved to the United States, Armenian groups assumed the primary responsibility for assisting them.

The earliest continuing organization designed to aid immigrants was the Armenian Colonial Association (ACA), founded in New York City in 1900. The ACA's founding membership included such prominent Armenian businessmen and clergy as Mihran Karagheusian, M. Dadrean, Gullabi Gulbenkian, Sarkis Minasian, Hovannes Tavshanjian, L. Gosdigian, Sarkis Telfeyan, A. Kitabian, A. Aleon, the Reverend Hovagim Hagopian and the Reverend Mashtots Vartabed Papazian. Establishment of the ACA may have been sparked when four Armenian orphans were debarred from landing in New York City in 1899, and the incident was publicized in the immigrant press. In any case, in 1900 the group hired the Reverend Hagopian as an agent charged with assisting Armenian newcomers at Castle Island and later at Ellis Island.[37] Although Reverend Hagopian could not render all the assistance required by the large influx of immigrants, he and his organization provided transportation, jobs, medical help, and other assistance to many. According to its first annual report, the ACA in 1900 arranged inexpensive transportation for 112 persons; found jobs for 99 persons; assisted 5 poverty-stricken Armenians to return to Marseilles; placed 5 Armenian children in orphanages; provided free medical help for 48 persons; secured release from the "Barge Office" of 8 families and 15 young persons; and assisted 9 persons in trouble with the customs officials. The annual report lamented the association's failure to find jobs for another 180 unemployed Armenian immigrants.[38]

The ACA grew with time, and with the generous financial support of Mihran Karagheusian of New York and Garabed Pushman of Chicago, agents were hired in Chicago (1911) and Marseilles (1912). The statistics of the 1912 annual report tell a success story, for in that year the ACA placed 1,521 Armenians in jobs in factories, hotels, hospitals and schools; assisted 83 immigrants with problems at Ellis Island; provided legal assistance to 35 Armenians; found work for 253 immigrants in Chicago; sought to improve the deplorable conditions in Marseilles; and distributed over $2,000 to needy Armenians en route to America.[39]

Despite the good it accomplished, the ACA did not lack critics. Some called it inactive and inefficient, and in 1913 the socialist-oriented Tashnags accused the association of swindling Armenian laborers, of misleading workers with inaccurate information, and of "harboring strike-breakers." One writer stated that the ACA was prejudiced in favor of Protestant as opposed to Apostolic Armenians, and that its officials were growing fat on the funds of Messrs. Karagheusian and Pushman.[40] But the record bears out none of these accusations.

The unstinting efforts of humanitarian groups from Marseilles and Liverpool to New York eased the trials of the indigent, sick, and exploited newcomers. But the work of the humanitarians subsided with the onset of World War I, as hostilities necessarily halted passage to America. Not until 1919 was it possible for substantial numbers of Armenians again to flee Turkey for America. A great wave of migration had crested and fallen, and one phase in the story of the odyssey of the Armenians was now history.

Characteristics of the Mass Migration. In 1899 the United States Commissioner General of Immigration began identifying newcomers by ethnic categories in addition to the national and geographic categories used hitherto; "Armenian" was thereafter employed as well as the category of immigrants from "Asiatic Turkey." In 1907 the United States Government, troubled by the nativists' fears of a "rising tide" of immigrants from eastern and southern Europe and the Middle East, undertook a massive study of the current immigration to America. The reports of the United States Immigration Commission shed light on the demographic and socio-economic character of the Armenian emigration to America, and they provide an illuminating view of that emigration in relation to the numbers of other immigrants from southern and eastern Europe.

Between 1899 and 1914 51,950 Armenians entered the United States. This figure does not include the 2,356 Armenians debarred from entry for medical or other reasons during these years. No prior wave of Armenian immigration approached the magnitude of this brief period from 1899 to World War I. Careful estimates place the migration bet veen 1891 and 1898 at 12,500 and in all periods prior to 1891 at 1,500. Thus, a total of approximately 65,950 Armenians were admitted to the United States prior to World War I.[41]

The annual volume of Armenian emigration to America between 1899 and 1910 (the period examined by the Immigration Commission) in relation to the total Old World population was very low, and far below that of such groups as the Southern Italians, Poles, and Eastern European Jews. The figures for Armenians exceeded only those for the nonemigrating peoples, the French and Spanish, as noted below:[42]

	Estimated Old World population	Average annual no. of immigrants, 1899–1910	Number of immigrants per 1,000 Old World population
Armenians	5,000,000	2,127	.4
Eastern European Jews	8,000,000	88,232	11.0
French	39,000,000	6,671	.2
Southern Italians	20,000,000	157,300	7.9
Poles	4,500,000	35,086	7.8
Spanish	20,000,000	2,451	.1

Overwhelmingly, the Armenian immigrants were male. As the table below shows, males (20,282) outnumbered the females (6,216) almost four to one. In this particular, Armenians were exceeded by the Bulgarians, Serbians, Montenegrins, Greeks, Rumanians, and Russians. Even so, the high percentage of Armenian male immigrants in the total exceeded that of the average of all immigrant groups of the period.

	Percent Male	Percent Female
Armenians	76.5	23.5
Bulgarians, Serbians and Montenegrins	95.7	4.3
Greeks	95.1	4.9
Rumanians	91.0	9.0
Russians	85.0	15.0
Average of all immigrants	69.5	30.5

The vast majority of the Armenian immigrants were young or middle-aged. Those under 14 years of age numbered 4,726, or about 9 percent of the total; fully 87 percent (45,269) fell into the 14–15 age category; and 4 percent (1,955) were over 45 years of age.[43] Generally speaking, it was the young, the ambitious and the strong who emigrated to America, leaving the weaker and older folk in the Old Country.

The socio-economic characteristics of the Armenian immigrants distinguished them as a group. Available data for 18,543 immigrants, from United States immigration records, reveal that over 40 percent of the Armenians admitted to the United States during the period 1899 to 1910 who had been employed in Turkey were in the "skilled" or "professional" classes. Among these the most numerous were the skilled tradesmen: the shoemakers, tailors, carpenters, and weavers.[44] (Examination of the passenger lists of ships entering New York Harbor in 1897 indicates an even higher percentage of skilled immigrants among the Armenians). Although the number of skilled workers was high, just over one-half of the Armenian emigrants were classified as "farm laborers" or "laborers."[45]

These figures indicated that between 1899 and 1910 there were far more skilled workers and professionals among the Armenian immigrants than among the other southern and eastern European groups such as the Southern Italians, Greeks, and Rumanians. Indeed, as the chart below shows, the numbers of skilled and professional Armenians exceeded the comparable numbers even from such "old" immigrant groups as the Germans, and Scandinavians. Of the "new" immigrant groups, only the Eastern European Jews surpassed the percentages of professional and skilled backgrounds attained by Armenians.[46]

	Percent professionals	Percent skilled workers	Percent farm laborers	Percent laborers	Percent other occupations
Armenians	2.3	39.3	23.5	17.8	17.1
Eastern European Jews	1.3	67.1	1.9	11.8	18.0
Germans	3.5	30.0	17.9	19.8	28.8
Greeks	.3	7.7	19.4	66.8	5.8
Southern Italians	.4	14.6	34.5	42.5	7.9
Rumanians	.2	2.7	59.4	34.4	3.3
Scandinavians	1.2	20.5	7.6	36.2	34.5

How is the exceptional socio-economic distribution of the Armenians to be explained? First, the nonagricultural classes were less rooted to the land by endemic poverty and debt than the peasantry. Up to 1908 observers regularly stated that it was "only the comparatively well-to-do who are able to emigrate, because it is quite impossible to obtain a teskere (passport) from the police authorities without the payment of a heavy bribe, which, of course, is beyond the means of the poorer classes."[47] In fact, during the period when passage costs were highest — prior to 1908 — a still greater percentage of immigrants than for the whole period came from the professional and artisan classes. After 1908, when permission to leave

Turkey was to be had for the asking and passage costs declined, the proportions of agricultural workers and laborers in the emigrating population increased substantially.[48] Second, it must be remembered that the petty bourgeois Armenians of Turkey played a role parallel to that of the Jews of eastern Europe; they formed the backbone of the middle classes — the bankers, traders and handicraft artisans — of Turkish society. For generations the empire's business and artisan crafts had been largely in Armenian hands. The large proportions of Armenians from the professional and artisan classes in the exodus thus reflected their important economic role in Ottoman society: simply, in proportionate terms, there were greater numbers of them to emigrate.

Third, emigration was more readily seen as a viable alternative by the educated classes. Significantly, the Armenian immigrant was considerably better educated than the average eastern or southern European immigrant of the period. Among the 51,950 Armenians entering the United States between 1899 and 1914 approximately three-quarters of those 14 years of age and older (35,391) were able to read and write in their own language. As the compilations of the Immigration Commission in the period 1899 to 1910 reveal, the literacy rate of the Armenians exceeded that of the Eastern European Jews and many other immigrant groups, and was surpassed only by three "new" immigrant groups (the Bohemians and Moravians, the Finns, and the Hungarians).[49]

	Percent literate
Armenians	76
Eastern European Jews	74
Bohemians and Moravians	98
Bulgarians, Serbians, and Montenegrins	58
Finns	99
Hungarians	88
Southern Italians	46
Poles	65
Average of all new immigrants	64

Indeed, the unusual socio-economic characteristics of the Armenian immigrants are especially important in understanding the nature of their experience in America.

PART THREE

The Terms of Settlement

6.

The Economic Base:
First Employment

In the beginning the vast majority of the newly arrived Armenian immigrants joined other newcomers from southern and eastern Europe as unskilled laborers in the factories and mills of the United States. They had arrived without capital or any knowledge of English; however, in time, the immigrant Armenians generally proved to be successful in their adjustment to the economic life of the adopted country. The new arrivals had a number of advantages: many had skills or backgrounds in business. Their literacy rate in their own language was exceptionally high. Their long experience as a minority group in their native land had taught them the techniques of survival in an alien environment. Finally, the devastation of Turkish Armenia during 1894–1896 and 1909 had compelled the vast majority to regard their move to the United States as a permanent break with the homeland, and not simply as a temporary, money-making sojourn.

Factory and Foundry

When they arrived in New York, most Armenians were too poor to open a business or purchase a farm. Of the 14,583 arriving between 1899 and 1907, the average per capita cash holding at dockside was $31.67. And the pattern persisted: in 1912 when 5,222 Armenians entered the port of New York, approximately 90 percent, excluding children under 14 years of age, debarked with less than $50 — hardly enough to pay rent and buy food for a family for a month.[1] Moreover, they lacked skills which were readily adaptable to American industry. But because they entered the country in a period when rapid industrial growth was opening jobs to unskilled laborers, the vast majority of the immigrants were able to find work in factories, foundries, and mills.

To understand their economic adjustment, it is useful to consider the character of the American industrial system at that time. Beginning in the 1880s, when the Armenians and the southern and eastern Europeans began to arrive en masse in the United States, the country's iron and steel, boot and shoe, rubber, textiles, building, and mining industries underwent sweeping technological innovations. Industrialists, stimulated by rising demand for products and hampered by the high cost of British and American hand labor, transformed their industries from handicraft production dependent upon a highly skilled labor force to mass production, which enabled them to exploit the tides of unskilled, docile immigrants.

The boot and shoe industry, which came to employ many Armenians, was a classic example of technological change. Although the sewing machine and the metal fastener had been invented by 1885, as of that date Yankee cobblers in Lynn, Massachusetts, still arduously nailed heels and sewed buttonholes by hand — a skilled nailer could fasten only 100 to 125 pairs of heels per day. After 1903, however, there were important improvements in nailing machines which permitted a semiskilled laborer and an apprentice to nail over 1,080 pairs of heels in a mere three hours, and this saved the wages of 48 additional shoe workers per day.[2] Similar developments occurred in the iron and steel, mining, textile, furniture, rubber goods, cement, and countless other industries.

Demographic studies and occupational statistics clearly show that, having arrived at the port of New York, the Armenians and other southern and eastern European immigrants entered the principal factories and foundries of the industrial Northeast. Massachusetts provides an excellent study in microcosm because of the unusual detail and completeness of its statistical data and more significantly because it had the largest population of foreign-born Armenians in the national censuses of 1910 and 1920. The state decennial census of 1915 tabulated a labor force of foreign-born Armenians 14 years of age or older at 4,239 in Massachusetts. Virtually two-thirds of these (3,158) are shown employed in the following manufacturing and mechanical industries:

Iron, steel, and other metals	662
Boots and shoes	658
Textiles	651
Rubber manufacturing	465
Tanning	95
Machining	31
Other Industries	596
Total	3,158

Bay State census statistics also confirm that almost without exception Armenians joined the labor force as unskilled or semiskilled hands. The figures for these workers for the four largest industries are as follows:

	Gen-eral	Un-skilled	Semi-skilled	Skilled	Total
Iron, steel, and other metals	26	419	217	—	662
Boots and shoes	—	31	627	—	658
Textiles	—	164	487	—	651
Rubber manufacturing	—	53	412	—	465

Over all, of the 3,158 immigrants in manufacturing and mechanical industries, 691 were in unskilled positions and 1,903 were in semi-skilled positions; only 4 were in skilled positions. Interestingly, no direct correlation existed between occupational rank and earnings in cross-industrial examination; that is, the semiskilled shoe operative did not necessarily earn higher hourly wages than the unskilled mill laborer. Wages were much more directly related to the conditions within the specific industry and the locally available labor supply.[3]

The demographic profile of the Armenian communities in the industrial Northeast (Massachusetts, Rhode Island, New York, New Jersey, and Pennsylvania), and Midwest (Illinois, Michigan, and Ohio), areas of large immigrant, industrial populations, confirms this picture of industrial labor. The names of the largest settlements are a roll call of late nineteenth- and early twentieth-century industrial America: In Massachusetts in 1905, the ten most populous Armenian communities were in the following cities in descending order: Worcester, Boston, Watertown, Chelsea, Lawrence, Lynn, Cambridge, Lowell, Northbridge, Milford. In Rhode Island, Armenians were concentrated in the silk and paint factories of Providence and Central Falls, and the Pawtucket and Cranston textile mills. New York State communities developed around the General Electric and locomotive plants in Schenectedy, the shirt and collar mills of Troy, the aluminum plants in Niagara Falls, and the iron plants in West Troy. The Armenians formed parts of the laboring force in the silk factories of Paterson, Camden, and West Hoboken, New Jersey, the tanneries of Philadelphia and Pennsylvania's bituminous coal mines. They entered the iron and steel mills in Waukegan, West Pullman, and Granite City, Illinois, the slaughter yards of Chicago, the automobile factories of Detroit, the furniture factories of Racine, Wisconsin, and Grand Rapids, Michigan. Large contingents of Russian Armenians gravitated to the East St. Louis steel mills, and the cement works of Riverside, California; a few in St. Paul, Minnesota, were railroad construction laborers, and they were also found in the California canneries.[4]

A national study by the U.S. Immigration Commission in 1907–1909 of 686 foreign-born Armenians in the manufacturing and mining sector of the economy substantiates the occupational patterns indicated above, as follows:[5]

Woolen and worsted goods	192
Shoes	141
Cotton goods	104
Leather	74
Iron and steel	50
Agricultural implements and vehicles	42
Slaughtering and meat packing	37
Silk goods	22
Other	24
Total	686

How Newcomers Found Jobs. The specific plant entered by the newcomer usually depended least on prior experience; rather, Armenians found work through hearsay, because of the arrival of earlier immigrants, by chance, or through the work of various immigrant groups functioning as employment agencies. News of high wages — when compared with Turkish standards — traveled fast. An immigrant earning $1.50 per day in a Lynn, Massachusetts, shoe factory, for example, would be asked by a foreman if he knew other Armenians willing to work at his job for the same wages; and the immigrant thereupon wrote to relatives in the Old Country who then emigrated — not to the United States — but specifically to the White Shoe Company in Lynn for a job. In turn, immigrants established in the East who were informed by more adventurous immigrants of higher wages in the Midwest thereupon left their textile mill or shoe factory for jobs in Waukegan or West Pullman, and wages of $2 per day.

Word of mouth was what precipitated the large colony of wire mill laborers in Worcester. Mentioned earlier was the first Armenian wire mill employee in Worcester, who arrived in 1867 as a missionary's servant and whose letters regarding his high wages induced a flow of Armenians to the central Massachusetts industrial plants. In addition, the Worcester industrialists Philip Moen and Charles Washburn had ties with the local Protestant missionary establishment and welcomed Armenian laborers, who numbered upwards of 300 as early as 1889. Other Worcester Armenians, attracted to the factories of the city, found jobs in the Crompton and Knowles Foundry, the Assonet Manufacturing Company, the Winslow Skate Manufacturing Company, and the Norton Abrasive Company.[6]

Because of its proximity to the port of Boston, Hood Rubber Company in Watertown, Massachusetts, became a large employer of Armenian immigrants. And many Armenians in the Greater Boston area, including the later renowned abstract painter, Arshile Gorky, got their first jobs in Hood Rubber's fabricating or shipping rooms. At the peak of the migration, the sprawling plant employed about 500 Armenian men and women.

Silk mills would seem naturally attractive for the Armenians, renowned for their silk products in the Old Country, and predictably large concentrations were drawn to the Paterson, New Jersey, silk mills. Yet even this choice of place and occupation was based less on their prior skills than on the fact that Armenians had previously worked in the plants as strikebreakers. This naturally blackened their reputations in Paterson, and by 1903 significant numbers had left the city for the mills in nearby Camden, Summit, and West Hoboken, where there were other Armenian immigrants.[7]

After 1899 the immigrant press commonly carried advertisements for jobs in factories which promised excellent working conditions and wages. Dr. Bedros Torosian of West Hoboken urged his fellow Armenians to settle in a New Jersey town (population 15,000) which was "attractive, clean, and healthy" and which wanted to hire Armenian laborers. Wages began at $7.50 per week but could rise to $6 a day, rents were low, and the company paid traveling expenses.[8]

Humanitarian friends of Armenians as well as philanthropic groups, such as the Armenian Colonial Association, also found jobs for newcomers. It was probably through the ACA (discussed in Chapter 5) that Armenians found their way to the Pennsylvania bituminous coal mines. In any case, in 1910, the coal mines were publicized by the ACA as "not a picnic or wedding," but they had advantages — they were not "outdoors" or "in the rain," wages were $1.75 per day for loading coal cars and $2 to $2.50 per day for digging coal. The ACA stressed the financial advantages of mining communities — ten laborers could board for 50 cents a month each in company-owned cottages — and that other Armenian miners, though unhappy at first, had adjusted to the miners' life.[9] Prior to this, in the wave of the Constantinople massacres, the Women's Christian Temperance Union had placed large numbers of refugees on New England farms, in stores, or as domestics. "Vassar's President keeps only Armenian servants," reported *Yeprad* in 1897.[10]

Labor Conditions. Whether in the mines, in textile mills, or in foundries, the jobs the immigrants first took were noteworthy for their drudgery and health hazards; without an effective labor movement, the immigrants labored long hours for minimal pay; and, in short, they endured the classic abuses of the industrial revolution. In the boot and shoe industry, for example, only 8 percent of the labor force was unionized. The labor movement in the iron and steel industry had been crushed in the abortive 1892 and 1901 strikes; and labor organization among Massachusetts rubber workers was not viable until the 1920s. Textile workers in the 1880s were employed 60 hours a week, and as late as 1901 in the Bay State, a leader in labor reform, factory operatives worked 9½ hours a day, 6 days a week.[11]

The strict regimentation mandated by the new industrial processes and the attitude toward labor of America's captains of industry caused the immigrants from Armenia to chafe at the grinding monotony and control exerted over their lives in dreary mill and factory towns. The broad fields and open air to which they were accustomed in the Old Country were now replaced by the clock, the assembly line, and the machinery's whirring pace. The immigrant press described typical Armenian young men as "groups moving to the machinery's pace; moving by sounds from early rising to entry into the factory, to leaving. Even going to sleep at night is in the factory's shadow." Complained another, "It is a question of 'factory to restaurant to sleep to factory.' "[12] A frequent bitter comment was that the mill was "too much like a prison."[13]

What was it like in a typical mill? Lawrence's textile mills employed 300 Armenian carders, pullers, and weavers, and T. M. Young described the conditions there in 1902: "In the mills the air is, as a rule, very bad, and there is often no provision at all for proper ventilation. In many mills I have seen the condensed moisture streaming down the windows, and clouds of water-vapour, almost scalding hot, rising amongst the looms from open grids on the floor."[14] These conditions were better than massacre and starvation, but they certainly did not match the immigrants' visions of the promised land. Perhaps the most physically taxing work was across the country from Lawrence — in the Riverside, California, cement works. There hundreds of Russian Armenian laborers not only struggled with 94-pound sacks of cement all day, but also breathed thick dust and poisonous air spewing from the overhead cement grinders and kilns. The coaling yards and paint factories of Providence and the moist heat and foul chemical-laden air of Hood Rubber Company all had perfected their own special varieties of "living death."[15]

As a result of these conditions, immigrant laborers who were described as coming to America in the prime of their lives — "vigorous, ambitious and frolicsome" — became "discouraged, demoralized, and too exhausted to attend night school." And the immigrant press urged the young Armenians to leave factory work to "the Irish, who are stronger than we are," before it impaired their health and to try to open stores and businesses instead. One immigrant employed for four years in the East Providence coaling station said that he had "suffered enough in this foreign land," and wanted only to return to Turkey "to live [out his years] and die." Bedros Keljik's fictional

Galata Bridge, Constantinople, about 1905.

A young Armenian of Western Turkey about to enter medical school in 1913.

Kharpert, Eastern Turkey, the single largest source of immigrants to the United States. Prominent buildings are Yeprad College (top) and the Church of St. James (center).

Homes in village near Marash, 1912.

Armenian primary school children in the village of Mashgerd, Eastern Turkey, before World War I. Only the children marked with x's survived the genocide of 1915.

Silk mill workers in New Jersey.

Foundry laborers in Detroit around 1913.

Hagop Bogigian's oriental rug store at the corner of Park and Beacon Streets, Boston.

Market in Jamaica Plain, Boston, 1914.

Armenians harvesting grapes in Fresno.

Drying grapes in sweatboxes.

The Seropian Brothers' packinghouse, one of the largest and earliest of its kind in the San Joaquin Valley.

Scene from a packinghouse operation, Fresno.

Varaztad Kazanjian, M.D., pioneer in the field of plastic surgery during World War I and professor at Harvard Medical School and Harvard Dental School.

Rug merchant Hagop Bogigian as a young man.

William Saroyan, writer, in New York City.

Retailer, industrialist, and philanthropist Stephen P. Mugar at the age of 18.

Magar Aga returned to his native Kharpert after many years in the promised land just in time to die, "worn out, exhausted, by factory life in America."[16]

Another reflection of the debilitating pace of industrial life was the regularity of accidents to the inexperienced, fatigued newcomers. To cite a few examples: *Worcester Daily Telegram*, February 16, 1890: "At 4 o'clock yesterday . . . an Armenian employed at the Quinsigamond wire mill was caught in an elevator and had one leg crushed. He was taken to his home in the Armenian settlement, on Hanover Street, in the Police ambulance." *Worcester Daily Telegram*, April 7, 1892: "Garped Ahurian, 25 years old, who boards on Gold Street, and is employed at the Grove Street wire mill, met with a severe accident yesterday morning. While at work his left foot was caught in a machine and his heel was cut off before he could extricate himself. . . . He arrived in this country two months ago." Because of its high accident rate, the Bellings Spence Company foundry in Hartford, Connecticut, was termed a "human slaughterhouse." In Whitinsville, Massachusetts, in 1912 a factory elevator gave way, nearly killing four immigrant Armenian workers. In Detroit in December 1914 at the Ford Motor Company, an Armenian's arm was severed because a Polish immigrant co-worker lowered a machine at the wrong time. The newly elected mayor of Worcester, James Logan, remarked in 1908: "I have frequently stood in the middle of the accident wards [of the city hospital] and noted that the face of every single patient was that of a foreigner. That means that the hard, the dangerous work was being done by these citizens of foreign birth."[17]

Wages. The wage structure of the Armenians is especially hard to penetrate because of the high incidence of piecework in many trades, the industry wide variations, and the effects of unemployment. However, according to the Immigration Commission's survey of 670 foreign-born Armenian males 18 years of age and older, in random industries across the country, the average weekly wage was $9.73. The commission's study showed a range for the Armenian worker from $13.28 per week in the agricultural vehicles and implements industry to $7.85 per week in the cotton goods branch of the textile industry. The reports of the Massachusetts Bureau of Statistics of Labor substantiate these figures for the basic industrial wage structure in the Bay States. Table I is based on actual weekly earnings in 538 Massachusetts factories and mills, representing 6 of the industries where significant numbers of Armenian immigrants found employment. The figures confirm the depressed wages in the largely unskilled occupations in textiles and the relatively advantageous wage position of the semiskilled in the boot and shoe industry.[18]

Table I.   Actual Weekly Earnings in Selected
Occupations of Selected Industries in Massachusetts

Industry and occupation	Actual average weekly earnings[a] (in dollars)
Boots and shoes	
All-round hands (cutting room)	10.56
Cutters (lifts, linings, soles, etc.)	13.91[b]
General helpers	9.38
Heelers	13.40
Lasters	16.17[b]
Packers	10.30
Machines and machinery	
Apprentices	7.12
Laborers	7.81
Lathe tenders	11.05
Machinists and machinists helpers	13.75[b]
Metals and metallic goods	
Wireworkers	7.26
Cotton Goods	
Carders (grinders, operatives, strippers)	7.80[b]
Doffers	5.67
Operatives	6.98
Pickers	7.29
Weavers	8.68
Woolen goods	
Carders	8.47
Operatives	8.01
Spinners	11.19
Weavers	10.09
Worsted goods	
Carders	8.42
Finishers	6.88
Operatives	9.46
Weavers	10.31

Source: Massachusetts, Bureau of Statistics of Labor, Reports, 1904, Pt. I, Sect. II.

[a] Figures are based not on a presumed 60-hour work week, but on the actual weekly earnings of workingmen with actual average hours worked per week ranging from 54.00 to 60.31 hours.

[b] Figures derived from weighted averages of two or more specialties within an occupation.

With respect to other immigrant groups, the wage structure of the Armenians compared only moderately favorably. The study of the Immigration Commission, cited above, also gave similar data for southern and eastern European immigrants. Examination of these data reveals that the average weekly earnings of the Armenians was the same or less than that of the average weekly earnings of most "new" immigrant groups.[19] But, while the average *weekly* wage of the Armenians reflects a somewhat depressed position with respect to the other immigrant groups, the *annual* earnings of the earnings of the various groups reveals a quite different picture. As the chart below shows, only the Eastern European Jews, Slovanians and Northern Italians exceeded the $454 annual wages of the Armenians. At the same time ten of the other groups fell below the Armenians' average annual wage. (The average annual wage of all fifteen "new" immigrant groups was $386).

	Average Annual Wage		Average Annual Wage
Armenians	454	Rumanians	402
Bulgarians	255	Russians	400
Eastern European	531	Serbians	212
Jews		Slovaks	442
Greeks	300	Slovanians	484
Lithuanians	454	Syrians	370
Magyars	395	Turks	281
Northern Italians	480	Average of all	
Poles	428	groups	391

Thus, although the average *weekly* wage of the Armenians only equaled or fell below that of the average of most "new" immigrant groups, their average *annual* earnings exceeded virtually all other southern and eastern European immigrants' annual average earnings.[20]

The annual figures, which took into account "voluntary lost time or lost time from shutdowns or other causes," in part reflected the persistence of the Armenian immigrant as well as his avoidance of such work stoppages as labor disputes. He simply put in more days and more hours at his job. It was the conclusion of M. Vartan Malcom, an immigrant historian, that

the Armenian workmen in these industries have rightfully earned the reputation of being among the most industrious in our heterogeneous laboring population. Years of oppression and struggle for existence against untold economic barriers have made them accustomed to hard work. Temperance is the prevailing habit among them. . . . Moreover, every Armenian immigrant has some dependent to support, such as a father, mother, sister or wife and children. All these things add to their efficiency as laborers and explain the reason why they stand foremost in their capacity to earn comparatively high wages.[21]

It is also probably true, however, that comparatively few Armenian immigrants returned to the Old Country as seasonal laborers, and therefore they were able to spend more days of each year on the job and attain higher annual wages.

To gain perspective on the "comparatively high wages" of the Armenians, it is most important to remember that daily wages for comparable hours and work were far higher for native workmen. Whereas the average Armenian cited in the Immigration Commission study earned $1.62 per day, a "progressive" American could not marry because his daily wages of $3.60 (*twice* that of the Armenian) were "too low" according to Peter Roberts, a noted authority on labor conditions of the period; "if the average native-born family had to live on $1.50 a day in our large cities, there would be a revolution within a twelve-month, but thousands of foreign-born families live on less and suffer."[22]

Women as well as men made up the Armenian laboring class in the United States. The tabulations of the Immigration Commission recorded a study of 98 Armenian familes employed in manufacturing and mining. Just over one-quarter (26 percent) of these families reported income from the wife. This high percentage was exceeded only by that of the Portuguese (28 percent) and the Syrians (28 percent), and it far exceeded that of the average of all foreign-born families (7 percent). Because of these factors, the annual average *family* income of $730 of the foreign-born Armenians in the Commission's sample exceeded that of all "new" immigrant families except the Portuguese (the average annual income of all "new" immigrant families was $646).[23]

The highest incidence of female employment among the Armenians was in Troy, New York. In Troy — the center of the collar, cuff, and shirt manufacturing industry in the United States — upwards of 75 percent of the Armenian married women in the community were wage earners whereas the average of all foreign born married women in Troy was 35 percent. There the Armenian women, in their homes and tenements, were engaged in turning, folding, and ironing collars as well as sewing buttonholes. The Tenement Law of 1899 prohibited the use of rooms or apartments in dwellings for "manufacturing or repair of clothes without a license." However, the shirt and collar industry was exempt from this legislation. The high incidence of female labor was due to the very depressed wages of the male laborers in the factories, for after 1905 wages were reduced from one-third to one-half of their former levels. Also this work could be performed in the home, which permitted the women to avoid the "cheap, rough" talk of the factories. Women often worked at such jobs seven days and as many nights a week, under poor lighting, for weekly salaries of $6 to $8.[24]

More Workers, Fewer Jobs.   Ironically, the spectre of unemployment often haunted the immigrant settlements most powerfully during peak immigrant periods. It was during the aftermath of the 1893 depression that the first major wave of immigration from Turkey took place, and 1894 reports from the colony in Worcester indicated that two-fifth's of the city's laboring population were out of work (the Washburn and Moen Company, which employed large numbers of Armenians, laid off 800 workmen in 1893).[25] So many Armenians were without jobs and hungry that some returned to the Old Country, while spokesmen in Worcester sought to stave off further immigration to the United States. In January 1897, according to the *Boston Herald,* many 1895 refugees "without money or proper clothing suitable for the cold, stormy weather of a New England winter are at this time sorely in need." Those who had gotten jobs had recently been laid off, because the plants that had hired them were closing.[26] Only Moses Gulesian's repeated charity in putting up the jobless refugees in his cornice factory in Boston, and his provision of food, clothing, and instruction in English and "American customs" eased their burdens.

The pattern recurred in the wake of the crash of 1907. One journal estimated that in New York City alone 1,000 Armenians were out of work; a majority of the 300 in Waukegan were on the dole, and some there had been out of work for over six months; joblessness was especially high in Providence.[27] Similarly, the largest wave of immigrants peaked in 1912–1913, in the teeth of major American labor and economic unrest. Hood Rubber laid off large numbers of Armenians in December 1912; one-third of Providence's Armenian laboring force was out of work in September 1913; and in Detroit, in the early winter of 1913–1914, troubled immigrant leaders reported that over 200 jobless Armenians were damaging their health and reputations by gambling, drinking, and fighting in the coffee shops along Solway Avenue. Similar unsettling reports emanated from Worcester, Lawrence, and Milford in the Bay State, and from Providence, Binghamton and Troy, New York, and West Pullman, Illinois.[28] Over the years, leaders in New York City, concerned about the immigrants "tramping the streets," organized an Armenian Labor Information Bureau (1908), the Boston Chapter of the Armenian General Benevolent Union opened an employment agency to "establish ties between employer and employees"; and the *Boston Directory* (1915) listed an Armenian Charitable Association Employment Office. But they were able to offer little assistance.[29]

Joblessness cut deeply into immigrants' savings. Thrift was an indispensable Old World attribute carried on in the New. "They [the Armenians] have been born and raised in poverty and hardship, they are however thrifty and industrious and wonderfully saving, and the money they make while in America is carefully put away for future investment. While in America they live in colonies . . . on the cheapest rations, many of them crowded into one sleeping room, and their personal expenses are only for actual living."[30] On weekly wages of $7 to $8, it was estimated that a typical immigrant without a family could save about $4 (he spent about $2 a week for board and $1 for room). But in the mid-1890s, in 1907, and 1912–1914, the long lines of immigrants who were turned away from factory gates because there were no jobs meant that nothing was saved, and families especially went hungry and without coal. As Zaven Baikar's fictional character, Bedros, states: "If I am out of work for a week, like a fish I rise to the surface of the water."[31]

Strikebreaking and Job Selling. The immigrants' need to find employment and their ignorance of labor conditions in the United States promoted a network of industrial abuses; most despicable of these was the exploitation of Armenian by Armenian. And one of the most flagrant abuses was strikebreaking. When they landed at New York City or Boston, a group of newcomers (greenhorns) would be approached by a *lezu kidsu* (English-speaking Armenian), with orders from a manufacturer or his foreman to hire immigrants as strikebreakers (scabs). Brandishing the prospects of high-paying jobs before the immigrants, the unscrupulous go-between lured them to a New England or Middle Atlantic states factory, which they entered through a line of pickets, often with police protection.

The first instance of Armenians involved in strikebreaking occurred in 1890. According to Edward L. Daley, general secretary of the Lasters' Protective Union of America, testifying before the Immigration Investigating Commission in 1894, "the strikes in the leather trade, notably that at Lynn four years ago, and in the shoemaking trade at Auburn, Me., East Weymouth, Boston, Stoneham, Haverhill, and other places in Massachusetts, foreign labor in any desired quantity has been immediately obtained by employers who have had trouble with their old employees. . . . In the case of the morocco strike at Lynn, . . . hundreds of Armenians were obtained . . . through R. G. Soloman, a leather manufacturer at Newark, N.J."[32] According to the Immigration Commission, upwards of 300 Armenians were led by professional scabs to break a Paterson, New Jersey, boycott in 1902. The first Armenian families in Middleboro, Massachusetts, in 1892 were scabs, and Armenian strike-breakers figured prominently in the A. F. Smith Shoe Company strike in Lynn in August 1907 and the L. O. White Shoe Company strike in Bridgewater, Massachusetts, in August 1909. The Ladies' Garment Workers' strike in Boston in September 1909 was scabbed by 12 Armenians, including 2 women, and the Armenians comprised the largest number of strikerbreakers at the Salem strike that year. Bringing newcomers to crash picket lines had become a lucrative business.[33]

The onus of strikebreaking badly tainted the reputation of the Armenians. In Manchester, New Hampshire, a group of citizens refused to rent rooms to Armenian laborers because of their nefarious involvement in the Boot and Shoe Worker's Union strike in 1903.[34] One reporter cited Armenians as "more hated and insulted" in Lynn than anywhere else.[35] In Philadelphia "the only nationalities more disliked by other new immigrants . . . were the Armenians, Greeks, and Syrians, they were all sometimes lumped together as strikebreakers, in a class by themselves, and where employed in large establishments, as in one Philadelphia house of the time, they were so disliked that it was necessary to segregate them in departments by themselves."[36] One Armenian immigrant's humorous story that he had to eat "five *kuftehs* [meatballs of legendary energy-building capabilities], a big bowl of *madzoon* [yogurt], take a picket off my fence and knock down three Irishmen to get to my job at the mill" underscored the ethnic tensions produced by strikebreaking.[37] Testifying before a government committee on the subject of "foreign labour" and strikes, the assistant secretary of the Boot and Shoe Makers' International Union stated an opinion widespread among organized labor that "the Armenians are from every point of view a most undesirable class."[38]

Civic-minded Armenian leaders, sensitive to the backlash against the strikebreakers, sought to eradicate the practice among the immigrants in a variety of ways. In *Hairenik*, writers like Shahan Natalie pleaded with their readers to educate their fellow immigrants about the virtues of the trade union movement and the sorry plight of nonunion laborers. In 1907 the paper's pro-Socialist editors blacklisted the more notorious professional strikebreakers by publishing their names. Meanwhile, groups of Armenians in Lynn and Chelsea resolved to shun the professional scabs by closing Armenian establishments — coffeehouses, restaurants, and boardinghouses — to them. The Central Committee of the Armenian Revolutionary Federation supported this resolve.[39]

A phenomenon related to strikebreaking was the hiring of the immigrants in jobs held by Yankee or native labor at drastically reduced wages. This practice, which was usually termed the "pad-rone" or boss system, is described by an official of the Lasters' Protective Union in 1894:

In a number of our large shoe factories have our workmen been displaced by Hebrews and Armenians at wages so low that it is impossible for our citizens to compete with them and live decently. . . . In another large factory, that of I. Winchell and Co., about 40 Armenians were hired, displacing the same number of old workmen, at wages more than one-third less than the former men were receiving, and numerous letters have been received by manufacturers in this city from agencies in Boston offering to furnish any number of this class of help at their own prices.

According to an ex-president of Worcester's Central Labor Union, many of Worcester's unemployed mechanics during the 1893 depression had the Armenians to blame, for they had been supplanted by Armenians "brought here by the agents of the company. The Armenians work for 85 to 90 cents per day and take the places of men who formerly earned from $3 to $4 per day."[40] French Canadians, Russian Jews, and Armenians were charged with depressing the tinsmith and cornice-making trades in Massachusetts, in which they "supplanted native workers making $16 to $18 a week, by laboring for their board, and a few dollars."[41] Perhaps because of their reputation, Commissioner General of Immigration Herman Stump, lumped the Armenians with Assyrians, Arabs, Turks, and Greeks as entering the United States under the padrone system "(financed by 'little father,'), to peddle goods, to black boots, to be scissors grinders and actual beggars on the streets" — although no evidence exists to substantiate the allegation.[42]

More commonly, Armenians were forced to pay bribes to obtain work. Greenhorns paid from $5 to $15 simply to get a job in a factory, and if a man had no money, reported the *Worcester Daily Telegram* "but could give valuable articles of furniture or ornament, they were sometimes given."[43] In Worcester the newly arrived immigrants usually lacked the bribe money and were forced to borrow "sometimes paying 20 to 25 per cent for the use of the money." One such usurer employed in a factory was termed "viler than a Turkish bey."[44] In the plants in Niagara Falls which employed large numbers of immigrants from Van, a fellow immigrant from that city not only solicited bribes for jobs but he also required a second bribe to restore the job when an immigrant fell sick. During peak immigration periods, the bribetakers seemed to "spring up like mushrooms."[45] As one court officer ruefully said, "no Armenian immigrant will give up a cup of water to his brother without a bribe."[46]

Occasionally, these leeches were apprehended. One intrepid immigrant at the Thomas-Crooker Company in Roxbury, Massachusetts, boldly challenged the bribetaking intermediaries, and the factory owner fired the two culprits. A scandal shook the Worcester wire mill on Grove Street when Philip Moen, the plant superintendent, upon investigating the situation, fired an Armenian, a Yankee foreman, and his assistant for complicity in bribetaking.[47] On the other hand, most immigrants, fearful of losing their jobs and wary of the foreman's power, reckoned it wiser to keep still and tolerate the abuses.

Although many Armenians were victimized by bribetakers or participated in undermining union activities as scabs, others were staunch supporters of the rights of labor. For example, the Rug Repairers Union in New York City, an offshoot of the Carpet Layers' Union, was comprised almost entirely of Armenians.[48] Armenian laborers also actively supported the call of labor organizers in other trades. In a Chelsea, Massachusetts, strike against the Walton and Logan Shoe Company, Armenians assisted Jewish laborers in fomenting the unrest; Armenians in Haverhill in May 1912 led a walkout for higher pay in a local plant: one Armenian picketing the Liberty Silk Company in New York City in 1899 was shot by a Syrian scab.[49]

Armenians were likewise conspicuous in the famous Lawrence strike of 1912. In Lawrence, laborers went on strike in January 1912 after hours and wages (already at starvation level) had been cut. The 20,000 Lawrence strikers included 500 Armenians, who comprised no less than two-thirds of the entire Lawrence Armenian population. Led by B. Tashjian, labor-conscious Armenians organized an Armenian branch of the Lawrence Strike Committee. The Armenian press vilified the handful of Armenians participating in strikebreaking in Lawrence, while Armenian restauranteurs in Lawrence united to stop feeding Armenian scabs. Strikebreakers were also threatened with eviction from their lodgings. The long strike, which lasted through the bitter winter of 1912, left strikers' families without food or coal, and the Armenian Revolutionary Federation, the Boston Chapter of the AGBU, and private individuals donated much needed funds for their assistance.[50]

The pro-Socialist *Hairenik* steadfastly urged Armenians to join the ranks of the American Socialist Labor party. Even the bitterly warring Armenian political parties occasionally united to assist their countrymen's role in a strike. Thus, in 1912 the Armenian Revolutionary Federation, the Reformed Hnchag party, and the Ramgavar party dispatched speakers to a Detroit rally in support of striking Armenians in the Malleable Iron Foundry.[51]

Although there were such instances in which Armenians supported labor unions, generally the strike, walkout, and picket line were foreign to them. Armenians saw little use in marching out of doors in a picket line when jobs were available inside the factory, and many Armenians welcomed the opportunities as strikebreakers to get jobs in the United States. In one case, in Whitinsville in 1905, a few radical Armenians tried to lead their compatriots out on strike, but they failed and "ignominiously . . . departed." One writer said that Armenians generally cared nothing for striking or purchasing guns. They were simply hungry.[52]

Generally, Armenians did not consider themselves members of a working class. Nor, because of their foreign birth and the language barrier, could they aspire to supervisory or managerial positions in the factories. Rather, their ambition was to leave the factories to earn enough money to return to the Old Country (especially before the 1890s), or to open their own businesses. There were many reasons for this. First, like most other immigrants, they were not accustomed to the physically ravaging pace, sweated conditions, and regimentation of the factories. One Armenian who left his job in a mill to open a small restaurant gave as his reason for the change that "the mill was too much like a prison." And the Immigration Commission noted that Armenians "sooner or later desired to leave the factory life which was undermining their physique." Moreover, their culture encouraged them to be their own bosses; as one worker commented, "As soon as I could I started a business on my own for I do not like to work for other people."[53]

The immigrant press echoed this petty bourgeois strain. Nowhere, except in the atypical Russian Armenian labor press, like *Eridasart Hayastan*, was there systematic and genuine advocacy of the rights of the proletariat. Rather, most issues of *Azk, Yeprad, Gotchnag,* and *Asbarez* gave fulsome praise to turn of the century capitalism and the Protestant ethic of hard work, patience, saving, and seeking advancement. "Work has been continually man's greatest blessing," stated *Gotchnag*, in a typical editorial.[54] Even such nominally socialist journals as *Hairenik*, which regularly quoted Karl Marx and Daniel De Leon and sharply criticized J. P. Morgan and John D. Rockefeller, revealed procapitalist sympathies. Thus, *Hairenik* carried a weekly column by Berj Barou, "Lessons of Youth," which commended the following English language works to immigrants: "Samuel Smiles . . . *Self Help; Character; Thrift; Duty;* William McThayer's *From Boyhood to Manhood; From Farmhouse to White House; From Pioneer Home to White House; . . . Turning Points in Successful Careers; Men Who Win; Women Who Win; The Way to Succeed; Tact; Push and Principle . . .* Orison Swett Marden's *. . . Pushing to the Front; Architects of Fate; Winning Out; The Secrets of Achievement.*[55] Under the intellectual facade of socialism was a deepseated, emotional and psychological commitment to business and capitalism.

By the eve of World War I, immigrants in numbers were leaving factories and mills to enter small businesses or agriculture. Having arrived in the New World without capital, unable to speak the language and unfamiliar with American business skills, Armenian immigrants had naturally gravitated to the factories and mills of the industrial Northeast and Midwest. Their painful initiation into the new industrial order was the mandatory first step which permitted many of them to pass on to the broader opportunities of the promised land.

Shopkeepers and Artisans

Numerous Armenians became small businessmen and shopkeepers. Although data do not exist to tabulate the rate of their departure from the "working class," the Immigration Commission, among other bodies, clearly noted the success of the immigrant Armenians in doing so. "Being ambitious, disliking the wage relation, they [the Armenians] have as their goal the establishment of a business or independent farming," noted the commission.[56] As early as 1894 a Bostonian remarked that

in variety of occupation the Armenians must be placed first among all the races . . . in Boston. Barely eight hundred strong, they can show engravers, artists, electricians, photographers, furriers, carpet merchants, enamellers, jewellers, brass finishers, confectioners, plumbers, shoemakers, restaurant keepers, fruiterers, and members of many other trades, besides clergymen and students.

The observer added that the Armenians "pick up English in no time, at once look about for some trade demanding skill and yielding opportunities, and in two or three years are employing workmen under them."[57]

For the Armenian Trade.   What were their specific businesses? One important group catered to the needs of their fellow immigrants. For example, the English-speaking shipping agent and insurance man usually established an office adjacent to the Armenian or Middle Eastern quarter, his walls adorned with posters of steamships and European ports. This entrepreneur attracted newcomers because of his language abilities, his Armenian background, and his familiarity with the puzzling transportation and visa problems. Few Armenian-speaking immigrants who sought to buy tickets for families in Turkey entered the austere offices of old established companies like Thomas Cook.

In addition to selling steamship and rail tickets between Turkey and New York City, the agent transmitted money orders of American

Express checks to the Old Country, helped newcomers with correspondence and with shipping goods to Turkey or Russia, and gave
advice on immigration and legal problems. Agents also sold immigrants their first real estate and insurance policies.[58] The role of
banker for savings, which many agents filled for southern and eastern
European immigrants, was not as important in the early Armenian
community.

An "Armenian Grocery," "Oriental Grocery," or "Ararat Food
Store" became an important fixture in the immigrant community.
Typical of the variety, "Manoog's store" in Chelsea, Massachusetts,

had all the stinks and smells of a third-rate foreign bazaar. Everything in it
looked exotic, strange, and on the verge of putrefaction. There was merchandise strewn everywhere. Long, rigid baloneys and sausages hung from
hooks in the ceiling; barrels of nuts, flour, cracked wheat and squash seeds
lined the walls. Tubs of olives and swimming Greek cheese had been shoved
under tables on which rested tins of Armenian pastry, herbs and all sorts of
canned stuff. A battered counter piled high with miscellaneous merchandise,
newspapers and wrapping paper, completed the storekeeper's unkempt
realm.[59]

Immigrant women crowded the stores especially on the eves of
religious holidays, shopping for the special herbs, spices, and pas-
tries for Christmas and Easter dinners; women also found the stores
convenient centers for exchanging news, not unlike the men's coffeehouses. Armenian was the language predominately used in the
stores, but since most groceries were also close to the Greek or Syrian
communities, it behooved immigrant grocers to learn a few words of
those languages. The immigrant groceries also functioned as communal news centers by posting notices of forthcoming church
bazaars, concerts, and productions of the immigrant theater.

In time enterprising immigrants began to manufacture the impor-
tant staples of *matzoon* (yogurt) and *boulghur* (wheat germ). In fact,
Armenians were credited with the introduction of "Zoolak, Matzoon,
Fermillac, and other forms of fermented milk" into the United
States.[60] The earliest marketing of matzoon was in 1885 by Markar
G. Dadirrian, a graduate of New York University Medical School.
According to Dadirrian, fermented cow's milk had been used in
Armenia, Persia, Turkey, and Arabia by all classes since the earliest
periods of history not only to quench thirst but also "as an antidote
for all kinds of poisonings," and a panacea in all "acute febrile
diseases." Meanwhile, in Fresno, California, V. A. Krikorian began
to manufacture the wheat germ staple in a plant which eventually
produced about 125 tons per year; his East Coast counterpart was the
Cilician Bulgar Company in Worcester.[61]

A third type of business intended for an exclusively immigrant clientele was the Armenian restaurant, boarding house, and coffeehouse. These institutions appeared as soon as handfuls of bachelors or married men without families formed a colony in a New World mill town or city. (Their important role in the immigrant milieu is discussed in Chapter 9.)

For the General Public. Although many immigrants opened businesses for their fellow countrymen, others pursued enterprises beyond the confines of the "Little Armenias" and "Little Orients." Tailor shops, shoemaking and shoe repairing establishments, groceries and confectionary shops run by Armenians were particularly prominent in the largest East Coast cities. A study of the occupations of the 843 identifiable Armenians gainfully employed in New York in 1915 and 620 Armenians in Boston reveals the following:[62]

	New York	Boston
Barbers	4	13
Clerks	22	56
Confectioners	12	27
Cooks	5	17
Engravers	13	14
Grocers	78	69
Jewelers	19	6
Restauranteurs	12	22
Shoemakers	26	56
Tailors	130	47
Tobacconists	9	4
Variety store keepers	2	15
Total	332	346

In all, over 46 percent of the identifiable, gainfully employed Armenians in Boston and New York in 1915 were to be found in the "artisan and shopkeeping category."

In the East Coast mill and factory towns, the percentages of immigrants in such callings were lower, though not negligible. According to the Immigration Commission's study of New Britain, Connecticut, 18 of the 300 Armenians dwelling in the city were placed in the "skilled trades" category. Table II indicates the comparative rank achieved by the Armenians with respect to New Britain's other ethnic groups—a smaller percentage of people in business than the Jews but a larger percentage than the Germans, Swedes, Poles, Italians, Lithuanians, Slovaks, French Canadians, Persians, Ruthenians, and Russians. Investigation by sociologist Lloyd Warner of "Yankee City" (Newburyport, Massachusetts) in 1913 revealed a high percentage of Armenians in the "skilled craft occupations." The tiny Armenian colony in Richmond, Virginia, included 16 grocers,

**Table II.   Armenians and Other Immigrants in
Business in New Britain, Connecticut, 1909**

Immigrant group	Estimated population 1909	Number of immigrants and children in business[a]	Percentage in business
Irish	12,500	91	0.72
German	7,500	112	1.50
Swedish	7,200	24	3.75
Polish	4,000	16	4.00
Italian	1,300	44	3.40
Lithuanian	1,200	11	0.90
Jewish	1,000	66	6.60
Slovak	400	3	0.75
Armenian	300	18	6.00
French Canadian	300	7	2.75
Persian	250	1	0.40
Ruthenian	250	2	0.80
Russian	80	3	3.75

Source: U. S., Immigration Commission, Reports, vol. XVII, 231, 295–296.

[a] Street trades not included.

2 tailors, 1 billiard parlor operator, and 1 rug merchant, and Gotchnag boasted in 1913 of Armenians there running small groceries, restaurants, pool and billiard parlors, barber shops, and shoe stores. Evidence gleaned from immigrant censuses of Worcester, Lowell, Cambridge, and Bridgeport, Connecticut, on the eve of World War I, confirmed the pattern of entrepreneurial drive.[63]

It is interesting that many of these businessmen had had no earlier experience in the specific trade they followed in the United States. Indeed, many of the so-called "tailor shops" were merely dry cleaning and hand blocking establishments which required little skill. Some immigrants testified that they knew nothing of tailoring or cleaning and pressing clothes (their first customers were often less than enthusiastic about their work), but many opened these stores because the work in them was less physically demanding and more remunerative than factory labor. Thus, a grocer who opened his store in Brighton, Massachusetts, after six years in a Lynn shoe factory, didn't know "corned beef from roast beef," but because he detested factory work, he started in the grocery business. Becoming one's own boss and escaping from the mills were powerful incentives in the immigrant world.

Some enterprising newcomers combined an immigrant and an "American" clientele, or managed a group of businesses. M. S. Kondazian began in the wholesale clothing manufacturing business in Boston in 1890, spurred by the belief that Jewish immigrant success was built on the garment industry. Because of access to fellow immigrants, he employed Armenians to merchandise his clothes in their own establishments or as peddlers. In addition to this line, in 1908 Kondazian opened the offices of the firm of Harpootlian and Kondazian in Boston and nearby Revere, which specialized as travel agents and immigrant bankers. Another immigrant who performed many functions was Kevork Bedros Thomajan, proprietor of the Star Men's Furnishing Store in Worcester and "counsellor, employment agency, interpreter, scribe, best man, notary, exporter of funds and importer of families."[64]

It is easy to romanticize the immigrant shopkeepers' achievements. To survive, the Armenian tailor or grocer worked an average of 60 to 70 hours a week. (His and his family's only cheap asset was their own labor, and there was no sparing that.) He rented a store in a poor neighborhood (often in a basement because of the low rent); to economize he often lived in the cramped quarters at the back of the store. Poor lighting, close air, and long hours on damp concrete floors were routine. "The tailor's shop, damp, and dark, was a disagreeable place," went one typical description. "There was no tailoring done there, only its name. . . . It was a place to dry clean and iron clothes. An old sewing machine sat in the corner. A decrepit presser was near the door. . . . On top of everything was a bitter, compacted odor which is peculiar to basements and old houses."[65] But the immigrant worked unceasingly expending his and his family's labor to become independent of the factory and the factory boss and to achieve the beginnings of respectability in the New World.

Nevertheless, many business ventures failed. According to the Massachusetts Immigration Commission, one 20-year-old immigrant spent his first five years in the United States working in a cotton machinery factory to repay debts incurred for passage to America and for a down payment on a fruit store. He opened the store and ran it for three months, at which time he went into bankruptcy, losing his five-year $450 investment. The plucky immigrant returned to the factory job at $8.55 a week to start saving for another business.[66] Shifts in occupation, especially among the inexperienced and younger immigrants, were common; eight to ten different jobs in a decade were not unknown. One Armenian who arrived in New York City in 1891 and first worked in a piano factory for $3 a week took on the following jobs in the next nine years: candy store proprietor, peddler, cotton mill laborer, "Arms and Cycle" factory laborer in Fitchburg,

Massachusetts, grocery and meat store proprietor in Worcester, a wire mill operative, fruiterer and confectioner in Providence, and an ice cream factory owner. Then, from 1901 to World War I, he went into vegetable peddling, life insurance, shoe repairing, and finally, into ranch labor in Fowler, California.[67]

Success Stories. Most of the immigrant businessmen remained little people, but there were some noteworthy successes. Jacob Arakelyan, for one, arrived in the United States in 1867 as a destitute immigrant. His first job was at a Cambridge, Massachusetts, printing plant; in time he opened his own printing business. Ambitious, hardworking, astute, he built his Pilgrim Press over the years into one of the Bay State's largest, and at his death his estate was worth between $250,000 and $300,000.[68]

The Star Market chain, now a subsidiary of the mammoth Jewel Tea Company, grew from a small store in Watertown Square, where the boy Stephen Mugar, worked with his sisters in the family's grocery. The Mugar family had emigrated from Kharpert to Boston in 1905, and Stephen was a born merchandiser. Once, when he advertised "specials" to the Watertown neighborhood by "running" (he was too ambitious to walk) from door to door, he handed leaflets to housewives saying "Here is a dollar for you." The woman, who saw only a printed circular and no money, was told "Shop at Star Market, and you will save a dollar." That week, the crowds patronizing the market astonished everyone. In later years, Mugar recalled how during the Depression, Star Market, through Mugar's faith in the newly adopted country, always accepted personal checks — and won many lifelong customers. Mugar understood the vast potential of supermarket merchandising and, through his brilliant business mind and enormous energy, established a major merchandizing chain in Massachusetts.[69]

Photoengraving was another important field for immigrant craftsmen largely because of Bedros Aznive, who taught many fellow Armenians this highly specialized skill. His Harvard Engraving Company of Boston became one of the largest, and most prestigious in its field.[70]

Emigrating to America in 1883 at the age of seventeen, Moses Gulesian got a job in a New York City carpet-weaving shop for $2 a week. Moving to Worcester, he worked at the famous wire mill and saved money to attend Worcester Academy. After learning coppersmithing, he moved to Boston where in 1889 he opened a coppersmith shop on Harrison Avenue. Two years later he purchased a six-story factory on Waltham Street (where he housed refugees from the 1890s massacres). The firm produced cornices for Boston's most important buildings, grew steadily, and brought Gulesian into close contact with Boston's business elite.

Gulesian eventually sold his factory and ventured into real estate and theater building. He became president of the Huntington Avenue Improvement Association, was known as a "good mixer," born executive, and "genial personality," and exemplifying his "complete Americanization," purchased a handsome late Georgian estate on Commonwealth Avenue and a summer home, "Waterside," at Falmouth.

But there was more. In 1905 Gulesian read of the decision of Charles J. Bonaparte, Theodore Roosevelt's Secretary of the Navy, to junk the frigate, *Constitution* and perhaps use it for target practice. Gulesian wired Bonaparte: "Will give ten thousand dollars for the *Constitution*, Old Ironsides. Will you sell?" Gulesian's offer for the historic vessel stirred the nation's imagination — one paper queried whether it "might worry the Sultan of Turkey if word reached him that an Armenian had purchased an American warship." Gulesian's theatrical gesture eventually helped to preserve the *Constitution* as a historical museum and brought him the presidency of the Old Ironsides Association (its members included Calvin Coolidge and A. Lawrence Lowell), and membership in the Sons of the American Revolution.[71]

Professionals and Aspiring Professionals

According to the Massachusetts Decennial Census of 1915 about 2 percent or 79 of the 4,279 gainfully employed, foreign-born Armenians 14 years of age or over were found in "professional service." A further breakdown of this category indicated that the largest numbers were in the fields of photography (25), the church (12), and medicine (10).[72]

Whether in the Bay State or elsewhere, Armenian professionals trained in the Old World often had difficulty attaining that same position and status in the New. As for the Armenian clergy, after the mid-1890s, there were too many of them for the number of livings available in the United States, and as a result many experienced bitter struggles. One example was the Reverend Onan Gaidzakian, a preacher and physician from Adana. Arriving as a penniless refugee in 1896 with a family of six, he was unable to find a pulpit. To keep the wolf from the door, he resorted to selling books, including his *Illustrated Armenia and the Armenians* (1898) and his chart of the Lord's Prayer in twelve different languages.[73] A student from the Theological Seminary at Marash was similarly hard pressed: his first job in the New World was working "hard day and night in a rag felt factory in the Bowery," and he ended the day sleeping "on the rags on the floor."[74] Armenian teachers and intellectuals likewise encountered problems. A few became political leaders or journalists of the Armenian American press, but their status was substantially diminished. Other teachers, writers, and editors were forced to take on jobs as tradesmen, janitors, and laborers, which they bitterly resented, and despising their new jobs made them "touchy foreigners."[75]

Although Old World immigrants contributed to the professional class, the more important segment of this social group in the United States was comprised of men and women educated in the United States. Education was eagerly sought by the newcomers; in 1921 the author of *Foreigners or Friends* observed that "love of learning was a marked characteristic of" the Armenians. "Although the bulk of the Armenians in America are from the peasant class, yet they are the most literate of the more recent immigrant groups. In proportion to their total numbers they have the largest number of students in our colleges, averaging about two hundred and fifty a year."[76] Corroboration of these impressively high figures is available from a 1916 survey which revealed that a total of 234 Armenian students were enrolled, in order, in the following: University of California, Yale, Columbia, Harvard, MIT, the University of Michigan, Ohio State University, Temple, and the University of Pennsylvania. Prior to their migration, most students in the survey had received a secondary education in the American "colleges" at Kharpert, Marsovan, Aintab, Tarsus, Constantinople, Smyrna, and Beirut. With respect to their careers, the young students indicated preferences for engineering (25), the clergy (16), medicine (11), dentistry (10), education (7), the law (5), and agriculture (4).[77] The survey indicated a relative lack of interest in the humanities and social sciences, probably because these fields required greater proficiency in English, were less materially rewarding, and were less studied in Turkey.

Students also received financial assistance from the Armenian Educational Society, which was founded in 1906 by Garabed Pushman of Chicago. A wealthy Oriental rug dealer, Pushman established the "Marion L. Pushman Fund" in the amount of $25,000 in his daughter's memory, and interest from the fund was loaned to needy, deserving Armenian students. In its first decade the society loaned over $18,000 to seventy-two students.[78]

To assist their countrymen, Armenian American students in 1910 organized the Armenian Students Association and by 1914, it had established chapters in Philadelphia, New York, New Haven, Boston, Chicago, Ann Arbor, and Columbus, Ohio. The purposes of the association, whose membership included 250 high school, college, and postgraduate students, were to publish a monthly newspaper, revise the curriculum for schools in Armenia, prepare modern textbooks in the Armenian language, and send properly trained Armenians to educate youth in the Old Country.[79]

Medicine. Numbers of Armenians became dentists and physicians in the United States, although their numbers were limited by the rigid certification requirements of the state licensing boards, the language barrier, and the costs of acquiring medical and dental degrees. (One estimate of 200 Armenian dentists and physicians in the United States in this period seems exceedingly high, especially since large Armenian colonies in Boston, Worcester, and New York City supported only a handful of Armenian doctors each.)[80]

In addition, academic medicine and the laboratory interested a few. Dr. Hampartzoom D. Garabedian, a graduate in 1879 of the "upper school" in Smyrna and the University of Michigan, conducted research among American Indians in connection with United States Senate investigations. Dr. Menas Gregory, a graduate in 1894 of Aintab College, and of Albany Medical College in 1898, became a professor and chief of Bellevue's Department of Psychiatry; Dr. Eliza Melkon, a graduate in 1916 of Tufts Medical School, was a pioneer among women in medicine.[81]

A few Armenians in medicine achieved national or international reputation. The most distinguished of these was Varaztad Kazanjian who arrived in the United States at the age of sixteen, in 1895. His first job, which lasted until 1900, was as a laborer in the Worcester wire mills. During this time he was encouraged by the Reverend H. G. Benneyan of the Armenian Protestant Church of the Martyrs in Worcester to continue his education, which he did through night school and correspondence courses for seven years. In 1902, with $400 in savings, he enrolled in English High School in Boston, and a year later he entered Harvard Dental School. Though "handicapped . . . by unfamiliarity with the language, and in the eyes of the provincial New Englanders, by being a foreigner," he graduated with distinction and was appointed a part time assistant in prosthetic dentistry at Harvard Dental. Thus began a lifelong teaching career.[82]

With the outbreak of World War I, Harvard equipped a hospital unit for the British Expeditionary Forces in France, and since the British Army had no dental corps at the time, Kazanjian was appointed chief dental officer; as such he "laid the foundation for some of the most remarkable services to be rendered in military hospitals." The war, fought largely in open trenches and close combat, produced many "highly destructive and disfiguring gunshot wounds of the face," which few were prepared to treat. Kazanjian, assuming the leadership of prosthetic surgery, had more than 3,000 cases pass through his hands. Using novel surgical techniques, he became extremely well known among the Allied armies. "A short, black haired, soft-spoken man with kindly eyes, he went quietly about his business and performed marvels upon the soldiers. His stature and appearance made him almost insignificant, yet in his presence one felt . . . a vitality, a force, a genius . . . that gave him extraordinary powers. . . . It is small wonder that the stricken British soldiers, suffering untold agonies from splintered jaws and mangled faces, believed implicitly in his ability to help them."

After the war Kazanjian was knighted by King George V for his battlefield endeavors; he then returned to Harvard Dental School as Chairman of the Department of Oral Surgery and Professor of Plastic Surgery at Harvard Medical School. His many published writings included the authoritative text, *Surgical Treatment of Facial Injuries*.

Others also received national recognition. Mihran Kassabian, who was born in Caesaria and graduated in 1898 from the Medico-Chirurgical College of Philadelphia, conducted important research in the field of x-rays. Tragically, Kassabian's promising career was cut short in 1910 at age 42, when he died of cancer contracted from his x-ray work. Haroutiun Dadourian a physicist at Yale, and H. H. Chakmakjian, who taught chemistry at Tufts, were also well known.[83]

Arts and Letters.   Perhaps the most illustrious Armenian American intellectual of the period was M. M. Mangasarian. A graduate of Robert College in 1878 and Princeton Theological Seminary in 1882 and an ordained minister, Mangasarian renounced the pulpit for ethical culture and free thinking and was for many years affiliated with the Independent Religious Society of Chicago. According to *Who's Who* (1926–1927), Mangasarian's publications included *A New Catechism: What is Christian Science; Morality Without God; Brave Thoughts from Brave Minds; The Truth about Jesus — Is He a Myth; The Story of My Mind; The Bible Unveiled; Is Life Worth Living Without Immortality; The Story of Joan of Arc; What Is the Trouble with the World; Marriage and Divorce; The American Girl; What Has Christ Done for the World*, and many others. Mangasarian's most important intellectual moment came in 1908, when he publically debated the Reverend Algernon Crapsey on the question of the historicity of Jesus, in a famous encounter which presaged much of the internationally famous Bryan-Darrow debate in the *Scopes* trial of the 1920s.[84]

Nor were the pseudosciences unrepresented. L. D. Kallajian, a hypnotist, advertised in the Boston press of his prowess in curing "almost every sort of disease and malady," including "smoking, drinking, nervousness, madness, fear," and "sleep talking and sleep walking."[85]

The largest single group of Armenians in the performing and studio arts were studio photographers. This was due in part to the enormous influence of Mgerditch Garo, of Boston. A student at the American College at Kharpert, Garo emigrated to Worcester where he worked in the famous wire mill. Later employed by a commercial printer, he settled in Boston in 1888 to become a painter; to earn a livelihood, however, he decided to learn photography. Within a few years Garo became one of the foremost photographers in Boston, and he trained a number of talented young immigrants in the art. His most famous pupil was Yousuf Karsh, who established a world famous career in Ottawa and New York.[86]

There were a few recognized painters, of whom the most famous was Haig Patigian. A resident of San Francisco, Patigian held successful exhibitions on the West Coast, was commissioned to execute a heroic bronze statue of President McKinley for Arcata Park in Humboldt County, and was awarded a prize for his monument commemorating the rebuilding of San Francisco. Nishan Tour, who emigrated to the United States in 1905 and furthered his education at the Hopkins College of Architecture and Arts in San Francisco, taught at John Muir College and was a prolific artist.[87] And Hovsep Pushman, the son of the Chicago oriental rug dealer and philanthropist, attained an international reputation for his paintings at Paris, Milwaukee, and Chicago showings.[88]

The role of music in wealthy Armenian homes in Turkey lived on in the immigrant world — especially the music of the church liturgy and the heritage of folk music. Agnes Chopourian, a dramatic soprano, and Zabel Mangasarian, daughter of the celebrated freethinker, attracted favorable reviews in American journals for their renditions of classical and Armenian music; Philip Bennyan and Paolo Ananian became noted concert artists; Rose Zulalian of Boston, who gained national attention for the Armenians for her rendition of the National Anthem at the Democratic National Convention in Chicago in 1932, was beginning her career in this prewar period.[89]

But certainly the most popular singer of the period was Armen Shah-Mouradian, the "bard of Daron," whose personal appearances and recordings were especially well known among Armenians. "Shah-Mouradian," recalled William Saroyan, "sang like fire and lived like it ." He sang for a time in Parisian operatic circles, but he was chiefly a "singer of the songs of Armenia." "When he sang," said Saroyan, "the nation lived and the soul of it burned and made light." Shah-Mouradian died in Paris in 1939.[90]

Although Armenians were represented in professions and arts, small business and unskilled labor were the principal callings of the immigrant generation before World War I. Whatever the occupation, the Armenians retained the Old World attributes of tenacity, thrift, and hard work.

7.

The Economic Base: Success on Both Coasts

In the period prior to World War I there were two major instances of very rapid upward economic mobility, one on the East Coast, in the oriental rug business. The other was on the West Coast, in agriculture, in Fresno, California.

The Armenians were eminently successful in both instances because of their backgrounds and talents in business, and because of the opportunities afforded them in the booming late nineteenth- and early twentieth-century American economy.

The Oriental Rug Business

By 1914 Armenians could be found in almost every large city in the East in the oriental rug trade, which, along with the rug cleaning business, they virtually monopolized.

The exceptional success of the dealers in orientals arose in part from the late nineteenth-century consumer interest in that commodity.[1] Commodore Matthew Perry's epoch-making trip to Japan in 1854, the diaries, letters, and speeches of missionaries to far off Syria, Turkey, and Armenia — all informed interested Americans about the bizarre, splendid, and exotic wonders of these ancient lands. The writings of Washington Irving (especially *Tales of the Alhambra*), the paintings of Mary Cassatt and James Whistler, Japanese calligraphy, all whetted suppressed Puritan appetites for the romantic, luxurious Orient. In architecture Richard Morris Hunt, architect of the Gilded Age, designed "Moorish" and "Byzantine" rooms, replete with oriental objet d'art, and P. T. Barnum, the greatest showman of all time, dazzled cheerless Bridgeport, Connecticut, by dwelling in exotic splendor in a "minaretted glory called 'Iranistan.' "[2] At the Philadelphia Centennial Exposition of 1876 "the exhibit ... of English, Turkish, and other Oriental kinds of rugs, ... aroused the liveliest curiosity."[3]

Home furnishings of the wealthy were promptly influenced by the new craze for the "oriental nook": Striped material, curtain rods spiked with spearheads, a cot, and pillows simulated a Turkish tent. The "Turkish corner" included a hookah, mother-of-pearl furniture, ottomans, and imitation oil lamps issuing a "dim mysterious light." Handsome Turkish and Persian carpets, rugs, and tapestries lavishly splayed on walls and floor completed the decor. Simultaneously, the increasing use of hardwood floors and the practical considerations of an increasingly mobile generation converted consumers to the virtues of "rugs," as opposed to full-floor coverings.[4]

During the 1880s, oriental rug stores were opened in New York, Boston, and Chicago; the largest firms, led by Gullabi Gulbenkian, Arshag and Mihran Karagheusian, Sarkis Telfeyan, Hovannes Tavshanjian, Bedros Kazanjian, and Topalian Brothers, opened in New York City in the 1890s or shortly thereafter. In 1909 A. H. Topakyan, later consul general for the Persian government in New York, gave President Theodore Roosevelt an oriental rug studded with "pearls, turquoise, rubies, and other oriental stones ingeniously embedded in the silken mesh of the fabric." In 1910 President William Howard Taft was also given a "valuable Persian rug," and a hit Broadway play of the 1913 season, *Blackbirds*, revolved around the theft of a $40,000 Persian rug.[5] Enthusiasm for orientals was such that by 1915 over 75 Armenian oriental rug firms were listed in the New York City Directory, while another 200 smaller retailers in orientals were located in major New England, Middle Atlantic, Midwest, and California centers.[6]

Backgrounds of Prominent Importers.   Who were the most prominent oriental rug dealers and how did they get started? Hagop Bogigian, Boston's earliest and most prestigious oriental rug merchant, began selling rugs in a Harvard Square basement in 1881 after an earlier trip to the United States during which he picked up the rudiments of English. Bogigian's success was facilitated by Henry Wadsworth Longfellow, who took a fatherly interest in Bogigian and introduced him to Charles Eliot Norton, other Harvard faculty members, business people, and "several influential ladies, wives of former college professors. . . ." Also assisted by a successful immigrant printer, Jacob Arakelyan, Bogigian expanded his business, importing a vast array of oriental carpets and exporting to Turkey, Persia, and Egypt "stoves, sewing machines, cotton goods, farming implements. . . ." Outgrowing the Harvard Square location, he moved to a handsome store on the corner of Park and Beacon Streets in downtown Boston, which was a city landmark for twenty-seven years; his customers included Marshall Field, George Pullman, the Vanderbilts, the Astors, "most of the steel men of Pennsylvania, and many well-known railroad men, manufacturers and newspaper men all over the country.[7]

Bogigian's success arose from his native talents, fortunate connections, and prior experience in the United States; other rug merchants had the advantages of experience and capital from the Old World. Probably the single largest enterprise in orientals in America was that of Gullabi Gulbenkian. Originally merchants from Talas, with connections throughout Anatolia, Persia, and the Caucasus and with Turkish officialdom in Constantinople, the Gulbenkians established trading houses in Constantinople and Smyrna in the mid-nineteenth century. In the 1890s they expanded to London and New York where, on Fifth Avenue and 26th Street, they were known as the "oldest wholesale dealers in Oriental rugs."[8] Similarly, the very important firm of Arshag and Mihran Karagheusian of New York and Freehold, New Jersey, began as an offshoot of the parent firm in Constantinople; other branches were set up in Manchester, England, and in Chicago, St. Louis, and Philadelphia. Costikyan Freres (later Kent-Costikyan) was founded in 1894 by Mihran Costikyan, whose family had "operated looms for the Sultan of Turkey and was responsible for many developments in the making of Oriental rugs," and had offices in Constantinople, London, and Chicago.[9]

Other founders of oriental rug firms in the early years had the benefit of education at missionary colleges in Turkey and were, thus, familiar with English. Garabed Telfeyan, founder of the Telfeyan rug business, moved from Caesaria to Constantinople in 1866 and sent his sons, educated at Protestant schools in Turkey, to the United States to found the New York firm of Sarkis Telfeyan and Company. Chicago's most important oriental rug dealers, the Pushmans, were educated at Yeprad College in Kharpert, moved to Constantinople, then emigrated to the New World in 1884. Hagop Isganian, who had attended Marsovan College, arrived in the United States in 1864, began manufacturing domestic throw rugs out of rags, and later expanded into importing and selling orientals.[10]

The Oriental rug business was a complex enterprise which depended heavily on careful preparation of marketable goods, annual trips to the Middle East, and judicious marketing. It is not surprising, then, that the career histories of the most prominent oriental rug dealers thus revealed a very high incidence of prior experience, connections, and assistance in establishing their businesses. Only a few Greeks, Jews, and Persians competed with the Armenians, because the Armenians had long standing in their markets, connections in Constantinople, familiarity with the languages, and capital reserves to finance the five-month buying tours through Persia. Until World War I, Armenians controlled well over 70 percent of the American market in imported orientals.[11]

Profits and Practices. Profits made by the major New York importers and retailers were healthy. The value of imported orientals rose from $300,000 in 1892 to over $4,000,000 in 1907, and rug imports maintained this level until 1914. These import dollar amounts represented wholesale import values and not the final retail price, which often rose from 100 to 500 percent of the wholesale buyer's cost. One oriental rug authority stated that a rug valued in Turkey at $100 cost a New York dealer about $200 because of shipping costs, insurance, and tariff; and it might retail for $1,000.[12]

Indeed, the physical opulence of the half dozen large New York City importers' showrooms reflected the profitability of the trade. Karagheusian's emporium was described as follows: "No Oriental showrooms in New York . . . have been more lavishly or exclusively decorated and prepared. . . . The walls, ceiling, and woodwork are specially treated by no less a firm than the Tiffany Decorating Company." Kent-Costikyan's showroom for the "ultra trade" had a ceiling "exquisitely furnished in gold bronze, rubbed with a dull sky-blue, while the side walls and pillars are treated in Roman gold, with the cornice in a brighter shade of gold bronze." The Pushman Brothers building in Chicago was "perhaps the most beautiful exclusive Oriental and domestic rug store in the Middle West," and Hagop Bogigian's Georgian establishment was fashionably situated to look out on Boston Common and Bulfinch's State House.[13]

Because of his large profits, his manner of business, the unscrupulousness of a handful of dealers, and the gross ignorance of the American clientele regarding imported rugs, the oriental rug dealer soon became an object of deep suspicion and prejudice. A classic example of this view is found in John Kimberly Mumford's *Oriental Rugs*, a turn-of-the-century guide to the English-speaking world on the subject of orientals. Here is Mumford describing one experience in rug buying:

The writer saw, among five hundred fabrics in a New York establishment, a dark, stout rug, perhaps five feet by ten. The befezzed Oriental who was in charge urged its purchase.
"It is a fine rug, that" he said; "a very rare variety."
"Of what variety is it?"
"That," he responded with impressive gravity, "is a Lulé."
"Ah! A Lulé. And from what does the name come?"
"From the old city of Lulé in Persia," he answered; "My father was born there; it is a fine old town." It was plain he was going on to tell the threadbare narrative, as venerable as the city of Lulé, and as fictitious, of how this particular bit of carpet was more than a century old — was, in fact, an heirloom in his family; of how his father had died just after bringing it all the way to this country, and it could now be had for the wretched sum of fifty dollars, because its associations made him so sad.

As a matter of fact, the name "Lulé" is a corruption of the French *roulez*, and is given by Levantine dealers, whose business is largely transacted in Gallic, to a class of carpets so thick, so tightly woven, that they cannot be folded, but must . . . be rolled up for shipment. But the part of this anecdote most germane, perhaps, to the present discussion is that the rug was not in the least a "Lulé," but a somewhat down-at-heel Kurdish product from the sand-hill districts of Mosul.[14]

On the other hand, gullible buyers who valued orientals only by their price sorely tempted scrupulously honest oriental rug dealers. Hagop Bogigian, whose offer of orientals to the wife of a former Harvard College president was rejected because the samples were "inferior," sold the rugs three weeks later to the same customer when he trebled the prices of the goods, thereby making them "nicer rugs." Henry Wadsworth Longfellow, Bogigian's patron, considered the story the "greatest joke in Cambridge," and Bogigian refunded the customer's money.[15]

Oriental rug dealers were also charged with "doctoring" rugs. Both Turkish and Kurdish weavers used raucous, raw looking vegetable dyes to color their products, but these were unsuited to Gilded Age tastes. Accordingly, the large importers washed the pieces in a mild acid bath to subdue their hues into a semiantique appearance. Sometimes rugs were also dotted and colored after the bathing process. Mumford castigated the "astute vendors of the East and, undoubtedly some in this country" for their "unnumbered tricks of chemical . . . to add the appearance of age, and consequent value."[16] To be sure, oriental rug dealers occasionally did indulge in such sharp practices; by and large, however, Armenian rug dealers were highly respected businessmen whose profits were not gleaned by swindling the public. The most prominent New York dealers — Tavshanjian, Gulbenkian, Karagheusian, and Costikyan — were men above reproach, who were charitable and socially concerned. One observer termed them "interesting, intelligent, and engaging . . . mostly trained by early adversity to hard work, independence of thought, tenacity, frugality, and self-respect."[17]

Manufacturing.   The enormous success of the orientals among the ultra trade influenced the development of the domestic rug and carpeting business in a number of ways. First, the "oriental craze" stimulated the popularity of domestic floor coverings, which rose in production from $48,000,000 in 1899 to $69,000,000 in 1914.[18] Second, the American consumer became attuned to specific sized rugs — as opposed to the more traditional roll form of carpeting — so that by the late 1920s about four-fifths of all wool floor coverings domestically produced were of the specific sized rug.[19] More important, the oriental boom sparked the demand by middle- and lower-middle-class consumers for a cheaper "domestic oriental."

The domestic oriental was pioneered on a large scale by the Bigelow-Hartford Company of Thompsonville, Connecticut, which became well known for its excellent oriental reproductions. Other domestic rug manufacturers soon vied with each other in designing "more and more exotic patterns."[20] In 1904 the Karagheusian brothers also entered the field of manufacturing both domestic orientals and broadlooms. Lacking carpet weaving machinery and skilled weavers in the New World, the brothers, in Freehold, New Jersey, turned to England where they purchased a battery of looms and imported skilled British weavers and carpet makers. Soon Armenian operatives were also trained to tend the humming looms. Using the capital, credit, and reputation of the oriental rug branch, the young manufacturers quickly established a flourishing business. Gradually, with increased production and branch offices in other parts of the United States, the firm became primarily involved in manufacturing machine-woven carpets under the trade names of Monmouth Wilton and Lakewood Wilton, and a domestic oriental, the Karaban. Their most important product would later become (in 1928) "Gulistan" carpet, a machine-woven rug that nearly rivaled fine imported pieces.[21]

By the 1890s the oriental rug business had also fostered an important sideline, for ambitious Armenian immigrants, who lacked capital but who possessed strong arms and sturdy backs, entered the oriental rug cleaning and repairing business. Many immigrants got their first taste of rug cleaning, as did Nazareth Barsumian, by laboring for $2 per day in an Armenian oriental rug store in New York. "I was instructed how to prepare the soapsuds, and how to scrub and rinse the rugs with a hard brush, on my knees, and how to hang the rugs on poles to dry," recalled Barsumian. Soon after, Barsumian opened his own plant for merchandising and cleaning oriental rugs in Evanston, Illinois, where he became well known for his tremendous devotion to work: "It was a common occurrence at the . . . plant . . . to wash and hang outside 200 or more large and small rugs on every sunshiny day, excepting, of course, Sundays. . . . Many nights we slept in the plant to be ready for an early start, usually about 2 A. M." Like most other operations, the Barsumian plant bowed to mechanization by purchasing an electric rotary rug cleaning machine in 1915.[22] Virtually every major city in the United Stated listed a few Armenian rug cleaning and repairing businesses; in 1915 New York City alone counted about twenty-five.[23]

It became part of the American myth that all Armenians were involved in the oriental rug business in the New World. And although only a few hundred were in fact actively in the trade, the oriental rug business did become the most significant single contribution of the Armenians to American commerce. This contribution exposed America to the luxury and opulence of texture and design of Middle Eastern rugs, tapestries, and objet d'art, which thereafter helped transform American interior design.

Raisin Country: Fresno, California

While some Armenians were finding exceptional success in importing, selling, and cleaning oriental rugs, others were seeking their fortune on the West Coast in agriculture. The most important farming colony grew up in Fresno, California, which soon became renowned among Armenians and non-Armenians alike for its prosperity.

Fresno County lies in the great San Joaquin Valley of Central California and is cut by the San Joaquin and Kings Rivers, which flow from the snowcapped Sierra Nevada Mountains on the east. The soil, which varies from a "loose, sand loam and white ash to the heavy red earth," is very fertile, and the near tropical climate of long hot summers, with temperatures to 110 degrees, and wet, cloudy winters, is ideally suited to the growing of grapes and fruits.[24]

Despite its agricultural potential, Fresno remained uncultivated until the post-Civil War decades. In 1872, however, the Central Pacific Railroad drove a feeder line from Sacramento south through the valley. At the same time a pioneer rancher, Moses Church, brought water from the Kings River to his ranch by irrigation canals. As a result, railroad officials were convinced that the Fresno area could be supplied with sufficient irrigation water, the town of Fresno was laid out by the railroad people, and it became the county seat. Ambitious irrigation projects and excursion trains from San Francisco contributed to the area's growth until Fresno became a "bustling, bright, prosperous city. . . .[25]

The focus of growth was vineyards, in which experimentation had begun in the 1870s. By the 1890s, the county raised at least 70 percent of the nation's raisin crop, surpassing the chief international producer, Spain. In addition, in 1896 the *Fresno Morning Republican* trumpeted that the valley produced sixty other varieties of fruits and vegetables, or every variety known outside the tropics.[26] Linked by the Southern Pacific and the Central Pacific Railroads to a national market, the valley had become an agricultural wonder.

It was in 1881 that the first Armenians settled in Fresno. Hagop Seropian had been advised by a physician to move from Worcester for his health. He and his brother Garabed traveled to San Francisco, then to the San Joaquin Valley, which "reminded Hagop of the Armenian heartlands, watered and drained by the Tigris and Euphrates and where the sun rose each morning over the twin peaks of Mt. Ararat." Three younger brothers joined the Seropians a year later and the family opened a variety and grocery store. In 1883, as a result of their enticing letters to the Old Country, the first large group of Armenian immigrants arrived directly from Marsovan.[27]

The Seropian brothers prospered and even attained notoriety. In 1892, when they wanted to ship goods to San Francisco by rail, the Southern Pacific imposed prohibitive freight charges. The aggressive immigrants, "in a dramatic counter move," rented a team of twelve mules and two wagons to carry their produce over Pecheco Pass to San Francisco. These mules, which "must have had somewhat the appearance of donkey caravans one meets in Palestine, aroused a great amount of curiosity in the villages through which they passed. . . . Pictures and accounts of them were published at the time in the *San Francisco Examiner* and created interest throughout the state."[28] Despite the Seropians' success, the Armenian population in the county remained small, estimated in 1894 at 360 souls.[29]

The mid-1890s were bitter years in the valley. Broken by the depression of 1893, farmers uprooted vast acres of vineyards and abandoned their farms.[30] By the late 1890s, however, good times had returned. This, and the exodus of Armenians from the Hamidean massacres in Turkey, spurred movement to the valley.

Like the Seropians, many of these settlers sought the valley's healthy air and healing sun, or had been told (*Gotchnag*, 1901) that it resembled a desert plain between Killis and Antioch in Cilicia.[31] Others were attracted by its fabled productivity. (Fresno Armenians wrote to relatives about "boat sized watermelons, egg sized grapes and 9 to 10 pound eggplants" — this, a dramatic reversal of the immigrants' constant lauding of Armenia's "world renowned" fertility).[32]

The movement to California was most frequently a second uprooting. That is, it usually occurred after immigrants first settled in Boston, Worcester, Providence or another East Coast city. According to one study of 67 Armenian males in Fresno, 31, or 46 percent of them, had obtained their first jobs in America as factory laborers in the East or Midwest.[33] Supporting this, 165 of 192 Armenians or 84 percent of another study resided an average of 5.7 years in the East prior to settlement in Fresno.[34] In 1909 the Immigration Com-

Table III. Population of Armenians and Other Foreign-Born Groups in Fresno County in 1900 and 1908

Group	1900[a]	1908[b]
Armenian	500[c]	3,000
Chinese	1,634	1,000
German	785	1,000
German-Russian	734	3,000
Italian	430	1,000
Japanese	601	3,000
Portuguese	309	600
Scandinavian	1,418	4,000
Austrian	112	500
Miscellaneous	2,611	3,000
Total	9,134	20,100

Source: U.S., Immigration Commission, *Reports*, vol. XXIV, 565.
a) The figures for 1900 are quoted from the census.
b) The figures for 1908 are estimated.
c) Estimated.

mission summed it up in this way: "The vast majority migrated to Fresno after spending years in Armenian colonies in the eastern industrial centers. However, they sooner or later desired to leave the factory life which was undermining their physique. Those who moved west were attracted to the new Armenian colony which enjoyed favorable climate and good opportunities." Like the German Russians in the Valley, but unlike the Japanese or Chinese there, the Armenians came chiefly in "whole families . . . to settle permanently upon a new soil."[35] A band of intrepid but luckless Armenian prospectors from the Klondike also headed south to California.[36]

The proportion of Armenians in the valley population as a whole increased over the years prior to World War I. Table III estimates figures of the various ethnic groups in Fresno in 1908. By the war's outbreak, the estimated Armenian population had tripled to about 10,000, which meant that the Armenians there constituted about 25 percent of the county's total foreign-born population.[37] An authentic "Little Armenia" was in the making.

Farmers and Laborers.   The Armenians of the San Joaquin Valley were unlike its other ethnic groups in two significant respects. First, many of the Armenians came from commercial backgrounds.[38] Second, many arrived with capital. An Immigration Commission study focused on seventeen Armenian farmers entering the valley between 1900 and 1908 whom they thought to be "typical of the land-owning Armenians in the county." Of these, sixteen brought a total of $47,291 to the Valley. The single largest amount was $10,000, while at the other extreme, one immigrant brought $150. The average amount of savings imported into the Valley by the sixteen farmers was $2,800, no little sum.[39]

The large amounts of capital brought to the valley by the Armenian farmers contrasted sharply with those of the "typical" German Russian, Japanese, and Danish farmers.

	No. of farmers	Total Cash	Average Cash
Armenians	17	$47,291.66	$2,781
Danish	25	35,120.00	1,405
German Russians	17	32,370.00	1,904
Japanese	34	16,780.00	494

Of the seventeen Armenian farmers in the study, five arrived in the United States with cash of at least $1,000 and eleven possessed that sum or more upon arrival in Fresno. By contrast, only one Dane and no Japanese or German Russians arrived in the United States with cash of $1,000 or more.[40]

Once they arrived in Fresno, the Armenian farmers quickly invested in vineyards and took large risks in doing so. They outbid each other and the more aggressive of the Japanese by sinking their entire savings — and incurring large debts — to secure the most profitable land available. In fact, the Armenians "have been so desirous to purchase . . . that they have bid up prices beyond what the land was really worth as a means of making a living and accumulating property. This fact and the further fact that they have usually bought soils good for viticulture, and frequently if not generally with bearing vines, explain [why] . . . the Armenians have paid a higher price per acre for the farms purchased by them than any other race investigated."[41]

After down payments often amounting to 50 percent of the purchase price, only three of the seventeen farmers retained sizable savings, while all the others sank every penny into their farms. All seventeen farmers carried heavy mortgages, with an average indebtedness of $5,702. This figure contrasted sharply with that of the "typical" Danish farmers investigated by the commission, whose average indebtedness was $2,500, or that of the German Russians ($2,576) or the Japanese ($2,982). Thus the Armenians began farming deeply in dept.[42]

In addition, some Armenian farmers leased land for farming. In 1900, of a total of 3,214 farms of non-Asians in the county, 730 were leased or rented, and a portion of these were "no doubt Armenians who had begun to farm on their own account." One of the 17 Armenians leased 110 acres, although leasing land was less common among the Armenians than among the Japanese. The Immigration Commission found that leasing land in some cases constituted a "stepping stone to the purchasing of farms," but that much of the leased land was "in addition to farms owned and cultivated by the Armenians."[43]

Although many Armenians migrated to Fresno with capital and immediately bought farms, a near majority brought only their own physical resources; this required them to take the only jobs available, as manual laborers in the vineyards or packinghouses. Some became regular farm hands on the larger ranches. Thus, according to the Immigration Commission: "The work with teams — cultivating, and hauling of boxes, and trays, harvested crop, and prunings from vines and trees — is done on the smallest ranches by the rancher himself, but on the larger ranches by 'hands' regularly employed throughout the year." For $2 a day immigrants did "unattractive" hand work — pruning the dormant vines during the winter months, hoeing, weeding, snipping suckers, "leeching" (washing) the soil of alkali, dusting for insects, and repairing boxes. Since American farmers preferred to hire "native" or western European hands because of their alleged versatility and skill over the Armenians and Asians, the immigrants often labored for fellow Armenians.[44]

In addition, Armenians toiled as grape pickers or stoop laborers, under arduous, dirty conditions:

The grapes as picked are placed upon trays, one layer deep, in order that they may be "cured" by the sunshine. These facts make it necessary that the picker should assume a stooping or squatting posture while engaged in clipping the bunches of grapes and placing them upon the trays. The work is commonly said to be "backbreaking," and this is one reason which most "Americans" give for their absolute refusal to engage in grape picking when other employment can be found. Moreover, the vineyards are dry and dusty, so that the employment becomes objectionable upon the ground that it is "dirty." . . . The harvesting of grapes falls during the hottest months of the year. At times the official records show a temperature of 105 or 110 in the shade. . . . Working in the sunshine close to the ground in the vineyards, the laborer finds it much hotter.[45]

Because Fresno's ranchers had not succeeded in getting "white men . . . [to] work all day in a stoop over position" in 110 degree heat amid flies and other insects, they had hired Chinese immigrants as Fresno's first stoop laborers.[46] (Many of the Chinese had been discharged from the Central Pacific Railroad construction gangs in the early 1880s.) Because of the Chinese Exclusion Acts soon after, these industrious, patient, and orderly sojourners were increasingly supplanted by turbaned East Indians, patient German Russians, Italians, Japanese, Mexicans, and Armenians.[47] Armenian children commonly labored in the fields to assist their struggling parents.

In the city of Fresno, wives and children of the poorer families worked in the fig and raisin packinghouses. Prior to the 1890s, this work was "clean and agreeable" but the introduction of raisin seeding machinery made it "unclean." According to the Immigration Commission, "great speed is required to keep up with the machinery, and . . . the men in the 'seeder rooms' work in a very high temperature, due to the escape of steam from the seeder machines, and the work of the women around the tables is disagreeable, because the soft steamed raisins drop from the chutes and tables and make the floors slippery and dirty." Fig packing conditions were worse. "The figs are usually passed through a solution of salt water before they are packed, and in handling them the salt works in between the fingers of the packers, and as a result the constant rubbing of the fingers against each other produces in a few days a painful ulceration of the skin."[48] (Because of these conditions, the large numbers of Northern European and American women in packinghouse work gave way to the immigrants; according to a 1917 survey, 455 workers, or about 15 percent of the entire Fresno packinghouse labor force, were Armenians.)[49]

In addition to the "sweated" conditions, Armenian women found the packinghouse atmosphere distasteful. Some complained of the lack of respect "on the part of the foremen," and the rough language. Bred to a "very high standard of propriety," the Armenians often sought to dissuade the younger women from seeking packinghouse work.[50] And wages were low. In one survey of 80 Armenian female packinghouse employees, 52 earned between $2 and $2.25 for a ten-hour day; a few earned up to $2.50 a day.[51] Nonetheless, packinghouse labor brought badly needed funds to the Armenian families to buy clothes and pay off mortgages. In 1913, under the rubric "Despised Work," *Asbarez* encouraged newly arrived Armenian women in Fresno to seek packinghouse jobs, despite their odious reputation, for there newcomers in need could save $300 in three short months to assist their families.[52]

Immigrant families kept a horse, cow and a small vegetable patch; a few peddled cucumbers in town or harvested the leftover second crop (passed over by pickers) to be sold for a pittance as wine grapes. Economies were made in their living quarters. Unlike the homes of well-to-do Danish farmers, which boasted carpeted floors and pianos, those of the Armenians were small, crowded, two- and three-room affairs with sweat boxes (in which raisins were dried) and cartons made into furniture. Armenians, said the Immigration Commission, devoted little effort or cash to keeping farm houses painted or in good repair — although the interiors were "on the whole very good." To the Armenians "making money is regarded as of primary, living well of secondary importance." Or in Armenian parlance, "no house can produce a farm, but a good farm can produce a house."[53]

Whatever sacrifices families made to gain a foothold in Fresno, the most critical factor in viticulture was the profit yield for raisins. In fact, a one- or two-cent change in price could spell success or catastrophe.

In the fifteen seasons between 1890 and the outbreak of World War I, prices fluctuated sharply. The worst markets occurred in the aftermath of the 1893 depression, when a record crop (of 103,000,000 pounds as compared with a normal crop of 85,000,000 pounds) together with the importation of 32,000,000 pounds of duty-free Greek currants and Spanish malagas glutted the market. Three cents a pound normally brought a profit to the grower, but prices dropped to less than one-half of that, finally bottoming at the disastrous level of three-fourths of a cent a pound. With no market for raisins, embittered farmers fed their surpluses to horses and cattle, 20,000 acres of vineyards were uprooted and foreclosures swept the valley.[54] By the late 1890s, however, raisin markets recovered for a variety of reasons: the United States government levied tariffs on imported raisins and currants; production dropped to 68,000,000 pounds (1896) and levelled off thereafter to about 80,000,000 pounds annually; and the domestic recovery eased conditions. Finally, the Fresno farmers organized a raisin cooperative, the California Raisin Growers' Association. The cooperative signed up about 90 percent of the California raisin acreage, and with this powerful weapon, collectively bargained with packers and buyers.[55] Because of these factors, prices between 1898 and 1903 held at three cents a pound or rose to four and five cents a pound. (Production costs of native growers were estimated at two cents a pound, those of the Armenians were reckoned to be one and one-half cents a pound.)[56]

The period from 1903 to 1908 was one of continuing prosperity for Fresno growers despite the collapse (in 1904) of the raisin growers' cooperative. For in 1904, late fall rains damaged a third of the crop and thus sustained prices; short crops in Fresno in 1905 and 1906, and damaged harvests in Europe in 1906 and 1907 resulted in four- and five-cent prices, with a few months seeing prices at the unheard of level of six cents a pound.[57] The nine years from 1898 to 1907 were healthy for most valley growers.

A second cycle of bad years began with the 1907 crash and a large crop in 1908. Armenians with heavy investments bitterly attacked the local Fresno packing interests.[58] A Fresno reporter in *Gotchnag* labeled the packers "men of no conscience," and one sixty-year-old Armenian farmer, who had amassed savings as a factory laborer in Worcester and Hartford to become a raisin grower and was wiped out in the depressed 1908 market, took his own life.[59] The bitter slump lasted for two full years. But in 1909, the Fresno Chamber of Commerce instituted a "Raisin Day" and parade to publicize the local product, and it cleared the "large surplus which growers had looked on as almost a total loss."[60] At the same time, shortages in Spanish and Turkish crops, and a second growers' cooperative, the California Raisin Exchange, which enlisted 75 percent of the local growers, introduced stability into the markets. Because of the cooperative especially, yields remained profitable until World War I.[61]

What was the relationship of the Armenian growers to the cooperative movement? The Armenian journal in Fresno, *Asbarez*, first published in 1908, and the Armenian-language journals in Boston repeatedly urged their readers in Fresno to "sign up" their acreage with the cooperatives. In 1901, the first California Raisin Growers' Association (1898–1904) included approximately 200 Armenian growers, surely a majority of the valley's Armenian ranchers. In 1902, because of alleged discrimination toward them, all but 50 of the Armenians left the cooperative, and it was perhaps because of this that an industry authority later claimed that the valley's foreigners — the Armenians, Italians, Japanese, and Chinese — were ignorant and suspicious of the cooperatives and thus boycotted them.[62]

In 1907, before the organization of the second cooperative, four substantial Armenian growers, John M. Seropian, Krikor Arakelian, Hagop Nishkian, and B. M. Rustigian, gathered forty to fifty Armenian farmers into their own cooperative, and also in 1907 twenty-five Armenian growers planned joint use of B. H. Paul's new seeding process to sell collectively in Fresno or the East to eliminate the detested middlemen packers.[63] Once the second cooperative began, the immigrant spokesmen on the staff of *Asbarez*, and the larger Armenian growers labored hard to induce fellow immigrants to join the new combine. Hagop Nishkian, leader of the procooperative forces among the Armenians, was active as one of the fifteen governors of the new cooperative. It is probably true that in this period some smaller Armenian growers, already "burned" by the failure of the first cooperative and able to receive higher prices outside the cooperative umbrella, failed to join the movement, but it is certain, as the *Fresno Morning Republican* pointed out, the larger Armenian growers were stalwart cooperative supporters.[64]

In addition to their activities in the cooperatives, Armenian growers were reputed to be hard bargainers and even "gamblers." One representative example is of their selling tactics in the chaotic market situation of 1907. August prices were holding at a profitable three and one half cents to four cents a pound when news arrived that sudden rains had destroyed the principal foreign competition, the Smyrna Sultana crop. As a result, prices shot up to five and one half cents a pound — a record level. However, a large group of Armenians, which sought to control 32,000,000 pounds of the 40,000,000 pounds of raisins still unsold, held out for still higher prices — to six cents. Led by Paul Mosesian, a noted "gambler" in raisin prices, the Armenians were termed by the *Fresno Morning Republican* as "strong players of the game of hold on as long as they have a steady market." According to the paper, the Armenians "pay big rentals and big prices for land," and "it is probable that many of them will see the whole fight to its ultimate outcome." The upshot of the speculation was handsome profits for those unloading holdings in late 1907.[65]

Because of their business abilities, work ethic, frugal living, and good management, all in a generally prosperous economic climate, the Armenians in and around Fresno achieved considerable success before World War I. One useful index of their progress is the amount of property accumulated by the seventeen typical Armenian farmers in Fresno investigated by the Immigration Commission. These seventeen farmers had arrived in the valley between 1900 and 1908 with total assets of $52,150 (average assets were $2,800). However, by 1908, less than a decade after the arrival of the first of the seventeen farmers, they owned property with a total estimated value of $246,150. After deducting their outstanding mortgages of $79,825 and a "few other debts," the net value of their property was $185,337 or a collective increase of $133,187. Individual net worth had increased from $2,781 to $11,587 per farmer, or as the Immigration Commission conservatively remarked, the farmers had accumulated between "three and four times as much property as they had at the time of the settlement."[66]

As a group, Armenians in the San Joaquin Valley by 1908 held 25,000 acres of land, owning about three-fifths of the total. Estimates of their vineyards ran between 16,000 and 20,000 acres, or roughly one-sixth of the acreage devoted to raisin grape production. "They are very industrious," stated the Immigration Commission, and "by business shrewdness, economy, have made rapid progress in the accumulation of wealth." The Armenians, concluded the commission, "have usually succeeded better than any other race in accumulating property. Not even the Japanese about Fresno have succeeded as well as they."[67]

At the same time, the Armenian immigrants who first labored in the fields or packinghouses were escaping "from the wage-earning classes" and were becoming independent farmers and businessmen. By 1908, for example, the combined total of Armenian and Italian grape pickers in the region equaled no more than 500 (and a survey in the same year of 838 random pickers included 508 Japanese, 109 Chinese, 55 East Indians, 50 Mexicans, 42 American Indians, and only 25 Armenians, or about 3 percent of the total).[68] The only appreciable supply of Armenian day labor in the pre-World War I period was provided by the female hands in the packinghouses.[69]

Indeed many Armenians became prosperous in the valley, but many also paid a heavy price. Falling markets, sudden August storms during drying season, and spring frosts and blights were frequent occurrences. In 1908 many Armenian farmers suffered severe setbacks when dampness and mildew damaged stored raisins; during a prolonged freeze in April 1911 Armenian growers took an estimated $200,000 loss.[70] According to *Gotchnag*, one elderly Armenian whose crops were devastated by August rains (1904) poisoned himself. Moreover, there were family sacrifices.[71] As noted earlier, Armenians became packinghouse laborers and even neglected their children's education to "get ahead," a practice which contrasted sharply with their national belief in education for the young. And there was the unending, backbreaking labor in the fields.

Other Commercial Interests.   In addition to raisin production, Fresno Armenians pioneered the development of the fig and melon industries. In the late 1800s, members of the *San Francisco Bulletin*, in conjunction with the American consul in Smyrna, sought unsuccessfully to grow Smyrna figs in the United States. However, a resourceful Armenian farmer, Henry Markarian, and his son, successfully cultivated the white Adriatic fig. In time they produced other varieties as well. However, a national market for figs did not develop until the early 1890s when a cholera scare led to an embargo on Smyrna figs and created a demand for the home-grown variety; about 500,000 pounds of figs were packed and shipped East in this period. From this beginning the Markarians became the largest fig growers in the United States with control of 20 percent of domestic production.[72]

At the same time Krikor Arakelian pioneered melon production in the United States. Arakelian and his family had emigrated from Marsovan to Fresno in 1883 when he was a boy of twelve. He worked for his father for $10 a month peddling fruit and melons around Fresno. In 1892 he returned to Marsovan, but with the outbreak of the Hamidean massacres he escaped to the United States. Beginning from nothing, Arakelian initiated large-scale melon growing in the San Joaquin Valley. Within a few years he had become the Melon King of America. Venturing also into raisin production, he soon owned thousands of acres of vineyards, as well as his own packinghouses. He also entered the wine industry under the soon-to-be-famous "Mission Bell" wine label.[73]

In addition to Arakelian's achievements, the Armenians, according to the Fresno Daily Republican, also introduced the "yellow watermelon, sometimes called locally the ice cream watermelon, the Persian melon, the Kassaba melon, . . . the Diarbekir melon, the Turkish melon, and the Armenian cucumber." Armenians also became involved in animal husbandry, hay production, vegetables, berries, and poultry raising. And, encouraged by the American Tobacco Company, by 1912 they had put 300 to 400 acres of tobacco under cultivation.[74]

Agriculture was not their only occupation in Fresno, for they were also involved in the city's businesses. In 1901, for example, there were 34 Armenian establishments engaged in shoe repairing, tailoring and men's furnishings, dry goods, and other businesses. But by 1915 the number of Armenian establishments had jumped to 162, the most numerous of which were shoe repair shops, barber shops, and tailors and haberdashers, as listed below.

	1901	1915
Barber shops	1	20
Cleaning and dying	0	13
Dry goods shops	4	8
Furniture stores	2	9
Groceries	1	14
Restaurants	2	8
Shoe repairing shops	8	25
Tailors, men's furnishings	4	15
Watchmakers and jewelers	3	7
Other	9	43
Total	34	162

(Other businesses included blacksmith shops, billiard and pool rooms, real estate agencies, drug stores, automobile shops, bicycle shops, confectionary and soft drink stores, and furrier shops). Probably the only rojig (Middle Eastern grape juice and nut candy) in the

United States was manufactured by the Kenderian Brothers in Olean-
der, 6 miles from Fresno, and when oil was discovered near Fresno,
Armenians formed the Fresno Oil Development Company. The
Armenian professionals in Fresno included 2 doctors, 4 lawyers, and
2 dentists.[75]

Because of their progress in Fresno's businesses and agriculture,
Armenians waxed eloquent over their community. "We are progressing when we contrast ourselves to the older days. Any comfortably
established person's table is more rich in delicacies than an ancient
Persian king's tables. Any Fresno Armenian who has a good 40 acres
or a brisk trade can dress in his Sunday shoes and clothes more
healthily, comfortably, and attractively than King Solomon. Our
rooms, sheltered by glass windows, illuminated by electricity, gas or
coal lamps, are certainly richer and more comfortable than Nebu-
chadnezzar's palace."[76] Their early struggles had turned the desert
into acres of productive and profitable vineyards. They had sunk
roots in *chamichi yergir* (raisin country).

Although there were relatively few Armenians in the United
States in the period to World War I, they acquitted themselves hon-
orably in the new industrial economy; and they helped to pioneer
America's development in new enterprises — rugs and raisins. Thus,
many had succeeded in their first challenge in the New World.

8.

The Physical Adjustment

While the Armenians were adjusting to the economic order of factories and farms, they also had to adapt to the harsh physical and social demands of immigrant life in America. It was an iron-clad law of late nineteenth- and early twenty-century America that poverty-stricken immigrants first congregated together in ethnic enclaves in the urban centers and mill towns in which they found their first jobs, and the Armenians were no exception. The statistics of the U.S. Commissioner General of Immigration and the federal and state censuses reveal a preponderance of Armenian settlements in the industrial East Coast, in the Midwest, and in California, and especially in the poor, congested, badly run, and violent neighborhoods in these regions. Daily life entailed facing terribly overcrowded tenements and boardinghouses, poor sanitation and hygiene, the onus of being "foreigners" and "immigrants," and harsh discrimination—especially in California. But it was a beginning from which the newcomers re-established their Old World communities in the New.

East Coast Settlement

Because of their jobs in the factories, mills, and farms, and because they settled where Armenians before them had settled, the immigrants were concentrated chiefly in the New England, Middle Atlantic, and Midwest states, and also in California. (Their destinations on arriving in the United States are detailed in Appendix Table IV).

Indeed, the East Coast urban centers were receiving grounds for all the masses of newly arrived immigrants from southern and eastern Europe and the Middle East. According to the Census of 1920, New England and the Middle Atlantic states claimed fully 48 percent of the nation's foreign-born; by the end of 1907 over two-thirds of Worcester's nearly 147,000-person population were foreign-born or of foreign-born parentage (in the same year, Worcester elected its first foreign-born mayor); the populaces of Boston, Providence, New

123

York, and Philadelphia averaged 66 percent foreign-born; and Paterson, New Jersey's 87 percent foreign-born population placed it first among "immigrant cities."[1]

Wherever they settled, the Armenians clustered together in "Little Armenias" or, lacking sufficient numbers, they became part of a "Little Orient." Such communities soon took on regional as well as national characteristics; that is, immigrants from the same Old Country region, city, or town settled together because, through the chain-link migration (chapter 4), they had relocated with relatives or neighbors from the Old Country. The single largest Old World group to emigrate to the United States was from the Kharpert Plain, and they naturally comprised the largest single regional group in many communities such as Boston, Worcester, Lynn, Providence, and Whitinsville.[2] Because a few early immigrants from Arapgir and Malatia settled in Philadelphia, the City of Brotherly Love soon attracted the single largest aggregations of Arapgertzis (Armenians from Arapgir) and Malatatzis.[3] Similarly, Pawtucket and Niagara Falls drew Armenians from Van, and the majority of the Armenians in Charlestown came originally from Hivsinigi.[4]

This stamp of regionalism was so strong that an Armenian writer in *Azk* in 1913 declared that "a visitor to West Hoboken who hadn't visited Dicranagert wouldn't need to."[5] Said another writer, "Not only are the women dressed in Old Country ways, but they eat pumpkin seeds in the streets" of West Hoboken.[6] Similarly Russian Armenians colonized apart from the Turkish Armenians, with their largest groups settling in Yonkers, New York; East St. Louis, Illinois; and Riverside and Los Angeles, California.[7]

Mercantile Centers.   In the mercantile centers of New York, Boston, Philadelphia, and Portland, the "little Armenias" were to be found in the poorer, although not the poorest, older working-class neighborhoods. Often these had been sections of "swell front" brick-faced homes of Yankee businessmen, each with its city garden and rooms for domestics. Not long deserted by the rich and near rich, they housed the nineteenth-century waves of immigrants, first the Irish and then the southern and eastern Europeans, among whom were the Armenians.

Boston's largest contingent of Armenian immigrants lived in the once fashionable South Cove, especially in its northern portion, bounded by Tyler, Hudson, Kneeland, and Dover Streets, and Shawmut Avenue.[8] In the 1870s businesses and "factories belching smoke" began encroaching hard on the Cove's northern boundary of Kneeland and Eliot Streets, as the district saw the final flight of the upper and middle classes to the newly filled Back Bay and to Roxbury. In their stead came an influx of Irish Americans and Irish immigrants. By 1900 the Cove yielded to yet another wave, thereby becoming part of the "Orient of Boston" with its principal denizens the Syrians, Greeks, Chinese, and Armenians. To house the ever more dense immigrant population profitably, ingenious contractors and builders converted the once stately three- and four-story brick, single-family residences into lodging houses and eventually subdivided the majority into miniscule apartments so that four to eight times the original number of occupants could be crowded into the original space. And where an area was left in back or to the sides — sometimes for alleys or courts — additions were made, blocking off the sun and light such that some buildings on the lower floors "never lost their green mold."[9]

One pocket, the area between Dover Street and the Boston and Albany Railroad, became "more compactly built with dwellings than any similar area in the city," housing 157 persons to the acre. By 1904–1905, the South Cove overall, now fully a lodging house district, had the comparatively heavy population density of 12.3 persons per dwelling. This density was exceeded only by the city's extremely congested North End (19.6 persons per dwelling) and West End (16.2 persons per dwelling). And outside the South Cove the most sizable clusters of Armenians were found precisely in the foreign tenements of the city's most congested wards, the West End along Cambridge Street, and in the North End, with scattered numbers in the relatively moderate congestion of South Boston.[10]

In New York City in 1900, the major Armenian colony was found on Manhattan's Lower East Side in Wards 18 and 21, wards comprising neighborhoods of comparatively moderate density.[11] Ward 18 with an average 30.78 persons per tenement and Ward 21 with 29.55 persons per tenement ranked as low as 15th and 17th from the highest densities of the 22 wards. Moreover, these wards were two of only four wards whose average population per tenement shows a decline (in both cases considerable) in a comparative study between earlier (1864) figures on average number of persons per tenement and the 1900 figures. By 1915 roughly half of the city's Armenians lived or worked in these two Lower East Side wards.[12]

The major concentration of the Armenians in these wards, and especially along Third Avenue distinctly resembled the South Cove, Kneeland Street settlement in Boston. Both Third Avenue in New York and Kneeland Street in Boston were demarcation lines dividing tenement districts from business districts. And it is precisely along this quasi-business-residential borderline that there was a clustering of Armenians with a preponderance of their numbers employed in small businesses: tailor shops, shoemaking and repair shops, rug repair shops, jewelry stores, and neighborhood groceries.

Finally, Philadelphia's small Armenian community perhaps best exemplified the trend. As early as 1902, *Gotchnag* noted that Philadelphia's nearly 350 Armenians (including 65 families) worked mostly in stores, generally their own, or as artisans and lived nearby. "Few are forced to do factory work." Clearly, in the mercantile centers the number of Armenians engaged in small business was out of proportion to their aggregate numbers (Chapter 6).[13] In each case, these were districts whose immigrants were already considered "once removed from poverty and on the way up the economic ladder."[14]

Factory and Mill Towns.   In direct contrast were the Armenian colonies of the nineteenth-century eastern factory cities and mill towns. Lawrence, Lowell, Worcester, Haverhill, Northbridge, Fitchburg, Lynn, and Fall River typify those towns in Massachusetts alone, whose single industry — textile mills, shoe factories, or wire goods — attracted sizable colonies of Armenian laborers. All exhibited a common history and character. Lawrence, whose textile mills dotted the Merrimack River shoreline, 11 miles downriver from Lowell, was a classic example.

An immigrant city long before its inundation by southern and eastern European immigrants, Lawrence endured a population explosion of 500 percent in the five decades from 1860 to 1910, including a doubling in two decades from fewer than 40,000 in 1880 to almost 86,000 in 1910. Despite enormous expansion of total numbers, the percentage of foreign-born population actually rose over the period to only 48 percent, but by 1910 7 of every 10 births recorded in the city involved parents who were both foreign born. As the floodgates widened, however, the ethnic backgrounds of the newcomers evidenced several changes. The early native stock, "mostly rural New Englanders," had encountered first the Irish, from 1847–1848 on, then a wave after the Civil War, primarily of Germans, French Canadians, and Scots, and finally, from the 1890s on, the Armenians scattered among the multitudes of Italians, Russians, Poles, Austrians, and Syrians.[15]

The huge population buildup grossly over-burdened the city's existing facilities, directly affecting the newest immigrants. "The very buildup dwarfed the city's capacity to tackle and successfully resolve such issues" as the need for "wholesale improvements in health and housing,"[16] Further, the incapacity was fed by native arguments that "Lawrence was industrial" and "that the city was overrun by foreigners who cared little for America or cleanliness, anyway."[17]

The history of Armenian settlement began in the 1890s when handfuls of Armenians took "miserable" furnished rooms on Common Street. Indeed in 1893, the first Armenian restaurant opened on Common Street in the very heart of Lawrence's traditional receiving ground for immigrants and, accordingly, the city's poorest section — Ward 2. Employed in the textile mills (the American Woolen Company, the Arlington, and the Pacific were among the largest) the Armenian colony, approximately 600 in 1907, grew to nearly 1,000 by 1915. Throughout this period, the focus of settlement was always the city's oldest and densest sections, now heavily immigrant wards. In the predominantly Italian and Irish wards — Wards 1 and 2 — the Armenians formed pockets along the arteries immediately north of the river and the mills; fewer of their numbers ventured out in the relatively less congested "plains" — Ward 3 — with its bulk of Irish and Syrian immigrants.[18]

Specifically, in 1913 of the 375 Armenian heads of households listed in the *Lawrence Directory*, 148 listed residences along Common Street, most in the lower east end, in the 100's (37) and 200's (70).[19] Conservatively estimated, easily half of the Armenians in Lawrence lived on or in close proximity to Common Street. This area, the two half blocks of lower Common Street east and west of Newbury, was "in 1911 the most congested . . . in the state, except for a small part of Boston," with population densities of 603 persons per acre to the east and 462 persons to the west.[20] The individual apartment held an average of eight persons on this portion of Common Street and over six persons on Valley Street — another area of Armenian concentration — compared with the four to four and one half persons per apartment in Boston and New York's Armenian neighborhoods. Similarly, extreme congestion characterized the smaller pockets of Armenians along other main arteries — Brook, Elm, Essex, Jackson, and High Streets — and here Armenian boardinghouses flourished.[21]

Indeed the omnipresent Armenian boardinghouse served as "home" to an inordinately large proportion of Lawrence's Armenians, relative to other immigrant groups. Causes for the widespread adoption of the boardinghouse system were two: first, the factory community's typically large percentage of bachelors — 40 percent of the adult male Armenian immigrants; and second, and even more important, the wives of as many as 70 percent of the married Armenian males as late as 1907 were still in the Old Country. By comparison only 18 percent of Lawrence's total foreign-born, married male population had wives still abroad.[22] Thus, typically, the boardinghouse at 31 Allen Street housed 23 Armenian men, 16 shared "furnished" rooms at 47 Mechanic Street, and similarly the 11 Armenian laborers residing at 65 Lawrence Street and the 13 at 19 Summer Street still lived "cooperatively" in 1915. *Gotchnag*, reporting on the "more than 365 Armenian men" patronizing Lawrence's six Armenian restaurants in 1913, found that more than half of them lived in furnished rooms.[23] And throughout the immigrant period, the boardinghouse reflected unquestionably the worst conditions of density, lack of sanitary facilities, and squalor.

Whether in bachelor boardinghouses or tenements of families, Lawrence's Armenians characteristically resided in three- and four-story wooden buildings — 97 percent of Lawrence's housing was wood construction, or "hastily constructed firetraps." The tall, narrow buildings predominant in Wards 1 and 2 occupied every available bit of land. Inadequate regulations specifying a minimum of three feet between sides of buildings and lot lines had long been circumvented with the result that wall to wall tenements covered former yards, courts, and rear spaces. In some cases, lots were so fully occupied with buildings that there was "not room to place a garbage can on the same lot with the house."[24]

Lawrence's congestion represented the extreme condition. Referring to the density crisis exacerbated by this rear-building construction, the *Lawrence Survey* reported: "Lowell and Salem have sections of blocks . . . equaling the worst congestion in Lawrence, but . . . their maps do not display the conditions on the Lawrence map. The center of Lawrence has the largest number of large frame houses and the largest number of rear houses. With Boston's brick center excepted, the map of Lawrence's center is the worst in New England."[25]

However, one "health hazard" in Lawrence markedly improved during this period. Until 1893 Lawrence's water supply had come unfiltered from the Merrimack River. All raw sewage, rubbish, and industrial effluents dumped by New Hampshire and Massachusetts cities and towns along the river flowed freely. The city of Lowell, directly upriver and a carbon copy of Lawrence on a slightly larger scale (107,000 population), became the prime culprit in Lawrence's pollution problem. Once a "clear-cheerful, hardworking Yankee River" (Whittier), the Merrimack was killing people by 1885 with its typhus bacteria at the alarming rate of 92/100,000 annually. Filtration introduced in 1893 lowered deaths from typhoid fever to 24/100,000 for the period 1894–1910.[26]

The Midwest

Early Armenian colonies in the Midwest were scarce. As late as 1910, the United States Census recorded only 2,195 of the 23,938 foreign-born Armenians — a scant 9 percent of the national total — located in midwestern states. Illinois in 1910 claimed the highest state population with its 1,402 foreign-born Armenians, almost half of whom settled in Chicago. Other tiny Illinois colonies appeared in East St. Louis, Waukegan, West Pullman, and Granite City-Madison. In the following decade, through overseas and internal migration, the Midwest's Armenian population increased both absolutely and proportionately. As a result, the 5,545 foreign-born Armenians there in 1920 accounted for 15 percent of the total 37,647 Armenians then in the United States. This growth reflected as well a shift in the pattern of migration toward the newly burgeoning motor city, Detroit. With impetus from Henry Ford's 1911 broadcast of $5 per day wages and the city's rapid industrial spurt after World War I, Detroit's 337 member Armenian colony of 1910 increased five-fold to 1,692 by 1920. Accordingly, the Armenian population in Michigan as a whole rose from a total 472 foreign born (1910) to 2,606 (1920). Sizable Armenian colonies appeared in Madison and Racine, Wisconsin, Grand Rapids, Michigan, and Cleveland, Ohio.[27]

These immigrant colonies were composed chiefly of young laborers, generally without their families, who, "disappointed at the low wages" in the eastern factories and "anxious to receive the higher wages in the midwest," set out for factories in Illinois, Michigan, and Wisconsin, as the Armenian language journal *Gotchnag* noted in 1902.[28] That this was a migration of laborers without families is borne out by *Gotchnag's* 1913 census of the fast-growing Detroit community: "Approximately 820 Armenians, including 51 families and 650 bachelors."[29] This phenomenon repeated the identical immigration pattern established in the East Coast colonies in the early decades of the 1880s and 1890s.

Within the broader context of economic incentive, the origins of several Armenian settlements in the Midwest can be pinpointed to specific events. In 1891 a major employer of immigrant Armenians, the Washburn and Moen Company of Worcester, later the American Wire and Steel Company, opened a wire manufacturing plant in Waukegan, Illinois. To build a labor force, immigrants in the Worcester plant were induced to migrate to the new plant, hence the establishment of Waukegan's Armenian community.[30] Similarly, many Worcester Armenians moved to Cleveland with guaranteed jobs in the American Wire and Steel Company's new plant in that Ohio industrial center.[31] Favorable reaction to midwestern settlements spurred their growth. In Cleveland, wrote one enthusiast, factory conditions were superior to those in the East: immigrants were not called "dagoes" or "foreigners" since all laborers were of foreign birth, and Armenians were closer to the Yankees than most other immigrants. Weekly wages, no small inducement, ranged here from $8 to $12, instead of an average of $6 to $8 in the East.[32] Personal and family connections, too, accounted for some communities. The small colony of about one hundred Armenians in Grand Rapids, Michigan, employed in the furniture factories there, were largely from the town of Palou and were related to the Kurkjian family.[33] As in the East, the Russian Armenian laborers settled apart from the Turkish Armenians, largely in East St. Louis.[34]

A smattering of immigrants pushed on from the Detroit community across the Canadian border into the industrial areas of Hamilton, Bradford, and St. Catharines. Records indicate the presence of other unexpected groups in such locations as Omaha and Kansas City, and the immigrant press made much of these. Their favorite exception, however, was the hardy band of gold prospectors who trekked to the Klondike to strike it rich. *Hairenik* and *Yeprad* of 1899 reported their progress with interest, but finally acknowledged with some disappointment that Eldorado had eluded the intrepid immigrants.[35]

Information regarding detailed conditions of housing in midwestern colonies, while scanty, covers a broad spectrum. In Detroit, the Midwest's largest Armenian colony was clustered in the dockside slums of Delray. This area, part of Detroit's Ward 18, was the city's heavily populated immigrant quarter, with dense concentrations of Russians, Slavs, Bulgarians, Lithuanians, and Hungarians, as well as Armenians. Peter Roberts, an authority on this period of immigration, said that when Detroit incorporated Delray as its 18th Ward, "it was the same as if a part of backward Europe were attached." To no one's surprise, much of Delray's housing was constructed without adequate sanitary facilities, and the serious health problems ensuing received considerable publicity but little action. Detroit's second sizable Armenian community concentrated in "better neighborhoods" — in Highland Park, Henry Ford's early domain.[36]

The 800 Armenians in the combined populations of the southern Illinois steel center of Granite City-Madison lived chiefly in the pejoratively dubbed "Hungary Hollow" sections of the adjacent communities. In these quarters, separated by a distance of four or five city blocks from each of the two regularly constituted towns, "the immigrants lived together and entirely apart from any American influences." Home to Bulgarians, Magyars, Hungarians, Serbians, Rumanians, and Armenians, this area grew from the immigrants' desire to be near their jobs, and, accordingly, was situated "along the tracks of the railroad . . . between the plants of the two steel companies and a short distance from the car shops and corn products manufacturing establishment." The Immigration Commission described the "Hungary Hollow" district of 1910:

Some of the lodging houses are located almost under the shadow of the car shops and along the main line of an important railroad system. The entire section is unhealthy. The atmosphere, on account of the proximity to the car shops and railroad, is filled with dust and dirt. The streets even along the electric line [railway] are unpaved; here and in the open lots mud and pools of stagnant water abound.[37]

Although several Armenian boarding houses were located within the American section of the towns, in Hungary Hollow the Armenian bachelors or families occupied company-owned cottages. The cottages, built in rows, were small, one-story frame buildings situated on 50' × 150' lots with yards suitable for gardening. Describing the cottages, the commission said: "The buildings themselves are small, one story in height, and usually are in great need of repair. They contain three, and four, and in some instances, five rooms. ... The dimensions of the rooms are about 8' by 6' with one room 10' × 12'."

The outstanding aspect of the life of the Armenians in Granite City-Madison was their relatively high standard of living. The Immigration Commission mentioned that "the Magyars, Slovaks and Armenians usually have more furnishings than the other races." Also, the "sleeping quarters of all races, with the exception of those of the Armenians, are overcrowded and unhealthy. ... Rooms are stuffy, unclean, and unhealthy, except the Armenians."[38]

Immigrant housing in less-congested Racine, Wisconsin, and Grand Rapids, Michigan, was adequate. On the other hand, the Armenian laborers on Chicago's North Halstead and Market Streets, near the packinghouse and slaughter yard district, were described as inhabiting "half furnished, dirty, and disgraceful boardinghouses." Finally, at the bottom end of the spectrum were the housing conditions and accommodations endured by the Russian Armenian laborers in East St. Louis. Reporting on these, an Armenian newspaper in 1910 attested to the arrest by local police of some sixty Armenians on charges of overcrowding, dirtiness, and gambling.[39]

The West: Fresno, California

Armenian settlements in the West were virtually synonymous with Fresno County, California (Chapter 7). Although a few of California's 10,112 "foreign stock" Armenians in 1920 had settled outside of Fresno, notably in Russian Armenian colonies in Los Angeles and Riverside, perhaps 95 percent dwelled in the San Joaquin Valley about Fresno. Fresno's and by extension, California's growth from 4,464 "foreign stock" Armenians in 1910 to 10,112 in 1920 accounted for 19 percent of the total Armenian population in the United States in 1920 and placed it second only to Massachusetts, with a population of 13,204. The growth of California's Armenian population represented the growth of families — as opposed to the migration of individuals. According to the federal census of 1920, of the 10,112 "foreign stock" Armenians in the state, 4,036 or fully 40 percent were born in the United States. This extremely high percentage of children to the total population exceeded that of all other states, including that of Massachusetts, whose 33 percent "native born" placed it second in that category.[40] What explained the concentration of families in California was the region's salubrious climate, the fact that farming provided jobs and prosperity for the entire family, and the opinion among many Armenians that settlement in California, away from the city, strengthened family ties. Indeed, migration to California soon became synonymous with families "sinking roots." But if California by 1920 appeared to be a utopia to many Armenians, this had not always been true. Many immigrants, poverty stricken and without marketable skills, had been forced to live in congested, unsanitary conditions, amid rank housing and social discrimination.

In Fresno proper, which housed the single largest community, the early immigrants clustered together in shanties and tenements in the city's southwestern area — just south of the Southern Pacific Railroad tracks and north of Peter's Addition, a farming division named after an early Armenian settler. At the same time, handfuls of immigrants were located immediately to the north and east of the railroad tracks, chiefly in the Emerson School district.[41] In the 1880s, the city's entire southwestern area, of which these settlements formed a part, had housed native Fresnans, but the period 1890–1900 brought an influx into the area not only of Armenian immigrants but also of German Russians (from the Volga), Chinese, Japanese, and Mexicans. As a result the early denizens fled to better residences in the north and west while their single-family residences were hastily converted by profiteering builders and landlords into small, multi-family tenements, and "Mexican shanties" of tar paper and 2" × 4"s were wedged into the alleys between the converted buildings. The resulting congestion and deteriorating housing were scathingly criticized in the 1915 and 1916 reports of the California Commission on Immigration and Housing. Specifically, in one area densely populated by Armenians and Mexicans, fully 105 of the 110 buildings under inspection were in a "state of bad repair," and the prevalence of stables, the unsanitary disposal of rubbish and garbage, and congestion offered every "advantage for the breeding and spreading of disease." The commission also condemned the profusion of "old privy vaults" in a "neglected and broken condition."[42]

The southern and southwestern parts of the city were plagued in addition by overflow of effluent from the overtaxed sewers used by adjacent packinghouses and ice factories. A report in 1906 in the *Fresno Daily Republican* noted that on D, E, and G Streets, from Santa Clara Avenue "down to the ditch at the city limits. . . . the water . . . backs up and flows often into the yards. In the alleys adjoining D and F Streets from Monterey Avenue south, the alleys are covered with pools and the stench is almost unbearable." The foul smells and water six inches deep, in an Armenian section in 1907, led to an embittered mass protest meeting against the irresponsible actions of the local ice companies.[43]

In time Armenians with savings naturally sought to obtain housing in better neighborhoods, but these immigrants encountered harsh legal, social, and psychological barriers to doing so. The movement west into Germantown, for example, was resisted by the hostility of the resident German Russian immigrants toward the Armenians. According to the Immigration Commission, there was an intense prejudice of native Fresnans toward the Armenians, and this led to a depreciation in real estate values. "If property in a new quarter of the district is sold to them it impairs very seriously the value of nearby property for the personal use of the members of other races," continued the commission.[44] Restrictive land covenants against the sale of property in the city's more desirable sections to Armenians (as well as Japanese and other "undesirable races") became the law of the day and the principal instrument of discrimination against the Armenians in Fresno. This first instance in the United States of legal discrimination against the Armenians helped preserve the existence of their "Little Armenia." In addition, the high profits accruing to landlords from the tenements and shanties in the foreign colonies kept alive the foreign neighborhoods in Fresno.

Rural conditions were certainly less congested, at least in terms of outdoor living space. Little information exists on the character of rural housing, but the Immigration Commission noted that the Armenians generally invested little in upkeep of their property. "It has not mattered greatly if the house was too small and is very much crowded when the weather is such that they can not live largely out of doors. Perhaps half have separate living rooms and separate dining rooms. The others use the kitchen for dining and any room as a living room."[45] Without electricity, most immigrants used gas lamps, and cooked on wood stoves, or out of doors.

The Impact of Urban Living: Disease and Crime

Immigrants felt the impact of urban living on their daily lives. The cold statistics of the boards of health revealed high mortality rates, especially among infants, and death from tuberculosis. The

Table IV. **Mortality Rates of Armenians in
Worcester, Massachusetts, in 1910 and 1920**

Year	Number of Armenians (foreign born and native born)[a]	Deaths of Armenians (excluding stillborn)[b]	Number of deaths per 1000 population	City mortality rate (excluding stillborn) per thousand)[c]
1910	1,585	21	13.3	16.96
1920	2,012	25	12.4	13.81

Sources: (a) U. S., Department of Labor, Bureau of the Census, *Thirteenth Census*, 1910, and *Fourteenth Census*, 1920; (b) Worcester, *Vital Statistics*, 1910, 1920; (c) Worcester, *City Documents*, 1910, 1920.

high infant mortality rates were chiefly caused by the lack of adequate prenatal and postnatal care of mothers and children, and by the reliance on midwives. Deaths from tuberculosis and other lung diseases were symptomatic of the immigrants' poor housing and working conditions. Many Armenian physicians and newspaper editors devoted considerable energy to educating the newcomers in the rudiments of hygiene as health concerns became an important theme in the immigrant world.

Mortality Rates. To be sure, mortality rates of the immigrants and their native-born children did not at first glance appear to be high. Table IV is derived from mortality statistics from the community of Worcester for the sample years 1910 and 1920. According to this table, the crude mortality rate of the Armenians in this community did not exceed the municipal mortality rate in any single period examined, although the Armenian death rate never fell much below that of the municipal rate.[46]

The usefulness of such crude rates must be questioned, however, for the foreign- and native-born generations in these years did not represent a normal population distribution, owing to the abnormally large number of young people within the group. Further, the preponderance of young, strong adult bachelors was hardly a representative population and would not be expected to succumb at the same rate as a population with a full age spectrum. If these rates are adjusted to compensate for the comparative youth and strength of the immigrants, their mortality rate might well equal or exceed that of the municipality in which they lived. It seems fair to conclude that the immigrants and their children were not favored by longevity when compared with a general population.

Certainly the appalling incidence of infant mortality substantiates these disparities. Table V, also derived from the vital statistics

Table V.   Mortality Rates of Armenians Under the Age of One
in Worcester, Massachusetts, in 1905, 1910, and 1915[a]

Year	Armenian live births	Armenian deaths under one (excluding stillborn and premature)	Armenian infant mortality rate (deaths per 1,000 live births)	City infant mortality rate[b]
1905	31	5	161	116
1910	59	9	153	148
1915	50	5	100	89.1

Sources: (a) *Vital Statistics*, Worcester, Massachusetts, 1905, 1910, 1915; (b) *Worcester City Documents*, 1905, 1910, 1915.

of Worcester, clearly indicates the abnormally high rate of deaths of infants born to Armenians in the years 1905, 1910, and 1915. In each of these three instances in Worcester, the death rate of the Armenian children exceeded that of the city at large. Another study, in Fresno, reported that almost 25 percent of all Armenian deaths were of children under one.[47]

The principal reason for the distressingly high incidence of infant mortality among the immigrant families was the families' reliance on Old World practices rather than on professional medical care for the mothers during the prenatal and postnatal periods. First, most immigrant women relied on Old Country midwives instead of physicians, because they were embarrassed before male physicians. Others lacked confidence in modern medicine or thought physicians were too costly. And only a few Armenian communities in the United States had the services of an Armenian physician before 1915. In place of modern medical care, immigrants used superstitious Old World practices to allay troubles during pregnancy. One such old practice was for a woman who had experienced miscarriages to safeguard the unborn child by collecting forty pieces of silver or cloth from neighbors, then attaching them together as a bracelet or dress. Such a garment or piece of jewelry was credited with powers sufficient to carry the pregnancy to term. Once born, the infant was customarily protected from the evil eye by the parent's sewing a piece of blue cloth or a collection of small pieces of blue crystal to the infant's clothing.

The percentage of immigrant women using midwives for delivery, though indeterminable, was probably very large. State health officials in Massachusetts and elsewhere sought to outlaw the practice, but they enjoyed little success.[48] So common was the practice among the Armenians that more enlightened groups finally organized to instruct the Armenian communities on its dangers. In one such instance in Fresno in 1909, Dr. B. A. Tufenkjian addressed a meeting of married Armenians on the "unsanitary, dangerous, and even fatal practice of midwives." He urged, "Spend a few dollars to secure a doctor's service," rather than rely on these women. The group thereupon elected a committee to employ legal means to outlaw midwives as medical practitioners for the poor.[49]

Health Hazards.   Among adults, the dreaded tuberculosis and other pulmonary diseases were prevalent. It is difficult to determine the incidence of the "white plague" among the immigrants upon arrival in the United States — it was not unknown in the Old World. But, certainly, urban industrial conditions — stifling, lint filled rooms of the New England textile mills; the dust of the grinding machines in foundries; and the dampness and congestion of the tenements — helped immigrants contract it and aggravated the conditions of those already afflicted. According to one study, over 30 percent of all of Lawrence's textile mill spinners died of tuberculosis or pneumonia; moreover, these diseases and other respiratory infections carried off large proportions of the city's weavers, dyers, and combers. The heavy concentration of Armenians in the New England heavy metal, abrasive, and leather goods industries likewise increased the incidence of tuberculosis.[50]

Through the medium of the immigrant press, Armenian spokesmen continuously implored their countrymen to safeguard their health by maintaining proper hygiene and diet. Commonly, physicians warned immigrants in the sternest language to get sufficient fresh air and exercise. Thus in many newspaper columns, Dr. D. M. Yazedjian sharply criticized the immigrants' living quarters because the rooms lacked air and light to combat germs. Tailors and shoemakers he especially urged to avoid the dust from their daily work. "Wash constantly" was another injunction.[51] For it was the "closed in life, the strenuous factory routine, and sleeping in an airless room" warned another writer, which encouraged tuberculosis to spread. Instead, immigrants should take deep breathing exercises — before breakfast and after dinner.[52] Another warning was leveled at the immigrants' poor diets. Thrifty immigrants scrimped by eating in Armenian restaurants and boardinghouses, which had deservedly bad reputations for their food.[53] A report on Armenian laborers, probably in the Portland Cement factory in Riverside, California, noted: "their diet was principally bread and meat, but fruit, butter, eggs and other ordinary necessities are bought by them only occasionally."[54] Spokesmen admonished newcomers to spend "a few cents more" to afford a balanced diet, and at the same time avoid the poor food, and cigarette and cigar smoke of the Armenian restaurants and boardinghouses. Dr. M. Smpad Kaprielian of New York also cautioned immigrants against the Old Country superstition, nurtured by midwives, that fresh air carried colds. (The universally held notion that night air was dangerous to the health meant that all windows in tenements were closed from evening to morning.)[55]

One peculiar aspect of Fresno was its early attraction as a health spa for those with respiratory illnesses. Directed by doctors, many left the eastern mills and factories and migrated to Fresno to live out their last years or more bluntly to die. In 1915, in Fresno County, for example, of the 24 deaths of male Armenians, 16 were attributable to tuberculosis, influenza and pneumonia, bronchial disease, or more generally "lung troubles." In 1920, of the 37 male deaths in Fresno, 19 were attributed to these pernicious causes.[56] Because of the tubercular victims among the immigrants, community leaders in Fresno urged their colony to establish a tuberculosis sanatorium. The first such proposal was made by the Board of Trustees of the Armenian Apostolic Church in Fresno in 1902. The appeal called for a rest home on a 40-acre tract which could provide proper medical care for the afflicted. The institution was also necessary, stated a *Hairenik* writer in 1906, because Armenian families in Fresno shunned immigrants among them who had contracted tuberculosis or consumption. Plans for the sanatorium failed to materialize, however, because the community could not afford one.[57]

Welfare. Living in such extreme poverty, some Armenians might have been expected to seek public assistance. In fact, one of the most interesting facets of the social life of the Armenians in America was their avoidance of public municipal charities or "handouts," a fact testified to by their absence from the rolls of public charities, outdoor relief, and other welfare institutions. In Worcester, for example, the annual reports of the Overseers of the Poor noted only one solitary Armenian name over the entire period 1880 to 1901; this was one Margaret Aslan, age 24, who, the report of 1898 cryptically noted, remained a ward of the charity for two weeks before dying of consumption. The reports of the Associated Charities of Worcester noted a total of eight new cases involving Armenians for the years 1896 to 1900.[58]

In Fresno, the demands on public charities by Armenians were trifling in terms of the immigrant population. A report of the California Commission on Immigration entitled "Fresno's Immigration Problem" noted that of the applicants to the Fresno County Relief and Employment Commission for the years of the report (1917) about

6 percent of those identifiable by nationality were Armenian. Study of selected charity cases of Armenians in the period 1917–1929 revealed that the total of Armenian cases never amounted to more than 2 percent of the total cases, while the total Armenian population in Fresno was in excess of 15 percent.[59]

In Boston, in the depths of the 1893 depression, the *Boston Evening Transcript* reported: "It speaks volumes for the characteristic qualities of the Armenian people that with all the Armenian refugees in this country, neither of the city institutions at Deer Island or Long Island numbers an Armenian among the inmates. . . . An Armenian will work for whatever he can rather than beg or stay idle."[60] No other sentence better sums up the pride, self-reliance, and shame at public charity of the Armenians.

In view of the above, it was all the more galling and humiliating for the immigrants to be accused of appealing to the American public for charitable donations for Armenian refugees and massacre victims, but then using the funds for personal uses. According to the English language *Armenia*, in 1912, both members of the Roman Catholic hierarchy in the United States and the Protestant *Missionary Herald* accused Armenians of soliciting for bogus purposes. Cardinal Farley, for one, included Armenians in the reprehensible category of "suspect Orientals" who raised money from the public under false pretenses. Although Armenians refuted the charges, the Cardinal failed to retract them.[61]

The men responsible for such fraud, noted the *Boston Evening Transcript* in October, 1896, were often "BOGUS ARMENIANS." In this instance, it was a group of Syrians who, posing as Armenians, were "selling Armenian and Turkish goods the proceeds of which were to go to the Armenian relief fund." Armenians also charged, in the same period, that "a certain Syrian from Urmieh, Persia, [had] toured the United States and gathered a fortune of $20,000 from charitable people, under the plea that it was for missionary work in Armenia."[62] Another publication reported that an Assyrian, posing as an Armenian clergyman, and collecting funds for Armenian orphanages, had been apprehended near Boise, Idaho, by a group of Armenians. (No mention was made of the actions the Armenians took against the charlatan.) With some bitterness, *Armenia* concluded: "Scratch an alleged Armenian who, with a sad tale, either solicits charity, or peddles Oriental goods, and you will find a Syrian."[63] That such allegations against Armenians may have contained a kernel of truth, however, was conceded by *Gotchnag*; in 1914, it wrote, "among the peddlers, knaves and deceivers," there were "Syrians, Nestorians, and we blush to say, Armenians" who "fleeced the public . . . fund raising for starving Armenians."[64]

Temptations of City Life.   Not all problems of ill health were imposed by the factories or cities directly, Many immigrant spokesmen feared the less tangible but in many ways more troubling phenomena of social deterioration and the breakdown of Old World communal standards.

There was considerable apprehension among the immigrants regarding the "social health" of the community, especially that of the young male immigrants without families who were exposed to the many temptations of American cities. Much debate ensued about the incidence of gambling, especially in Armenian coffeehouses and Chinese gambling dens in Fresno, the contracting of social diseases, and the appearance of violence in the ethnic ghettoes.

Another problem the immigrants in the cities did not have was alcoholism. This fact not only spoke in the favor of the Armenians but spared them from the problems of such groups as the Irish whose indulgence in drink was the bane of their life in America. Certainly Armenians did not abstain from drinking (as did, say the eastern European Jews), for any Armenian could find beer, wine, or the omnipresent *raki* (a white-colored alcohol distilled from raisins) in most Armenian coffeehouses, restaurants, and clubs. Drinking was a common feature of Sunday picnics as well, for immigrants wanted strong drink to wash down the soot of the factory and city. And drinking remained popular well into prohibition days when immigrants manufactured *raki* (oghie) in homemade stills.

On the other hand, there were strong communal pressures and traditions which curbed the excessive use of alcohol. Drinking to excess, which was frowned upon in the Old Country, became associated in the United States with the boorish manners of the Irish, who were characterized as drunkards, profligate with money, and unfaithful to family virtues. For an Armenian, there was no more contemptible insult than to be called a "drunken Irishman," unless, of course, he was labeled a "Turk." Many Armenian Protestants were staunch prohibitionists, who frowned on drinking even at picnics and weddings. Those who abstained from drinking thereby became the butt of the standard joke: "Eh, Pohokagan es?" (Well, are you a Protestant?) Some even labored against legalizing drinking. In 1909, when Fresnans battled over the issue of licensing saloons in the municipality, *Asbarez* supported the "anti" group on the grounds that public drinking (not drinking per se) led to drunkenness and squandering money, while a group of Armenian women campaigned from a streetside stand against the Fresno licence law.[65] To be sure, some Armenians found consolation in alcohol, but by and large excessive drinking was not a social problem of the immigrant generation.

Rather than drinking, the greater threat to the immigrants' social health was the temptation of the tenderloin districts which were fixtures in the eastern cities and in Fresno. The South Cove in Boston near the "Little Orient" was a thoroughfare for criminals and prostitutes, and Robert Woods wrote that "behind a millinery, or a manicure or masseur's sign, was a shop dedicated to less wholesome trade: prostitution."[66] The United States Industrial Commission reported that red light districts operated brazenly and at full blast in many sections of New York.[67] The presence of a flourishing and menacing tenderloin in Fresno was due to the fact that the county seat was the geographical and economic center of the San Joaquin Valley and that lumberjacks and throngs of migrant agricultural laborers flocked to the city, especially on Saturday nights, in search of liquor and illicit pleasure.[68]

Immigrants in Fresno and elsewhere frequented these areas, and the red light districts and the diseases which immigrants contracted there drew the fire of normally reticent Armenians. Public spirited writers and physicians especially urged the community and the churches to inform the youth about the perils and snares of city life. One physician warned young men of the diseases by describing their stages, and another urged the clergy, the journalists, and the politicians to foster medical attention among the young, since those in trouble often cloaked their "diseases in silence."[69] Launching a broadside against all the city's vices, Arpagsat Setrakian, an outspoken reformer in Fresno, reported with consternation that immigrant males patronized the local brothels and Chinese and Japanese gaming tables; that women and young girls mixed with a "rough, ugly, dirty crowd" in the city's packinghouses; that the California climate made young people reach puberty at an earlier age than in the Old Country; and that, scandalously, the three local Armenian churches in Fresno had totally failed to caution or educate young people about the many pitfalls of the new environment. "Prayers, holy services, salvation of the soul, or sermons . . . are not enough" he sternly admonished.[70] Despite the exhortations of Setrakian and others, there is little evidence that religious leaders in the Apostolic or Protestant churches undertook special programs or took any other steps to educate the young men especially about the tenderloins. And this failure rested in good measure in their lack of preparation for the city's problems, their inherent modesty about such matters, and the general ignorance about America of older clergy educated in the Old World. The problem of the tenderloin remained a real one in the immigrant milieu.

Crime.   To the credit of the Armenian character, comparatively few were implicated in major crimes; the transgressions of the Armenians were chiefly in the petty vices of gambling or assault and battery. The Immigration Commission noted of the Fresno community: "A few Armenians have been convicted of serious crimes, such as murder and arson which have generally grown out of property considerations. It is to be noted, furthermore, that they are far more conspicuous in the civil than in the criminal courts, the disputes bringing them there being with reference to water rights and similar things. Aside from suits at law, they find little place upon the calendar of the courts if the large number of them in the community is taken into consideration." It is revealing that the Fresno County Jail Register of 1910, for example, listed no Armenians arrested for serious crimes.[71]

However, one of the most cold-blooded murders of the period before World War I was committed by an Armenian terrorist, Bedros Hampartzumian, who assassinated Hovannes Tavshanjian on the streets of New York, because Tavshanjian refused to contribute political blackmail to the terrorist's political cause. Two Armenians were implicated in the killing of a Turkish Armenian in New York City in 1904, and the mysterious death of "Harry the Turk" (Mehemed Moustapha) in 1896 in the wake of the bloody Turkish massacres of 1894–1896 led the American State Department to suspect the work of Armenian immigrants.[72] On the whole, however, these were exceptions which stemmed from Old World feuds; major crime was not a feature of the Armenian immigrant experience.

On the other hand, Armenians were frequently hauled into court for violating city ordinances against gambling and disturbing the peace. To be sure, immigrant spokesmen frequently warned that gambling was the most direct path to ruination. Thus, Arpagsat Setrakian, an editor of *Asbarez*, related the story of the young immigrant who was lonely in the new country but who took consolation in the fact that after one year he had at least saved the sum of $80. However, the young Armenian was attracted to the Chinese gambling dens in Fresno and in the space of one evening lost his entire year's savings.[73] Newspapers like *Hairenik* sharply criticized the young men without families who squandered their hard-earned savings in playing cards from "Saturday night to Sunday night," asserted that the frequent arrests of Armenians for gambling injured the ethnic group's reputation in America, and threatened to expose the guilty parties by printing their names in the Armenian newspapers.

A pack of professional Armenian gamblers made the rounds of the Armenian colonies, and *Hairenik*, terming them "parasites and leeches" warned the immigrants in Lawrence, Troy, and elsewhere to be wary of these "high priests of gambling." Despite these repeated warnings and the threats of public censure, the laborers were willing to be arrested and face public exposure for their gambling, since the card games and *tavloo* (backgammon) helped them, at least momentarily, to escape the loneliness and monotony of their factory and boardinghouse existence. Indeed, the allure of the gaming table was so great, said one observer, that the tavloo players would not leave their game even if a fire broke out in the coffeehouse.[74]

Not only the cardplayers got in trouble with the law, for violence also erupted frequently in the coffeehouses and immigrant quarters. One of the most frequent causes of violence was the animosity between Armenian immigrants and other ethnic groups, who called them "God damned Turks" and bullied and assaulted them. Worcester's tough North End, which was "so far removed from police surveillance that law-abiders are handicapped by the lawless element who use this as a safe hiding place" — was one ethnic battleground between Armenians and Irish. The earliest and most heated clashes took place in the late 1880s and early 1890s when, noted the *Worcester Daily Telegram*, "the slumbering dislike of the Irishman for the Turk [sic] was aroused." The fights arose when the Irish attacked the Armenians on their way to work, and after church (at the Protestant Armenian services), and when they stoned the immigrants' lodgings. Within a short while Irish and Armenian gangs were fighting each other in Worcester. In one episode, one Kapriel Garabedian, who had a rock thrown at him, retaliated, and was "thrown down, battered and kicked" by his Irish assailants. In another, two Irish youths suspected of membership in a gang were slashed and knifed by Armenians wielding a eight- to ten-inch doubled-edged dirk.[75]

The bad blood between the two warring groups was not purged by the local police. On the contrary, in a later incident when local Armenians sought police protection for their persons and homes, one Armenian was told by a Worcester policeman: "Go on about your business, you Armenians are getting too fresh. I've a good mind to smash your heads and then run you in." As a result, at their mass meeting in Worcester in September 1891 the Armenians voiced bitter complaints about police indifference to their plight. In order to seek protection, 400 Armenians meeting in the church on Laurel Street, formed a branch of the Armeno-American Ameliorating and Protective League to further the interests of Worcester's Armenians. A. De Kreko, agent of the league, which maintained offices in London, New York, and Boston, urged the local Armenians to become citizens as soon as possible to lend weight to their grievances in Worcester.[76]

Old World troubles also racked some communities. In East St. Louis, for example, immigrants from Caesaria battled with Kurds inhabiting the same boardinghouse; in Lowell, E. Agnooni, (Hachadoor Maloomian), a leader of the Armenian Revolutionary Federation, noted that in cities such as Lowell "some Armenians and Turks have quarrelled with one another, and both parties have sent word to their relatives to the same effect, and as a result of that instigation the two elements in the same village — Armenians and Turks — have been quarreling, devouring each other."[77]

The deep-seated antipathy of Armenians for Turks became a diplomatic issue in 1896 when a group of Muslims in Providence bitterly complained to the Turkish minister in Washington of alleged wrongdoing toward them by local Armenians. Their petition, forwarded to United States Secretary of State Richard Olney, read:

We are Ottoman subjects who have come to America for the purpose of engaging in commercial business. There are fifteen of us residing at Providence. The Armenians use insulting language to us and maltreat us. Day and night we have no rest, either in the streets or at our homes. They have slandered us. They demanded two hundred dollars from one of us, and fifty dollars from another. They induced the authorities to interfere, and these Mussulmans were imprisoned. Five or ten Armenians testified against them, and won their case. The authorities, however, do not realize our situation. Complaint was made against one of the Mussulmans on the grounds that he had inflicted blows and drawn a knife, and he was put in prison. . . . Finally, they circulated baseless slanders, and they have caused some of us to be notified by the Sheriff that they would be arrested.[78]

The streetcorner brawl in defense of their honor thus constituted one aspect of the immigrants' introduction to American urban life; far more psychically damaging to the community, however, were the battles among the Armenians themselves — in their coffeehouses and restaurants. These local brawls erupted most commonly in periods of heavy unemployment when jobless and embittered men let their hot tempers get the better of them. In Granite City, Illinois, there were frequent barroom fights in which immigrants assaulted each other with chairs, smashed heads, and "beat up a policeman." (This, the press ascribed to the "Asiatic habits" of the sudden influx of immigrants into the industrial center — "in bad times.")[79] A reporter from Milford, Massachusetts, noted that the local police had grown increasingly weary of arresting Armenians in such free-for-alls.[80] And *Hairenik*, in disgust, chronicled the series of altercations which had disturbed the Armenian quarter in Detroit's Delray section. Other unedifying frays had taken place in Watertown, Worcester, and Newburyport, Massachusetts.[81]

The Armenians, who were extremely sensitive about their reputation in the local community and who attempted to solve their problems privately instead of dragging them into public view, sought assiduously to quell such outbreaks. The writer who blamed the altercations on the immigrants' "Asiatic habits," urged his countrymen to live "as Americans." Others denounced the behavior as disgraceful and dishonorable, while, in Detroit in 1912, the local *gomide* (committee) of the powerful Armenian Revolutionary Federation resolved to intervene itself to stop the unseemly behavior.[82]

The self-monitoring of the Armenians extended beyond public brawling to other matters involving the immigrants' reputation in the larger community. One such incident involved a possible homocide. In Richmond, Virginia, in 1912 an Armenian who had married a girl considerably younger than himself suddenly died, and rumors flew that his widow and his younger brother had been lovers for some time and that she had poisoned her husband. The two alleged lovers soon married. Promptly thereafter the Armenian colony in Richmond gathered together to deliberate on the situation and then resolved first to ostracize the young pair and then to notify the local police of the suspected homocide.[83]

Exemplifying the more usual civil arbitration was the situation in the small California farming community of Yettem (in Armenian, "Eden"), founded in 1901 and populated exclusively by Armenians. There, to keep Armenians out of court, five immigrants established an arbitration commission with the right of hearing and pronouncing sentences on matters of possible litigation involving their country-men. A glowing report in 1913 indicated that the townspeople and the officials of the county court were well pleased with their work, for the commission successfully arbitrated at least five knotty ques-tions involving the sum of $5,570, and the immigrants proudly observed that not a single cent of Armenian money had gone into the pockets of American lawyers.[84] In Worcester, the Board of Trustees of *Surp Prgich* Church adjudicated a long standing financial dispute between two church members to the satisfaction of both parties, which stopped the "disputants from resorting to the local courts"; and it also brought a gift to the church from one disputant. In such ways, then, the immigrants protected "their own" from public expo-sure, solved some vexing intracommunal quarrels, and, in addition, saved lawyers' fees.[85]

Discrimination. Despite the strife of Armenians among them-selves and with other ethnic groups, it was only in Fresno that the immigrants encountered overt racial discrimination. There they were prohibited from owning land in Fresno's "better neighborhoods," they were excluded from social groups, and they suffered the igno-miny of ethnic sterotypes and slurs.

The most direct discriminatory weapon against the Armenians in Fresno was the restrictive land covenant, alluded to earlier in this chapter. Incorporated in a deed, lease, or buy and sell agreement, the covenant restricted the parties' rights to sell the property to or permit its use by "undesirables." ("Neither said premises, nor any part thereof," read the standard form, "shall be used in any manner whatsoever or occupied by any Negro, Chinese, Japanese, Hindu, Armenian, Asiatic or native of the Turkish Empire, or descendant of the above named persons, or anyone not of the white or Caucasian race.")[86] The convenant successfully circumscribed the settlement of the urban Armenians to the center of Fresno proper. And before World War I, Fresno real estate brokers not only abided by the covenants but blatantly advertised property with such restrictions. In 1913, Aram Hovsepian, a burly Armenian wrestler, was so angered by the restriction that he physically assaulted a Fresno broker for the practice, but by and large Armenians accepted the restriction and, in this sense, remained second-class citizens in Fresno until after World War II.[87] Then, in the case of *Shelley v. Kraemer* (1948) the Supreme Court rendered the covenants unconstitutional.[88] However, even with the high court ruling, informal discriminatory arrangements persisted in Fresno for some time.

In addition to discrimination in property holding, Fresno Armenians were excluded from or made wholly unwelcome at the city's many churches, clubs, fraternal organizations, and civic groups. Although "several Armenians belong to the Young Men's Christian Association," observed the Immigration Commission, "such membership is not encouraged." Routinely, the local Woodsmen, Elks, and Lions' groups refused to accept Armenians as members. Even as early as 1894, Armenians were forced to withdraw from a church they helped to build because the local Fresnans in the church objected to "the growing membership of the Armenians."[89]

The prejudice and antipathy toward Armenians in Fresno found expression in insults and schoolyard fistfights. Behind their backs, the Armenians were termed "dishonest, undependable, arrogant, greedy and tricky." Some compared them to "Jews," or "lower class Jews." Made to feel unwelcome and inferior in the school yards, Armenian children kept to themselves, avoiding the Americans. Virtually nowhere were they befriended by classmates or were their parents welcomed as newcomers to the land.[90]

A powerful combination of social and economic forces underlay the hostility toward the Armenians. First, noted the Immigration Commission, it was a case of native jealousy against an unusually successful class settling in the community in increasing numbers. Quickly becoming the city's largest ethnic group, the Armenians rapidly leased and bought choice land, and successfully ventured into the city's businesses. To native Fresnans, it appeared that these outlandish newcomers, who knew neither the language nor the customs of the country, were rapidly taking the land from the original settlers.[91]

Second, the stubborn pride and fierce independence of the Armenians seemed inappropriate to the native Fresnans who expected immigrants to assume servile attitudes. One Yankee authority contrasted the Armenians with the German Russians in this respect (using racist language the while). "The Armenian, who is generally a superior person, is unpopular because his success is for himself, in his own business. The Russian peasant, who is often an inferior person, is popular because his labor is useful to us, in our own businesses." Or a school girl's comment about young Armenians: "They are the only foreigners in Fowler [a neighboring town to Fresno] who think they are just as good as we are. I don't know why they aren't, but we think they aren't."[92] Moreover, noted the Immigration Commission, there were differences of skin color and dress and difficulties with English.[93] Finally there remained the racist frontier mentality of California itself, which since the 1870s had spawned nativist movements against the Chinese, culminating in the Exculusion Acts of 1882, the restrictive legislation against the Japanese after 1900, and the anti-alien land legislation of 1912. The legacy of racist hatred had deep roots in California soil.

Elsewhere in California racism erupted into riots against the Chinese and Greek communities; the Armenians in Fresno were spared this bloodshed. What were the possible reasons? First, anti-Armenian sentiment lacked newspaper support in Fresno. In fact, the Fresno Morning Republican, the county's most important journal, was staunchly pro-Armenian, and it helped defuse anti-immigrant sentiment in the county.[94] Second, although the prejudice against Armenians presented a volatile situation in Fresno itself, there were too few Armenians in the state of California to stir a regional or statewide anti-Armenian movement which could have sent agitators to ignite the local situation in the San Joaquin Valley. Finally, it was perhaps a matter of good fortune that the Armenians avoided a confrontation there.

Until World War I, the Armenian colony in Fresno, with the exception of instances such as the Aram Hovsepian episode noted earlier, did little to confront the anti-Armenian enmity in the community. On the contrary, writers in Asbarez and the East Coast Armenian language papers apologetically urged the immigrants to rid themselves of their Old World habits in order to convince natives of their ability to become assimilated as "good Americans." These feelings of inadequacy and even self-contempt engendered by the natives, and the desire by Armenian leaders to improve immigrant conditions, led to Americanization groups in Fresno after World War I.

In Fresno, then, the immigrants were subjected to harsh nativist feelings, manifested in discriminatory housing covenants, exclusion from social and religious organizations, and social ostracism. Like Fresno's Blacks, Asiatics, and East Indians, they were the social pariahs.

Leaving the Ghettoes

The early days of the Armenians were often harsh. Living in congested, unsanitary tenements, they economized to the point of depriving themselves of decent accommodations and diets; their poverty and exposure to unhealthy air in the tenements and mills produced weakened bodies and lungs; and their toil showed in their faces, hands, and lives. Certainly at first, America was no land of "gold in the streets." But by the eve of World War I, the worst was over for many immigrants: they were moving their families from the ghettoes into more desirable neighborhoods; they were succeeding in their work (some quite rapidly); and they were highly optimistic about the future.

In 1911 a writer in *Asbarez* underscored their successful adjustment: "Poverty and trouble is always with us, but the Armenian family here is ever progressing toward comfort."[95] The move to better housing was one unmistakable sign. In Boston, for example, the center of the initial Armenian settlement in the South Cove had shifted to tree-lined streets to the south. The names of Armenians in the *Boston Directory* of 1915, as the immigrants moved south along Huntington Avenue and Tremont Street, were most frequent in Roxbury, Dorchester, and Hyde Park; lesser numbers were by then also apparent in Jamaica Plain and West Roxbury. And according to the 1920 federal census there were Armenian communities in suburban Malden, Medford, and Somerville (a demographic trend which carried second generation Armenians into the more affluent suburbs of Greater Boston).[96] In New York, the distribution of the total "foreign white stock" of Armenians was as follows:

Borough	1910	1920
Bronx	197	644
Manhattan	2,102	2,648
Queens	86	477
Richmond	4	34
Brooklyn	227	897
Total	2,616	4,700

Between 1910 and 1920 the numbers of Armenians grew in each New York borough, but the increase was most appreciable in Brooklyn and the Bronx — traditional areas of settlement for immigrants leaving the lower East Side. There was an especially sizable community of Armenians in airy Washington Heights, around 180th Street.[97]

In Fresno it will be remembered that the major urban settlement lay in the city's southwestern section, near the Southern Pacific Railroad tracks. In 1900 its geographical center was in the old, weatherbeaten houses in the 300 block of "G" Street, south and west of the railroad, while a few householders were located to the east of the tracks. Moreover, settlement outside this area was singularly restricted — to the west and south by the German Russian colony; to the north by the central business district; and beyond that to the choice middle-class neighborhoods of northern Fresno by restrictive land covenants. Therefore, the more prosperous immigrants moved eastward, around the Emerson School. Here, the existing homes had been left by native Fresnans fleeing north into the new real estate development made possible by the Fresno Traction Railway, which linked it to the central city. By 1910, perhaps one-half of the entire Armenian population in the city had crossed the tracks into this district; a decade later, the absorption was virtually complete, with only the poorest or oldest of the Armenians left to the west of the railroad. In the meantime, still other Armenian settlements developed further eastward and south of Ventura Avenue toward the county hospital.[98]

At the same time, increasing numbers of Armenians populated the surrounding Fresno County communities of Sanger, Parlier, Selma, and Reedley, and Dinuba, in Tulare County. By 1920 over one-half of all Armenian householders in Fresno County lived outside the city limits, and indicative of their inclination to move together, four of the eleven Rural Free Delivery routes contained over 70 percent of the total rural Armenian population.[99]

Geographical mobility was one reflection of their physical adjustment by the outbreak of World War I; another, which underlay this movement, was the immigrants' optimism and sense of belonging to the New World. One Armenian proudly proclaimed that "Armenian families have begun slowly to build fine homes and furnish them in expensive good taste in the towns and farms; and they keep splendid carriages and automobiles."[100] Writers spoke of young men migrating to the foothills of the Sierra Nevadas to become rich in oil prospecting, or helping to transform the hamlet of Wautoke from a "barren uninhabited field, where only mice, rabbits and jackals freely roamed," into a "fertile paradise."[101] At the same time, Armenians in the East boasted of the achievements of their countrymen in opening shops, stores, and other independent businesses.[102] "In comparison with their . . . parents," another went on to say, "the new generation of Armenians in America are prettier to look at, taller, lighter, educated and graduated from school, and speak better English than their parents." "We are hopeful," he concluded, "that our sons will surpass us in everything, instead of being laborers, tomato growers, small farmers and small shopkeepers. They shall be prominent men in business, in banks, offices . . . in government . . . or architects . . . and professors [in service] for this country, for Armenia, for the world and all mankind."[103]

9.

The Social Matrix: Family, Societies, Clubs

Social institutions, as well as economic and physical realities, were important mediators between the immigrants and their new environment. The family, compatriotic societies, and clubs brought countrymen together in a strange land, provided fellowship and recreation, and reminded the newcomers of home; together, they sustained immigrant society against the shocks of the new culture. Inevitably, however, these institutions were reshaped by the pressures of American life.

The Family in the New World

The immigrants' most useful adaptive institution and their central unit of social organization was the family. Nonetheless, family life in the immigrant colonies developed slowly because Armenians did not emigrate as family units. For example, according to the Immigration Commission's study in 1909 of 637 Armenian male immigrants 20 years of age or older (in manufacturing and mining industries), fully 58 percent reported "married" (an additional 2 percent reported "widowed"). Yet, when asked whether their wives were in the United States or abroad, 51 percent of the married men replied "abroad." Moreover, a further breakdown of the study demonstrated the preponderance of family men in age groups where large proportions were likely to have had several children before emigrating. Thus, in the 30–44 age category, more than 75 percent reported "married or widowed," while among those 45 years of age and over, 90 percent so reported.[1] Clearly, one out of every two Armenian immigrants lived in America for a time without his family.

Many of the married men expected to save $200 or $300 and then return to the Old Country villages to enjoy their families and property. But because of harsh Old World conditions (especially after the mid-1890s massacres) and their gradual adjustment to the new land, "days passed into weeks, weeks into months, and months into years"; and relatively few of these sojourners returned to their native soil.[2] In fact, even after the 1908 Turkish constitution opened frontiers to travel by immigrants to Turkey, out of a population of about 50,000 only 600 Armenians returned annually prior to World War I.[3] Accordingly, they began to send for their long-separated wives and children.

In the meantime, the wives of immigrants lived with their husbands' families in the Old Country, and a rigid family and village code, developed over centuries of exposure to migration, governed their lives. Thus, the English traveler Lynch noted in 1894: "Although husbands leave their brides when they migrate to Constantinople, infidelity is uncommon."[4] Within these households, harsh Old Country conditions took their toll. The presence of a husband in America meant a flow of cash to his wife, but this was often put to the family's use. Absences of ten to twenty years were not unknown, and many a man, upon his return was greeted by a son whom he had left during the early period of pregnancy, now grown to manhood.[5] Most probably the absence of the husband induced a variety of tensions, not the least of which were the fears of illness, desertion, or worse.

In time families were reunited. However, many families seeking to travel to America were frustrated by insidious delays and petty oppressions perpetrated by the Turkish government. This was especially true in the years 1900–1903. As noted in Chapter 4, until 1908 Turkey did not recognize its subjects' right to emigrate. In 1900, however, the sultan's regime, under pressure from the American government, exempted the wives and children of naturalized American citizens from that restriction. But despite this concession, and after long and tedious negotiations by the American State Department on the matter, permission to emigrate was granted on paper only.

Indeed, three full years passed without a single American family gaining such permission to leave, with the result that in 1902 the "number of women awaiting the opportunity [was] exceedingly great, mounting probably in the hundreds," with equal numbers of children. Finally in 1903 the American minister unilaterally ordered the suffering families to be taken under the protection of consular cavasses (guards) to the sea and placed on steamers for America.[6] Soon after this show of force, the Turks officially sanctioned the departure of the first group of families to the United States.

Individual instances of harassment continued, however. One naturalized American citizen sought State Department assistance in freeing his wife from Turkey because her request for permission to leave had not been acted on for a year. The State Department, after lengthy correspondence with local authorities, informed him that "emigration is rarely obtained in less than six months, and is often delayed for a year or more," but that — no small comfort — "there appears to be no reason to believe that your wife's emigration will not be accomplished *eventually.*"[7] Desperation forced another's hand. Caught in the complexities of the Turks' policy, this Armenian American left the New World and traveled 5,000 miles to Batum in hopes of extricating his wife from Turkey. He remained in Batum for six months, but even after this long stay he was unable merely to obtain permission to see his wife, let alone take her to America. Then he was advised to return to America *alone* in order to secure her release.

This turn of things strikes me too much, because . . . I came to Caucasus by the only purpose of getting my wife from Turkey and to return back together. By doing so I caused myself so much trouble and waste of money, but for not leaving my poor wife to journey, all alone, over the oceans; a woman who never has been away from her native country, and does not know a single foreign word.[8]

This unconscionable state prevailed for these families until the Turkish constitution of 1908, which liberalized regulations governing permission to emigrate to America. It went without saying that the much larger number of wives and children of *unnaturalized* Armenian immigrants in America had even greater difficulty in joining their menfolk in the New World.

New World Marriages

Old World custom held that all able-bodied men and women should marry; an unmarried Armenian was a misfortune. Marriages were arranged between families, and social and financial considerations were important. Females married from the age of fourteen on whereas males married beginning in their twenties. But in the New World important changes took place in marriage patterns and attitudes.

In the first place, for the considerable immigrant bachelor population (40 percent of all males over twenty years of age), there was little likelihood of contracting a "suitable" marriage in the United States, chiefly because of the large proportion of males to females. The chart below, compiled from a contemporary study of ethnic intermarriages in New York City, illustrates the imbalance between male and female Armenians of marriageable age at the time of arrival in the United States in the period 1910–1917 and the ratio of marriageable men to women.[9]

	Total Number	Number per 100 of opposite sex
Armenian men	15,595	668
Armenian women	2,334	15

Obviously, the demand for eligible Armenian females in the United States far outstripped the supply.

New Marriage Arrangements. What were the consequences? If one believes the immigrant press, marriage became a big business in which parents auctioned their few eligible daughters to the highest bidders. In 1900 *Hairenik* reported that one Armenian father who was fortunate enough to have two unmarried daughters bartered each for $200 to prospective bridegrooms.[10] Another immigrant parent sold his fourteen-year-old daughter for $100 (the "highest bidder") to a forty-year-old male, in a marriage sanctioned by an Armenian priest. And Fresno writers mimicked the practices in the San Joaquin Valley:

> My wife and I have decided
> We shall marry our daughter to someone
> Who owns chickens, goats, cows and sheep.
> His own tail makes no difference to us.[11]

Thus, the reduction of arranged marriages to a system of "bidding" for brides was one byproduct of the migration.

In addition to bidding, bachelors selected brides by traveling to Turkey (one immigrant sent his brother to the Old Country to investigate whether "this Anna" would make him a desirable wife).[12] However, this method proved extremely difficult before 1908 when many returning Armenian Americans, regarded by watchful Turkish authorities as suspected Armenian revolutionaries, were barred from entering the empire. The problem quickly subsided after the Young Turk Constitution of 1908, although within two years returning young Armenian males were in constant jeopardy of being impressed into military service in the Ottoman armies.[13] More commonly, immigrant suitors exchanged photographs with "picture brides" in the Old Country, using hometown friends or relatives as intermediaries.

However, these arranged overseas marriages were sharply criticized. Fifty-year-old men often sent photographs of themselves at age twenty-five, deluding the innocent young Armenian girls in Turkey. On the other hand, the marriageable Armenian women sometimes outsmarted the returning immigrant suitors. One of Hamasdegh's (Hampartzoom Gelenian) finest stories, *Vartan*, is about a lonely middle-aged Armenian immigrant who traveled to Constantinople in search of a wife. An aging milkman, Vartan was inveigled into financing the passage of his young bride-to-be to America, only to find upon her arrival in America that she rejoined and fled with her husband, who had emigrated earlier.[14] Speaking out against the disparity in ages, other writers were bitterly critical of the fictional forty-year-old Boston cobbler Bedros Aga who traveled to Marseilles, refused to marry one of many suitable Armenian widows in favor of the eighteen-year-old Sirpouhi. However, once in the United States, the young girl became involved with a handsome young Armenian businessman, and her marriage ended tragically.[15] Echoing this criticism, Shahan Natalie, on the occasion of United States Treasury Secretary William Gibbs McAdoo's marriage to Woodrow Wilson's twenty-five-year-old daughter, generalized that immigrant Armenian practices were as immoral as the Americans' in that Armenian parents asked the male suitor for cash for their daughter's passage, a gift for themselves, and "furnishings for the store"; an inevitable question put to the suitor was "bank book oonis?" (Do you have a bank book?)[16]

Marriages were arranged in the New World as well. In Fresno, Arpagsat Setrakian excoriated the Armenian mothers in Fresno's packinghouses for setting the arrangements with "the children having no choice." This "ancient and barbarous system," he said, in America was based primarily on need, with "agents" peddling the unmarried girls to the highest bidder and paying no heed to the bridegroom's suitability or lack thereof; "being old, ignorant, or unlearned" was irrelevant to the matchmakers.[17] The situation on the East Coast was no different. Upon a report from Providence that one immigrant father compelled his seventeen-year-old-daughter, at knifepoint, to marry a thirty-five-year-old man, instead of the younger man she loved, Shahan Natalie solemnly warned Armenian parents that such forced marriages would lead to secret trysts, separations, and divorces.[18]

What are the merits of these complaints? In the first place, although there may have been chicanery, compulsion, and sordid dealings in making arranged marriages, it appears that the vast majority of such unions lasted and provided some fulfillment. Certainly, the lack of divorce in the immigrant generation and the preservation of Armenian family life in America gave stability and comfort to the newcomers. Second, the writers' criticisms of the institution of arranged marriages with its Old World assumption that "love comes after marriage" meant that Armenian family life was already being influenced by a younger generation's New World ethos: the ethos of romantic love.

Intermarriage.   If contracting a suitable marriage was a problem for the immigrant generation, intermarriage (marriage with a non-Armenian) was not. Overwhelmingly, Armenians married within and not outside their ethnic group. The most thorough statistical sample of the incidence of intermarriage among first generation Armenian Americans is of 164 marriages contracted in Manhattan and the Bronx in the years 1908–1912 (Table VI). Of these only 16 Armenians, or 9.6 percent of the total, married non-Armenians, while

90.4 percent married within the group. Interestingly, no first generation Armenian females intermarried. By comparison with other ethnic groups in the study, the Armenians fell into the category of 5 to 9.99 intermarriages per 100 marriages (Class II), below which were only Jewish immigrants, blacks, and Syrians. Of these, the religious differences of the Jews and the color barrier rendered these groups exceptional cases and accounted for their extremely low intermarriage level. As Table VI indicates, the Armenians intermarried more than Italians and Hungarians (in Class II) did, but all the others — Finns, Russians, Irish, Greeks, French, Scandinavians, western Europeans, and Canadians — exceeded the level of intermarriage of the Armenians.[19]

Confirming this, a more restricted survey of 27 marriages among Armenians in Woonsocket, Rhode Island, conducted in 1926, revealed no marriages of Armenians to non-Armenians, and another sociologist recorded only one example of a first generation Armenian intermarrying among 200 to 300 first- and second-generation Armenians in Greater Boston. In Fresno the Immigration Commission found similar results: "In Fresno, certainly in nineteen cases in twenty, marriage has been of Armenian to Armenian."[20]

The low incidence of intermarriage stemmed from a variety of causes. Armenians intensely felt that marriages with *odars* (non-Armenians) would be unhappy, would occur with undesirables, and would lead to divorce. That is, as foreigners without knowledge of the language and customs of the new land, the young people could not discriminate between suitable and unsuitable mates and would be duped into unsuccessful marriages. Rather, it was better for newcomers to marry from among their own. Also, the community sternly believed that marriage with non-Armenians would dilute the ethnic purity of the Armenians and would lead to the extinction of the culture, or as one immigrant put it, within two decades the language would not be spoken by "anyone under fifty," and the "songs, literature, martyrdom, history, — two thousand, three thousand years" of the historic culture would vanish from the face of the globe.[21]

At the same time, external forces such as prejudice also discouraged intermarriage. In Fresno especially, residential and social segregation and social animus against the Armenians created barriers to intermarriage. Although a few Armenians in Fresno were married to non-Armenians, noted the Immigration Commission, these marriages had been "contracted in Eastern States," where "there is less feeling against the Armenian race."[22]

Thus the Armenian colony strongly favored marriage, but by this it meant endogemous marriage. And the stern strictures by Armenians on this topic, rooted in Old World views of family and fears of

**Table VI. Intermarriages by Nationality in New York City 1908–1912
(Men and Women of the 1st, 2nd, and 3rd generations)**

Class I
(0 to 4.99 intermarriages per 100 marriages)

Nationality	Intermarriages per 100 marriages
Romania (Jewish)	.45
British West Indies (Black)	.48
Russia (Jewish)	.62
United States (Black)	1.08
Hungary (Jewish)	2.24
United States (Jewish)	4.26
Syria	4.63

Class II
(5 to 9.99 intermarriages per 100 marriages)

Nationality	Intermarriages per 100 marriages
Germany (Jewish)	5.16
Italy (South)	5.83
Hungary	8.59
Armenia	9.63

Class III
(10 to 24.99 intermarriages per 100 marriages)

Nationality	Intermarriages per 100 marriages
Turkey	13.15
Italy (north)	16.73
Finland	16.82
Ireland	21.59
Greece	22.14

Class IV
(25 to 49.99 intermarriages per 100 marriages)

Nationality	Intermarriages per 100 marriages
Sweden	31.04
Spain	33.11
Germany (combined groups)	33.34
Norway	39.14
British West Indies (English)	39.86
Denmark	47.42
France	49.55

Table VI. (cont.)

Class V
(50 to 100 intermarriages per 100 marriages)

Nationality	Intermarriages per 100 marriages
Germany (North)	53.05
Germany (South)	55.98
Wales	59.44
Belgium	59.63
Scotland	59.79
Holland	62.58
England	62.70
Japan	72.41
Cuba (Spanish)	73.73
Canada (French)	75.60
Canada (English)	79.85
Portugal	88.23

Source: Based on Julius Drachsler, "Intermarriage in New York City; A Statistical Study of the Amalgamation of European Peoples," *Studies in History, Economics and Public Law,* 94, no. 2 (1921), 43–45.

disintegration of the community through intermarriage, were obeyed — at least for the time being.

Family Structure

When the family was established or resettled in the United States, the role of each member was structured by the Old Country models from which it was derived. At the head of the New World families were the immigrant fathers. Replacing the Old Country patriarch grandfathers who were left behind in the migration (Chapter 4), the fathers exercised strong, though not absolute, authority.

The . . . Armenian family . . . was a unified family, but a unity based not so much on common attitudes or interests as on a tight checkrein held by father which prevented the children from "riding off in all directions." This is not to say that father was unfeeling or cold. . . . He loved his children and was loved in return. . . . He was not an immovable tyrant . . . but he was authoritative with a power sanctioned by time-honored, Old Country tradition.[23]

Because of his position, his younger brothers deferred to him, young people stood when he entered the room, and he meted out punishment to errant children usually by an irritated glance.

Fathers received family respect and harbored considerable self-esteem. Scornfully accusing non-Armenians of placing their own interests above their children's, they prided themselves on their abilities — real or imagined — to nurture their families. "They were convinced of their moral superiority — their Armenianness; their ability to work hard, make sacrifices and survive. Didn't my father, who had his own business, work six days a week, twelve hours a day? Wasn't he willing to ride the subway for an hour every morning and every night so that we could live in a pleasant neighborhood."[24] And although not all fathers measured up to this ideal, the pattern rang true for much of the immigrant generation.

If the father was the outer face of the home, the mother was the inner. However, in America the relationship was not always so equal, for many immigrant wives suffered the disadvantages of having arrived in the United States later than their husbands and lacked their husbands' daily opportunity of contact with non-Armenians to learn the language and customs. On the other hand, many Armenian women were strong individuals who exercised considerable force in the new land. Many had emigrated to America without their husbands under extremely difficult circumstances and often with young children in tow. In America they had the responsibility of single-handedly feeding, clothing, and caring for households which included not only the immediate family but also relatives (usually on the husband's side), as well as neighbors and orphans of kin massacred in 1894–1896, 1909, and World War I. Thus, one Armenian home in New York became a way station for those Armenian émigrés who happened to come from the vicinity of Smyrna, the place of her mother's birth, or "from Antioch, which my father had fled. The house was large enough . . . and they flocked in — Ashodians, Bubukians, Casparians — singly or in families, of assorted ages and professions."[25] In addition, large numbers of immigrant households contained boarders. According to the Immigration Commission's survey of 120 sample Armenian households, roughly 21 percent housed a fee-paying boarder. (The number of households containing only boarders, though not surveyed, would have inflated this percentage.)[26]

Immigrant mothers, especially, faced the additional social problem of the boarders. Immigrant spokesmen, through the Armenian language press, warned immigrant families about the perils of such outsiders. In one case a 40-year-old "friend and family man" from the Old Country lured a young daughter into deserting her family. Another writer cautioned of the corruptions emanating even from kinsmen under the same roof.[27] Certainly there were many such incidents which were quietly endured away from public gaze. Boarders were an economic necessity for the poorer newcomers, but they were a special burden for the already crowded households.

Because of these large numbers, the immigrant mother's single most time-consuming household task was food preparation. To be sure, the daily preparation of Armenian meals — *boulghur, yalanchi dolma* (stuffed grape leaves), yogurt — was seen not only as a duty but also as an honor for the mother. Canning fruits and vegetables in season for winter use, pickling *turshu* (celery, tomatoes, and cucumbers) and preserving meats by drying and spices for *mezza* (appetizers), and finally handrolling the endless layers of sheet dough for the holiday specialties *paklava* and *bourma* attested to her talents as well as her frugality. The regular demonstrations of such *marifets* (accomplishments) were one of the few forms permitted by traditional custom for a woman to receive praise openly, especially from her husband. Still, the responsibility of feeding the household was a heavy one.

As homemakers, the immigrant mothers also struggled to collect essential furnishings for the tenement or farmhouse. Mention has been made of the skimpy furniture in the Fresno homes. But, most interiors were ornate, with artifacts and bricabrac of a strong nationalistic flavor. "Our living room was cluttered and noisy and bright, with blue plush chairs . . . and three paintings of Mount Ararat."[28] A hand-crocheted rendering or stylized painting of Mother Armenia weeping over the ruins of the country usually adorned the walls covered with faded wallpaper.

At the same time, women's roles outside the home expanded. Although the culture did not approve of women working outside the home — it was preferable if women brought work back to the dwelling, as in Troy, New York, where they stitched collars and shirts in the tenement sweatshops — poverty and improvident breadwinners forced women to take jobs in factories, stores, and packinghouses. Moreover, women assumed vital community duties unknown in the old culture, primarily in the church, Sunday schools, charities, and education for children. "Whereas the women had no formal function in the Old World village community," noted one sociologist, "the husband father representing the family in all village matters — in America the women were carrying out definite and important community roles." In one colony, "they have an association of their own, the Armenian Welfare Corps, which is the sole charity-dispensing structure of the community; and the committee having complete authority over the Armenian school is composed entirely of women."[29] Women's communal responsibilities thus grew significantly in the New World.

In contrast to the women's enhanced roles, the status of the elderly eroded in America. Many households included an elderly uncle, widowed aunt, or grandparent. In the Old World they were paid the highest respect for their superior knowledge, long experience, and able leadership in the familiar Old Country environment. However, this position inevitably deteriorated in the new surroundings, owing to their inability now to learn the new language or establish contacts outside the family. Not that the older family members were without roles. Indeed, their main function was to resist the forces of assimilation. Grandparents kept the old language alive, especially for the American-born generation which, thereby, was forced daily to speak the native language despite outside pressures to adopt English only. Then, too, the oldest women clung tenaciously to the Old Country dietary customs and continued the use of Old World foods. Still, the grandparents, though accorded the ingrained respect paid to the elderly, were often shunted off into lesser roles — a fact which engendered frequent mutterings, laments, and nostalgic accounts of the glories of the Old Country and their exalted positions therein. Unfortunately or not, "grandparents were no longer the autocrats they had been."[30]

Similarly, the position of the Old Country *ginkahayr* (godfather, literally baptism father) lost its importance. Old World village custom held that the "best man" or another member of his family acted as godfather for the children of the couple at whose wedding he assisted. A godfather was considered a very close kinsman, so much so that the Armenian Apostolic Church prohibited the marriage of godfather to goddaughter. As godfather a man became a pillar of the family, serving at the child's baptism, betrothal, and wedding. Responsible for this godchild's religious and moral training, he was also entrusted with the child's financial well being in the event of catastrophe to its father. Accorded utmost respect, "given a seat of honor when he visited" his godchild's home, he, alone was "permitted to criticize, censure, and punish the child without interference from the family."[31] In the New World, however, because families often lost touch with each other, neither this intimate relationship nor its accompanying veneration was re-established; the role dwindled to that of ceremonial attendant at the child's baptism.

In many of these social respects, differences of religion were critical. That is, the Protestant community, which composed about one fifth of the immigrants, more rapidly embraced American ways. For example, the Protestant Armenian journals, especially *Gotchnag*, forcefully advocated rapid adoption of New World ways, especially in family relationships and childrearing. Thus, criticizing the Old World adage, "the talking [of children] at the table is a sin," an editor of *Gotchnag* urged immigrant women to assemble the entire family around the table twice daily for "mutual pleasure and companionship," and to encourage the children to express their ideas, explain their problems, and describe their experiences to their parents.[32] Similarly, parents were urged to treat Armenian girls and boys equally.[33]

And on the notably provocative issue of intermarriage, "Protestants, more than Apostolics, feel the religious barrier removed since they consider themselves of the same religion as American Protestants, whereas Apostolics feel themselves a group apart, religiously speaking." The available data on intermarriage confirm this view. According to one California study, intermarriage among Protestant Armenians was fully 50 percent higher than among Apostolic Armenians.[34] Finally, the use of the Armenian language in the home was given higher priority by the Apostolic family (strongly supported by the Apostolic Church) than by the Protestant family.[35]

The Second Generation

Immigrant homes were adult-oriented, not child-oriented. Children were strictly supervised in their many home duties and outside activities, often to their discomfort. Fidelity to Armenian traditions by attendance at Armenian language schools and Armenian church services, as well as speaking Armenian in the home and honoring their parents and grandparents, were firm requirements. In time the second generation was admonished to marry fellow Armenians and rear their children in Old World ways.

The painful, time-honored dilemma of second generation children was that the outside world often demanded quite opposite things of them. Children of the pre–World War I years grew up amidst a virulent nationalist atmosphere characterized by 100 percent Americanism, which held in contempt most foreign habits and foreign-born peoples. Public schools and their teachers taught impressionable youngsters that the preservation of Armenian names and Old World customs and ideas was both totally wrong and un-American. Immigrants' children learned perfect English while their parents spoke with an accent. The children winced under the exquisite torture of the school teacher's reference to those "immigrant children." Armenian children were taught, in effect, to be ashamed of their Old World culture, their olive skins, and their "funny foods.'" "The children, the poor children! We were torn in half by the conflicting demands of our Armenian homes and our American environment."[36]

Children first learned of the difference between their Armenian home and the American environment on the streets or in the first grade. There they were called "foreigners," "immigrants," or "Turks." This shocked children whose parents had inculcated in them pride in their ancestry, their language, and their culture. The children instinctively fought back against the insults, but few escaped the self-doubts implanted by the American milieu.

Parents added to the children's confusion by their persistence in clinging to the old. One conspicuous sign of immigrant status was speaking the foreign language in the home. In doing so, parents embarrassed the more sensitive or insecure children when they entertained their American friends at home. In fact, some children were so ashamed of the language that they sought to ignore or cover up their mother's call upon arriving home with friends. Parents also relied on Old World methods of bargaining in stores to the chagrin of the children often present as interpreters. The Old Country method of transacting business was to "haggle" and bargain, a custom which immigrants accepted and enjoyed. To non-Armenians, however, this seemed to be "cheating" and a desire to rob the shopkeeper of his last cent. The Armenians "always want eggs, butter, sugar, etc., at lower prices than others pay and haggle over little things like a cent or two more than they think a thing is worth."[37] The Armenian parent who succeeded in gaining a discount in price often promised to bring back his other children for the same shoes or clothes at the same price. The English-speaking son or daughter employed as interme-diary was mortified by the experience, especially by the exasperation of the American shopkeeper. "We learn to believe that a certain practice is the 'only way' from our outside contacts," commented one second generation Armenian; "our parents must be wrong since they are foreigners and old-fashioned. . . . [they] have much to learn. . . ."[38]

Classrooms were also scenes of tribulation. In Fresno, American teachers, despite laudable intentions, were often unable to suppress a cordial dislike for the more aggressive Armenian children; the pejorative phrase "you foreign children" was commonly used. One Fresno teacher went on the charge that "in school, the boys, with but three or four exceptions, have been liars and sneaks."[39] Immigrant children were reproved for eating onions and garlic, and speaking Armenian with peers in the schoolyard. Boys suffered the scorn of classmates for their family allegiance and obedience to the "old lady." "Some afternoon after school is out my classmates decide to go on some boyhood adventure. I refuse to join them because my mother has told me to always come directly home from school. The American children, however, scoff at the idea that I take my mother's orders seriously. . . . They even brag . . . about the lickings they have gotten for disobedience. They may even jibe me of being afraid to disobey."[40] Although some teachers were sympathetic to their Armenian charges, most were grossly ignorant of any immigrant people's history or culture.

The children's routine at home was far from recreational. Sacrificing the opportunities and pleasures of other youngsters on the sandlots and football fields and in extra-curricular clubs and debating societies, Armenian children returned home immediately after school to attend Armenian language school or to help with family chores. In Fresno, boys cared for the livestock, repaired sheds and sweatboxes, and assisted in the summer harvests; even girls remember pruning grapevines. And their help was unpaid, as parents followed the Old World precept that it was *amot* (a sin) to be remunerated for family work. The weekly allowance of a later period was a sure sign of Americanization.

Armenian girls were more sheltered than the boys, because parents feared for their "purity" and because they had a lower regard for their education. As a result second-generation Armenian American girls tended to be submissive and compliant toward their parents' wishes; most of their time outside school was spent at home in countless household chores or caring for younger siblings. Young second-generation males criticized the lack of social graces among the second-generation girls — "they do not learn what to do, how to act, what to say, in social contacts" — yet they often felt that the girls' training in housekeeping, child care, and household economy were important compensating factors; in short, that they made good wives and mothers.[41]

Controls on both sexes extended to activities outside the home. Dancing in the American manner was strictly forbidden. To be sure, children were encouraged to take part in traditional Armenian group dances at picnics, socials, and at home, but the "cheek to cheek" and "breast to breast" American variety was considered immoral and vulgar.[42] Teenagers were not allowed to go out at night except when parents accompanied them to evening events such as choir recitals and dramatic presentations, and boys were strictly warned to avoid poolhalls, drugstore corners, or the "bums that hang around." Armenian parents had few fears stronger than that their sons would become "good for nothings."[43]

A respect for "hard times" and family sacrifice was also inculcated at home. Children were rarely shielded from news of misfortunes — layoffs, business failures, or poor crops. The lack of privacy in cramped quarters and a less genteel attitude toward childbearing brought them into intimate contact with sickness, childbirth, pain, and personal conflict — despite the Armenian family's ingrained modesty. Accounts of cruelties at the hands of the Turks were common, and these stirred a life-long hatred of the historic oppressors. That life was a serious business full of "hard times" was a common lesson.

The second-generation Armenian who, from his earliest days recognized the enormous sacrifices made in his behalf, likewise was cognizant of the burdens thus placed on him and his generation. It is to the second generation's credit that they did not strenuously object to the hubbub and sacrifices of their home life. If they occasionally resented their fathers' broken accent, Old World mannerisms, and foreign way of dress, and furtively longed for the respectability of "Americans," they also deeply admired their parents' sacrifices in their behalf. Here is how William Saroyan wrote of his father's odyssey in America:

He was desperately poor; poverty trailed him like a hound, as the expression is. Most of his poems and stories were written on wrapping paper which he folded into small books. Only his journal is in English (which he spoke and wrote perfectly), and it is full of lamentations. In New York, according to this journal, my father had only two moods: *sad* and *very sad*. About thirty years ago he was alone in that city, and he was trying to earn enough money to pay for the passage of his wife and three children to the new world. He was a janitor. Why should I withhold this fact? There is nothing shameful about a great man's being a janitor in America. In the Old Country he was a man of honor, a professor, and he was called Agha, which means approximately lord. Unfortunately he was also a revolutionist, as all good Armenians are. He wanted the handful of people of his race to be free . . . and so he was placed in jail every now and then. Finally, it got so bad that if he did not leave the old country, he would kill and be killed. He knew English, he had read Shakespeare and Swift in English, and so he came to this country. And they made a janitor of him. After a number of years of hard work his family joined him in New York.[44]

Conversely, although they did not immerse themselves in their children's activities or join local PTAs or Girl Scout troops, the parents sincerely appreciated and loved their children's world:

They were dazzled by the success of my sorties into this strange America. "Ays darorinag Amerikan" ("This strange America"), they would say, looking heavenward for comfort. They would listen as I bragged about the size of trees I climbed, the daring games I had invented, the ready challenge I had shown in responding to the challenge of a larger, bossier child. Sometimes, assuming a more worldly manner, I would bestow upon them bits of information — about Shirley Temple ("They say she has a solid-gold doll house") ice-cream flavors, varieties of penny candy, comic-strip characters, Eddie Cantor; I would sing snatches of songs ("The music goes round and round. . . ."); and they would laugh and nudge each other and jump up to squeeze me. "Those foreign children have to keep awake to keep up with her," my father would say. . . . "Let them all see what an Armenian is."[45]

The most important crises in families occurred over the subject of intermarriage. According to the Immigration Commission many second-generation Armenians not surprisingly preferred "American institutions and ways" to the prearranged marriage system of the Old World.[46] They also objected to their parents' strictures against "dating" per se. "Our high school dating," recalled one Armenian American, "aroused anxiety and desperation in our parents. 'I want you should grow up marry nice Armenian gel,' my father admonished."[47] On the other hand, the second generation, which drew its ideas about marriage from American education, Hollywood, and magazines, "for the most part . . . gave wholehearted allegiance to the American ideal of romantic love."[48]

Because few second-generation Armenians had reached marriageable age before World War I, the issue of intermarriage was not widely faced. However, the handfuls who did confront it learned what anxious consternation the issue aroused in troubled parents. A most bitter expression come into common use in the period: "*Americaii mech, zavagner her che gai*" (in America, children are of no worth).[49] To Armenian parents, intermarriage was tantamount to broken homes, brought on by American women interested only in clothes and high society.

Parental censure convinced many young people to reach a compromise between Old and New World values. Fresno second-generation Armenians who believed in romantic love also "were realistic enough to think that it would be much more convenient if they did fall in love with someone from their own group." Few of them appeared to resent the stratagems their parents employed to bring about marriages with other Armenians and many, secure within family loyalties, made their first homes as couples within the physical boundaries of their parents' neighborhoods.[50]

Some, however, bitterly resented their parents' chronic, blatant, nagging injunction to "marry a nice Armenian" as an abridgment of their freedom and an insult to their intelligence, and the insistence on marriage only with an Armenian often kept young people from marrying at all. Very possibly offspring who left the Armenian colonies for the anonymity of the larger city did so to avoid the constant embittered clashes over their choice of husband or wife.

The Armenian family maintained itself as a tightly knit unit which sought to preserve the more enduring values of filial piety, sacrifice, and love. It was a highly moral entity. "The Armenians are unusually temperate, have a pure family life, and their women are chaste. . . . Their moral standard is higher than that of the communities they live in," concluded the Immigration Commission.[51] Children learned from their parents about sacrifice, responsibility, and hard, unending labor. Uncomfortable, not always joyful, the experience of growing up in an Armenian home inculcated strict values of character and family. Practically no children experienced a home broken by divorce, though divorce was permissible in the Apostolic Church, and juvenile delinquency was a rare phenomenon in the Armenian community.

Immigrant Social Life

The Armenian family in the United States was the fundamental social unit of the community and as such was the arena for the deepest emotions, ambitions, and drives of the newcomers and their children. But the newcomers did have broader affiliations. Social activities such as visits and picnics and the social institutions of the immigrant theater and charities were important areas in which newcomers received strength and enjoyment from their fellows in meeting the challenges of the New World. The Armenian restaurants and coffeehouses, although sharply criticized in the period, also were critical refuges, especially for the bachelors and other immigrants without their families in the New World. In all these activities and institutions Armenians found support for enduring this "strange new America."

Sunday Calls and Outings.   The most common Armenian social activity was visiting among families and friends. Every Sunday and holiday, immigrants with their children and other household members in tow arrived unannounced and uninvited at a relative's home, in accordance with time-honored Old World tradition. (One of the most vivid memories of any second-generation Armenian is of the hordes of fellow Armenians descending weekly on his home to spend the day.) The central event of the visit was the Sunday meal, which the women had prepared in advance "just in case" relatives arrived. A recitation of the Lord's Prayer in Armenian by the eldest family member began the ceremony, and this was followed by toasts with small glasses of homemade wine.

Each week for many years, a group of my father's friends took Sunday dinner with us. . . . One of them — perhaps the journalist who wore pince-nez, with his stiff white collar and striped shirt — would say, "Comrades, let us drink to our beloved comrade and his bride who offer the warmth of Armenian hospitality to us in this foreign land." My mother, who had married at sixteen, and was regarded for years as a child bride, would murmur welcomes. My father would frown and shake his head, as if he were trying to shake off the kind words. The men would raise shot glasses of *oghie* to their lips. . . . "To the Armenian spirit." "Let the massacrists beware." "Eh, toward Armenia. Let us see Ararat and Sevan Lake soon."[52]

After the meal, the men smoked their *narguilas* or *hookahs* (Middle Eastern water pipes) and sang sad Armenian songs, while children performed on musical instruments or recited poetry in Armenian and English. In all, the ritual let men enjoy each other's company after the week's hard work, and it gave women relief from their daily routine in the immediate family and neighborhood; the visits also fulfilled the moral obligation to care for one's family and to be hospitable ("as ye sow so shall ye reap").

In addition to Sunday visits, picnics were extremely popular; five hundred or more Armenians would gather in a rented grove or field on a Sunday afternoon. Sponsored by religious, political, or social organizations, these outings permitted immigrants to escape from their sooty mill towns and crowded tenements for a variety of locations — West Hoboken's Sheffers Field or Hudson County Park; Waverly Grove in Waltham, Massachusetts, or Franklin Park in Boston.

The picnics were festive occasions. First, there were huge quantities of Armenian food — shish kebab, pilaf, Syrian or Armenian bread, *yalanchi dolma* and salad. Beer and *raki* (oghie) were also plentiful, even during Prohibition. Inevitably, too, an immigrant orchestra played Armenian, Turkish, and "oriental" music on the oud, doumbeg, and clarinet, to which picnickers performed traditional Armenian and Turkish group dances.

Picnics also featured competition among marching societies. Composed of brightly uniformed boys and girls, and often accompanied by a tuba, cornet, or drums, these groups — patriotically named after such national symbols or dynasties as the Araratian or Rupiniantz Marching Societies — paraded for prizes awarded for their precision, dress, and physical fitness.[53] (One writer, commenting on one society's "mock warfare" at a 1899 picnic, expressed the hope that the group would one day demonstrate their skills against the Turks in the Old Country.)[54] Games and races were organized to keep the younger children from getting underfoot; the adult males set up tables and chairs for card games, usually pinochle or tavloo.

Picnics were often forums for political parties, whose following they naturally drew. Occasionally, this resulted in havoc when four or five picnics were carried on simultaneously, "each by a different group featuring public speakers who would present diametrically opposite poin_s of view"; more frequently, the Hnchag, Tashnag, or Ramgavar picnic selected different dates or locations for their outings.[55] Inevitably, spectators heard a long list of speakers and appeals for funds.

Picnics were enthusiastically endorsed by most immigrant spokesmen as salubrious and fun. One writer, publicizing a picnic in West Hoboken in July 1899, noted that unlike the affluent who could afford vacations far from the city, the poor should take advantage of the nearby outings, away from New York's "festering atmosphere," and in the "clean, invigorating air of the Jersey fields."[56] Immigrants crowded within four walls in the city, stated another, required the sights of "flowers, and the sounds of birds."[57] According to Hagop Kuyumjian, whose *Aha Kezi Amerigan* (Here Is America) is an important source for the period, the Armenian colony in Philadelphia enjoyed the George's Hill picnics because they could "restore broken ties," breathe clean air, and speak Armenian without any embarrassment. Indeed, the babble of spoken Armenian, and the aromas of Armenian food were so pervasive at the park, noted Kuyumjian, that hoisting an Armenian tricolor there would have claimed it for the Armenian Federation.[58]

In contrast to this fulsome praise, the Protestant Armenian ministry sharply criticized outings because of their drinking, gambling, and political and personal quarrels. Others asserted that picnics had no place on the Sabbath.[59] Needless to say, members of the Armenian Apostolic churches paid little heed to the complaints of their Protestant evangelical brethren.

There were other outings, too, like the boat rides on the Hudson River or across to Staten Island enjoyed by New York Armenians. One child of immigrants remembered a glorious trip on a ferry boat, accompanied by the Local 53A of the Pipefitters Union. On this occasion the Armenian musicians on the ferry were assisted by a group of Irish musicians and an Armenian singer, whose Old Country songs were followed by "Hail, Hail, the Gang's All Here."[60] Yearly, the Armenian Union of New York sponsored a free Labor Day picnic–boat ride on the Hudson, which in 1902 drew 500 adults and 200 children. A 13-piece Italian band played "Pomp Vorodom" and "My Armenia Who Calls Me" during the trip to River View Grove, which recalled the "shores of the Bosphorus."[61]

One special American and Armenian commercial fete took place in Fresno. Commencing in 1909, the Fresno Chamber of Commerce sponsored a Raisin Day parade to promote the local crop.[62] William Saroyan recalled that "the biggest public entertainment in Fresno came on Raisin Day early every summer. The long parade of that day, beginning around ten o'clock in the morning, was not unlike the present-day Rose Bowl parades of Pasadena. A Raisin Day King would be hired from Hollywood and he would drive a horsedrawn chariot, accompanied by a Queen, a local girl. . . ."[63]

The most significant year-round social event was the *hantes* (festival or celebration). Occasionally, a hantes commemorated a national holiday or anniversary of a preeminent historical event. In May 1914 some 2,000 spectators gathered in the Fresno Auditorium to celebrate the 1500th *Hopelian* (anniversary) of the discovery of the Armenian alphabet.[64] In 1909 a number of communities sponsored joint mass meetings in commemoration of the death of the beloved patriarch, Khrimian Hairig. More commonly, the hantes was an annual or semiannual social and fundraising event sponsored by one of a variety of social, political, or religious groups within a specific community at which plentiful Armenian food, dancing, and a long program of patriotic songs and speeches, climaxed by an appeal for donations to the society's cause, were the ritual.[65]

Dramatic Arts and Athletics. In addition to the hantes, immigrant dramatic groups put on readings and plays in the old language to large audiences. The earliest immigrant production probably took place in the Grand Army Hall in Worcester in 1890 for the benefit of the local Armenian Young Men's Association.[66] But the influx of immigrants after the mid-1890s so expanded the number of the drama groups that by 1905 virtually every major colony in the United States supported an immigrant Armenian theatre. (Among the most popular were the troupes at the Dudley Street Opera House in Boston and New York's Carnegie Lyceum.)

With the exception of the Eastern Theatre, which toured the Armenian colonies in the United States in 1913, most thespian societies were composed of amateurs. Critics constantly lambasted actors as being "awkward," "amateurish," and "poor."[67] The immigrant theater's weakest link was the acting of women, because in the Old World women avoided the theater as a "debasing institution."[68] Shirvanzade (Alexander Shirvanzade), the distinguished Russian Armenian playwright who toured the Armenian American colonies in the early 1920s, agreed that the drama was of poor quality, although the choral accompaniments were passable.[69]

Despite the rank amateurism of the troupes, immigrants crowded theaters "like teeth on a comb," because there, in their native language, they relived the former glories and aspirations of their people, as well as the heartache of the immigrant experience.[70] For example, immigrants reveled in the romantic, historical dramas of Raffi — *Samuel*, *Sheik Jellalledin*, and *Khente* (The Fool). In the *Defence of Van*, performed in Boston in 1908, Armenians shared in the brave exploits of their countrymen in the face of overwhelming Turkish odds.[71] Immigrants also wept at stories of persecution in the ancient period; in Bedros Tourian's classic *The Destruction of Ani* (capital of ancient Armenia), "Mother Armenia was represented as weeping over the fall of the city and calling for vengeance on the invaders." Nor were New World themes neglected. *Card Players*, by the immigrant playwright Zaven Baikar, was deemed essential viewing for all young men, as it depicted the career of one Barsam who gambled and drank away his life while his family was left starving.[72] On a lighter note, *Kabork Tivjara*, a farce written in Turkish, was presented in Boston in 1908 ostensibly to appeal to the Turkish-speaking immigrants from Cilicia and Adana.[73]

The atmosphere of the immigrant theater was sketched by the *Fresno Morning Republican* (January 1906): "The little theater was crowded to the doors, the audience composed of men, women and children — most Armenians — who listened eagerly to the words from the stage given in their native tongue." The play was preceded by an introduction by a community leader, Dr. A. Tufenkjian, who spoke of the history of the Armenian people. The "Garden of Eden, according to tradition, was situated in Armenia. . . . The nation was over five thousand years old, its first patriarch was Haig, the great grandson of Noah. . . ." Further, "There have been contemporary empires of the Persian, Babylonian, Grecian, and Roman, but today there is not one to represent them, while the Armenians have a living history. While the nations of Europe were yet barbarians the Armenian empire was a civilized and law abiding government." The play, *The Dawn*, which dealt with Kurdish depredations on an Armenian village, received "frequent," and "lusty" applause, although the critic of the *Fresno Morning Republican*, who knew no Armenian, deemed it "wordy."[74]

Some theatrical productions included sideshows. In May 1914 in Fresno the Tourian Dramatic Society of the Armenian Revolutionary Federation, which staged Shirvanzade's *For Honor* before 700 spectators, opened its presentation with a fifteen-minute wrestling match between Aram Hovsepian and an American opponent, whom he "toyed with."[75] Choral groups, whose activities sprang from abiding national traditions of folk and liturgical singing, were also popular. Perhaps the most impressive was the Fresno Armenian Choral Union which on one occasion in 1904 performed before an audience of 600.[76] Slide shows were also well attended throughout the communities and in 1913 the only extant Armenian film, *Kelishe*, was brought to the United States by the Egyptian Armenian Vahan Zartarian.[77]

Sporting events were also important in immigrant society. In the Old Country national sports were unknown until the Turkish Constitution of 1908 when the "Armenian General Athletic Union came into existence in Constantinople. . . . Athletic field days and Olympiads were held until the advent of the World War." Soccer was also introduced into many Protestant colleges in Turkey.[78] In America the immigrant generation lacked the leisure to participate in sports, but there were some athletic activities. One of the earliest athletic organizations of Armenians was the thirty-member Worcester Armenian Bicycle Club founded in 1896. The club competed in the annual Worcester Fourth of July bicycle competition, and its entire membership, according to the *Worcester Daily Telegram*, was "ambitious to be heard in the racing world."[79] The *Armenian Review* noted an Armenian Athletic Union formed in 1911, also in Worcester, for the "promotion of sports," and Worcester Armenians took part in municipal track and field competitions in the 100-yard dash and the weight toss.[80]

Then, in April 1911 the Boston Chapter of the Kharpert Union Educational Association sponsored a Boxing and Athletic Night at the Knights of Honor Hall in Boston with the following card:[81]

1.	Young Jannet (Armenian)	156 lbs.	Watertown vs.
	K. K. Manoog (Armenian)	165 lbs.	Watertown
2.	Phil Sully (Italian)	184 lbs.	Barrie, Vt. vs.
	Young Hassan (Syrian)	178 lbs.	Lowell
3.	Flannagan Bros. (Irish)	51-48	New York
4.	Kid Richards (Armenian)	138 lbs.	Cambridge vs.
	James McCarthy (Swede)	135 lbs.	Neponset
5.	Young Kirby (Jewish)	135 lbs.	Roxbury vs.
	Joe Rucher (Jewish)	135 lbs.	Boston
6.	Dan Danielson (Armenian)	135 lbs.	S. Boston vs.
	Young Popis (Greek)	135 lbs.	Worcester

The most renowned of Armenian American athletes of the period were the professional wrestlers, and the most successful of them competed for considerable stakes. In Illinois in 1905, twenty-two-year-old Avak M. Manoogian from Morenig, Turkey, who was billed as a champion wrestler, offered any opponent $150 if he could survive for fifteen minutes in the ring with him and $500 to any stalwart who could pin him. One "giant American" who paid the mandatory challenge fee of $25 reportedly cried for help from the "lion like paws" of the Armenian within one minute of the starting bell.[82] Aram Hovsepian, born in the rugged mountains of Bitlis and "built like a buffalo," in 1912 defeated Mike Athens, then champion of the San Joaquin Valley, to become the "muscular knight of the Valley." Hovsepian's fifteen consecutive victories by 1914 gained him "national reputation as a wrestler."[83]

Despite these sorties into athletics before World War I, the full Americanization of the Armenians in these fields did not fully begin until the 1920s. In that decade a few gifted members of a college-educated generation figured prominently in amateur collegiate competition, especially in football at Harvard, Brown, and Williams.[84]

The Coffeehouse.   Still another significant social fixture of the immigrant world was the Armenian coffeehouse. Notwithstanding its unsavory reputation in the community, the coffeehouse played an indispensable role in catering to the needs of a solitary social group: the Armenian males without families.

The coffeehouse was first and foremost a social center of bachelors and married men without families in the New World. What characterized these men, noted the Massachusetts Immigration Commission (1914), was "their general forlornness. They do not touch the outside world, they have no formal family or social relationships in their own group, they work long hours for low wages and are open to every temptation."[85] It was at the Armenian coffeehouse that a lonely workingman found what he needed: a place where fellow immigrants spoke his language and where he could spend his hours away from his work, access to immigrant newspapers, communications from the Old Country, gossip about the local community, and most important, "warm, genial company." There, too, he found a free meal when he was out of work, and news about job openings.[86]

Coffeehouses were opened in communities with a few hundred immigrants by an enterprising Armenian with a little capital. Renting a small store near the Armenian settlement for which he customarily paid a week's advance rent, the immigrant then purchased second-hand tables and chairs and some sturdy dishes, and laid in a supply of powdered Turkish coffee and its accompaniments: *lokum*, the sticky sweet Middle Eastern confection, pistachio nuts, and pumpkin seeds. Alcoholic beverages, for which a license was sometimes secured, soon followed. Ostensibly, the staff of the coffeehouse included a manager, chef, dishwasher, waiters, cashier, and custodian, but in practice the aproned proprietor and either his wife or an elderly male compatriot assumed all of these roles. If the bitter complaints about the food in most coffeehouses or coffeehouse-restaurants are accurate, most "chefs" were certainly ill-named.

Entertainment was often a feature of the coffeehouse. An aggressive proprietor hired special entertainment to increase flagging patronage or quash competition. One such attraction might be a wrestling match performed by a touring group. Middle Eastern belly dancers and jugglers were sure crowd pleasers, while more routine entertainment features were Armenian musicians — groups, singers, and instrumentalists. Then, too, spontaneous sidelights were provided by a fistfight, gambling, or verbal combat; in times of economic depression, coffeehouses degenerated into hotbeds of embittered, restless, unemployed male immigrants.[87]

Coffeehouses also became political arenas where émigré politicians and their followers heatedly argued every political issue facing Armenians in Turkey, Russia, and the United States. As revolutionary activity sharpened the rivalries between different factions, members or sympathizers of the partisan political organizations often frequented separate Armenian coffeehouses. At a later period, in Boston, Watertown, New York, Fresno, and elsewhere, the political parties themselves established separate coffeehouse-clubs for adherents.

Frequently without proper sanitary conditions, ventilation, or maintenance, these premises left much to be desired. Epilents, a novelist of the period, depicts the coffeehouse as "smoky, unpleasant, crowded, dirty, with a few Armenian musicians, men drawing on hookahs, pinochle players . . . tavloo games, and beer, raki, and lokum served to the customers."[88] A cynical, experienced coffeehouse patron remarked that "there are a number of foods [there] whose makeup the intellect of Pasteur couldn't analyze."[89] Another complained that "in the summer there are swarms of flies and in the winter legions of termites in the kitchens."[90] The lack of experience of many proprietors and the heavy traffic of immigrants accounted for much of the neglect. There were efforts to form a "cooperative" restaurant in Chelsea, Massachusetts, to improve on matters there, but it failed.[91] And competition and free enterprise prevailed; one proprietor encouraged patronage by hiring an experienced chef from the world famous Tokatlian Restaurant in Constantinople — or so he proclaimed in Philadelphia's immigrant press.[92]

More "respectable" elements of the community sharply censured coffeehouses for being hangouts for gamblers and drunkards. In February 1913, *Gotchnag* sought to protect young Armenian immigrants from "such corrupt elements" by exposing proprietors who permitted gambling and alcohol "in full defiance of the law." Such "reform measures" — and they were plentiful — bore meagre fruits.[93] The institution of the coffeehouse, however imperfect, provided a sorely needed atmosphere of sociability, honesty, and comfort to lonely men without families. One regular patron succinctly stated, "my coffeehouse is my church."[94]

Giving: Immigrant Charities

Compatriotic Societies. Another important aspect of the immigrants' communal life was their charities. By World War I hundreds of charities and compatriotic societies had been formed to assist in educating and caring for the homeless refugees and orphans in the Old World and the New. The most prolific of these organizations were the compatriotic societies, which were founded by Armenians of the same Old Country village, town, or region to support educational efforts in Turkey. Dating from the 1890s, the societies began as local groups but soon founded branches in all of the larger Armenian communities in the United States and Canada, and these met annually in regional or national gatherings. In time the larger groups also incorporated the smaller ones; thus a compatriotic society formed of immigrants from a village in Sivas would become part of the Greater Sivas Compatriotic Union. Invariably, however, strong-willed or intensely parochial groups "went it alone" and personal feuds among immigrant factions led to frequent schisms within the unions.

Most important of the compatriotic societies was the Kharpert Union Educational Association, with headquarters in Boston and branches in many other American cities. In 1901, eight years after its founding, the society convened its first national representative assembly in Providence, with representatives from Boston, Lynn, Worcester, Fitchburg, and Providence. Its object was to promote education in eastern Turkey by supporting the existing Armenian church schools and to raise an endowment fund for higher education.[95] By 1906 the endowment fund had reached $5,000 and the society was annually contributing $500 for the maintenance of schools and their 1400 pupils.[96] A local society more typical in size was the Tzack Village Educational Association, founded in 1910 in Watertown, Massachusetts, with a membership of 36 and assets of $201.65.[97] Most societies derived their financial support from monthly dues of 25 to 50 cents; special fundraising drives and solicitations at weddings, picnics, and hanteses supplemented their purse. By 1906, 27 compatriotic societies were active in the United States.[98]

The structure and goals of the compatriotic societies derived from Old World educational societies like the Araratian and United Societies, which had been established in Constantinople in the 1870s and 1880s, with branches throughout the provinces. However, in addition to their stated educational and charitable purposes, the compatriotic societies in America took on the new social function of enabling widely scattered immigrants from the same Old World town or village to reconvene, at least annually, to reminisce and relay news to each other. A historian of the Gesaratzi (Caesaria) Compatriotic Union, founded in 1905, remarked that the society's meetings were the only occasion where Gesaratzis got together to talk about the Old Country and take pleasure in their small donations to the town.[99] One immigrant, when asked about his society (Tzack Village Educational Association), said nostalgically that he was "sorry it had dissolved; it was good to see the people from the village at the meetings."[100]

Armenian compatriotic societies differed from the societies of other ethnic groups in not providing sickness or death benefits for their members. This peculiarity stemmed from the Armenian precept that such contingencies were the responsibility of the immediate family only and not of the community.

Societies and Drives. In addition to the compatriotic societies, Armenians organized countless charities for the orphaned, needy, and destitute scattered throughout Turkey. One of the earliest was the New Jersey Women's Orphan Association, founded in West Hoboken in 1892 to raise money for Dicranagert's orphaned Armenians.[101] Institutions like Our Saviour's Hospital and Charity in Constantinople, with its 2,000 patients a year and 250 orphaned children, were assisted by an annual collection of about $300 from Armenian churches in the United States.[102] One of the most humble societies was a group in Allston, Massachusetts, which pledged a penny a day per person to support an orphan.

Charities extended alms to immigrants in the United States as well, in part because an Armenian anywhere on relief degraded not only himself but all Armenians. Chapter 5 noted that the Armenian Colonial Association, founded in New York in 1901, assisted many bewildered and penniless immigrants at Ellis Island. The Armenian Benevolent Association of Boston helped Armenians within ten miles of Boston to secure jobs, care for the sick, and aid the needy.

At the same time, the more fortunate, humanitarian-minded Armenians raised funds for specific calamities. Thus the "fearful earthquake in Garin" in 1901 and 1902 or the famine in Van (1904) sparked fundraising drives.[103] The largest charitable efforts arose in the wake of the massacres of 1894–1896, 1904, and 1909.[104] And in the United States, the disastrous fires in Chelsea (1908) and Salem (1910), Massachusetts, prompted large-hearted moves by Armenian leaders.[105]

Armenian General Benevolent Union. Overshadowing all the compatriotic unions and individual charities, however, was the charitable work of the Armenian General Benevolent Union. The AGBU was headed by the eminent Egyptian-Armenian, Boghos Nubar Pasha. Boghos Nubar's father had served as Egyptian premier for three terms and for a period acted as regent. His son, a distinguished and imposing personality, declined to enter politics in preference for agriculture, engineering, and business; he became president or director of about twenty banks and corporations, served as director general of the Egyptian railways, and revamped the entire Sudan irrigation project. Because of his engineering and commercial contributions to Egypt, he was awarded the Order of Leopold of Belgium, and the "Nile," "the highest medal the Anglo-Egyptian government could award a civilian. As with his father, he was also given the title 'Pasha' by the Egyptian government."[106]

After the 1894–1896 massacres, thoughtful Armenian leaders sought to establish a strong, nonpolitical national philanthropic organization capable of extending immediate aid in times of disaster "if the nation was to survive its ordeals." At first they considered basing the organization in Turkey, but instead resolved to set up "a society on the free soil of a foreign country, with sufficient capital and resources for emergency relief, and to put through a long-range program of philanthropy, with a strong emphasis on education." The community spokesmen stressed the need for unity among the widely scattered and splintered Armenian communities, although it might involve the "vicious factional struggles among Armenians in the Dispersion." Boghos Nubar, himself troubled by the tragic fate of his countrymen in Turkey, became the leader and driving force of the Armenian General Benevolent Union.

The specific purposes of the organization, founded in Cairo in 1906, were to "establish or subsidize schools, libraries, trade schools, workshops, hospitals, dispensaries, orphanages and other institutions of the kind . . . provide assistance to needy Armenians in the homeland without distinction of religious faith . . . assist the peasantry . . . with land, seeds, animals, and implements . . . encourage the progress of local industries, disseminate knowledge in modern agriculture and . . . extend immediate help to victims of famines, fires and any other disasters."[107]

The AGBU received a prompt and favorable response in the Old World, partly because of the personality and the magic name of Boghos Nubar Pasha. Then in 1908 the Young Turk revolution and the ensuing constitutional government opened wide vistas for the fledgling union. Within the next few years it founded chapters in all the principal Armenian provinces, cities, and towns of Turkey and in Europe and Africa, and by 1914 it had the following membership:

Africa	4 chapters	828 members
Turkey	59 chapters	4,215 members
Europe	25 chapters	1,016 members

Notwithstanding the enthusiastic endorsement in the Old World, the United States became the "foremost stronghold" of the AGBU. The organization of its first chapters lay in the hands of Vahan Kurkjian, an educator and director of an Armenian orphanage in Cyprus, who emigrated to the United States in 1907 as the AGBU's personal representative. Despite competition from existing revolutionary parties, Kurkjian founded the first New World AGBU chapter in Boston in October 1908. With the assistance especially of Armenian Protestant clergy, chapters were established in 1909 in New Britain, Worcester, Providence, Brockton, and Pawtucket. In 1910 under the leadership of the prominent oriental rug importer and manufacturer, Mihran Karagheusian, the most pivotal chapter — New York City — was established, with the support of the colony's grandees. In the same year the first West Coast chapter was formed in Fresno. By 1912, when the New World chapters convened their first consultative assembly in Boston, 39 chapters had been formed, and that number jumped to 54 chapters with a total membership of 2,407 by the end of 1913.

A monthly publication, the Armenian, was born and died in 1909. But in 1914 the American branch began publication of another Armenian language monthly, Hoosharar (The Awakener), which continues in print in the 1980s as the official organ of the organization. Clearly, by World War I the AGBU had captured the community's enthusiastic support.

The AGBU's initial thrust in 1906 lay in alleviating the deplorable political and economic situation in Turkey — through grants and subsidies to a number of schools and orphanages, food and seed for planting for Armenian peasants stricken by famine, and relief funds for Russian Armenian victims of the Armeno-Tatar clashes. But the sudden and overwhelmingly catastrophic massacres in Cilicia in 1909 "forged the will and tested the finances of the fledgling organization." Parekordzagan (Benevolent Union), as it was known, rushed funds to provide tents, blankets, food, clothing and medical assistance; and for the many new orphans, it established its first orphanage, the Kelegian, at Deort Yol in Cilicia. Education was also nurtured as the AGBU established, maintained or supported thirty-four schools in Armenia and Cilicia, and in order to provide them with qualified teachers established a normal school in the city of Van. By 1911 the AGBU's capital fund stood at $110,000, with total disbursements for relief at $90,000.

Contributions from the Armenian community in America rose dramatically from $2,340 in 1909 to $23,689 in 1914.[108] Some of the funds were kept in the United States. In 1908, for example, in its funding year, the Boston chapter, which donated $60 to the Old Country, raised $284.75 for emergency aid to the Armenian victims of the disastrous Chelsea Fire and stationed an interpreter in Chelsea for ten days to assist the homeless Armenian victims of the tragedy. Annually, thereafter, immigrants who needed help with back rent, employment, or traveling expenses to the Old Country (for one

Armenian with an incurable disease who hoped that "the clean air might prolong his life") were assisted.[109] In all of its works, the AGBU consistently stressed its motto: "An Armenian must not open his hand before an American." (The Boston chapter, especially, bristled at the charge that "Armenians coming [to America] are a burden on public welfare.")[110]

The AGBU actively sought to remain a nonpartisan organization, free from political or religious ties and entanglements. Nonetheless, the Armenian Revolutionary Federation (Tashnags) soon attacked it for alleged affiliation with their opponents, the Ramgavars. According to the Tashnags, the AGBU's benefactions discriminated in favor of "pro-Ramgavar organizations, schools and persons." The Tashnags also charged that the AGBU enriched its own officials, especially Vahan Malezian and Souren Bartevian, in Boston. For this reason, *Hairenik*, the Tashnag journal, urged its readers in 1912 to "stay away from that anti-humanitarian, so-called benevolent association." Later charges that the AGBU were "parasites . . . negligent in their calling . . . inefficient . . . the pawn of bureaucrats . . . a juggler of figures" continued through the immigrant and second generations.[111]

Armenian Red Cross.   While the Tashnags leveled criticism at the AGBU, they also formed their own charitable organization, the Armenian Red Cross (*Hai Garmir Khach*). This organization, which in 1946 became the Armenian Relief Society, was established in 1910. Like the AGBU, its avowed purposes were to extend relief to the suffering and needy Armenians in the Old Country and to assist in building and supporting educational institutions in Turkey and Russia. However, the ARC differed from the AGBU in three major respects: it lacked the AGBU's strong financial backing and numerically impressive membership; it was distinctly an arm of a political party (the Tashnags), and it was entirely administered by women.[112]

According to its historian, relief efforts of Armenian women in the United States antedated the formation of the ARC by half a dozen years: in 1903, handfuls of women in New York, Philadelphia, Troy, Boston, Providence, and West Pullman had formed auxiliary groups under the mantle of the local Tashnag gomides (committees), often calling themselves the "Armenian Red Cross"; but such groups were largely informal. The real impetus for a permanent and cohesive relief organization came from the tragic Adana massacre of 1909 and the tremendous assistance required to alleviate the suffering from the appalling loss of lives, homes, and property in the region. Accordingly, on January 1, 1910, the first Armenian Red Cross chapter was formed in New York. The formalization of the Armenian Red Cross as part of the Armenian Revolutionary Federation occurred in late 1910 when E. Agnooni (Hachadoor Maloomian), a powerful agent of the Armenian Revolutionary Federation's Western Bureau in Geneva, arrived in the United States on a speaking tour of the various Armenian colonies. A charismatic speaker, with an unequalled reputation among Tashnags in the United States, Agnooni within one year organized chapters of the Armenian Red Cross in Boston, Worcester, Providence, West Hoboken, Philadelphia, Hartford, West Pullman, Chicago, Fresno, Troy, Lynn, Paterson, Portland, Watertown, Waukegan, and Brantford, Canada.

The Armenian Red Cross, whose activities, budgets, and disbursements are unavailable for the years 1910–1914, contributed much to Old World hospitals, outdoor relief, food, clothing, shelter, and aid to educational institutions. The very first donation of the New York Chapter in 1910 was 50 Turkish pounds for the opening of a new Armenian school in Talvorig, outside Mush, in Eastern Turkey. During and after World War I, it continued its vital assistance to the needy, orphaned, and blind in the Middle East, Greece, Cyprus, and elsewhere.

As a charitable institution wholly run by women, the Armenian Red Cross significantly advanced the education and skills of immigrant women in organizational activities. Prior to its founding, Armenian women were unfamiliar with communal activity and lacked "the audacity to enter the public arena." However, the sponsoring Armenian Revolutionary Federation "brought [them] valuable assistance . . . and like a big brother, accustomed its sisters to serve the work of the Armenians."[113] In all, the immigrant charities rendered valuable assistance to the Armenian nation in times of need. The AGBU, the Armenian Red Cross, and the compatriotic societies were critical social institutions aiding the immigrants and their families overseas. Together with the families and social pastimes, they were important facets of the immigrants' complex and vigorous social life, brought into being or reshaped by the demands of the newcomers' world.

As yet, however, no consideration has been given to the oldest of Armenian social institutions — the church.

10.

The Churches of the Immigrants

Like other immigrants in a strange and distant land, the Armenians sought to rebuild their familiar traditions of worship in America. The immigrants brought with them two religious heritages: the historic Armenian Apostolic Church, which embraced the vast majority of the newcomers, and the Armenian Protestant Church. Each church functioned in important ways for the immigrants: each bridged the gap between the old and the new; each used priests or ministers to act as intermediaries between the immigrants and the American society; and each church and service reminded the sojourner of home. The Armenian Apostolic Church, especially, linked the widely scattered Armenians to their long and troubled past, their homeland, their language, their literature, and their faith.

As other immigrant groups discovered, however, the transplanting of the churches involved enormous financial, social, political, and religious decisions. The struggle to recreate the ancient Armenian Apostolic Church 5,000 miles from its historic home was a special trial.

The Apostolic Church in Armenia

The Armenian Apostolic Church was as old as the nation. Tradition held that the Apostles St. Judas Thaddeus and St. Bartholomew visited Armenia in the middle of the first century A.D.; however, the true apostle to the Armenians was the evangelist Gregory, who converted the nation to Christianity in A.D. 301. Armenia was thus the first entire nation to embrace the new faith, a fact which the Armenians are proud of to this day.

In its infancy the church shaped Armenia's destiny. The early church fathers acted in concert with Rome and Byzantium in sanctioning the decrees of the first three ecumenical councils of Nicea (325), Constantinople (381), and Ephesus (431). But in 491 the Armenians broke with Rome and the Greek church over the doctrine of Christ's combined divinity and humanity set at the Council of

Chalcedon (451) and were independent thereafter. A few years before (406) its clerics had developed a thirty-six-letter alphabet for the Armenian language and then translated the Bible, liturgy, and literature into Armenian, ushering in the "Armenian Golden Age." These momentous events sealed the Church to the nation. Divorced from the great Christian communions, which regarded Armenians as heretics for avowing that Christ had a single, divine nature, the nation and church pursued their joint culture independent of outside influences.

Politically, too, the church represented a continuum of power, from the medieval period when the clergy more than the kings dealt with foreign powers and led the nation to the Turkish conquest in the fifteenth century, when Ottoman rule fused its Armenian subjects into a virtual nation-state because of their religion — a condition which endured for four hundred years.[1]

The church, though hierarchical, was mixed with democratic elements: at each level of organization, lay elements participated with the clergy in the selection of the priests, bishops, archbishops, and the catholicoi, or heads of the church. It was administered by its celibate clergy, the *vartabeds* (doctors of theology) who, after arduous religious training, cared for important parishes, were scholars, and became bishops, archbishops, patriarchs, and catholicoi. They also governed the lower, married clergy, the *kahanas* — studious men with rudimentary educations — who mixed their religious duties of administering the sacraments and visiting the poor with ordinary work as craftsmen or farmers.[2]

In later times the church lost its strong position. Until the twelfth century, for example, the sovereign head of the church was a single hierarch, the Catholicos of all Armenians. But because of troubled political conditions, this Holy See had wandered with the people. It was finally situated at Echmiadzin in 1441, where it has remained to the present. But other hierarchical sees developed from the twelfth century, one, at the island of Aghtamar, on Lake Van, and another at Sis in Cilicia. These sees, in addition to the patriarchate of Jerusalem (1311) and the patriarchate of Constantinople (1461), although subordinate to Echmiadzin, became rival centers of power and influence.[3]

The long years under Turkish rule further weakened the church. "Having filled an important place in another age," wrote one modern historian, "the monasteries today are utterly inadequate to meet the demands of a modern ministry."[4] Office seeking, simony, quarrels, schism, and rival patriarchs were common. Self-complacency was another hallmark. Thus Ormanian, patriarch of Constantinople in 1910 and cognizant of the church's persecution of the Protestants in the nineteenth century, could still write: "In the matter of liberalism and religious tolerance, the Armenian Church yields to no other church . . . nothing is easier for an Armenian writer than to defend his own Church."[5] Not surprisingly, late nineteenth-century Armenian intellectuals in Turkey and Russia assaulted the church for its corruption, outmoded educational network, social conservatism, and blind self-assurance.

Despite its infirmities, the Apostolic Church prevailed over its attackers. Over the centuries the church had acted as an asylum and rallying center, especially in troubled times; it nurtured and preserved Armenian traditions, customs, language, and literature; and it stood as the only symbol of unity among the Armenians which had endured over the centuries of trials and dispersions. However imperfect, it was the only transcendent focus of Armenians in the homeland and the diaspora.

Origins of the Apostolic Church in America: The Worcester Parish

Desire and First Steps. In the late 1880s the Worcester community included about 1,000 Armenian immigrants, mostly laborers in the city's wire mills. Before the founding of the first Armenian Apostolic Church in 1891, Armenian churchgoers attended English-language Protestant services. On occasions, however, they were ridiculed as foreigners or chastised for practicing their inherited faith. In one instance, an Armenian Baptist minister told the Armenian Apostolics that their mother church's rites were "idolatrous."[6] At other times the local population called Armenians "scabs," "foreigners," or "Turks."[7]

These troubling events coincided with the fortuitous arrival in Worcester in 1888 of a prominent Armenian leader, Mgerdich Portukalian. An intellectual firebrand who had been exiled from Turkey in the 1880s for his revolutionary writings, Portukalian had fled to Marseilles where he commenced publication of *Armenia*, a soon-to-be famous journal of the Armenian revolutionary struggle. In Worcester, Portukalian urged the small immigrant community to keep their faith by establishing an Armenian church and an Armenian school. The Armenians, roused by Portukalian's stirring presence, soon formed an Armenian Academy or club, the kernel of the embryonic church, with a membership which quickly grew to 250.[8] Thus, the first steps toward establishing a church sprang from high political and nationalistic feelings.

Church affairs in America at the time fell under the jurisdiction of the Armenian patriarch in Constantinople. In January 1889 the Worcester Armenian Academy petitioned the patriarch for an

English-speaking or French-speaking vartabed, who might spread "correct" knowledge about the Armenian people among the Americans. Kahanas were also needed, said the petition, for the Armenians in New York, Philadelphia, Boston, and Jersey City. By mid-1889 a forty-year-old vartabed, Joseph Sarajian, educated in Mush and Jerusalem, was en route to America.[9]

It takes little imagination to reconstruct the joyful scene in Worcester on Sunday afternoon, July 28, when hundreds of Armenians crowded into the Reform Club Hall to hear the newly arrived priest conduct the first Armenian mass in the New World. Sarajian, described as medium in height, with an "abundant crop of hair and a voluminous black beard" bestowed the church's blessings and sacraments on the "Armenian pilgrims" of Worcester. The celebration of "joy and comfort" was a historic moment in the community.[10]

Soon after a *hokapardzutiun* (parish council) was elected. It resolved: "Whereas the Armenian people, by reason of persecution and abject poverty, are immigrating to America, in order to preserve these immigrants from being alienated, we hereby decide to build a church. . . ."[11] A new church was thus to be founded in accordance with its centuries' long function: the preservation of the culture from assimilation. The first religious services were held in rented halls, but on June 18, 1891, several hundred Armenians from Worcester, Boston, Salem, Haverhill, and New York joined Father Sarajian in consecrating *Surp Prgich* (Holy Saviour) a modest, attractive wooden structure on Laurel Hill near Worcester's Armenian quarter as the first New World parish of the ancient Armenian Apostolic Church.[12]

After 1891 other communities followed Worcester's example. Inspired by Father Sarajian's personal visits, church groups soon formed in Boston, Providence, New York, Lawrence, and Fresno. In most cases the procedure followed Worcester's: first, a committee was formed by the priest and a prominent local Armenian. Once assembled, this parish council canvassed the community for donations to start worship and form a church. In these years before churches were purchased or constructed, communities in New York and Lawrence made arrangements for weekly services with neighboring Episcopal churches, with whom the Apostolic Armenians felt kinship; services were led by itinerant priests or laymen.[13]

Political Turmoil.   While other communities were struggling to establish churches of their own, the newly founded church in Worcester discovered that it had inherited deep-seated political problems from the Old World. The context was that by the early 1890s Armenian intellectuals in the Old World had established paramilitary nationalist-socialist committees in Eastern Europe and Turkey for the purpose of setting up an autonomous and eventually independent Armenian socialist republic in Eastern Turkey. In agreement with conservative and liberal opinion, the Apostolic Church hierarchy in Turkey feared that the nationalist movement, despite its obviously desirable ends, would goad the Turks into destroying the Armenian population. Church officialdom also bitterly opposed the nationalists' strident anticlericalism.[14]

In the early 1890s the Armenian Academy in Worcester began receiving copies of revolutionary literature — Portukalian's *Armenia*, *Hnchag* (The Clarion), the organ of the social Democratic Hnchagian Party, and works of the great patriotic novelist, Raffi. Father Sarajian, probably on orders from the patriarchate, banned these works from the Armenian Academy despite their popularity. Apostolic and Protestant Armenians immediately opposed his efforts. Then in December 1892, Sarajian arbitrarily set aside a recent election of the president of the Armenian Academy — a nationalist — in favor of his conservative colleague Michael Tophanelian. The ill-advised move sparked bitter protests and the call for Tophanelian's ouster.[15] Then, according to the *Worcester Daily Telegram*, Sarajian "declared an open animosity toward the majority of members who withdrew, and who were the most enlightened members of his own church."[16]

The unfortunate dispute climaxed in a fracas during the Sunday, March 26, meeting of the academy in 1893. Despite the numerous resignations, many anti-Tophanelian members were present. When one Armenian rose to urge Tophanelian's ouster, Sarajian shut him off, and this began a free for all. The Armenians, "with blood running down their faces, were swinging chair legs through the air."[17] Another account noted that Sarajian, when the lights went out, was "like a general of darkness, leading the fray" by passing chair legs to the Tophanelian supporters. The police were soon called in to quell the riot; then more people were injured and the vestry furniture was smashed. Soon after, a second fight erupted on Arch Street, in the heart of the Armenian quarter.[18]

The long-festering dispute, the brawls, and the bold headlines of the *Worcester Daily Telegram* "PRIEST WAS IN FIGHT!" "Bloody Riot" "ARMENIANS SMASH EACH OTHER WITH TABLES AND CHAIRS" — prompted prominent New York Armenians to come to Worcester to arbitrate the dispute.[19] The arbitration committee sharply reprimanded Tophanelian and his followers, recommended that the Armenian Academy be dissolved, that there be no further political discussions in the church, and that Tophanelian be discharged from his post. The committee also criticized Sarajian. The report was unanimously accepted by the "anti-priest" faction meeting in the Worcester Grange Hall, and Sarajian, though unhappy, nonetheless accepted the committee's recommendations.[20]

In the long run Sarajian's activities against the revolutionary sympathizers gravely diminished his influence in Worcester and paved the way for his resignation. Complaining about the mounting administrative and religious duties he carried and irritated by the church's refusal to hire an assistant, Sarajian resigned his post on August 15, 1893. The *Worcester Daily Telegram* concluded that Sarajian had quit because of the dispute over the revolutionary materials, his friendship with Tophanelian, and the March 26 fracas — an explanation which surely fits the immediate situation.[21] But others later ascribed Sarajian's troubles also to the religious and psychological conditions of American life. That is, the strong competition from rival Protestant sects and the Armenian immigrants' "wrongly understood freedom" or "peculiar licence" in "free America" promoted unrestrained criticism of the church unknown in the Old World.[22] This explanation was also close to the mark.

Sarajian's resignation did not end the political problems of the parish; his immediate successor, Malachia Vartabed Deroonian, also hewed to the conservative line. Aged 48, "short and rugged in stature, . . . [with] a broad, high forehead, prominent Grecian features, a full beard and hair of grey iron," Deroonian promptly argued that political emancipation of the persecuted Armenians in Turkey could come "by diplomacy [rather] than Bloodshed." His declaration — "my view of the matter may be antagonistic to those of the majority of Armenians in America" — was a classic understatement.[23] The revolution-sympathizers replied: "He is nothing less than a Turkish agent, for a Turkish molla (priest) could not do or say more than this." The *Worcester Daily Telegram* noted in early 1894 that only cooler heads were averting another breach in the congregation.[24] In less than three years Deroonian also resigned.

Religious strife was renewed during the brief, stormy tenure of Mashtots Vartabed Papazian, Worcester's third priest in a decade. Papazian, a young zealot who led the Worcester flock for only one year (1897–1898), alienated every group in Worcester. In a gathering which included Protestant Armenians, Papazian stressed: "Those who bring their wives over [to America] are faithless to the country and those who entice countrymen to migrate are hirelings of the missionaries."[25] In Boston, *Yeprad* noted with dismay that Papazian made decisions on several important church matters without the knowledge or consent of the local parish council. He also ardently and openly sympathized with the nationalist Tashnag cause, with the result that three separate parish councils were elected and resigned in only five months, and a writer bitterly complained of the "shame reigning among Worcester Armenians." Papazian's arbitrary conduct, ill-chosen remarks, and political sympathies turned the parish into a cauldron of animosities and tensions. No services were held in *Surp Prgich* for two and one-half months for fear of fights; and the Armenians gained a reputation as unruly and incorrigible troublemakers. Peace was finally restored in August 1898 when Papazian resigned his post, just ten years after the founding of the first American parish.[26] For a decade, instead of the consolation of the venerable church and the comfort of its traditional hymns, chants, sermons, and sacraments, Worcester immigrants had found the parish repeatedly embroiled in political and personal strife.

The Armenian American Prelacy: 1898–1914

The First Bishop.   The year 1898 marked the beginning of the second decade and the second stage of the Apostolic Church's history in the New World. In that year Khrimian, Catholicos of All Armenians, in Echmiadzin, cognizant of the growing numbers of Armenians streaming out of Turkey to America after the Hamidean massacres (1894–1896) and of the need for order among the far flung, embattled parish councils, raised the United States to the status of a missionary diocese; Joseph Vartabed Sarajian, America's first Armenian Apostolic priest, was chosen as her first bishop, reputedly, said the Catholicos, because *"oorish choonim"* (I have no one else). Worcester was designated the diocesan seat.[27]

Sarajian's task was to organize and minister to the rapidly growing community. Parish councils were promptly formed in Hartford and Lynn and Manchester (1898); others followed in Chicago and Troy (1899), West Hoboken (detached from the New York City community) in 1900, New Britain (1900), and Philadelphia (1902). The second Armenian Apostolic edifice was completed in Fresno in 1900, the third in West Hoboken in 1906. By the latter date Sarajian, virtually single-handedly, had established embryonic church organizations in another twenty communities from Massachusetts to California.[28]

In 1901 Sarajian held the first meeting, in Worcester, of the six regular Armenian Apostolic clergy in the United States under his charge. Then in 1902 Bishop Sarajian brought the scattered communities into a church council or assembly, under a church constitution, which demarcated the powers, rights, and jurisdiction of the Church clergy, hierarchy, and laity. The constitution organized the immigrant colonies into seven pastorates — "the nuclei of future dioceses" — over which a pastor was to be appointed by each local congregation; stipulated that all communities which fell outside the seven pastorates, designated "mission stations," lay under the direct supervision and care of the bishop in Worcester; carefully ruled

(Article 17) that "no pastor . . . may conduct the services or assume the spiritual office of another parish without the consent of its pastor and board of trustees, or the knowledge of the prelate" — a probable reference to the interference in 1897–1898 of Mashtots Vartabed Papazian in the Boston Parish Council. In addition, formal documents, a secretariat, and annual assemblies were duly instituted by the new prelate.[29]

Sarajian's tenure as prelate, like his career as a priest, was plagued by bitter quarrels with the revolutionaries, who disputed the legality of his selection by the Catholicos in Echmiadzin. Normally, bishops were selected by the diocesan assembly from a list of three candidates drawn up by the local assembly, the Catholicos, or both. But in Sarajian's case, only two of the four fully organized parishes in America (New York, Worcester, Boston, and Fresno) had been represented.[30] Moreover, Sarajian was criticized for catering to wealthy Armenians in America, failing to honor a martyr to the "Armenian revolutionary cause" and — preposterously — with pocketing moneys collected for the relief of famine victims in Van.[31] Then in 1906 various communities waged an all out campaign in the immigrant press to discredit Sarajian. A letter in *Tzain Haireneats* from Philadelphia in February called a service by Sarajian the work of a "veritable juggler, in which he left no impression on the disheartened group. In the sermon he is no different from the *kahanas* who also farm, who have memorized a few lines from the Bible."[32] In March 134 Armenians in Lowell petitioned that Sarajian be removed for personal failings and his "illegal" election; 101 Armenians in Waukegan and 178 petitioners from Chelsea in April voiced strong objections to his activities or lack thereof.[33] In August, "exhausted by my labors and tired by the New World," Sarajian submitted his resignation, thereby ending the first eight years of the prelacy.[34]

Sarajian, over this long period, had been responsible for the entire North American diocese from Boston to Fresno. Founding churches in West Hoboken and Fresno, supervising a ministry of 11, and establishing countless parish councils, he ministered to nearly 20,000 communicants. Notwithstanding Sarajian's failings — he was probably unimpressive from the pulpit, and a later prelate complained about his record keeping — his tenure as bishop was productive.

Sarajian's resignation spelled a new crisis in the fledgling church. Despite interim replacements, it took seven years before order returned to the North American diocese. In the meantime organized religious life was enfeebled. In fact, events in the diocese could be described as chaos relieved by confusion; however, the worst situation occurred in 1910.

The Self-Selected Bishop. The two major Armenian political parties, the nationalist-revolutionary Tashnags and the conservative Ramgavars, were at each others' throats. Partisans of each faction found places on local parish councils. The path of wisdom among the church hierarchy would have been to neutralize the factionalism in the separate churches, restore order, and minister to the parishioners' religious and social needs. Instead, in 1910 as never before, the church became totally immersed in the political struggle of the émigré parties.

At the heart of the debacle was the controversial Musheg Seropian, bishop of Adana since 1905. According to Turkish sources, Seropian bore partial responsibility for the notorious Adana massacres of 1909, which claimed 30,000 Armenian lives, by heightening Armeno-Turkish tensions after the Young Turk Constitution of 1908.[35] In any case, Seropian, who fled Cilicia in late 1909 or early 1910, was an inveterate political intriguer with a sense for the theatrical. (Immigrants proudly remembered him — tall and handsome — as he rode through the Adana diocese on horseback.)

Seropian arrived in the United States in late 1910. Lacking the sanction of the Holy See in Echmiadzin and summoned by no one in America, he had come to the New World ostensibly "for study"; but his eye was certainly on the vacant prelacy.[36] Large crowds from Worcester to Chicago turned out to offer warm greetings to the famous bishop. Without much delay he plunged into politics by avowing the Ramgavar cause — the front page of the Ramgavar journal *Azk* (November 30) carried his full portrait and words of welcome. Later he said, "If I were not a priest, I would join the [Ramgavar] Party; I encourage them, I praise their direction, I speak at all their pulpits where I am invited."[37] Such was his open invitation to trouble.

An obvious choice for the prelacy and supported by conservative forces, Seropian, at a religious assembly convened in March 1911 to elect a prelate, succeeded in having his name inserted on the already prepared list of candidates (a step of dubious legality); when the session ended (it was conducted in private to avoid heated arguments from outsiders), Seropian had been elected prelate of the American diocese.[38]

Seropian's high-handed tactics and his political affiliations ignited a turbulent struggle in the church between the "probishop" and the "antibishop" factions. Parish councils, instead of ministering to the needs of their congregations, engaged in verbal arguments over whether to permit the newly elected bishop to preach in their pulpits (Boston, July 1911). The Worcester probishop faction sought to oust its parish priest to install Seropian in his place — if his election as prelate were not sanctioned — while the local priest himself led a group of 40 parishioners to disband the probishop parish council (October 1911). In Chicago (April 1911), opposition to the bishop led to fistfights and the flight of Seropian and his colleagues through a rear door. In West Hoboken (February 1912), Seropian, forewarned of trouble, relied on the attendance of the local police force at the Divine Liturgy to avert trouble.[39]

Meanwhile, Seropian's election brought bitter complaints from abroad. As Bishop of Adana under the Sis Catholicate, Seropian had no jurisdiction outside his diocese, and in late 1911 the Holy See in Echmiadzin, which had jurisdiction over the Armenian diocese, refused to sanction his election as bishop in the United States. However, Seropian's immediate superior, the Catholicos of Sis and thus a traditional rival of the Catholicos of All Armenians, in Echmiadzin, tacitly sanctioned Seropian's activities in America on the dubious grounds that the Holy See in Echmiadzin was vested with no authority over a prelate from Sis.[40] Old World feuds thus boiled over again in the New. Under powerful sanctions from Echmiadzin, however, the newly elected Seropian stepped down from his post, thereby ending the most disgraceful chapter in the history of the Armenian diocese.[41]

Order Restored. The problem of finding proper leadership for the strife-ridden church was not solved until the election in late 1913 of Arsen Vartabed Vehooni. Quickly dispatched from the Old World after his election, the new prelate came upon quarreling parish councils, closed parishes, and a prelacy with no archives, no secretariat, no seals, no addresses of parish councils, and no records since 1889. However, Vehooni made visits to the East and West Coast parishes with unusual and commendable speed, even established contacts with South American parishes, and sought to reconcile differences among the "dissident" parishes.[42] For the prelacy, it was the light at the end of the tunnel.

The story of the Armenian prelacy in the United States until World War I was thus characterized by rival ambitions, neglect and ignorance on the part of the Holy See, political splits which disrupted church life, rivalries among Old World jurisdictions, and feuds unleashed by "free America." The situation in 1912 was summed up by one intelligent observer:

The Armenian Church . . . our chief representative and trustee . . . is a feeble, breathless creature. . . . The great majority of the Armenians in America are not in communication with its influence. . . . In Eastern states, the churches in Worcester and Hoboken, in California, Fresno, Fowler and Yettem . . . lack regularity and discipline. . . . [This is] . . . the Armenian Church, the first flower of Christianity, whose apostleship, devotion and martyrdom we vaunt. . . . I know of many who scoff, for whom religion means ignorance, retrogression, and melancholy. . . . But where are the believers? . . . In Boston of 2500 Gregorian [Apostolic] Armenians barely 25 have paid their $2 annual dues. . . . Our pews remain empty, except for Easter and Christmas, and [many are nominal Christians]. The church is leaderless.[43]

The Local Parishes and Priests

Clearly, the survival of the church depended not on the tortuous history of the prelacy, but rather on the efforts of the local priests and their faithful parishioners. Who were the local priests, what circumstances brought them to the United States, and how well did they preserve the religious life and traditional religious observances in the New World?

An accurate estimate of the numbers of priests in the immigrant church can be derived from the federal census of Religious Bodies of 1906 and 1916. In 1906 the Armenian Apostolic community supported three church edifices (Worcester, West Hoboken, and Fresno) and a priesthood of one archbishop, seven resident pastors, three missionary priests, and one deacon.[44] By 1916 seven church buildings had been added (New York, Troy, Philadelphia, Providence, Lowell, Fowler, and Yettem); the clergy stood at seventeen. In addition to communities with church buildings, in 1916 twenty-four communities with parish councils made arrangements for religious services with local American churches, usually the Episcopal, or they rented halls fitted up as churches.[45]

In places without regular Armenian church buildings, missionary priests conducted biweekly or monthly services; the sacraments of baptism and marriage were occasionally performed in private dwellings. (The tiny Armenian community in Chicago which had had no religious services for nearly five years, turned out en masse on a Sunday afternoon in November 1909 to attend a two and one half hour *badarak* (mass) conducted by Boghos Vartabed Kaftanian of the Worcester parish; amid the confusion, crying of infants, laughter and numerous baptisms, the immigrant community, it was reported, "seemed to have found a long lost treasure.")[46] Communities without permanent priests, such as New Britain, Connecticut, held services with the aid of "group designated lay priests."[47]

Of the quality of the Armenian priesthood in the United States, Bishop Seropian rather coldly remarked that the eight Armenian priests under his jurisdiction in America (1911) "have been rather ignorant and inefficient and unable to do much for the people in the way of uplift. They do not speak English and hardly know their own tongue. Some speak Turkish."[48] According to another authority, the priests "come here at an advanced age and never seem to grasp the changes ... in the temper, outlook and demands of the Armenian immigrants, and so adapt themselves and the churches to meet these changes."[49]

Whatever his qualifications, the routine and demands placed upon the local priest were trying. Often poorly educated, as in the Old Country, sometimes merely able to "mumble through the mass," he was expected to attend to the many requests for religious and social consolation and service in the community. One specific task was to visit the sick and infirm, not only in his own community, but in the neighboring towns as well; the death of an Apostolic Armenian even in a faraway state called for an Armenian priest to administer the last rites. Priests also received hundreds of requests from orphans, immigrants in difficulty with the courts or the police, or seeking housing, hospital care, or money. Priests were also responsible for the local Armenian church school.

The local priest occasionally battled with his parish council, and sometimes members of the parish council sought to use the church for political ends. Often, too, the self-made men who comprised the majority of the parish councils felt that their financial support of the priests ("we pay his wages") permitted them to dictate policy about the governance of the church. In response, the more educated priests bristled that parish councillors did not comprehend how much they, the priests, sacrificed for the parish; that Armenians in America were "too free" and "too critical" in comparison with the Old World; and that the priest, as president of the parish council and spokesman of the Holy See in local parish deliberations, was the principal authority in the parish with virtual veto power. One result of such clashing conceptions of authority and the unremitting and bitter political struggles was a very rapid turnover of priests on the local level. In Providence nine different priests served the parish in the years 1897–1913 (one embittered parishioner termed six or seven of them "mediocrities"), and a historian of the Worcester parish listed a total of eight different parish priests between 1900 and 1912.[50]

Uneducated parish priests were often objects of ridicule and scorn. Some few were unethical and shamed the immigrant community. One priest in California was implicated in the abduction of a fourteen-year-old Armenian girl from Fresno to Arizona. The episode ignited the age-old debate about celibacy among the higher clergy. One writer editorialized that "When a group of Armenians gathers, and the conversation turns to the ... priests, practically everyone has a Boccaccio-like episode to tell."[51] The most sordid episode of the period implicated an ordained Armenian vartabed in the blackmailing and subsequent murder of a distinguished Armenian merchant, Hovannes Tavshanjian in New York in 1906. Hevont Vartabed Martoogesian, a professed member of the Reformed Hnchag Party, was also convicted of blackmailing another prominent oriental rug dealer, Mihran Karagheusian, for which crime he served a two-year prison sentence. (Martoogesian returned to the cloth a few years after his release from prison — but in another denomination.)[52]

The second generation also bitterly criticized the priests' "old fashioned ways and service." Specifically, American-educated children bewailed the unintelligible services in the ancient Armenian language (krapar) and the sermons in modern Armenian (ashkharapar). They disliked the torture of sitting on hard wooden benches or standing at long intervals during the liturgy. Some felt nausea from the incense-laden air of the poorly ventilated churches and rented halls. They chafed at the scoldings of outspoken priests for squirming about during the service, and they objected to the "Sunday schools" which were often inadequately equipped and poorly taught.[53]

For every tactless, old-fashioned priest, however, a saintly, self-sacrificing, though perhaps poorly educated cleric administered the sacraments to his flock. Perhaps the most impressive of these was Aharon Vartabed Markarian, who arrived in the United States at the advanced age of seventy, and who successfully ministered to the large parish in Fresno for seven strenuous years.[54]

Armenian communities, like other immigrant communities far from the authority of the mother church, were also afflicted by "hawking clerics." These itinerant, self-proclaimed priests, often with forged papers testifying to their "good character" and years of service in "such and such" a parish, sought the care (and comfort) of a vacant New World parish; others had been defrocked and disgraced in the Old World. In 1913 one George Sarajian even advertised in the Boston Transcript for clerical employment, and thereby disgraced Armenians before the American community.[55] To combat these practices, in 1901 the Armenian Catholicos dispatched to the New World parishes a pastoral letter (gontag) warning communities of such "hawkers", and in 1907 the Armenian Religious Assembly in Constantinople alerted New World parishes to a certain priest in flight from punishment in Turkey. Despite such admonitions, not a few "wandering" priests probably served communities as their clerics, as these colonies, which had been without regular services for often a decade, eagerly hired the imposters to perform the sacred rites of baptism, marriage, and the liturgy.

The Religious Life

Whatever the capabilities of the individual Armenian priests in the United States, it is certain that the religious culture of the Old World was not transplanted to the New. This was reflected not only in the diminution of the numbers of faithful parishioners, but also in the failure of immigrants to observe the rich cycle of religious festivals, holidays, and practices. Such a falling away was, of course, to be expected in view of the geographical scattering of the Armenians in America, the competition of other ethnic agencies such as political parties and lyceums, the trials of the prelacy, the weakness of the priesthood, and the more general secularizing nature of a modern urban industrial society.

To be sure, the great religious festivals of Christmas and Easter did not lose their appeal. Yearly, especially at Easter, hundreds of immigrants flocked to the metropolitan centers to celebrate the Resurrection and worship with their friends and relatives. There they crowded into the tiny, incense laden churches and rented halls to hear the celebration of the ancient mass: to join countrymen and priests in singing the *Hyre Mer* (Our Father) and chanting the *Der Vorormia* (Lord Have Mercy), to receive the *mas* (unleavened bread) and wine, and to hear the priest deliver a sermon on the meaning of the Resurrection.

Easter was also an important social occasion. Upon meeting, Armenians greeted each other with the ancient ritual, saying *"Christos Hariav i Merelotz"* (Christ has risen from the dead) and were answered *"Orhnial e Haroutiun Christosi"* (Blessed is the resurrection of Christ). After the service, on the churches' front steps and overflowing onto the walks, men in black derbies and starched collars, women in long black dresses, and multitudes of children — exchanged greetings, conversation, and gifts. In the church vestry, basement, or social hall, immigrants also took part in the traditional practice of cracking the eggs, symbolically dyed red (with onion skins).

As a ritual, the observance of the Armenian liturgy, celebrated on every Sunday — and on Saturdays, too, if the congregation were sufficiently large — as well as on the major religious holidays, remained unchanged as the central rite of the Armenian Apostolic Church. To this day the only important alteration in the ancient mass is the use of English in the sermon. Churches in the United States also added to the long calendar of days of penance and mourning by the adoption of a day of grieving for the 1894 "Dead of Sasun", and the holocaust of World War I was commemorated on April 24 — the anniversary date of the Turkish governmental edict instituting the deportations of 1915 which resulted in the annihilation of over 1,000,000 Armenians during the war.

On the other hand, much of the Old World religious practice lapsed. For example, the long calendar of Saints' Days, fasts, and festivals was no longer observed in its entirety. One Old Country custom was the celebration of one's patron saint's day instead of one's birthday; thus, a son born near St. Sarkis' Day celebrated that day and not the anniversary of his birth as his "birthday." This practice was shortlived in the United States. Further, although church canons forbade it, saints days celebrated in the Old World on Saturday were instead commemorated in the New World on Sundays, to accommodate immigrants working on Saturdays.[56]

Furthermore, fasting was practiced in the New World only by the older people, especially the women. The Armenian calendar prescribed 160 days of abstinence. (One immigrant remarked that his grandmother, despite her illiteracy, knew all the fast days by rote.)[57] On these days, only vegetables were permitted, for "everything which belongs to the animal kingdom is regarded as meat diet; honey is the only exception."[58] In the Old Country, women in the summer prepared the vegetables and dried fruits consumed on these days. In America, however, the young men without families, and especially immigrants without grandparents, ignored the injunctions about abstinence; working people felt that the strenuous work day of the immigrant required a hearty diet.

More important, the daily matins and vespers, and the worship by the average Armenian on a daily basis for five or ten minutes, the practice of kissing the walls of the church, or at least crossing oneself on passing the sacred building — all these lapsed in busy, industrial America. The decline in Sunday church attendance, everywhere alluded to in the literature of the period, confirmed the growing secular behavior of the immigrant generation.

Clearly the old religious culture weakened and in some respects disappeared entirely. However, much more would have been lost had it not been for the handful of dedicated priests, parish councils, and the hitherto neglected immigrant women. For it was the Armenian women who staunchly supported the mission of the church and its ancillary institutions to preserve the old ways. Specifically, the Sunday schools and Armenian-language schools, though supervised by the local priest, in fact were the sole responsibility of the female parishioners who staffed them, prepared their materials, and furnished their budget. Women also supported church-based charities.

Perhaps because of their greater responsibilities, women's rights in the church were enlarged in the years before 1914. In some cases women assumed a greater role in the conduct of church work itself, as deaconesses. Besides "devoting themselves to general works of mercy," they took a "limited part" in the public services of the church, including assisting the priest during the mass. However, this innovation found little "general favor with the Armenians."[59] Further, in a gontag issued by the Catholicos in 1906, women of age were permitted to vote in parish matters, although their political rights did not extend to participation in the election of the diocesan bishop or the Catholicos.[60]

Despite the advances made by women in the Church, the Old World stricture of segregation of the sexes remained intact in the New. To be sure, the ancient prohibition against women sitting in the nave of the church lapsed. (Prior to the twentieth century women were required to sit only in the galleries, which were screened from the body of the church by a heavy trellis, thereby symbolizing their inferiority).[61] Nevertheless, the principle of female inequality persisted as Patriarch Malachia Ormanian exhorted (1910): "The separation of sexes in the church is always indispensable." Accordingly, in most New World congregations, one half of the nave was given over to women, the other half to the men.[62] However it treated them, the church owed much to the dedicated women who worked ceaselessly — amid all the turmoil of the Apostolic Church — for the preservation of the religious life and the preservation of Armenian culture in America.

The Armenian Protestant Evangelical Church

The second important religious tradition of the immigrants was the Armenian Protestant Evangelical Church, to which 15 or 20 percent of the Armenian American community belonged. The majority of the Armenian Protestants were Congregationalists by denomination; a few were Presbyterians. In addition to Armenian Protestants, there were handfuls of Seventh Day Adventists and Armeno-Catholics.[63]

As newcomers in a strange land, the Protestants fared better than the Apostolics, for they were closer to their historical roots in American Congregationalism, their clergy were well educated, and they lacked the disabling political battles of the Apostolic Church. By the eve of World War I the small minority of Armenian Protestants, with as many churches as the Apostolic, had successfully taken hold in the New World.

Historically, the Armenian Protestant Church was an outgrowth of the nineteenth-century activities in Turkey of the American Board of Commissioners for Foreign Missions, described in Chapter 3. Having arrived in the United States, the Protestant Armenians established their own, separate Armenian Protestant churches. Some joined native American Protestant church groups, but their humiliating experience — in Fresno — taught many of them otherwise.

In 1883 and 1884 a small band of newly arrived Armenian Protestants was encouraged by the San Francisco Congregationalist missionary association to combine with native Fresno Congregationalists to establish a first church in the frontier farming community. The Armenians, who had arrived "poor and friendless" had found "good friends," said an Armenian leader, and "our industry has bettered our condition." The combined communities completed their edifice in 1887, after which Armenian families journeyed on horseback, by wagon, or on foot to the First Congregationalist Church for separate Armenian-language services or joined the English-speaking natives in the Sunday morning services. "We were all happy in the kindness exhibited us," recalled one Armenian. The harmonious union, however, soon succumbed to prejudice and bigotry. As the number of Americans in the congregation grew and the balance of power shifted, the Armenians were no longer welcome. Specifically, a "system of discrimination and persecution against the Armenians" was initiated. The newcomers were ordered to sit by themselves in the church; all hymnbooks and Bibles were removed from their pews; no new Armenians were permitted membership in the church; and finally, their names were stricken from the church membership rolls. All this occurred in the church which they had been invited to help build and support.[64]

The ousted Armenians, who blamed their old clothes, their meagre financial resources, and even perhaps their garlic eating, were publicly defended by the Fresno police chief and in the columns of the Fresno Daily Republican. Editorials in their defense in national religious journals such as the Boston Congregationalist and the New York Outlook made the situation a cause célèbre — to no avail. Instead, the bewildered, outcast Armenian Protestants of Fresno undertook fund raising anew and by 1900 consecrated their second church. This time, however, it was an Armenian Presbyterian Church. In time, a dissident group from the newly formed Presbyterian church started the Armenian Pilgrims Congregationalist Church. After years of services in Edgerly Hall over the Fresno Post Office they purchased their own building, and in 1912 they bought back the original Congregationalist church which had ousted them in 1894, as the native American congregation moved out of the now mainly immigrant neighborhood.[65]

Rising Armenian immigration into California created the need for more Congregationalist churches, which were erected or purchased in the neighboring San Joaquin Valley communities of Fowler

(1907), and Parlier (1911); a Presbyterian church was established in Yettem in 1912. In 1905 Armenians consecrated the Congregationalist Gethsemane Church in Los Angeles. Many Armenian Protestant churches relied on lay or itinerant preachers; all were established wholly independently of the local native American congregations.[66]

In the years after 1890, evangelical activity on the East Coast was no less forceful, but there state and local missionary societies played much more critical roles in founding the immigrant parishes. Like the first Armenian Apostolic Church, the first Armenian Protestant Church in the East was built in Worcester. The earliest services for the Armenian Protestant community took place in 1881 in the immigrant lodgings of an Armenian theology student. With increasing immigration, Sunday prayer meetings were held in the Congregationalist church.[67] In the next years, when the Armenian Apostolics established their own church in the city, the small Protestant group sought assistance from the local Protestant Missionary Association. The American Protestants, some of whom had been missionaries in Turkey, became the critical link in building this religious community and church.

In 1891, for example, American missionaries were holding three Armenian-language services each Sunday in Worcester. They used Bibles and question books written in Armenian and obtained help in singing from American "ladies of other churches." A moving force of the early Worcester community was the Reverend Albert Hitchcock, a former missionary in Turkey who, well-versed in the language and history of the Armenians, had himself written an Armenian prayer book. Throughout the 1890s, the Worcester Missionary Society contributed to the local church group's expenses, including the pastors' entire salaries. Preachers and laymen were also active in Providence, Salem, Lawrence, Whitinsville, Millbury, and Nashua.[68]

The same missionary assistance helped the church structure. In 1900 the Armenian Protestant community in Worcester tried to raise a staggering $9,000 for its first Protestant church in the city. The meager seventy-member congregation's dramatic efforts raised $1,500 from dollar-by-dollar donations and solicitations. The local Protestants, impressed by the "heroic sacrifices" of the small band of immigrants, thereupon donated $6,000 (on the condition of a further Armenian contribution of $1,500) so that on July 14, 1901, the Worcester Armenian Protestant community, which had wandered for twenty years from homes to church halls for worship, joyfully celebrated the cornerstone laying of its Armenian Evangelical Martyrs Church on Pink Street.[69]

During this period, politics played almost as disruptive a role in the Protestant church as in the Apostolic. In 1892 the community had obtained its most popular preacher, Karekin Chitjian, a fiery, inspired nationalist who had been exiled from Turkey. Chitjian attracted many Apostolic brethren into the Protestant fold because of his passionate sermons against the Turkish oppressors. However, Chitjian's unrestrained attacks on the Turks deeply troubled the American Board, which feared repercussions against its personnel and property in the Ottoman Empire for permitting Chitjian to preach in a Protestant pulpit. The missionaries did not scruple to interfere in the church, and Chitjian was dismissed from his post — an act which robbed the parish of its most stalwart supporters. Eventually the diminution of political tensions in the late 1890s and the accession of the "genial and accomplished" Reverend H. G. Benneyan to the pulpit restored the evangelical movement.[70]

By 1900 other Protestant Armenian parishes had been founded in the East. In New York City, for example, the first regular Protestant services were conducted in 1897, through the aid of the Home Mission Society. The YMCA and other missionary groups tried to enroll the immigrant Protestants into native American congregations, but the tiny group did not want to pray in "an *odar*'s (stranger's) church"; the community finally moved into its own church building in 1923.[71]

The only Presbyterian church in the East was established in Troy, New York, in 1906. There the American Board (Congregationalist) discouraged the immigrants from building their own Armenian Congregationalist church. At the same time the local Presbyterian synod offered financial assistance if the Armenians adopted the Presbyterian affiliation — which they did. By World War I Congregationalist churches had also been built or purchased in West Hoboken, Boston, Lawrence, Lowell, Providence, and Philadelphia.[72]

The only Protestant congregation in the Midwest was established in 1901 when Garabed Pushman, the philanthropic oriental rug dealer in Chicago, rented a hall in the Chicago Commons to preach once a month to the local Protestant Armenians. The Protestant communities in Chicago, West Pullman, and Waukegan, and East St. Louis were chiefly ministered to by itinerant pastors.[73]

The building of New World churches and the beginnings of religious services in rented halls or churches in smaller communities in the United States completed one major task for the tiny Protestant Armenian community. However, there remained other challenges — nurturing the religious life, and keeping their parishioners (especially the younger generation) in the fold. In striving for these goals, the Protestant Armenian approach differed sharply from that of their Apostolic brethren. The Apostolic Church stressed the preservation of the old culture in the New World. Repeatedly, the Apostolic priests emphasized fidelity to Armenian traditions, the language, the family, and marriage within the group. By contrast, the Protestants acted as a willing acculturating mechanism in the New World. The Protestants did not emphasize the need to keep the old language and culture. Rather, while seeking to bring the Armenians to Christ, they promoted the adoption of New World and American ways. The Armenian Protestant Church was a willing halfway house between the old religious culture and the twentieth century in America.

To be sure, Armenian Protestant ministers (*badvellis*) resolutely affirmed their Armenian patriotism. "We are not to grow just as a 'church' or any other church, but grow as an *Armenian* church," testified the Reverend A. A. Bedikian, a saintly and generous leader of the Armenian Protestant Church.[74] And the Old World language was exclusively used in the early services. In fact, there were also allowances for the Turkish-speaking members of the congregations who came from Adana or Marash. The Second Armenian Congregational Church of Philadelphia had the unusual distinction of a regular bilingual service: the badvelli delivered a sermon in Armenian, then one in Turkish, on different topics since some of his parishioners knew both languages. Hymns from Elmassian's bilingual hymnal were sung in Armenian and Turkish simultaneously which made it sound, said one young Armenian Protestant, like a Tower of Babel.[75] In any case, Armenian was an integral part of the earliest Protestant services.

In time, however, English supplanted Armenian in the churches, especially for the younger generation, who were insufficiently versed in Armenian to follow services in that language. William Saroyan recalled that in Fresno in the 1920s the entire service, except for the sermon, was carried out in English.[76] In the 1930s, the Philadelphia congregation, which used Turkish and Armenian, added English for trilingual services for some years.[77]

In this connection it appears that the badvellis, unlike the Apostolic priests, rarely urged their parishioners to speak the ancestral language at home. Whereas in an Apostolic parish many sermons each year were devoted to encouraging use of the language, especially among the young, this was not true in Protestant congregations. Indeed, nationalistic Armenians berated the Protestants for permitting the language to lapse and quoted one badvelli as saying: "For me, there is no Armenia, only America. We left Armenian things in Turkish Armenia; here we must be Americans. I am an American and I teach my children no Armenian."[78] Religious themes rather than nationalistic injunctions or stories about Armenian history formed the core of the sermons of the Protestant Armenians.

More important, the badvellis were English-speaking, American-educated (in colleges in Turkey), and knowledgeable; this was of inestimable assistance in acculturating the bewildered and helpless immigrants to the demands of urban America. Again, by contrast with the Apostolic priests, many of whom encountered adjustment problems of their own, the Armenian badvellis aided newcomers in a host of ways: writing letters in English, making bank deposits, purchasing land or property, and dealing with immigration authorities, the courts, or the law. Armenians seeking work were placed in jobs. The well-educated and well-spoken Armenian Protestant ministers — William Saroyan recalled that one "spoke a crisp, almost classic English, with just a touch of dry, brittle style or accent, which made his English seem authentic and mine (for instance) haphazard" — also helped immigrants cleanse their reputations as strikebreakers.[79]

Indeed, by 1901 much Protestant effort had gone into immigrant assistance through the Armenian Colonial Association, which maintained offices in Marseilles, New York, and Chicago to aid newcomers. The ACA was of incalculable assistance to the immigrants at the major stopping port of Marseilles and at Ellis Island in providing funds, advice, and ultimately jobs.[80] Informally, the badvellis' close personal ties with prominent American missionaries and churchmen provided another vital resource for immigrants in America.

In addition, Armenian ministers adopted such American innovations as Sunday schools and Christian Endeavor societies to fuse evangelical Christianity and social ethics. These and the young men's and young women's lyceums, meeting once or twice weekly, were often devoted to informing immigrants about life in the American city and gave talks on such topics as the proper diet for the city family, life in the tenement, child care, and the necessity for exercise in the city.[81]

From the pulpits the badvellis also inculcated their congregations with the ethical core of modern American Congregationalism, and the temptations of the new urban environment were not neglected. Emphasis was placed on ethics, biblical literalism, and abstinence. Indeed, abstinence from drink was an eleventh commandment. Thus, badvellis severely rebuked Armenian picnic-goers who drank beer or raki (oghie); Armenian coffeehouses were termed places not of relaxation but of dissipation. Drinking, smoking, gambling, and modern "breast to breast" dancing were all condemned.[82] Although criticized in California along with the Apostolic clerics for neglecting the education of the young regarding city temptations,[83] the badvellis generally administered a heavy dose of fundamentalist American morality. Indeed, the injunctions against such activities were so strong that one son of an Armenian minister remembered the feeling that "anything that brought supreme pleasure was wrong."[84]

The core of the badvellis' message emphasized modern American Protestant religious dogma and social ethics. However, it would be an error to equate the immigrant Protestant churches with the wealthy American Congregationalist or Presbyterian churches of the period. Most were small and poverty stricken, and not a few members of the younger generation, offended by the "immigrant" or "old country" status of the churches, sought religious consolation in American churches. Thus one girl wrote of the Protestant church services in a rented hall in Boston:

[The room] was sparse and wretched. . . . There were sparse old wooden chairs on a dirty wooden floor, . . . a huge old piano with thick legs and feet. . . . The pulpit was nothing more than a small wooden platform with an oak bookstand. On it sits a Bible with a worn out cover. . . . There are hymnals without covers scattered here and there. [As for the atmosphere of the place] there is the smell of smoke and onions. . . . There is confusion — women bring their children who play or quarrel . . . while the infants are being suckled. . . . The *badvelli* starts the service . . . assisted by a boy at the piano . . . and the congregation, out of tune, joins them.[85]

The distasteful associations of the immigrant church were so strong that one second-generation badvelli who was called to the pastorate of an Armenian Protestant church in New England insisted that the church discard all old furniture, hand-me-down lamps, second-hand pianos, rugs and dilapidated furnishings which recalled the immigrant days of rented halls and poverty.[86] Indeed the jump from the Old World to respectability took more than one generation.

The early history of the Protestant church in the United States sharply differed from that of the Apostolic Church. Relatively untroubled by the savage political disputes of the Apostolics, and assisted by American church bodies, the Protestant churches rapidly adjusted to the New World. Moreover, they represented, willingly and forcefully, an important mediating step between the Old Country and the New. Their parishioners more quickly learned English, adopted new ways, made their life in the United States, and became "Americanized." Thus, Protestant Armenians formed a separate social and psychological community in the United States. Unquestionably, with respect to the role of the Armenian churches in the New World, the paramount and undeniable difference between the two churches lay in the area of acculturation. One — the Apostolic — stood staunchly and resolutely for the preservation in toto of the Old; this was its historic justification, its rationale, and a source of its weakness. It was also its glory. On the other hand, there was the smaller, equally poor, but more modernizing Armenian Protestant Church, which stood halfway between the Old and the New.

PART FOUR

Politics: The Call of the Homeland

11.

The Hamidean Massacres, 1894–1896

Preparation: The Origins to 1894

The Old World Background. In the quarter century between 1890 and the outbreak of World War I, the Armenians in America threw themselves into the political struggle against their nation's oppressors in Turkey and Russia. That struggle stemmed from the harassment and plundering of the Armenian Christians in Turkey, an awakened sense among the Armenians of their rights, and the failure of Turkey and of the West to ensure conditions of stability and security for the Armenians. Chapter 3 discussed how the question of reforms for the Armenian population (the Armenian Question) first arose after the Russo-Turkish War of 1878 and how the European Concert (England, France, Germany, Italy, Austria, and Russia) agreed in the Treaty of Berlin (Article LXI) to alleviate the plight of the Armenians, who had suffered greviously during the hostilities. Unfortunately, despite the efforts of the British, no action was taken to make the sultan reform.

Despite Europe's betrayal of their cause, the overwhelming majority of Armenians clung to the Berlin Treaty as the way to obtain reforms. Repeatedly, they petitioned the signatory powers and even the United States to enforce Article LXI, in which the Sublime Porte had agreed to immediate, sweeping reforms for the Armenians. Increasingly, however, Armenian nationalists, frustrated by the Turks' intransigence and the failure of Great Power diplomacy, and buoyed by the example of the Greek and Balkan peoples in obtaining liberation from Turkish rule, moved to more radical steps.

The earliest liberation movements were the "defenders of the homeland," and the Armenagans at Erzerum and Van in Eastern Turkey.[1] By the late 1880s and early 1890s, however, full fledged paramilitary radical and socialist political groups had arisen to wrest Turkish Armenia from Ottoman rule. A terrible conflict ensued. And Armenian communities everywhere unceasingly contributed manpower, money, and political and diplomatic efforts for their brethren in Turkey; the Armenian community in the United States was especially important in these efforts. Indeed, few immigrant groups were so immersed in their countrymen's Old World struggles. But, as the bitter struggle over the momentous issues and events in Turkey progressed, it brought discord and division to the immigrant world. Driven by the frustration of exile and the sanguinary example of Old World tactics, the political groups did not hesitate to use violence and political assassination to support their arguments. Frequently they singled out as enemies fellow Armenians who disagreed with them. At the same time, to advance their respective causes, the parties also established important institutions in the United States. The immigrant press was the parties' creation: virtually every successful Armenian-language journal in the New World was the organ of a political party. The parties organized youth groups, reading rooms, and women's organizations, and they fostered educational forums. They also promoted repatriation to the Old Country.

The political struggles of the Armenians reached beyond ethnic enclaves to the wider non-Armenian community. The United States repeatedly expressed its political and humanitarian support for Christian Armenia, and the Armenian Question loomed large, especially during the massacres of the mid-1890s.

Early Stirrings: The Hnchags from 1888 to 1894. It was in the late 1880s, in the tumultuous decade following the Treaty of Berlin, that the Armenian Question was introduced to the immigrant community in the United States. Although revolutionary groups had been coalescing in the Old World, the first step in preparing for the immigrants' organization was taken in 1888 by Mgerdich Portukalian, the nationalist editor of *Armenia* who had been banished from Turkey for his political teachings in Van. Portukalian, who was not affiliated with the major revolutionary parties, had sparked the Armenians in Worcester to found the Armenian Academy (Chapter 10).[2] On the same trip, to raise funds for *Armenia*, he fired up immigrants in New York with his encouraging forecasts and news from the Old Country. In Worcester 250 Armenians crowded into a downtown hall to hear him describe Turkish outrages, then counsel preparation for the coming storm against the Turks. But his trip also raised the hackles of the local Protestants who feared that sponsorship of Portukalian would trigger Turkish reprisals against missionaries.[3] In Portukalian's view, the Armenians lacked the experience for immediate insurrection; rather, he urged long-range preparation, especially in military training, and the formation of a "large, strong and wealthy organization" to resolve the Armenian Question.[4] However, Portukalian's mission was a personal, discrete event which left no enduring party structure, cells, or political network. It was an incidental episode in the community's history. The challenge of developing political organizations lay rather in the hands of the major political parties.

The first permanent political organization to assert Armenian rights in Turkey and to set up a political structure in the United States was the Social Democratic Hnchagian Party, which was founded in Geneva in 1887 by the Russian Armenian Avedis Nazarbeg, his fiancée Maro — a dedicated revolutionary who had been exiled from St. Petersburg because of her revolutionary activities — and other Russian Armenian students, all in their twenties.[5] The Hnchags immediately began publishing their journal, *Hnchag* (The Clarion) in Geneva. In it they evinced a doctrinaire socialist creed which borrowed heavily from Marx, Lasalles, and especially Herzen (*Hnchag* was an obvious imitation of *Kolokol*). The objective of the Hnchags was to overthrow the Ottoman Empire and then usher in a socialist Armenian republic in which Armenians from Turkey, Persia, and Russia would all join.[6]

To effect such ends the Hnchagist leader Nazarbeg and his colleagues in Geneva planned to employ propaganda, terror, and assassination against Turks and Armenian traitors and spies. At the same time they would ignite a far flung insurrectionary movement among all Turkey's disaffected minorities, including the Cretans, Macedonians, and Albanians. Once Turkey's countryside was in flames and bloodied, the Hnchags believed that the European powers would intervene to establish an Armenian republic as they had intervened in the Balkans and Bulgaria in 1877–1878.[7]

Hnchag organizational activity began in Turkish Armenian centers in 1888 and 1889; in 1890, Hnchags fomented anti-Turkish demonstrations in Erzerum and Constantinople.[8] Soon after they set up New World branches of the party in New York, Providence, Worcester, Boston, Lowell, Lawrence, Lynn, Malden, and Nashua.[9]

The principal early Hnchag organizers in the United States were Nishan Garabedian and Karekin Chitjian. A Protestant minister in Turkey, Chitjian had been banished for his inflammatory activity against the Ottoman government. He settled in Worcester where the City Missionary Society placed him in the pastorate of the local Armenian Protestant congregation, but they removed him when he began again to preach the revolution to the immigrant parishioners. (See Chapter 10.) Chitjian thereafter devoted himself to Hnchag fieldwork.[10]

Chitjian's co-organizer of Hnchag activity, Nishan Garabedian, was also known as Khan Azad. Garabedian, who had been one of the party's founders in Geneva in 1887, had traveled through the Caucasus and Turkey organizing students and intellectuals. (When he consulted with the venerable Khrimian, Armenian patriarch of Constantinople and later Catholicos, the religious leader told him; "You are crazy; the Armenians are a very small nation, and how much blood will have to be shed.") Garabedian was dispatched to the New World by Hnchag founder Nazarbeg as his personal emissary, fund-raiser, and delegate of the party's central committee.[11]

The major instrument of early Hnchag activity in the United States was the public rally. In Worcester, passionate public meetings full of patriotic songs and fiery speeches attracted 600 to 700 immigrants. There, the hopeful audience heard Garabedian report that the revolution was near: "There are general imbroglios developing every day near Diarbekir, in Sasoon, Dersim and Bitlis. If they have not yet been favorable, they are to be in these three months" (July 1893).[12] At other meetings, Bedros Keljik, a Garabedian lieutenant, urged armed resistance; pointing to pictures of swords, cannon, and rifles on the walls, he intoned: "They show that liberty can be gained only by force of arms. . . . We can free ourselves from this slavery . . . only by resort to arms. Let us then drill with firearms."[13]

Hnchag followers also heard appeals for money. At a meeting commemorating the third anniversary of the Constantinople demonstration of 1890, Garabedian stated: "Revolutionary war requires excessive expenses. To send a revolutionary letter to any part of the country costs $2 to $3. If a man flees to the mountains, it costs money to support him there. Firearms must be purchased."[14] By 1894 Garabedian had raised $10,000 in the United States.[15]

The Hnchags' Marxist ideology soon stirred controversy within the party. Garabedian and his colleagues lectured to immigrants on "The Question of Class and Labor," "Bourgeoisie and Proletariat," and "The Landlord and the Landless," and they cultivated relationships with leading Russian and Jewish socialist intellectuals in the United States. Despite the powerful rhetoric of Garabedian and Chitjian, Hnchag followers in Malden, Lynn, and elsewhere objected that European socialism was irrelevant to the Armenian plight.[16] Others feared the stigma of an "anarchist plot." In response, in the wake of the Pullman Strike and the anarchist assassination of French Prime Minister Carnot, Garabedian in July 1894 stated that anarchy was directly "opposed to the principles of socialism," and that he abhorred Carnot's assassin.[17] However, pitched battles and fistfights broke up Hnchag rallies over these issues. Party regulars also attacked the Hnchag leadership for premature promptings of revolutionary demonstrations in Turkey which would only invite savage Turkish retaliation on innocent Armenians. Rather, these Hnchags counseled the party to plan and prepare, with utmost secrecy, in advance of further demonstrations.[18]

Notwithstanding the party's inner trials, the Armenian community responded enthusiastically to Hnchag rhetoric. According to the *Worcester Daily Telegram*, one-third of the Apostolic Church members in Worcester and a "majority of the Congregationalist converts, including the more intelligent of them, are leading members of the Huntchagist Party."[19] Even nonmembers of the party were enthusiastic: Dr. M. Smpad Kaprielian — physician; editor of *Haik*, one of the very few Armenian-language papers of the time in America; and no Hnchag regular — warmly endorsed the most radical "system of Hentchaguin, viz, to organize bands at once." "Experience has shown," wrote Kaprielian, "that the political reconstruction of the nation through diplomatic action is impossible. Positive and energetic means are needed in order to bring about diplomatic intervention. Those means are fire and sword. . . ." Kaprielian even sanctioned cataclysm: "We must lose, if necessary, one half of the nation for the sake of saving the other half." (1893)[20]

Opposition to the Hnchag effort.   In the early 1890s fierce external opposition to the Hnchags arose from three principal quarters: the Armenian Apostolic Church, American missionaries, and the Turkish government in Washington. Reference has already been made (Chapter 10) to the opposition of Father Sarajian and his successor, Father Deroonian, to Hnchag propaganda in the Armenian Academy in Worcester. Far more conspicuous was the unremitting attack on the Hnchags by the American missionary establishment. In 1892 inflammatory placards had been posted at the American college at Marsovan, a step which led local Turks to believe that the missionary institution was a "hotbed of revolutionary ideas and must be destroyed."[21] To counter these fears prominent missionaries entered the lists against the revolutionaries.

The most influential assault on the Hnchags was delivered by Dr. Cyrus Hamlin, founder of Robert College in Constantinople and a well-known authority on Turkey and the Armenians, who enjoyed the confidence of many statesmen and politicians. Hamlin charged in the *Congregationalist* in 1893 that an Armenian revolutionary party was causing "great evil and suffering" to the "missionary work" and to the "whole Christian population" of Turkish Armenia. To Hamlin, the Hnchag design was no less than a *deliberate* plot to foment revolution and *massacres* of innocent Armenians — to secure Western intervention in Turkey. A prominent Armenian had thus explained to Hamlin:

These Huntchaguist bands, organized all over the Empire, will watch their opportunity to kill Turks and Koords, set fire to their villages, and then make their escape into the mountains. The enraged Moslems will then rise and fall upon the defenseless Armenians and slaughter them with such barbar-

ities that Russia will enter, in the name of humanity and Christian civilization, and take possesssion.

Because of this, Hamlin urged all missionaries, "home and foreign" to denounce the Hnchags in the strongest terms imaginable.[22]

At about the same time, the Reverend Albert Hitchcock, working among the Armenian Protestants in Worcester and in sympathy with the plight of Armenians in Turkey, warned of the insuperable obstacles in the way of liberation as espoused by the Hnchags. First, the 2,500,000 Armenians in Turkey lacked weapons and military training, and they were grossly outnumbered by the 15,000,000 Muslim Turks and Kurds, some of whom were veterans of the Russo-Turkish War of 1877–1878. Second, a revolutionary movement would bring on a "very horrible massacre and suffering for the Armenians." Third, there was no possibility of a viable Armenian state carved out of Turkey, given the preponderance of Muslims in Turkish Armenia. In sum, Armenia was not Bulgaria, and revolution was a criminal error.[23]

By the early 1890s the Turkish minister in Washington was also mounting an attack on the Hnchags in the United States. One significant area aggravating the Turkish government was the rabidly anti-Turkish propaganda in the Armenian-language press. In 1893 the Turkish minister alerted the American Secretary of State to "articles in the Armenian journals published in London, in Marseilles, in Athens, and even in New York" — preaching resistance to the Turks. To thwart the propaganda, the minister proposed that "such Ottoman subjects as would come to the United States and attempt there to publish, with obvious malicious intent, newspapers or pamphlets . . . be delivered to us [emphasis added]."[24] That is, the United States government should voluntarily hand over Armenians to the Turkish government for justice. (It was a request the State Department categorically denied.)

Military recruitment and training of Hnchags on American soil for service against the Turks likewise angered the Turkish minister. In January 1894 Mavroyeni Bey complained to the Secretary of State that 30 Armenians in New York "proposed to engage in military drill in order that, upon occasion, they may be prepared, as they openly declare through their journals, to disturb order and tranquility in Turkey." In June, Mavroyeni, quoting the Hnchag Karekin Chitjian, charged that the Hnchag party was training Armenians in the United States to "spread the spirit of revolt" in Turkey. And in July, he rebuked the city of New York for permitting a band of Armenians to march and make "incendiary speeches" against Turkish misrule. All such charges were diplomatically turned aside by the State Department.[25]

Picnickers. Armenian group dancing often featured male soloists; the women are in the background only.

Tavloo (backgammon) players at an Armenian club.

Boghos Nubar Pasha,
distinguished Armenian
statesman and founder of the
AGBU.

The New York AGBU Orphanage Committee. Front, from left to right: Mrs. S.
Telfeyan, Mrs. M. Karagheusian, Mrs. H. Hagopian, Mrs. V. Kitabjian, Mrs. A.
Bedikian; standing, Mrs. H. Tavshanjian, Mrs. H. Gulbenkian, Mrs. B.
Costikyan, Mrs. H. Kelegian.

The Reverend Antranig
Bedikian (1962), pillar of the
Armenian Protestant Church
in America.

First Diocesan Assembly, July 1902, Clergy left to right:
Hevont Vartabed Martoogesian, Arsen Vartabed Vehooni,
Bishop Hovsep Sarajian, Mashtots Vartabed Papazian.

Surp Prgich (Holy Saviour), Worcester, built in 1891.

"**Արդեօք, գալու է
մի օր, ժամանակ՝
Տեսնել Մասիս
Գլխին մի դրօշակ...
Եւ ամէն կողմից
պանդուխտ հայազգիք
Դիմեն դէպ իւրեանց
սիրուն հայրենիք:** "

Raffi, literary father of the Armenian national movement. "Is it possible that a day or time will come when our flag will be seen on the summit of Mt. Ararat . . . and from every corner of the earth exiled Armenians will return to their beloved homeland?"

Karekin Chitjian, an ordained Protestant minister who was ousted from the church for his nationalistic speeches. He then became a founder of the Reformed Hnchag Party and an editor of *Tzain Haireneats*. A martyr of the revolutionary cause, he was assassinated in Odessa in 1903.

E. Agnooni, charismatic Tashnag leader, founder
of the Armenian Relief Society.

Souren Bartevian, writer and leader of the
Reformed Hnchag Party.

Arshag Vramian, editor of *Hairenik*,
Tashnag journal in Boston.

Young Armenian Americans training to
be *fedayees* (guerrilla fighters).

Armenian *fedayees* in Turkey.

Three generations of the Hovsep Gulesian family in
Marash, Turkey, in 1892.

The Gulesian family ten years later in Boston in 1902.

Certainly the most controversial action taken by the Turkish government against the Hnchags before 1894 was its attempt to bar suspected party members from returning to the Ottoman Empire, especially if they were American citizens. According to the Turks, an Ottoman subject could not become a citizen of another nation unless granted specific permission to do so by the sultan — a doctrine which all western nations — except Russia — refused to acknowledge. Any resident of the United States who complied with statutory requirements could become an American citizen. What troubled the Turks most was the fact that the Turkish American Treaty of 1830 (Article IV) gave American citizens on Turkish soil immunity from arrest and punishment by Ottoman officials. If Turkish officials acceded to this, the danger from returning Hnchags was crystal clear, and indeed, by the early 1890s, suspected Armenian revolutionaries began to debark at Ottoman ports with American passports — as American citizens — and claim that they were immune from Turkish law.[26]

Accordingly, in 1892 the Turks branded such naturalized returning Armenian Americans as "illegal charges" and forbade them to enter the empire; in 1893, they sought to debar most Armenians returning to Turkey, and in 1894 they imprisoned unoffending Armenians, "tore up, flung away" American passports, refused to permit jailed Armenians to contact American officials, and harassed returning Armenian women and children.[27] In response, the American government, which was furious at the "Sick Man of Europe's" contemptuous treatment of American nationals, defended their rights in Turkey but compromised with the Turks (1893) by permitting them to debar from the empire any Armenian Americans whom they deemed undesirable.[28] However, the troublesome question of the rights of naturalized Armenians of Turkish origin was not resolved until 1908.

Up until 1894, the primary manifestation of the Armenian struggle in the United States was the presence of the Hnchag party. The party had met with considerable opposition from the Ottoman regime, the American missionary establishment, and the Armenian Apostolic Church. Still, it had led the Armenian immigrant community to organize, raise funds, and issue propaganda for the Armenian cause.

Phase One: Sasun

While Armenians in the United States were organizing their rudimentary political parties, in the Old World a new and fearful chapter in the Armenian struggle was unfolding. In 1892, the Hnchag

Party selected Sasun, in remote Eastern Turkey, for the scene of their
first "grand coup" against the sultan.[29] For generations Armenian
villagers and shepherds in Sasun had dwelled side by side with
Kurdish nomads in a rough peace, the Armenians paying feudal dues
to Kurdish tribal chiefs in exchange for protection. But beginning in
1892 Hnchag leaders preached resistance—"an eye for an eye, a tooth
for a tooth"—to the rugged, warlike Sasunli villagers whom the
Hnchags reckoned would "put up a hard fight."[30] Then, in August
1894 the Sasunlis raised the Hnchag standard of revolt by withhold-
ing feudal dues and resisting Kurdish demands for them. It was the
first such uprising in the Armenian revolutionary movement.

The Ottoman response was prompt and brutal. Probably forewarned of the uprising, the Turks rushed their cossack-like Hamidié
regiments (Kurdish cavalry) and an Ottoman army to Sasun with
instructions to spare "neither man, woman nor child." Whole Armenian settlements—Shenig, Semal, Gueilligeozan, Alants, Dalvorig—
were destroyed, and villages wholly innocent of the insurrection
were decimated. Cattle and sheep were stolen; inhabitants were rout-
ed from their homes, then cut down; buildings were plundered and
then burned. In all, the Turkish and Kurdish attackers obliterated 25
villages and massacred between 10,000 and 20,000 Armenians.[31] The
fears that Hnchag demonstrations would lead to rivers of blood had
been realized.

News of the massacres did not immediately reach the western
world because the region of Sasun was remote and entry was restricted by a Turkish military cordon. By late November 1894, however,
English and American newspapers were carrying missionary and
refugee accounts of massive losses of life amid fearsome atrocities.

The most immediate reactions came from the outraged Armenian
communities in the United States. Immediately all factions—Apostolic and Protestant, Hnchag and liberal—united in protest marches,
petitions to Congress, mass public meetings, and feverish declamations. In Chicago during the week of November 20 "several hundred"
Armenians and sympathizers, although disavowing the use of arms
against the Turks—"it would be folly to rise up against our oppressors"—staunchly protested the atrocities at Sasun and vowed to propagandize their message among Americans and the American
press.[32]

On November 25 in Worcester at the "largest Armenian meeting
ever held," where "every Armenian in the city was present, including
a number of women," a united front led by the Apostolic priest,
Father Deroonian, the Protestant Rev. K. G. Kemalian, and the
Hnchag M. G. Seron, after five hours of fevered, "exciting debate"
resolved to petition the British government and the other signatories

of the Berlin Treaty to enforce Article LXI to "put an end to the rule of anarchy and lawlessness." The meeting, which held "Perfidious Albion" responsible for the Sasun massacre by her utter neglect of Article LXI, appointed a committee of prominent Armenians to present Armenia's case before the European powers. Three days later, on Thanksgiving Day, mourning Armenians attended services at Worcester's Armenian Protestant and Apostolic churches, and a *Worcester Daily Telegram* reporter noted in *Surp Prgich* "cloaked in black" a "low sobbing of the minority of women in the gallery mingled with strange restlessness among the men." Then nearly 400 Armenians with black armbands solemnly paraded through downtown Worcester.[33] Similar protest meetings in Boston, Lynn, Chelsea, Lowell, and Lawrence dispatched resolutions to Washington and collected funds, some down to the immigrants' "last penny," to finance the committee's tour of Europe on behalf of Bleeding Armenia. At Christmas a national assembly of prominent Armenians of all affiliations convened in Worcester under the chairmanship of Father Deroonian to "work for the promotion of Armenian political aspirations and justice in Turkey."[34]

Although their reaction was prompt and unified against the outrages at Sasun, the Armenians by themselves lacked the numbers, the experience, and the wherewithal to influence western policy toward the Turks. More powerful voices were needed to sway the American response, and those voices came from a surprisingly militant Protestant establishment.

The American animus toward the "Terrible Turk" was longstanding. Since the eighteenth century, writers, political figures, and publicists had labeled the Ottoman Empire the perfect example of a corrupt and vicious oriental despotism. And the atrocities which the Greek and Balkan peoples suffered at the hands of the Turks in the nineteenth century sharpened the image of the Turks as bloodthirsty infidels capable of the most barbarous killings of Christians. These factors and the atrocity stories flowing from Sasun (little was said of the role of the Hnchags in stirring the crisis), set amidst the growing nationalism of America in the 1890s, soon produced a bellicose outcry among a host of Protestant and pro-Armenian groups.[35]

In Worcester in November, for example, several hundred agitated Americans, led by the mayor and the city's most prominent bankers, attorneys, and clergy, in an atmosphere like a revival meeting, denounced the "unspeakable Turk," chanted for "Armenian home-rule" and "Armenia for the Armenians," and drafted militant resolutions to President Grover Cleveland. The meeting called the Sasun massacre "unprovoked" and contemptuously dismissed the possibility of an Armenian uprising at Sasun.[36] Like many others of its kind, a petition to Congress signed by the ministers of the Congregational and Methodist churches in Marlboro, New Hampshire, called on the United States government to "secure investigation by an accredited representative of our government into the recent massacre of Christian Armenians . . . and to secure redress for and prevent any such brutalities." In early January, the Young Men's Baptist Social Union of Boston remonstrated "against the recent atrocious crime against Armenian Christians." Even the State Grange of Delaware united in prayer urging Congress to enact federal "legislation to prevent the cruel and barbarous treatment of the Armenian Christians by Turkish soldiers."[37]

Joining the outcry were the influential Friends of Armenia. Founded in 1893 as a cultural society dedicated to Armenian literature and folklore, its leaders included Alice Stone Blackwell—the gentle, determined, wispy haired daughter of the eminent humanitarians, Lucy Stone and Henry Blackwell—thereafter America's single most important champion of the Armenians; the Reverend Samuel Barrows, editor of the *Christian Register*; the Reverend Edward Everett Hale; and America's foremost crusader for human rights, Julia Ward Howe. In 1894 assisted by two Armenian businessmen, Hagop Bogigian and Moses Gulesian, the Friends of Armenia flooded Washington and the American press with pro-Armenian petitions and letters on the crisis.[38]

The State Department in Washington had received no word from Judge A. W. Terrell, its eccentric minister in Constantinople, as late as the last week in November. In its absence, the government relied on the atrocity stories in the press and petitions streaming into Washington. At the same time, it received the official Turkish version of the events: the criminal acts of "Armenian brigands" had instigated the trouble, and their deliberate torture of neighboring Kurds incited the disturbance. According to the Turkish version, the Armenians, to cast a bad light on the Turks, had looted their own villages in Sasun. Instead of the 25 villages purportedly "wiped out," the Turkish forces had merely "restored public order and tranquility to the satisfaction of all."[39] When Terrell's report came on November 28, it embraced the official Turkish account: "Reports of American papers of Turkish atrocities at Sassoun are sensational and exaggerated."[40] In the meantime, the Turkish government, though categorically denying any wrong-doing, acceded to English and European demands for an inquiry and the punishment of wrongdoers.[41]

The United States Congress did not let the subject rest. On December 3, Senator Newton Blanchard of Louisiana labeled the "indiscriminate massacre of thousands of men, women, and children" a "blot upon the civilization of the age, meriting the severest condemnation of mankind." On the same day, Congress passed a joint resolution calling on the White House to provide full information regarding cruelties to American citizens or to those declaring their intention to become naturalized citizens, and further, a report on any diplomatic steps taken by the United States.[42]

To the congressional resolution, President Cleveland replied that he had no information regarding injuries to American citizens, or citizens-to-be, therefore he made no "expostulations . . . to the Government of Turkey." Further, because the United States was not a signatory of the Berlin Treaty, Cleveland maintained that American interference might be "embarrassing." Finally, Cleveland offered no sympathy for the Armenian victims of Sasun. It was no wonder, therefore, that the Armenian community, outraged over Cleveland's inertia, retorted: "There is a saying in the old country that Mr. Blaine [Secretary of State, 1889–1892, and a staunch America-Firster] is dead, but there may yet be a man like him in the presidential chair. Day by day they [the Armenians] count the remaining days of Grover's reign."[43]

At this point the pro-Turkish forces in the United States sought publicly to vindicate their government and discredit the pro-Armenian propaganda in the United States. In mid-November 1894 the Turkish minister, Marvoyeni Bey, in a letter to the *New York Herald*, was the first to defend his country. Seeking to refute step by step the widely held accounts of the massacres, he blamed the killings entirely on the "criminal acts of Armenian brigands." To fortify his argument, the minister recalled the testimony of Dr. Cyrus Hamlin prior to Sasun that the Hnchags were preparing to incite bloodshed to erect an Armenian state in Turkey. If Hamlin, a pro-Armenian, called the Hnchags bloodthirsty fanatics, *surely he knew the truth.* On the following day, Hamlin charged in anger that the minister had distorted his earlier criticism; to Hamlin, "the plots of the revolutionists were harmless" and the work of a few "hair-brained young men." Accordingly, Hamlin bitterly regretted that the "Ottoman Ambassador should attempt to cover up the . . . horrid atrocities which have agitated the whole Christian world. . . ."[44]

Soon afterward General Lew Wallace, former American minister to Turkey and author of *Ben Hur*, took to the lecture circuit to discredit the Armenians. To Wallace, a massacre of the Armenians ordered by the sultan was unthinkable, for Abdul Hamid was a humanitarian. Had he not contributed to the Jamestown, Virginia, flood victims in 1893? In fact Wallace even likened the sultan to Abraham Lincoln! (In rebuttal, Alice Stone Blackwell of the Friends of Armenia, among others, vigorously refuted the general's incredible contentions.)[45] Then, in early 1895 an interesting, anonymously written pamphlet, *The Armenian Troubles and Where the Responsibility Lies*, appeared. The pamphlet, probably penned by the Turkish minister, not only exonerated the sultan but lashed out against the "pro-Christian and pro-Armenian journalism" in the United States. Ascribing the entire responsibility for Sasun to the Hnchags, it argued that the sultan had no alternative but to suppress the uprising. "The mere idea," claimed the apologia, that "the Sultan would order a massacre of his Christian subjects, Armenians or no Armenians, is ridiculous in itself, and denotes a credulous belief in the falsehoods and calumnies propagated by the Armenian revolutionary committees."[46]

Whatever effect the pro-Turkish charges had was undercut in early 1895 by the growing stream of reports and books on the atrocities at Sasun. One critical source was Emil Dillon, the highly respected British correspondent of the *London Daily Telegram*, who traveled to Turkey just after Sasun. Dillon's widely circulated accounts carried detailed horror stories from eyewitnesses and refugees. More important in the United States was Frederick Greene's *The Armenian Crisis in Turkey*, which appeared in April 1895. Greene, a missionary in Turkey for many years, published sixteen accounts of "refugees from that region or of Kurds and soldiers who participated in the butchery and who had no hesitation in speaking." Like Dillon, Greene reported multiple instances of killings and tortures: Armed assailants captured Armenian children and "hacked them to pieces with their swords." Soldiers "stood the boys in a row and shot them, to see how many could be killed by a single bullet"; or "wrenched babies from their mothers' arms, cut their throats while the mothers shrieked and pleaded," and boiled them in kettles. To Greene, the "cumulative and overwhelming evidence" conclusively proved that "a gigantic and indescribably horrible massacre of Armenian men, women and children did actually take place" at Sasun and was ordered by the sultan himself.[47]

The commission of inquiry in Turkey finally reported in mid-1895. The official Turkish board of inquiry, unswayed by the overwhelming evidence of atrocities, faithfully affirmed the original Ottoman position: a *revolution* had occurred and had been suppressed; however, *no massacre* had taken place, and the atrocities and looting were the work of the Armenian revolutionaries.[48] Diametrically opposite findings were presented by the separate "Report of the [European] Consular Delegates attached to the Commission." This report declared that the Armenians were guilty only of sheltering the Hnchags at Sasun; they had indulged in a "few isolated acts of brigandage"; and they had "resisted the government troops under conditions that were not entirely clear." The European commission found devastation in vast areas of the Armenian homelands, "far in excess of what the punishment for the revolt should have been." Certainly, "the misery to which the Armenians were reduced could not be justified."[49] The European report and the evidence from other sources spurred European diplomats in Constantinople to propose reforms to the sultan. However, Abdul Hamid, well skilled at playing off the Powers against each other, carefully manipulated their rivalries, ambitions, and fears to his advantage. The spring and summer of 1895 came and went with no resolution of the Armenian Question.

Phase Two: Increased Devastation in 1895

By the summer of 1895 the Hnchag party had been girding for some months for new uprisings; its chief, Avedis Nazarbeg, considered that the uprising at Sasun had successfully awakened Europe to the sufferings of the Armenians. Hnchags from the United States and Cyprus smuggled themselves into Turkey to organize self-defense units. In the United States the talk was of "Revolution; Bullets and Blood" (April).[50] In August, the Hnchag M. G. Seron called on 250 immigrants in Worcester to be "near the scene of battle when" the signal for revolt is given. "Heroic resistance to Moslem oppression," said another, "would eventually compel the powers . . . [to send] a coalition army into the Armenian provinces to prevent, *by a timely appearance on the scene*, a repetition of the massacre of Sassoun."[51] A major demonstration by the Hnchags against the Turks took place in late September in Constantinople itself.

The details of the September 28 Hnchag demonstration in Constantinople can be briefly told. On that date, the Hnchags, many of whom were armed, after due warning to the sultan and the foreign embassies in the city, marched en masse in a "peaceful" demonstration to dramatize their demands for reforms. Not long after the march of perhaps 1,000 Armenians commenced, "severe fighting and violence broke out." "For several days ensuing, hundreds of demonstrators were imprisoned. The prisons became crowded with wounded men, and scores of dead bodies were collected from the streets." Over 100 Armenians were killed as bloodshed and violence finally reached the imperial capital. The slaughter in Constantinople itself brought a new note of alarm to the Powers and the city's European enclaves. Demands arose for implementation of the reform measures sitting on the sultan's desk. However, the bloodletting soon spread— on October 3, the Armenian community at Ak Hissar, to the northeast of Constantinople, was subjected to a preplanned massacre; on October 8, newspapers reported fighting and atrocities against unarmed Armenian women and children in Trebizond.[52]

In Constantinople, owing to strident demands from the European powers, the sultan on October 17 finally issued an *irade* sanctioning the reform measures proposed the preceding summer. This was the only significant concession to the Armenian Question the Sublime Porte had made since 1878. "My own conviction," noted the American minister Terrell of this major step, "is that . . . permanent security and order in the Ottoman Empire are made impossible by the rancor of race and religious hatred, now more bitter than ever. . . ."[53] Terrell for once was right, for there now ensued a thoroughgoing, preplanned, and merciless program of massacres and physical devastation of the Armenian communities in Turkey. Using the Hnchags as a pretext, angered over European intervention on behalf of the Armenians, and confident of his ability to immobilize the Powers, the sultan determined to settle the Armenian Question—by exterminating the Armenians.

Fall Massacres. The massacres commenced at Erzingan and Baiburt on October 21 and 25, respectively; then, they moved to Bitlis on the 27th and Erzerum on the 30th. The major centers of Arapgir and Diarbekir erupted with pogroms on November 1, and Malatia was hit on November 4. The important education and trade centers of Kharpert, Sivas, Marsovan and Aintab were devastated on November 10, 12, 13 and 15 respectively; Marash was put to the sword on November 18. In the meantime hundreds of villages and towns were similarly devastated. Exhausted and consumed by their own internal fury, and under intense foreign pressure, the massacres terminated at Caesaria on November 30; but reports of sporadic violence and atrocities continued through the winter and the following spring.[54]

Destruction of life and property was beyond belief. Commerce ground to a halt. In the heavily Armenian vilayet (province) of Mamuret-Ul-Aziz: "the trade of this vilayet since the troubles of 1895–96 has been practically at a standstill. All the principal towns, viz., Kharpert, Malatia, Arabkir, Eghin, Peri and Khozat, were, with the exception of the last-named, devastated by the disturbances. At Kharpert, the whole of the Protestant quarter was destroyed and the goods carried thither from the market by the Armenians for safety, were all lost." At Arapgir, 1,561 out of a total of 2,182 Christian houses were burnt, and at Eghin, 90 percent. At Malatia, "a great part of the Armenian Quarter was ruined, and the whole of it looted. About 90 percent of the Armenian villages throughout the vilayet were pillaged and a larger percentage of them were burnt. The wave of anarchy and destruction which swept through Mamuret-ul-Aziz in the autumn of 1895 reduced the majority of the Christians to sheer destitution. . . ."[55]

Other Armenian provinces were likewise desolated and silenced. A tabular estimate of the total destruction of the Armenian communities follows:[56]

Armenians in the ten provinces	1,192,000
Total houses and shops plundered and destroyed or burned	62,661
Number killed	83,895
Number forced to accept Islam	40,950
Number destitute	315,060
Number widowed	65,650
Number orphaned	55,000

Accompanying the statistics were accounts of horrible atrocities. Emil Dillon of the London Daily Telegram declared the outrages to be infinitely worse than Sasun. Innocent Armenians were "hung up by their heels, the hair of their heads and beards plucked out one by one, their bodies branded with red hot irons . . . their wives dishonored in their presence"; men were put on "spits" alive and skinned and roasted.[57] The atrocity accounts of the autumn and winter of 1895, which were daily fare in the press and filled such works as W. W. Howard's Horrors of Armenia, Edwin Bliss's Turkey and the Armenian Atrocities, and Dr. M. Smpad Kaprielian's Facts About Armenia, seared the minds of the western world.[58]

American missionary property was also attacked in these later atrocities. The Porte, exploiting the populace's deepseated suspicion that missionaries were secret allies of the Armenian revolutionary committees and aware of Hnchag propaganda at the missionary colleges, did little to deter mobs bent on destroying mission property. At Marsovan in mid-November 1895, Minister Terrell intervened from Constantinople to prevent a Turkish mob from entering the grounds at Marsovan College, but at Kharpert and Marash Turkish mobs openly looted and burned the property in the presence of local Turkish militia. Many missionary families fled for their lives; damages amounted to over $100,000.[59]

Reaction in the United States. The barbarous events of 1895 now convinced many westerners that the sultan was treacherous and that the only way to treat Turkey was to change it root and branch. In the United States Protestant church organizations, led by the American Board and the Evangelical Alliance, whipped up a systematic public outcry against the Turks now even more vehemently than in 1894. From September to December, weekly sermons denounced the "unspeakable Turks" and called for total condemnation of the Red Assassin. Religious journals like the Independent, Outlook, Christian Register, Congregationalist, Baptist Philadelphian, Commonwealth, Christian Herald, and Lend a Hand demanded deeds and not words.[60] In England, Lord Bryce argued that if the Powers could not agree on concerted action, then the British should appoint Russia as mandate nation to rule Armenia. An absolute demand of many influential Americans was to secure protection and respect for American nationals in Turkey by dispatching the fleet to the Eastern Mediterranean.

It was the duty of the government, exhorted Governor Nelson Dingley of Maine and the Reverend Washington Gladden, to protect missionaries in foreign lands. The Baptist Pastors Association of New York urged the country to join others in "teaching Turkey a lesson."[61] And on September 30, even before news of the attacks on missionary property, an Evangelical Alliance meeting in Boston resolved that the United States should "keep such a naval force in Turkish waters as shall make the American name respected on the Mediterranean or on the Kurdish mountains."[62]

State legislatures and mass assemblies joined the hue and cry. In February 1896 the general assembly of the state of Ohio, decrying the "brutal murders" by "Moslem savages" of 75,000 Armenian men, women, and children "for no other or better reason than because of their devotion to the Christian religion" petitioned Congress to adopt "such measures as will show to all the world our abhorrence of such atrocities as have been committed in Armenia, and extend to them such protection and material aid as is within the power of this Government...."[63] On January 15, 1896, a mass meeting in Haddonfield, New Jersey, solemnly declared that "the Sultan of Turkey has forfeited all right to rule over the Armenian people."[64] In Washington a Connecticut representative described the furore in his constituency: "During the past four or five weeks — yes, for a longer time — the people of my district and of the city of New Haven have been holding mass meetings upon this question of Armenian outrages. They are fully roused. Not only have they held mass meetings, but they have memorialized Congress; they have sent here letters and resolutions. ... Not only are my constituents adopting resolutions, not only are they sending petitions to this body, but during the last few weeks they have been passing subscription papers from house to house for the purpose of raising money to send it to these suffering Christians. The people of my district ... are ready to take any step they can legally, properly, and morally take, which will suppress, or assist in suppressing, the Armenian outrages now practiced by the Turks and Kurds."[65]

On Capital Hill the Senate first took up the issue on January 22, 1896, when the Foreign Relations Committee resolved that Americans should protest the utter neglect of the Berlin Treaty and that President Cleveland should urge the European Concert to "stay the hand of fanaticism and lawless violence." Senator Shelby Collum of Illinois, sponsor of the resolutions, argued that Europe's power in Turkey was so great that "they could have in six days put a perfect and absolute stop to the reign of terror." There were, however, limits to America's power. Despite America's sympathy for the slain and suffering Armenians and her support for the earlier Greek and Balkan struggles against Turkish oppression, the United States could not, "consistent with its declarations in the past," dispatch a fleet and an army to Turkey to stop the slaughter of the Armenians. Although other Senators longed for stronger action, in the final analysis Europe and not the United States bore the responsibility for the salvation of the Armenians of Turkey. With respect to American interests, however, it was a totally different story. There, Collum's resolutions forcefully supported the president "in the most vigorous action he may take" to protect American citizens and obtain redress for damages.[66]

Others longed for stronger action for the Armenians. Senator William Frye of Maine, whose circle of friends included American missionaries, longed for intervention: "If I had my way, after the powers of Europe have waited now a solid year looking each other in the face with suspicious eyes and neither one daring to make a move lest the other shall receive a benefit . . . I would have Congress memorialize Russia and say to her: 'Take Armenia into your possession. Protect the lives of these Christians there. And the United States will stand behind you with all of its power.' "[67] Then, Senator Wilkinson Call of Florida, a fiery Democratic supporter of Cuban independence against the "military barbarism of the Cuban regime," labeling the resolutions "very feeble and emasculated," urged his colleagues to support an *Independent Armenia* "by peaceful negotiations or if necessary by force of arms . . . with such guarantees by the civilized powers of its own authority and permanence as shall be adequate to that end."[68] Such objections were overruled, however; the appeal to the Berlin Treaty signatories stood as the Senate's action on the Armenian crisis.

In the House, a rancorous debate before packed chambers lasted for four days. According to Charles Henry Grosvenor of Ohio, the Senate resolutions were unworthy of the United States. But, the most explosive came from Iowa's Representative William Hepburn. The Armenians, thundered Hepburn, "do not want sympathy; . . . they want rescue. They do not want our mere words; they want Christian people to come to their relief." Accordingly, Hepburn urged America to show its detestation of the atrocities by dismissing the Turkish minister from his post in Washington and severing all diplomatic ties with the government of Turkey.

Hepburn's broadside, which some deemed tantamount to a declaration of war, sparked a heated exchange in the House. Unfortunately for the Armenians, Hepburn's militancy was out of place. A few years later America went to war over similar issues in Cuba, but to the House of Representatives Turkey was too far away and in the province of the European powers. Hepburn's fiery remonstrance was voted down as the House concurred in the moderate Senate resolutions.

In the meantime, what steps had the administration taken? President Cleveland's first response to the massacres of 1895 was directed only to the protection of American lives in Turkey. In September, as the first rumors of killings appeared, Minister Terrell in Constantinople strongly advised the Porte to safeguard all Americans in Turkey by stationing armed, uniformed militia at missionary establishments throughout the empire. Terrell's forceful action was rewarded, for no Americans were killed or seriously injured during the three-month span of pogroms. Only at Kharpert and Marash was there extensive damage to American property with evidence of government complicity. Then in late December the State Department ordered Terrell to secure explanations for the callous and cynical behavior at Kharpert and Marash and to extract reparations; at the same time he was commanded to secure continued Turkish military protection for American citizens in the empire.[69]

The congressional debates of late January 1896 strengthened Cleveland's actions. With the Congress's determination to assist the president in defense of American lives and property, Cleveland in late January dispatched the cruisers *San Francisco* and *Marblehead* to Turkish waters as a show of force against further outrages against American citizens. Minister Terrell, with obvious relief, noted that the ironclads induced a real diminution in Muslim-Christian tensions. The Turks, however, hedged on the issue of reparations for damage to American property, thereby commencing a long standing controversy in Turkish-American relations.[70]

However, with respect to the Armenians and the European powers' obligations to the Christians in Turkey, Cleveland, the slow moving anti-imperialist, was tepid. At no time during the frightful crisis did the administration indicate any official disapproval to the Turkish government of the killings and atrocities. Indeed, the linchpin of Cleveland's policy was protection of *American* rights alone. Thus, in late December 1895, when the old Christian warrior and head of the American mission in Turkey, the Rev. H. O. Dwight, beseeched Terrell in Constantinople for assistance for the Armenians, the Cleveland diplomat told him that Washington could do nothing so long as the two nations were at peace and "so long as Turkey gives assurances for the protection of our citizens. . . ."[71]

President Cleveland himself spoke to the issue in early 1896. Terrell was told directly not to involve the United States in the Armenian issue so long as American citizens were safe. And Cleveland's trusted Ambassador in London, writing in late January 1896 to the president, probably echoed his views by saying that "on the Armenian question there seems to be an insanity on both sides of the Atlantic, and some of the propositions reported from the United States would wrap the world in flames if carried out."[72] The political response of the Cleveland administration to the Armenians was exceedingly conservative.

Relief Work.   However, America's popular outburst against the Turkish atrocities was expressed in many ways, including a humanitarian crusade to assist the Armenians in Turkey. For in the winter of 1895–1896 Armenia was desolated, with "thousands of helpless women, aged men and children, homeless, starving and destitute." A handful of missionaries and doctors struggled with the long lines of sick, injured, and malnourished in the refugee camps. And according to Cyrus Hamlin (*The Outlook*, December 1895) at least a quarter of a million Armenians would die of "cold, hunger, typhus and other diseases before the winter was over unless help on a large scale could be rushed to Armenia and administered by reliable American almoners."[73]

Relief efforts had commenced after the Sasun massacres when local Armenian relief committees were organized in New York by Bishop Alonzo Potter and Archbishop Michael Corrigan. Dr. Louis Klopsch of the *Christian Herald* and the Rev. Edward Everett Hale of the Friends of Armenia mounted fund drives through *Outlook* and *Lend a Hand*. Many churches held an "Armenian Sunday." And by December 1895, the New York Armenian Relief Committee had organized the National Armenian Relief Committee under the leadership of Supreme Court Justice David Brewer and the Reverend Frederick Greene.[74]

The National Armenian Relief Committee coordinated and distributed literature to its branch committees in Springfield, Worcester, Syracuse, Harrisburg, Baltimore, Washington, Detroit, Cleveland, Columbus, Indianapolis, Chicago, St. Paul, and other cities. It also arranged for speakers for the branch committees. (Explicit instructions for speakers commended the reading of missionary accounts of the atrocities to American audiences, but cautioned against "overreaching the mark," since "much harm has been done by painting the subject . . . so black as to paralyze all effort to relieve it" and urged Armenian speakers to dwell on relief topics and not on political diatribes.)[75]

Despite the National Committee's extensive canvassing, the funds raised were less than anticipated. Cyrus Hamlin deemed $1,000,000 an appropriate amount to be raised, but Robert Ogden of the Philadelphia committee dolefully conceded that "never in all the history of my connection with the . . . Committee was so much earnest, energetic, persistent and intelligent work done for any cause . . . with the result that we secured . . . twenty-five thousand dollars, a miserably small and meagre sum, and out of all proportion to the success met on other occasions with causes far less powerful."[76] Worcester raised $1,800 after a year's effort, and $600 of that came from two men alone. John D. Rockefeller donated $1,000 but few matched this. Philadelphia's public school officials refused to participate in a fund drive in the schools because the children would be distracted by horror stories; on the other hand, 2,500 children in Minneapolis raised over $7,000.[77]

The difficulties in fund raising were attributed to the mid-1890s depression, the suspicion that the Armenians, in traveler-writer Marion Crawford's view, were the "sharpest, shrewdest and trickiest of all eastern peoples," and the very genuine fear that the Turkish government would frustrate all relief efforts to the Armenians. Between 1894 and 1896 Americans contributed about $300,000 to the cause while the Armenian American community probably matched that figure.[78]

In Turkey, American missionaries and Armenian relief workers performed miracles at great personal risk. Dr. Grace Kimball fed about 1,500 persons daily and saved hundreds from dying of typhus around Van; Caleb Gates, President of Yeprad College in Kharpert, distributed relief from the Armenian and American charities to over 50,000 destitute refugees in 160 villages.[79] However, the single most important relief effort by Americans in Turkey came from Clara Barton and the American Red Cross. At the age of 74 she was thought to be incompetent, inefficient, and too dictatorial for the massive overseas undertaking, and Miss Barton herself had serious misgivings about a 6,000 mile journey into "disturbed" Turkey. Moreover, in early January 1896 the Ottoman government refused her entry on the grounds of a "lack of neutrality" of the Red Cross. (At this news, with atrocity stories in every daily journal, one American vowed that "one million men would be there with guns and knives to force a way.") However, urged on by the American public and especially the American Board, America's Florence Nightingale sailed for Constantinople in January 1896.[80]

Since her trip took place as Congress heatedly debated the massacres, the Cleveland administration through Minister Terrell in Constantinople strongly suggested to the Porte that Miss Barton be permitted to minister to the Armenians to "allay prevalent excitement and indignation." Moreover, upon her arrival Miss Barton promised the Turkish foreign minister that she would not discriminate in her relief efforts, write a book on Turkey, or commit surreptitious deeds; she was soon permitted to enter.[81]

The Red Cross mounted five expeditions into the desolated interior, two of which were headed by physicians. The objective of each was to distribute food, medicine, and tools to begin the massive reconstruction of the devastated towns and villages of Armenia. According to Miss Barton, who stayed in Constantinople to supervise the work and deal with the Porte, "with the help of Dr. Ira Harris, a resident American physician in Tripoli, remarkable results were achieved in the pestilence-ridden Marash and Zeitun areas. Dr. J. B. Hubbell, Ernest Mason, Charles King Wood and Edward M. Wister, who led expeditions, achieved equally remarkable results at the cost of hard work, difficult travel, and great exposure." In the Kharpert area, for example, where Turkish and Kurdish brigands had spared nothing, and where the survivors still quivered from the massacres, Wistar distributed 500 beds, 3,500 articles of clothing, 300 farm animals, 1,640 bushels of grain, and 3,000 farm implements. (In every case tools bore a Red Cross stamp so that they could be recovered if stolen by marauding Kurds.) During the spring and summer through "horrendous weather" and difficult terrain, the five expeditions covered nearly 300 villages and furnished permanent relief to probably 200,000 starving persons. As a result, thousands of lives were saved, crops were planted, and arrangements were made for harvesting. "Armenians worked again with hope."[82]

Phase Three: The Constantinople Massacre of 1896

The American Red Cross expedition to Turkey ended in late summer 1896 and stood as the nation's most dramatic gesture of support and compassion for Bleeding Armenia. But the crisis of 1894–1896 was not over.

Although the Powers had urged the sultan to institute badly needed reforms for the Armenian Provinces, by the late summer Abdul Hamid had permitted only the establishment of a European commission of reform which, though composed of "able and well intentioned men," lacked authority to achieve substantial results from its deliberations. Because of this, Armenian revolutionary committees again stirred demonstrations.[83]

In the summer of 1896 the initiative shifted to the Armenian Revolutionary Federation (Tashnagtsutiun or the Tashnags). Founded in Tiflis in 1890 by Christopher Mikaelian, Stepan Zorian, and Simon Zavarian as a composite of Marxist, socialist, and nationalist Russian Armenian groups, it had sought unsuccessfully to work in concert with the Hnchag leader, Nazarbeg. Though steeped in Marxism (it joined the Third Internationale in 1907), its dominant thrust was nationalism and liberation. Its methods were borrowed from Russian terrorist societies: violence, assassination, and blackmail of Turks and Armenians alike and armed uprisings to force European intervention; its aims were Armenian autonomy and security within the Ottoman Empire.[84]

Tashnagtsutiun limited its early activities to raiding parties, and establishing secret cells in Transcaucasia, Turkey, and the United States. In Turkey the first important guerrilla activity took place in Van in mid-June 1896; other outbreaks occurred in Eastern Anatolia, the Black Sea area, and Syria. But the major demonstration was reserved for Constantinople itself. There on August 26, 1896, a band of Tashnags dressed as hamals (porters) seized control of the Ottoman Imperial Bank in the heart of the capital to dramatize Armenia's demands for justice.

The upshot of the Ottoman Bank attack was more carnage — the third series in three successive late summers. The sultan, probably informed of the impending attack on the bank, prepared his revenge by arming lower-class Turks and Kurds with clubs to attack innocent Armenians in the city. Terror gripped the city streets as mobs controlled Constantinople for 36 hours. As the Turkish police stood quietly by, Armenians were "ruthlessly cut down and hunted through their houses 'like rabbits.' " Estimates of the dead ran from 5,000 to 8,000 in comparison with the 100 victims the previous autumn in Constantinople.[85]

Now, in September 1896 the English and Americans again wearily read of the wholesale slaughter of Armenians in Turkey while they were purportedly under the protection of the European powers. In England the diatribes unleashed against the Turks were of furious intensity. Everyone demanded immediate action, "either with Russia and France, or alone." Opinion in the United States, however, was divided and less shrill. The Republican party, leveling charges against Cleveland's supineness, resolved in their 1896 platform: "the massacres in Armenia have aroused the deep sympathy and just indignation of the American people, and we believe that the United States should exercise all the influence it can properly exert to bring these atrocities to an end."[86] The Presbyterian Synod, meeting in Boston in October heard its Dr. James Gardner proclaim, "An American ship must pass the Dardanelles, hoist the stars and stripes and fire a blank shot as a warning of what might follow." Another cleric exhorted, "The course of this government has been despicable. Turkey ought to be wiped out."[87]

On the other hand, conservative journals and some businessmen took another view of the country's obligations. Journals like the *New York Tribune* expressed sympathy with the Armenians but argued that the responsibility was Europe's and not America's. The fall and winter of 1896 saw no mass rallies as had 1895, many pious businessmen turned to other issues, and in his annual message to Congress (December 7, 1896) President Cleveland cautioned that the Americans' "deep feeling and sympathy" for the Armenians "ought not to so far blind their reason and judgment as to lead them to demand impossible things."[88]

Moreover, by the early spring of 1897 a new storm center had moved into the Eastern Mediterranean — the revival of nationalist aspirations in Macedonia and Crete. There, Muslim-Christian rivalries erupted into war between Greece and Turkey.[89] This spelled the end of the crisis of 1894–1896. The political demonstrations and uprisings and the brutal retaliations had come and gone. Despite their earnest professions, Europe and America had done little politically to assuage the sufferings or fulfill the aspirations of the Armenians. An important chapter in the Armenian Question had come to a close.

For three years the plight of the Armenians in Turkey had engaged Europe and America; the Armenian Question had become the diplomatic issue of the period. Repeatedly, however, the effort to institute reforms had been undermined by European power considerations and suspicions. And the United States, though roused to deep moral indignation, remained politically remote.

For three years, too, the Armenian Crisis had exercised the Armenian American community. Their political organizations, the Hnchags and the Tashnags, had sought at great cost to the nation and without an iota of success to resolve the Armenian Question. For them, however, the bitter struggle for reforms, autonomy, and liberation had only begun.

12.

Deterioration and Turmoil, 1897–1907

For thirty months Europe and the United States had extended their sympathy and philanthropic support to the cause of Armenia. At the end of it all, however, Armenia was abandoned, humbled, and silenced.

After the massacres of 1894–1896 a savage reassessment of the Armenian revolutionary movement took place in the diaspora. The Hnchag party was irreparably rent by schism. The Reformed Hnchags, a splinter party, and the Armenian Revolutionary Federation (Tashnagtsutiun) became the chief beneficiaries of the factionalism. In the ensuing political confusion and psychological vacuum, their activities amounted chiefly to maligning each other. But in time and under the impact of fresh Old World crises, they sought to purge the movement of its most radical elements, build support anew among the Armenian American community, and rekindle the once-ardent sympathy of pro-Armenian America.

Breakup of the Hnchags

Events in Turkey in 1897 signaled that revolutionary activity had been throttled for some time. Even so, in the summer two large Tashnag raiding parties crossed from Persia into Turkey, "surprised a Kurdish camp and [in retaliation for the massacres] killed or barbarously mutilated men, women and children." At the same time there were new "bomb outrages" in Constantinople.[1] However, little came of this as the Turkish Armenians had no taste for demonstrations after the carnage of 1894–1896. By late 1897 the hated sultan, having faced and triumphed over an uprising in Crete, enjoyed a heightened reputation for power in his domain. The American minister in Constantinople reported in July 1898 that fear of reprisals, coupled with jailings of suspected Armenian revolutionaries, controls over travel in the interior, and a greatly enlarged system of espionage dramatically curtailed political activity in Turkey.[2] The disillusioned and embittered Armenians, abandoned by the West, now focused on reconstruction of the homeland.

ppraisal. In the United States the Hnchag party was
appraised. Party members sharply criticized Nazarbeg
rebellion with an unprepared and unarmed peasantry,
ing Turkish officials to the "coming imbroglios" in Cil-
sun. Further, many bitterly concluded that the West had
intervene because the Hnchag party called for a socialist
Finally, in Worcester in January 1897, party members
hat while Armenians were being massacred in Turkey,
and his wife Maro had embezzled funds earmarked for
of the sultan's persecution that they might live "on the fat of
l in London."[3]
luential Armenians outside party ranks who were originally
warm to the idea of the revolution lashed out at the "gigantic folly"
of the movement. Dr. M. Smpad Kaprielian, editor of *Haik* in New
York, ridiculed the movement as "suicidal," because of its extrem-
ism, socialism, and anarchism. Its continuance, warned Kaprielian,
would "lead to greater dangers and disasters." A few others, following Archag Tchobanian in *Armenia* in 1899, believed the horrendous
charge that the Hnchags had deliberately provoked the Turks so that
"the victims would be their own people." On the whole, however,
the bulk of nonparty opinion regarded the Hnchags as inept and
premature, but not guilty of deliberate provocation to incite massacres.[4]

Within the Hnchag party, reformers strove to alter the party's
central committee, but Nazarbeg thwarted the moves. Accordingly,
in August 1896 the party's disaffected membership met secretly in
general convention in London to plan for complete disassociation
— in fact, for the establishment of their own party. In America in
1897 Nazarbeg was labeled a traitor to the Armenian cause, and
Karekin Chitjian, leader of the New World group, journeyed to London to dissuade Nazarbeg from factionalism — to no avail.

The Reformed Hnchags. The result of the dispute was the emergence of a new Armenian revolutionary organization. Dissident
Hnchags, led by the talented journalist Arpiar Arpiarian, formed the
Veragazmial Hnchagian Gusagtsutiun (Reformed Hnchag Party) in
October 1898 in Alexandria, Egypt. In the United States the organization was headed by Karekin Chitjian, and its journal, *Tzain Haireneats* (The Voice of the Homeland), was first published in Boston
in 1899 under the editorship of Garabed Papazian.

The dissidents quickly built a party and program. Through *Tzain
Haireneats* and *Nor Giank* (New Life) in Alexandria, they urged a
dedication to Armenian nationalism unalloyed with socialist ideology. For the Reformed Hnchags, rebuilding after the cataclysm of
1894–1896, the critical issue in Turkey was the Ottomans' political
oppression of the Armenians and not the economic exploitation of

one class by another. Equally critical was their renunciation of immediate insurrection. Cognizant of the numerical inferiority and lack of military training of the Armenians which produced the catastrophe of 1894–1986, they preached a program of careful, rigorous, and assiduous political training and education of the Armenians for the coming storm.[5] "The slaughter of the innocent lambs of 1894–1896 has taught us," said *Tzain Haireneats* ruefully, that "a revolution cannot succeed only by arming a few villagers."[6]

The Reformed Hnchags, whose chief base was in the United States, absorbed many rank and file Old Hnchags into their cells in the East, in Chicago, and in California. They also promoted unity with various nonpolitical Armenian organizations. Attracting many respected and influential political leaders, in September 1899 they met jointly with Protestant and Apostolic Armenian leaders in Worcester under the motto of "one army, one flag, and one fatherland's salvation." In 1900 the party's central committee called for a national congress of Armenian groups in the New World to revivify the Armenian Question on the American forum. And in December 1900, thirty-one representatives (from New York, Boston, Providence, Worcester, Lowell, Lawrence, Haverhill, Newburyport, Fitchburg, Springfield, Malden, Bridgewater, Milford, New Britain, Watertown, and East Weymouth) resolved: to assist Armenian orphans in Turkey, defend the honor of the Armenians and the Armenian Cause, establish relations with other Armenian communities in the diaspora, assist refugees in Marseilles and New York, and memorialize President William McKinley on the Armenian Question. A second national assembly followed in June 1901.[7]

It was logical that the Reformed Hnchags would seek an accommodation with Tashnagtsutiun, the second prominent Armenian political organization in the United States, for the tiny Armenian community warmly endorsed unity against the common hated foe. Thus *Nor Giank* in 1901 proposed preliminary discussions with the Tashnags with a view toward eventual union. However, Tashnagtsutiun refused to cooperate. Though acknowledging the popularity of a united front, its leaders nonetheless feared that the now deeply divided Hnchags (Reformed Hnchags and Old Hnchags) would be a millstone around their neck. They also clearly recognized that the Reformed Hnchag party, having been extirpated from Turkey and Russia, was viable only in the United States. It made no sense therefore to become allied with a schismatic organization.[8]

Instead of collaboration, Tashnagtsutiun embarked on a frontal attack on the Reformed Hnchags through weekly denunciatory editorials which criticized the "weaknesses, partisanship and worthlessness" of their rivals. It was Middle Eastern political invective at its worst. A classic example of the strident internecine warfare and its bitter fruit was the Armenian Self-Defense Committee, founded by the adherents of Tashnagtsutiun in January 1902. Its purpose was to propagandize and raise funds for the revolution. (The group was headed by one A. Aleon, its secretary was the pro-Tashnag priest, Father Papazian, and its masthead contained the names of many prominent Yankees, including many former Friends of the Armenians). In February 1902, a fund raising meeting of the committee, chaired by Father Papazian, erupted into an altercation between Papazian and the Reverend Hevont Martoogesian, a prominent Reformed Hnchag. The battle of words led to a free for all and the calling of the New York City Police. A year later, Mrs. Isabell Barrows, wife of the editor of the *Christian Register* and an original member of Friends of the Armenians, bitterly resigned her post on the Self-Defense Committee because the "whole scheme was impractical" and because "the Armenians are far from being in harmony with each other. I fancy if Americans could read the Armenian papers they would be shocked to see how far the Armenians of this country are from meriting the Biblical phrase 'Behold how good and pleasant it is for brethern to dwell together in unity.' Till they have learned that lesson it is useless to expect the cooperation of Americans. In the great cause of freedom every personality should be banished." Tashnagtsutiun's Self-Defense Committee was quietly interred in late 1903.[9]

Reunification Fails. Although the Tashnags and Reformed Hnchags remained antagonists, by early 1902 it appeared that the Reformed Hnchags had achieved the impossible — reunification with the Old Hnchags. In the United States large numbers of Armenians and their American sympathizers warmly greeted the prospect. In Boston in May 1902, over 2,000 Armenians and Armenian sympathizers gathered to celebrate the prospect of healing Hnchag wounds. The gala meeting, to which Boston's Mayor Patrick Collins; Edward Clement, editor of the *Boston Transcript*; William Lloyd Garrison; and George F. Hoar were invited, featured music, military exercises, and pro-Armenian speeches at the Boston YMCA building. Edward A. Horton applauded these "noble efforts in behalf of the Armenian Cause. Not only will good results come from this special agitation, maintained by your patriotic societies, but I believe that the [Armenian] cause will be helped by the enthusiasm for liberty of people throughout the world today."[10]

To Karekin Chitjian, at the same celebration, it was the instrumental first step: "We have united, we have joined arms, and we have embraced, forgetting the sad past events, burying the personal ... considerations." Chitjian also ventured that "tomorrow we shall join with . . . the Armenian Revolutionary Federation, and the Armenagans, the neutralists and the entire Armenian community." Cheers and thunderous applause greeted his words as Armenians in Lawrence, Bridgewater, Middleboro, New York, Chicago, and Fresno likewise feted the union.[11]

Events belied the promising picture of unity. In London, meetings between Old and Reformed Hnchags erupted into bitter disagreements over the shape of the unified organization. The rift deepened as both groups sought leverage by appealing to compatriots in Bulgaria and Russia.

Karekin Chitjian and Moho Sahen (Seferian) journeyed to the Caucasus and Bulgaria for the Reformed Hnchags but embittered Old Hnchags in London forewarned the Eastern European committees of the emissaries. Anxious to win at all costs, they labeled Chitjian as responsible for the party's 1896 split, and a "hypocrite, traitor, egoist and parasite on the revolutionary cause."[12] The poison soon found its mark. While seeking to convince Old Hnchags of the merit of the Reformed Hnchag criticism of the party, Moho Sahen was knifed to death as a traitor to the Armenian Cause in Poti in the Caucasus. Chitjian, after receiving word of Moho's death, was repeatedly warned not to travel to Russia, but the admonitions were thrust aside: "I wish to remain alive," he replied, but "it is necessary to labor . . . even in danger. . . . Perhaps this is the last letter I shall write . . . But the Armenian Revolution needs to be purified. . . . Should we retreat because they kill us . . . because my wife shall be widowed and my children made orphans?"[13] Chitjian died on the streets of Odessa on June 13, 1903, when he was assaulted by three assassins, who stabbed him eleven times in the chest, throat, and back.[14] The Old Hnchags, who had triggered the massacres of innocent Armenians in 1894–1896, were now devouring the revolution.

In the United States "all hell broke loose." In Boston at the offices of the Reformed Hnchag *Tzain Haireneats*, the beloved Chitjian's associates were "turned upside down" by their desire for revenge. In the black-bordered paper, editor Souren Bartevian blasted the Old Hnchags for exploiting the revolution for their bizarre socialist theories and personal gains.[15] In response, Sabah Culian, through the Old Hnchag *Eridasart Hayastan*, told Armenian colonies in the United States that the hatred arose from the "malcontents" Moho and Chitjian.[16] On July 7, 1903, at the corner of Dudley and Dana Streets in downtown Boston, two Armenians fired four shots which wounded Sabah Culian. In October, Nazarbeg was stabbed and nearly assassinated in Lucerne, Switerland, and in late October a Nazarbeg associate was killed in London. A fortnight later two other Old Hnchags fell before assassins' bullets.[17] Thus, the abortive attempt at union of the Hnchag party's two wings ended with the elimination of virtually the entire leadership of both wings.

The bloodshed naturally harmed the Armenian revolutionary cause both in the Armenian American and the American communities. Papers like the *New York World* printed headlines in November: "WORLD-WIDE PLOT TO SLAY ARMENIANS."[18] The assassinations, it quoted Old Hnchags as saying, were backed by "Turkish gold," which also created the Reformed Hnchag party. In Boston the Tashnags, caught in the backlash against the émigré parties, issued a lengthy explanation denouncing the killings:

A number of Armenians have recently fallen victims of political plottings in Europe and in this country. This was the result of factional quarrels, of the once so-called Hunchaquist Party, that date back to 1896 — the party that has long ceased to be the leader in the cause of the emancipation of Armenia. These crimes wrought in senseless vengeance by . . . ambitious individuals . . . do [no] credit to the Armenian name, or . . . the cause of the Armenian people. We . . . regret that . . . the American press . . . has given a national character to these crimes, for which neither the Armenian people, in general, nor those who are actively engaged in the struggle for their freedom, are responsible, and who are unjustly subject to such characterization.[19]

The communal bloodletting fostered the demise of the Old Hnchags and nearly destroyed the Reformed Hnchag organization. It also benefitted the party immune from the killings: the Armenian Revolutionary Federation (Tashnagtsutiun). The party, led by *Hairenik's* aggressive and tireless editor, Arshag Vramian, grew in size and stature in the United States even before the tumultuous events of 1904–1906.

Full Circle: 1904–1907

Sasun Again.   In 1904 Sasun again became a battleground of insurgents against the Ottoman regime. The immediate cause of renewed hostilities was the example of Macedonia. There the nationalist Macedonian revolutionary committees were "blowing up bridges and buildings with dynamite, [effecting] destruction of crops, burning of villages and the killing of hundreds of inoffensive people, including women and children" — all, to stir Turkish massacres and "possible consequent intervention of the European powers. . . ."[20] Anti-Turk agitation boiled over into Armenia where since 1901 Tashnag *fedayees* (guerrillas) had been infiltrating the peasantry and spreading incendiary propaganda; by early 1904 over 1,000 Armenian insurgents were reported in the mountain area about Van, Bitlis, and Sasun.[21]

The course of Armeno-Turkish clashes in the Sasun district in 1904 was well described in a lengthy communiqué from the American minister in Constantinople:

The present troubles in Armenia [wrote Minister John Leishman] resemble very closely the movement in Macedonia last year, and the revolutionists, no doubt, hope for the same result, i. e., foreign intervention; but this is not likely to occur unless a general massacre should ensue. . . . The action of the [rebel] bands is well calculated to bring trouble to thousands of innocent Armenians who are not directly connected with the revolutionary movement, as the bands swoop down upon a Turkish village, and, after committing what damage they can, seek refuge in some Armenian villages, and when followed by the troops flee to the mountains, where the Turks are unable to pursue them, and the consequence is that the troops generally fall upon the village and sack it.[22]

The immediate results of the 1904 uprising appallingly resembled those of the decade before. In the spring of 1904 trained Turkish regiments with field artillery completely annihilated a number of Armenian villages. Thousands of Armenians were killed or made homeless. The Turkish regulars, abetted by the wild Kurds who "have broke loose from all restraint," indulged in widespread looting and rapine.[23] As usual, the innocent were the casualties of the Armeno-Turkish rivalry.

The suffering of the survivors in the winter of 1904–1905 was severe. According to American Consul Norton, "the survivors of the massacre number about 10,000 and they barely escaped with their lives; every house almost without exception was plundered and burned, all their cattle and sheep — all their means of clothing and food — have been driven away. They suffer from fear, lack of shelter, and insufficient food."[24]

In Europe the outrages committed against innocent Armenian villages in Sasun drew strident protests as they had a decade before. Strong joint representations were made to the Porte by the English, Russian, and French embassies. Growing pro-Armenian feeling was manifest in France. Since 1901 Pro Armenia, a fortnightly published in Paris by such eminent men of affairs as Georges Clemenceau, Anatole France, Jean Jaurès, Francis de Pressensé, Théophile Delcassé, and Eugene de Roberty had lobbied for the Armenians, and in the summer of 1904 the French Chamber of Deputies heatedly debated the issue. In England senescent pro-Armenian groups became active, and a new organization, the Association on the Armenian Question — a joint lobby of Anglo-French pro-Armenians, Near Eastern specialists, and missionaries — took to the public forum on behalf of the Armenians.[25]

In the United States the news of Sasun rekindled the energies of the pro-Armenian faithful. In July 1904 Julia Ward Howe, keeper of America's conscience, urged Secretary of State John Hay to investigate the "recent troubles" in Sasun, whereupon Consul Norton traveled to the troubled regions. A revivified Friends of Armenia petitioned Congress and President Theodore Roosevelt for help. The National Armenia and India Relief Association and the National Armenian Relief Association spearheaded efforts to assist refugees and rebuild devastated Sasun and Mush.[26]

Reaction to Sasun in the Armenian American community was sharply split. Tashnagtsutiun, which fostered the uprising, argued that it successfully demonstrated Armenian resistance to Turkish tyranny, and a later apologist termed the uprising more successful than the Hnchag rebellion a decade before. Arshag Vramian, the Tashnag chieftain in the New World, proclaimed it the beginning of a new chapter in the story of Armenian resistance and freedom.[27] On the other hand, the majority of the community, while in sympathy with Tashnagtsutiun's goals, criticized the rebellion as totally ill-timed at the expense of thousands of innocent Armenian lives. Thus *Tzain Haireneats*, bitterly asked in July 1904: "Fight, yes, let us shed blood, yes, but shall we be slaughtered if we are weaponless, shall we be butchered when we are unprepared?" Referring to 1894–1896, it declaimed: "Are not 300,000 victims sufficient, when they were slaughtered like sheep?"

Mass meetings memorialized the "dead of Sasun," and in New York in the cold of February 1905, 250 Armenians solemnly chanted their liturgical Der Vorormia, and listened to the philanthropist Hovannes Tavshanjian (later assassinated by revolutionaries) criticize the defiance at Sasun. "Take care that your work is not shameful for you shall be judged by history. . . . Do not be hasty, overzealous. It is better that nothing be accomplished than such things as this happen. . . . We esteem brave men but bravery has its place." In addition, the Reformed Hnchags noted with sullen disappointment that England, France, Russia, and the United States took little note of Sasun; that Delcassé, the great French ally, had declared that the Armenians were unprepared as yet for revolution; and that American newspapers were tired of reporting "our massacres."[28]

The American minister in Constantinople in June 1903 summed up the dilemma of the Armenians:

It is greatly to be regretted that their native intelligence does not enable them to discover the difference between their impractical efforts to secure the freedom of an interior province, from Turkish Rule — single handed and alone, as against the successful efforts of some of their old compatriots in the Turkish European province, which was owing not so much to their own efforts as to the assistance given them by the European powers for purely selfish reasons.[29]

The 1904 Sasun uprising came and went with no palpable results for the Armenian Question.

The Armenian Church Crisis.   Between 1903 and 1905 Armenians in Russia also came under concerted attack. Since Czar Alexander II's assassination in 1881, Russian minority policy had been directed at assimilating its many restive non-Russian peoples. The Armenians, hitherto favored by the czars, now were forced to bow before Russification policies as expressed in the seizure of prominent newspapers, school closings, and the imposition of strict censorship. In 1903 the czarist autocracy, under the archconservative Prince Golitsyn, sought to crush the aspirations of the Armenians entirely by assaulting their nationalist stronghold: the church.

In June 1903 the government decreed that the church had squandered its revenues, in part on Armenian nationalists; its lands, therefore, were to be controlled not by the duly elected Armenian clergy and laity, but by the Russian government. Many feared a Russian episcopacy. When the aged Catholicos Khrimian refused compliance, czarist troops and police occupied the holy monastery at Echmiadzin and ripped open the catholicate's safe to seize all valuable title deeds of the church. The czarist rape of the Armenian church was underway.

However, the czarist program was a major miscalculation. Throughout the Caucasus outraged Armenians of every political persuasion rallied behind the nationalist but hitherto vehemently anticlerical Tashnags in protest demonstrations against the arbitrary and illegal seizure of the church. The protest turned the Caucasus into an armed camp, in which Tashnagtsutiun, whose members swelled to over 100,000, initiated a "bloody reign of terror" against the Russian officials. Golitsyn himself was nearly assassinated by Armenians in October 1903 and political murder became the order of the day.[30]

Armenians in America shared in the outrage. *Eridasart Hayastan*, organ of the Old Hnchag faction, first published in Boston in 1903, reiterated in January 1904 its strident accusation of the czar as the "true enemy" of the Armenians. "Not only does Russia not want an Armenian Bulgaria on her borders," criticized the journal, "but she desires to crush Armenia's fondest dreams." *Tzain Haireneats* issued declamations against the "illegal seizure," and *Hairenik*, organ of the belligerent Tashnags, vilified the Golitsyn regime while calling upon the Armenians in America to contribute funds to the Central Committee for Self-Defense in Russian Armenia. "All that Armenia can do," echoed the *Fresno Daily Republican* in early 1904, "is to do what the Revolutionary Federation is doing — arm those in

Armenia that they may protect their lives, their property and their honor."[31]

Armenian Americans expressed their deep concerns by frenzied work in assemblies and political organizations. In September 1903 Joseph Sarajian, prelate of the Armenian diocese in the United States, addressed a circular letter to Armenian American leaders to attend a representative assembly on October 3-4 in Providence to formulate strategy for the restoration of the church lands. In the early fall, 90 delegates from virtually every Armenian community and political and social group in the country convened to hear the archbishop, a gontag (circular letter) from the Catholicos, and a message from the Armenian patriarch of Constantinople. Then the disquieted assembly resolved to protest the illegal seizures of the national properties to the czar himself — through the Russian ambassador in Washington. Archbishop Sarajian, Dr. M. Smpad Kaprielian, and two other leaders, were appointed to deliver the formal protest. Another 800 Armenians attended a public protest meeting in Providence that weekend, while 6 months later, on May 28-30, 25 communities sent over 50 delegates to a second such assembly.[32]

The Armenian church crisis came to a head in the summer of 1905. By this time the Russian regime had suffered serious setbacks in the Russo-Japanese War and was in the throes of the 1905 Revolution. The paralysis of government in the Caucasus, largely caused by the assassination of hundreds of Russian bureaucrats, soldiers, and police by "bullets, knives and bombs of Armenian 'terrorists,'" added to the tottering regime's woes. To pacify the strife torn region, Czar Nicholas II dispatched the able Count I. I. Vorontsov-Dashkov to the Caucasus as viceroy to annul the hated edict of confiscation and thereby neutralize the opposition sparked especially by Tashnagtsutiun. The news in August 1905 of the return of the church properties brought joy and elation — unfamiliar emotions — to Armenians from Russia to California.[33]

Tashnagtsutiun's critical role in the smashing victory over the czar in the 1903–1905 crisis was amply rewarded; for the party now catapulted into the forefront of the nationalist movement in Russia, Turkey, and the United States. The Tashnags, jubilant over their victory, claimed with some exaggeration that it was their "nearly one million soldiers" in the Caucasus who accounted for the triumph.[34] The reputation of the party was unquestionably skyrocketing in 1905.

Hopes for the Hague Conference. Hopes rose, too, that the American colossus would intervene for the Armenian cause — in Turkey. Repeatedly, Theodore Roosevelt expressed his deepest personal sympathy for the suffering minorities, the Armenians and the Jews. "As for the Armenians in Turkey," he wrote to the historian

G. O. Trevelyan in 1905. "if I could get this people [the Americans] to back me I really think I should be tempted to go into a crusade against the Turks." And Roosevelt and Armenian Americans looked to the forthcoming second Hague Conference as the instrument to rectify the burning wrongs committed against the Armenians. (In September 1904, in fact, Roosevelt suggested to American minister Oscar Straus in Constantinople that Armenian entreaties for international help should be "left to be brought before that conference.")[35]

Religious bodies like the national Methodist Conference in Philadelphia in March 1906 pleaded with the president, who recently in the Russo-Japanese peace treaty had emerged as the "world's pacificator," to enter a "national protest against the continuance of the outrages and to request a permanent guarantee against their renewal, which seems imminent," before the Hague tribunal. The most prestigious petition to the State Department came from James B. Reynolds and influential leaders in France, Italy, Belgium, Sweden, Denmark, Great Britain, Holland, Germany and Austria-Hungary. These men also suggested that were the Hague tribunal unsuccessful, Roosevelt should convene a special conference of the Berlin Treaty powers to deal with the Armenian Question. Armenians in America were urged by the immigrant press to lobby in Washington for American representation at the Hague conference.[36]

Roosevelt's moral revulsion at Turkish misrule was as real as his hatred of Spanish oppression in Cuba, but his ardor for the Armenians at the Hague soon cooled. In 1905–1907 he confided to friends and diplomats that the Berlin Treaty was a stumbling block to American intervention or even American initiative in the troubled Ottoman Empire. Also intervention by the United States might lead to European "fishing expeditions" in the Western Hemisphere. Roosevelt feared too, that American initiatives would only exacerbate the plight of the Armenians (and the Jews). For these reasons, Roosevelt poured cold water on the proposal to defend the Armenians at the Hague or at a special Berlin Treaty conference.[37]

Roosevelt's decision eased the troubled mind of his minister in Constantinople. "The action of the President," wrote a relieved John Leishman, "in declining to offer any interference will . . . prove a great relief not only to the Sultan but also to the European powers, who find the Turkish question a most difficult problem to solve. The mere suggestion of a [separate] conference was sufficient to cause considerable worry and anxiety."[38]

On the other hand, Roosevelt's inaction angered Armenian Americans. In April 1906 *Armenia*, the widely circulated English-language monthly of the Reformed Hnchag party, bitterly pointed to America's recent intervention in Morocco at the Algeciras Conference (1905), and to the country's long history of resistance to oppression in Greece in the 1820s and during the uprising of Kossuth and the Hungarians in 1848 — all as incontrovertible proof of America's de facto intercession in Europe. Later, a lengthy petition from Armenians in California accused Roosevelt of gross inconsistency. In the *Strenuous Life* he had flatly condemned the Powers' indifference to the suffering Armenians; how, then, could he now wash his hands of the issue?[39]

Whatever the historical merit of these arguments, Roosevelt had no enthusiasm for the Armenians when the second Hague Conference convened in late 1907. Ignored once again by the West, the Armenian suppliants and their sympathizers were now thrust back on their own initiative. The cycle of oppression, protest, and neglect had been repeated.

Division in the Parties.   The postscript to the period 1897 to 1907 in the Armenian American political community was one of increasing bitterness, confusion, schism, and tragedy. In 1907 Tashnagtsutiun was deeply troubled by ideological divisions. Just as the nationalist-socialist dichotomy had helped split the Hnchag party a decade before, now it threatened to fracture Tashnagtsutiun. As early as 1905 the party's Midwest regional conference, meeting in Chicago in October, noted that its members were troubled that *Troshag*, the party's official journal, published in Geneva, proposed adoption of a socialist program. The conference leaders urged the American representative assembly to wage battle against the Ottoman tyranny only so long as socialism was kept out of the party platform.[40] In the spring of 1907, their worst fears were confirmed as the party's radical elements at the Fourth International Congress of Tashnagtsutiun, meeting in May in Vienna, officially adopted an explicit socialist program for the party. Later in the same year Tasnagtsutiun officially joined the Second Socialist Internationale.[41]

A staunch protest arose from alienated members in America. In November and December 1907, American Tashnag intellectuals, echoing Hnchag declamations of a decade before, voiced their bitterest apprehensions that the new socialist orientation would wreck the party.[42] Critics outside the party concurred. Berating Tashnagtsutiun for its new direction, the Reformed Hnchags charged that the party had abandoned Turkish Armenia for socialism. "Funds, instead of being disposed of for Turkish Armenia's self defense, go to increasing the number of socialist propaganda tools and newspapers." Where was Tashnagtsutiun headed, they queried — to the Caucasus and socialism or to Turkish Armenia. Wasn't the party risking the perils of the old Hnchag experience?[43]

Meanwhile factionalism and schism besmirched the Reformed Hnchags. In late 1905 news arrived in the United States that a wealthy Turkish Armenian in Constantinople had been assassinated by a Reformed Hnchag from the United States.[44] In addition, long-festering personal animosities broke out in early 1906. One wing of the party charged that the Reverend Martoogesian, a Reformed Hnchag official, had appropriated $33,000 in party funds for his group's personal benefit and thereby turned the "Hnchag Party's holy temple into a pigsty." In April 1906, the party's chieftains in Cairo backed the Martoogesian faction and dissolved the party's American central committee, which criticized the priest. The dissolution edict fell "like a bomb." A representative assembly that convened in Fitchburg, Massachusetts, on July 1, 1906, failed after eight days of "long and exhaustive labor" to repair the breach. It was "the blackest day in our party's history," wrote its official historian.

Schism followed. In late 1906, 100 to 200 members and a dozen cells of the dissident, anti-Martoogesian faction, followed by like-minded Armenians in Cilicia, Bulgaria, and elsewhere, left the Reformed Hnchag party to form their own wing. Their new journal, Azk (the Nation), edited by Souren Bartevian, was first published in Boston on April 20, 1907.[45]

Then came the most squalid blackmail. In New York in 1907, prominent Armenian businessmen were threatened with death for failure to contribute large sums of money to the revolutionary cause.[46] And on the afternoon of July 22, in Union Square in the heart of New York City, Hovannes Tavshanjian, an eminent and philanthropic Armenian businessman, was brutally assassinated by a Reformed Hnchag henchman, Bedros Hampartzumian, for refusing to contribute $25,000 to the party's coffers. The plot led to Martoogesian and his wing of the party, but it blackened the name of all Armenian Americans.[47] English language papers called the Armenians "undesirable citizens" (Providence Evening Bulletin), the Hnchags were termed counterparts of the "Italian Mafia or Chinese Highbinders" (Richmond News Leader), and Mrs. Madeline Cole and Alice Stone Blackwell urged Armenians to quit the party's ranks.[48] It was the nadir of the period. To what depths had the Armenian revolution sunk?

13.

The Political Parties: An Analysis

In the period from 1890 to World War I, the Armenian Question in the United States was kept alive largely through the Armenian political parties. These paramilitary organizations — the Old and Reformed Hnchags, the Tashnags, and after 1908, the Armenian Constitutional Democratic Party (Ramgavars) — inspired and channeled immigrant political support for the Armenian Question. They raised funds and manpower for the military and political struggle in Turkey, Europe, and America; they founded and supported the immigrant press; and they established ancillary social institutions to preserve Armenian identity in America. Their frequent recourse to violence notwithstanding, the parties were vital institutions in the community.

Armenian political parties operated on many levels. The inner core of the parties lay in their gomides (committees) and central committees, which controlled the dynamics of party decisions. Their excursions into violence, mayhem, and political murder were clandestine. And the parties also sponsored publications, public meetings, and fund-raising rallies lobbying for the attention and support of the American and Armenian communities. An analysis of the inner mechanisms of the parties will shed light on this important aspect of the immigrant experience.

The Anatomy of the Parties

Unquestionably, Tashnagtsutiun became the largest Armenian political party in the United States before World War I. According to the figures from its annual assemblies and circular letters of the central committee, it grew most rapidly:[1]

	Gomides	Members
1903	36	(unknown)
1907	48	1,005
1914	77	1,728

The total number of members in all the other parties — the Hnchag party (the "mother revolutionary party"), the Reformed Hnchags, and the Ramgavar party, which was founded in 1908 out of elements of the Reformed Hnchag party and other conservative elements — equaled or barely surpassed Tashnagtsutiun. The Reformed Hnchags in 1905 were estimated to number 1,000 whereas in the same period the Old Hnchags never surpassed 400 or 500 members; by 1914, the Ramgavar party, Tashnagtsutiun's only significant rival, probably numbered about 1,200 members.[2]

The structure of the political parties derived largely from Russian revolutionary societies like Narodnia Volia: they were hierarchical, pyramidical in shape, and committed to discipline and secrecy. At the base of the parties were the rank and file, gathered in individual chapters or gomides, one in each Armenian American colony. The gomide was composed of 10 to 15 dues paying members, who were well known to each other, met weekly or monthly and swore oaths to "do what we are ordered to do."[3] Most gomide members were recruited from the factory laborers. Women were enlisted as early as 1903 in West Pullman, Illinois, but their numbers remained very small; after the Armeno-Turkish entente of 1908, American Tashnag gomides welcomed liberal Turks and Kurds as members.[4]

Like the leadership of the Russian prototype, the leaders of the Armenian organizations were a small, professional, intellectual, and autocratic elite. They formed the central committee, which was elected by the party assembly and usually composed of five members of whom three were full-time, paid party functionaries. Among these was the editor of the party's journal. The central committee's responsibility lay in executing the party's mandate from the European headquarters, organizing its annual assemblies, administering its party finances, and supervising its press and propaganda.

It was alleged that the central committee possessed absolute power over the rank and file, mainly to protect itself from its many internal and external enemies. One source of fear was the constant surveillance by the Turkish government through the Turkish Legation in Washington. And after 1905 the Turkish government, embittered over the attempted assassination of Sultan Abdul Hamid, induced the American Secret Service to assist its spy efforts in the United States.[5] The purpose of the surveillance was to identify Armenian revolutionaries on their return to Turkey so that they could be imprisoned and executed or to visit retribution on their families in Turkey. A second source of danger to revolutionaries was their Armenian political rivals in the United States and abroad.

Because of this, the central committees' names, activities, and missions were kept secret, and they assumed fictitious names while traveling. It was also said that the central committee could condemn to death a member to enforce discipline or punish proven traitors. To do so, however, the vote in the committee was required to be unanimous, and the accused could appeal to the party's general convention.[6]

Although the central committees exercised great power over their rank and file, they were in turn subordinate to the European headquarters of their parties. The central committee of the American branch of Tashnagtsutiun lay under the jurisdiction of the "supreme body," the (western) bureau in Geneva. Tashnag central committees in the Caucasus and Eastern Europe were ruled by the equally authoritative eastern bureau in Tiflis. Each bureau was composed of five of the party's most powerful figures, who guided the party's most pressing affairs. Every four years, or more frequently when issues of transcendent importance dictated, the party convened its international congress composed of delegates from all national branches. The comparable institution in the Reformed Hnchag organization was its all-powerful convention, located at various times in Cyprus or Cairo.[7]

There were many links between the bureaus and the branches in the United States. One was the press. *Troshag* (The Banner), the international journal of the Tashnags first published in Tiflis in 1891, was widely distributed among party regulars in the United States. In fact, Tashnags were often referred to in the early years as Troshagists."[8] A second link was the kordzich (field agent). A paid agent of the bureau, the kordzich traveled in one region or another to give direction and zeal to the outlying communities, supervised party finances, adjudicated party disputes, revivified lifeless gomides, and generally executed central committee mandates.[9] The two together — the press and the kordzich — were important cohesive forces in the widely scattered party organizations.

Internal Dynamics: Money, Munitions, and Political Murder

Ever since the mid-1890s when Nishan Garabedian, the Hnchag leader, raised an estimated $10,000 in the United States, the chief function of the parties in the New World had been to raise funds for the struggles in Turkey and Russia. As the Tashnag central committee's report to the bureau in Geneva noted in 1908: "The American region if not physically at least morally and financially can promise a great harvest."[10]

Party funds flowed from two main sources: dues and public meetings. The members' regular party dues varied. One Reformed

Hnchag said "we paid as much as we could; some paid 50 cents, some $100."[11] According to the Tashnag writer Rouben Der Minasian, party dues were dependent upon the individual member's ability to pay; and ordinarily the quota fixed by the gomide for the member did not exceed 2 or 3 percent of his income.[12] However, individual dues were trivial in comparison to funds raised by the parties' public meetings in the various Armenian American colonies. Local cells held weekly or monthly public meetings on Sundays "because the majority . . . are working people, who cannot attend meetings on work days", and before audiences of from fifty to several hundred, "fiery speeches were made, full of patriotic sentiments and strong and encouraging words, which appeal to the hearts and feelings of the listeners." Vivid descriptions of massacres always aroused attention.[13]

The Armenian communities generously contributed to party appeals. According to the February 3, 1906, issue of *Hairenik*, for example, $1,700 had been raised the prior week at a public meeting in Providence, Rhode Island. In Hamilton, Canada, $400 was collected at a meeting held December 31, 1905, "the people handing in $10 and $20 notes with great enthusiasm." One Bedros Varjabedian, a party orator, informed the United States Secret Service that on one mission, "he raised $782 in Waukegan alone at two meetings, within three months, previously to which he had raised $290 at that place. In St. Louis he raised $172, and in Chicago $250 and $75, at two meetings." At such meetings, contributors usually gave fictitious names "so that it may not be known who the contributors are when acknowledgement is made in the newspapers of the money contributed."[14]

Money raised in the United States was promptly funneled to party headquarters in New York, then abroad for a variety of purposes. In 1906, for example, the Tashnag central committee of the United States spent $9,600 for weapons and $2,523 to train Armenians in guerrilla activity. Prussic acid, dynamite cotton, and shells — all unavailable in Turkey — were purchased in the United States or in European countries to be smuggled into Turkey disguised as lamp wicks (dynamite cotton), and machine parts (shells). Revolutionaries also expended large sums to bribe Turkish customs inspectors, police, and boatmen to smuggle party members and contraband goods into Turkey.[15]

Whie large numbers of party regulars and sympathizers were involved in propaganda efforts and fund raising, a more clandestine and exclusive cadre devoted itself to violence for party ends. Political violence, which was always disavowed in the United States by the party leadership, was a cardinal element of revolutionary terrorist organizations in the Old World. There it was directed against corrupt officials, informers, and others identified with the tyrannizing regime. Inevitably, violence and terror spilled over into the United States.

The most common form of violence was the political disturbance — disrupting meetings of opposing parties by haranguing the speaker, shoving, shouting, and finally the ubiquitous fistfight — but stopping short of bloodshed. For example, after the Tashnags opened a meeting in New York on September 16, 1905, a Hnchag approached the stage to speak. He was promptly refused, words were exchanged, and fighting broke out; soon there were "screams and chairs" thrown in the air.[16] A Tashnag-inspired brawl at a Hnchag rally was an inevitable result. Similarly, emotions ran very high in 1907 after the split of the Reformed Hnchag party, when it was reported that the Reverend Hevont Martoogesian, a central committee member and apostle of the schism, had sent a group of followers to Paterson, New Jersey, "to break up a meeting of Armenians who were opposed to the Martoogesian policy. With two others he succeeded in breaking up the meeting without killing anyone."[17]

Agitators were particularly active in disrupting speaking tours of prominent opposition field workers. An important instance of this took place during the very successful mission of the famous Hnchag General Murad (Hampartsoom Boyadjian) in 1907. Boyadjian, who preached reconciliation among the warring revolutionary parties, drew enormous crowds; and in Boston on February 23, a Tashnag cadre, purportedly "jealous of his attention," subverted the meeting by shouting questions at the speaker.[18] Tashnags also assiduously disrupted meetings and church services in 1910 in Paterson, West Hoboken, and Philadelphia on the occasion of sermons by the rival pro-Ramgavar bishop, Musheg Seropian.[19]

On occasion the political activities extended to blackmail or assassination or both. The first internecine bloodshed occurred in 1903 when rival Hnchag groups, learning of the murder of Karekin Chitjian in Odessa, began armed retaliation in the United States.[20] In 1907, a group of Reformed Hnchags blackmailed prominent Armenian merchants in New York to obtain party donations. "The executive of the Constantinople Armenian Revolutionary Terrorists' Organization" — as it called itself — "condemn to death Harutiun Gulbenkian, Gullabi Gulbenkian and Padrick Gulbenkian — these three brothers who have entirely deaf ears to all appeals for the national freedom of Armenia. Our executive board has given them 24 hours to decide between their duty and their death." Although the Gulbenkians escaped death without paying the $25,000 demand, a terrorist killed Hovannes Tavshanjian for refusing to pay the blackmailers (Chapter 12); Caspar Vartanian, an Armenian priest who advised other Armenians not to yield to the extortion, was also murdered.[21]

Terrorist activities also carried Armenian Americans across the Atlantic and Mediterranean to the Ottoman Empire. Naturalized Armenian Americans enjoyed unusual diplomatic protection from the United States government when on Turkish soil, and party leaders accordingly employed them to commit violent acts. Certainly the most chilling example of this imported violence comes from a sworn affidavit before an American consul general in 1905 in Constantinople by a naturalized Armenian American caught red handed in a political murder. His lengthy confession is also of interest in that it exposes his character, thoughts, and behavior:

My name is Charles Vartanian. My name before I was naturalized was Garabed Vartanian. I am a native of Harput. I am 33 years old. . . . I went to America in 1890. . . . I had there a couple of friends who went with me, simply we ran away. . . . I first went to New York. Then went to Worcester. . . . From Worcester I went to Buffalo. . . . From Buffalo I went to Chicago I worked . . . in a tannery, Warl Brothers. . . . The last place I worked in the Western Wheel Works. . . . I was naturalized in September 26, 1896, in the Cook Country Courthouse. I joined a secret society called the "Hintchak" in Chicago. I joined the society because they asked me to join it. M. B. Seronian, M. Gouregian, and Simpat Mouradian. . . . The object of the society . . . is to try and free Armenians. I joined . . . about 4 years ago. . . . Zeronian was general manager, sometimes I was treasurer, sometimes others. We collected money and sent it to Armenia. The money was given to Zeronian who gave it to the head committee; we don't know where they are. In Chicago we had about 12 members.

When I joined the society I took an oath to do whatever the society directed me to do. . . . About the 1st of April Zeronian told me Zarehcotchian wanted me in New York. I went to New York and met Zarehcotchian in an Armenian restaurant in East 27th Street. Afarian [an accomplice] had gone to New York before me. I met Afarian at the restaurant with Zarehcotchian. Zarehcotchian said we three were going to Constantinople. From Chicago to New York I paid my own expenses. I know I was going on the business of the Hintchak Society. Zarehcotchian furnished me with money to pay our expenses from New York to Constantinople. We arranged to meet Zarehcotchian in Marseilles. [There] . . . he told us to go on to Pireus and he came direct to Constantinople. Zarehcotchian's committee name is Ardavas. He is known in Constantinople as Ohanessian. We stopped in Pireus near the railway station. [Zarehcotchian] . . . gave us the name of Simon . . . who is a coffee dealer in Pireus, and is a member of the Hintchak and I told him we were going to Constantinople. Simon had orders to send us there. . . . I came on a Greek steamer and one of the men employed on the steamer took me off. When I came here I wore a cap, the next day I wore a fez. . . . Zarehcotchian told me to wear a fez.

About two weeks before I committed the crime Zarehcotchian directed me to go with him and he would show me Apik Effendi [Oundjian] and I was with him alone. He took me on the bridge where the steamers land passengers, about half past five in the afternoon. He pointed out to me Apik Effendi Oundjian. Three days afterwards I took Afarian to the bridge and showed him Apik Effendi. About a week after that I saw Apik Effendi at the same place. About 3 days later . . . Afarian was arrested. . . . Sunday afternoon following after the arrest of Afarian Zarehcotchian came to me and gave me a revolver. I was to murder the man he pointed out. I asked the man's name and was told it was Apik Effendi. He did not tell me why I was to murder him. When we take the oath we swear to do what we are ordered to do. If Zarehcotchian had ordered me to shoot you I should not have done it without knowing the reason, if directed to kill an Armenian I should do it without reasons. We assumed that he had done something that called for it. I took blindly the word of Zarehcotchian as to whom I was to kill. This was on Sunday that Zarehcotchian gave me order to kill Apik Effendi and on Monday I tried to find him but could not. I went to the landing place and did not see him. Tuesday I did not see him. Thursday I went to the bridge, saw him, following him through some streets, and did not shoot. On Saturday I went to the landing stage and saw Apik Effendi leave the boat, I followed him across the bridge to this side and into a side street and shot him I think four times.[22]

Vartanian and his accomplice, Afarian, were promptly tried and found guilty by the Turkish authorities. Afarian was sentenced to fifteen years' hard labor; Vartanian was given the death sentence. Because of their American citizenship, however, they were (reluctantly) protected by the American State Department. After a short time in prison, they were released in 1908 under the terms of the general amnesty of the reformist Young Turk government.[23]

The Immigrant Press

Even though the political parties made violence and terror a part of the immigrant community, they also made enormously important contributions to the Armenian American community. For the parties established a plethora of immigrant and public institutions which promoted the Armenian cause in the diaspora. They sparked pro-Armenian sentiments, keeping alive the attachment to the Old Country and old ways. They encouraged education through schools and lyceums, and they promoted social activities through clubs, picnics, and plays. The communal contributions of the parties was as important as their clandestine activities.

Foremost of all such institutions was the immigrant press. But the earliest immigrant newspapers, from the late 1880s and early 1890s, predated the formation of the political parties in the United

States. They were one man operations with small circulations and short lives.

The pathfinder of the immigrant press was Haigag Eginian, who emigrated from Turkey in 1883 to further his education. A part-time student and New Jersey silk-factory laborer, Eginian wrote articles for Armenian papers in Constantinople. In 1888 he imported Armenian type from the Catholic Armenian Mkhitarist monastery in Venice to begin his own paper. His first such effort was *Arekag* (Sunlight), which was published in Jersey City in 1888. The monthly continued for about a dozen issues. Then in 1889 Eginian began publishing *Surhantag* (The Courier), also a monthly in West Hoboken; in 1890 the paper became a semi-weekly in New York under the name of *Azadutiun* (Freedom). That also failed. Other successive Eginian published papers were *Tigris* (1897), *Kaghakatsi* (The Citizen) in Fresno, 1902-1908 (fitfully), and finally *Nor Giank* (New Life) also in Fresno in 1912.[24]

The efforts of Dr. M. Smpad Kaprielian, another pioneer independent, were more enduring. In 1891 Kaprielian, a physician and Armenian patriot, began publishing *Haik*. Although the paper got him into trouble with the Turkish minister in Washington (Chapter 11), his vehemently written weekly lasted for six years, until 1898.[25] Other less successful nonparty journals were *Yeprad* (Euphrates), published in Worcester in 1898 by A. Shagalian, a student at Worcester Polytechnic Institute, and *Gaidzag* (Lightning), a broadside out of Lynn, both of 1898.[26]

The achievement of these small, independent journals of the late 1880s and early 1890s should not be discounted, especially in view of the mountainous difficulties the individual publisher-editors faced; they were, after all, singlehanded operations which set the stage for the more permanent immigrant press. On the other hand, they never matched the party organs. For the parties, despite their early struggles in establishing their journals, always relied on paid, professional editors, a cadre of (unpaid) correspondents and reporters in the United States and abroad, and a distribution system in the Old World and New. Above all they were supported by their party's prestige and finances. The appearance of the party journals marks the true emergence of the immigrant Armenian press.

The first party papers were *Tzain Haireneats* (Voice of the Homeland) and *Hairenik* (The Fatherland). The first issues of *Tzain Haireneats* were published independently in New York then in Worcester in 1899 but without success. Its editor, the Reformed Hnchag leader, Karekin Chitjian, then turned the journal over to the party, and this brought it "prestige and popularity" throughout the country. It remained a very influential Armenian journal until the party's demise in 1907. *Hairenik*, journal of Tashnagtsutiun, also was first published in New York in 1899, then moved (in 1900) to Boston where, under the aggressive, tough-minded leadership of Arshag Vramian, it became the premier Armenian language journal in the United States. It is still published daily in Boston in Armenian.[27]

The purpose of each political journal was to advance its party's program for the liberation of Armenia. A single issue would reflect an impressive variety of bylines from Constantinople, the interior Turkish centers of Kharpert, Adana, Sivas, Van, and Erzerum, and such important European and Middle Eastern centers as Tiflis, Batum, Cairo, Athens, Bucharest, London, and Paris. Party-inspired editorials attacked the Russian and Turkish oppressors and lashed out at the *chezok* (neutralist) Armenians for their "callousness" and indifference to the cause of Bleeding Armenia. Writers also abused their party opponents for their *sudahosutiunner* (lies), *sevatrekner* (calumnies), and *borodahosutiunner* and *yesahosutiunner* (boastings and egomania), attacked their opponents' credibility, intelligence, and loyalty to the Armenian cause, and went to great lengths to prove indubitably the other writer's stupidity or ignorance with respect to Armenian history, literature, or language. It was a field day for the untrammeled, self-educated Armenian intellectual.

Although the political struggle comprised the bulk of newspaper copy, party journalists, who were deeply committed to their followers' intellectual enlightenment, published the finest of modern Armenian, English, and French prose in their papers. The novels of Raffi were extremely popular. Regularly, *Hairenik* devoted columns to the literature of Alphonse Daudet, Edgar Allen Poe, John Galsworthy, and Jack London. Leading continental and American socialists were also reprinted.[28]

At the same time columns regularly reported on the immediate and pressing personal concerns of immigrant readers. News of the migration (especially a report from the "hell hole" of Marseilles, the chief Mediterranean port of call) was a standard item. Information on immigration regulation, American laws and ordinances, jobs, health care, and the like was common. The back pages of the rapidly expanding newspapers were increasingly devoted to advertising the services and goods of Armenian American business and professional people.

The third newspaper to appear by 1900 was *Gotchnag* (The Church Bell) in Boston. Without political affiliation, *Gotchnag* was a serious religious weekly supported financially and morally by the American Missionary Association and the Armenian Protestant Church in America. Like *Hairenik* and *Tzain Haireneats*, however, it covered the Armenian Question in great detail, reported on Armenian life in the United States, and strove assiduously to assist the Americanization of Armenians through educating readers about American citizenship obligations, American history, and the virtures of republicanism. Its first editor was the Reverend Herbert Allen, an American missionary who had served in Turkey for many years. Ideologically, it stressed the evangelical Protestant message, serializing such prominent American Protestants as Lyman Abbott, editor of *Outlook*.[29]

Gotchnag's most serious liability was its tie to the Armenian Protestant minority. Because of this, it stressed its national over its religious character. A small, serious, intelligent, and modern journal which eschewed the vituperation and backbiting of the political press, *Gotchnag* lacked *Hairenik*'s and *Tzain Haireneats*'s circulation; in 1907 it moved from Boston to New York where it is published to this day as an Armenian-language weekly.

Hairenik, Tzain Haireneats, and *Gotchnag* laid the foundations of the immigrant press in 1899–1900; in the decade after 1903, a handful of important additions to the Armenian-language press in America were made.

The most interesting of the "second wave" of the political press, and the only important one from the West, was the semi-official Tashnag journal, *Asbarez* (The Arena), founded in Fresno in 1908. Like *Hairenik, Asbarez* was established by a cadre of dedicated Tashnags who burned with zeal for the party. Their four-page weekly published party news and writings, encouraged use of the Armenian language, and deepened the love of the Armenians for the fatherland. At the same time volunteer editors, who were taken under the wing of Chester Rowell, editor of the *Fresno Morning Republican*, stressed the "American" needs of the immigrants — citizenship, getting along with the natives, voting, and becoming "integrated American citizens." To *Asbarez*, the immigrants could be both "good Armenians" and "good Americans." This acceptance of America clashed with the Tashnag party line. To East Coast Tashnags, America was only a way station, a temporary exile, a brief resting place for the pilgrims until they returned to the fatherland. In California, the *Asbarez* Tashnags knew that Armenians were planting deep roots in American soil which would not be extirpated. *Asbarez* also differed from *Hairenik* in its devotion to local (California) news, and it had the only regular Armenian American humorous column, "Notes from Uncle Hadji."[30]

In 1907, as the Fresno Tashnags were founding *Asbarez*, the split in the Reformed Hnchag Party brought about the demise of *Tzain Haireneats* and the emergence of two new journals representing the separate wings of the schism. *Azk* (The Nation), appeared in 1907 under the editorship of Souren Bartevian, previously editor of *Tzain Haireneats*. *Bahag* (The Sentinel) was founded in Providence in 1908 to represent the second wing, and it became an important journal, edited by Hratch Yervant, a Boston University Law School graduate.[31]

Eridasart Hayastan (Young Armenia), organ of the "old" Hnchag Party of Avedis Nazarbeg, first appeared as an Armenian American publication in Boston in 1903 with Sabah Culian at the helm. It then underwent a peripatetic existence from New York to Chicago, to Providence, and back to New York — its wanderings symbolizing the trials of the "mother" revolutionary party.[32]

Armenian party journals published abroad also circulated in the immigrant colonies throughout the period. The first Hnchag journal, *Hnchag*, circulated in Worcester in the early 1890s, and *Troshag*, official journal of the Tashnag western bureau in Geneva, made its way through the colonies. *Puzantion* (Byzantium) published in Constantinople, reached as far as Fresno, and in 1912, when the bumper raisin crop exhausted the local supply of paper boxes, the freshly picked raisins were wrapped in the pages of this prestigious journal from Turkey.[33]

In the meantime, dozens of "fly by night" journals such as *Tailailig* (The Warbler), *Dzakhavel* (The Broom), *Nvirag* (Envoy) and *Hai* (The Armenian) appeared in the Armenian colonies; the best ran for perhaps a dozen issues. A student magazine *Hai Usanogh* (The Armenian Student) appeared in 1909.[34] According to one source, *Ardziv* (The Eagle), a literary-political periodical published as a weekly in 1905–1906 and as a semi-monthly in 1907–1908 "had a stormy existence, since it specialized in fiery invective and violently attacked individuals, organizations, and other publications." Its contemporary and rival, *Arax*, was founded in Boston by one H. Hagopian in October 1905. "It was Mr. Hagopian's ambition," writes the same source, "to make his paper the greatest literary medium of American Armenians, but he fell far short of his goal. Old-time Armenians still recall the heated controversies of these two Boston newspapers . . . which seemd to expend all their energy in blackening each other's reputations."[35] Both were shortlived.

The first English-language Armenian journal also appeared before World War I. This was *Armenia*, first published in 1904 as the influential organ of the Reformed Hnchag party. Under the able editorship of Arshag Mahdesian, *Armenia* sought to influence American policy and public opinion by disseminating information on the history, culture, and contemporary political crisis of the Armenians in Turkey and Russia. The well-prepared monthly relied on the generous editorial assistance of a host of pro-Armenians: Julia Ward

Howe, Alice Stone Blackwell, Charlotte Perkins Gilman, Lucy Ames Mead, the Reverend Charles Gordon Ames, Edward H. Clement of the *Boston Transcript*, Prof. Albert S. Cook, the Reverend Charles F. Dole, Rabbi Charles Fleischer, James Bronson Reynolds, and Prof. William G. War. The monthly regularly issued 2,500 complimentary copies to officials in New York, New Jersey, New England, Illinois, and California; Presidents Roosevelt and Taft also received copies. The split of the Reformed Hnchag Party in 1907 suspended publication, but the journal was resurrected in 1910, again under the editorship of Arshag Mahdesian, under the name *New Armenia*.[36] It remained a significant propaganda weapon and the most important link with the non-Armenian community for 20 years.

Clubs and Societies

Concurrent with the party press, the parties established numerous social and political institutions such as clubs, libraries, and societies which played important roles in community life. The first of these to appear in new communities were the ubiquitous clubs where political partisans gathered together to exchange views and enjoy each other's company. In the earliest days, the offices of the newspapers often served as clubrooms. In Fresno, noted the playwright Shirvanzade, the busiest social center was the office of *Asbarez*, which was "continually crowded with young men and women, carrying news and messages" and "quarreling with each other." [37] In time, parties rented separate rooms for social centers known as the "Tashnag," "Hnchag," or "Ramgavar" club. There gomides held regular meetings and partisans fraternized over cards, narguiles, newspapers, and small talk. "My father went to the Tashnag club," recalled a second generation Armenian American, "he had his cronies there; they respected him there; he liked them and they liked him; they played pinochle or cards, for a few cents." In the club, the second generation Armenian added, "they talked about nothing else except the Armenian Question; there was very little else they were concerned about." And he added, "where else was a man who had no home life to go, will you tell me? He was not a member of the larger community. He had difficulties in English to express himself, as an immigrant he was an Armenian who was forced to be an Armenian because of circumstances."[38]

Notwithstanding the important fraternal aspects of the social clubs, the parties also used them for the improvement and education of their members. They rented rooms for libraries or reading rooms which contained serious works on the Armenian Question, Armenian history, and literature. There conscientious political leaders sought to educate the newly arrived immigrants in the rudiments of Armenian history and language, as well as in English. A reporter of the Hnchag clubs in Boston noted that in 1914:

The clubs were extremely active. The coming of war increased the local enthusiasm. By 1914 Hnchags maintained clubs in Watertown, Chelsea, Cambridge and elsewhere. Boston was the center. At the Tremont Street club, the rooms were open day and night, receiving members from outlying towns as well as Boston. The tables were crowded with comrades reading papers, books, disputing. . . . It was a kind of school. One evening each week there were lecture groups, at which the educated comrades spoke on scientific, political and social questions; college and university students were invited to speak on their specialties. . . . Later the group turned into an educational hearth, which assisted the illiterate to be educated; we promoted the zeal for self improvement.[39]

Parties also organized their own drama groups and military societies. The purpose of the thespian groups (see Chapter 8), noted a Tashnag regional committee in 1905, was to edify fellow members and the community through the production of historical Armenian dramas as well as famous European and American plays. The first regular "military" school was established in Providence in 1899, and others followed in New York (1900), Boston, and elsewhere. The function of the school was to train young volunteers to fight the Turks. Financially the schools required considerable sums: the Tashnag party annually appropriated over $2,000 for their upkeep. Earlier, in the mid-1890s, Hnchags in Lynn hired a retired United States Army captain to train their partisans. Shortly thereafter, the Turkish minister in Washington lodged an official protest with the State Department regarding the Lynn activities. A report of the 14th Annual Representative Assembly of the Tashnag Party (1909) noted with offense that "protests" from the Russian and Turkish legations to the State Department had forced the closing of the Providence Tashnag military academy.[40]

It was said that "whenever a few Armenians find themselves in a foreign land, their first thought is to publish a newspaper. . . ."[41] While the independent press universally failed to survive in the United States, the parties did successfully establish the tradition of Armenian American journalism. And the papers were widely read: George Mardikian once remarked that a copy of *Asbarez* reached at least 200 hands, and even many nonpolitical Armenians who could read no English read the Armenian newspapers.[42] Admittedly, the journals, with the exception of *Armenia*, neglected the interests of American-born Armenians, a fact belatedly recognized by the rise of English-language Armenian papers in the 1930s. And certainly the papers — as party organs — dissipated too much energy in fighting each other. But the political press constituted the major thrust for the Armenian Question in the United States, inspiring and galvanizing the immigrants to assist in the cause of Bleeding Armenia and educating a generation of newcomers.

For twenty-five years the Armenian Question had agitated the Armenian community in the United States and elsewhere. Frustrated by the broken promises of the European powers, and strangled by the yoke of Turkish misrule, the Armenians founded paramilitary organizations to champion their political rights in Turkey. In the United States these organizations played critical roles in raising funds and material for the military effort in Turkey; they also strengthened the community's political will through their propaganda, their all important presses, and their host of ancillary organizations. The political parties were what kept alive the hopes and ideals of a Free Armenia. At the same time, they stirred bloody conflict in Turkey while contributing much discord, turmoil and violence to the New World.

14.

To World War I, 1908–1914

The Armenian Question in the United States spanned the quarter century from 1888 to World War I. By 1907 the Armenian immigrants had witnessed or been part of the development of Armenian nationalist political parties in the United States (1888–1894), the fevered reaction to the Hamidean massacres (1894–1897), and a decade of disillusionment and demoralization (1897–1907). In 1907 the political parties were beset by schism, dissension, and political murder.

All this, however, was only a prelude to the next chapter in the saga of the Armenian Question. For the startling events of 1908 brought new hope for peace and justice in the Ottoman Empire.

The Young Turk Revolt: 1908

After two decades of struggle, political prospects for Armenian rights in Turkey appeared bleak in 1907. Past efforts had borne bitter fruit. Moreover, the Armenian political parties in Turkey and the diaspora foundered in a morass of extortion, schism, and internecine warfare. Although journals in late December carried stories of a congress of Ottoman and Armenian liberals in Paris which deliberated on the overthrow of the hated sultan, Abdul Hamid's entrenched power made these hopes seem chimerical.

Suddenly, dawn broke in mid-summer 1908 with the Young Turk revolt. In July disaffected Turkish reformist army officers and European-educated Turkish progressives engineered a stunning, bloodless takeover of the sultan's autocratic regime. These steps culminated the long-brewing reform movement which had expressed itself in the Ottoman liberal congresses of 1902 and 1907. Taken wholly by surprise, Sultan Abdul Hamid capitulated on July 24 and a military and civilian coalition seized the reins of power.[1]

Reform and Rejoicing. Liberal reforms soon expressed the modern temper of the Young Turks. First the Constitution of 1876, suspended by the sultan in 1878, was revived. The press would now be uncensored; controls over travel and education would be relaxed;

and the security and political rights of all Ottoman subjects, including the Christian minorities, would be guaranteed. The Ottoman parliament, prorogued since 1878, was recalled. The government began to remove corrupt officials from power, declared a general amnesty for all political prisoners and exiled subjects, and legitimized all political parties hitherto proscribed by the sultan.[2] Small wonder, then, that astonished European and American observers termed it "Daybreak in Turkey."[3]

The immediate response of Armenians in Turkey and the diaspora to the Young Turk revolt was ecstatic. Turks and Armenians embraced each other in frantic demonstrations in the streets of Constantinople. In Paris in August, Jews, Greeks, Turks, and Armenians joined in a "great celebration" of the rapprochement in Armeno-Turkish affairs.[4] In Fresno, at a rally of 1,500 Armenian Americans (the largest gathering in the colony's history) young men in fedayee (guerrilla) outfits and girls carrying Turkish and Armenian revolutionary flags, climaxed a series of coast to coast demonstrations in Armenian American communities in salute to the regime's principles of "Liberty, Equality, and Fraternity."[5]

The Young Turk coup deeply stirred Armenian party circles everywhere. In the first place, Tashnagstutiun, which had played conspicuous roles in the 1902 and 1907 congresses of Ottoman liberals and which had co-chaired the second congress, enjoyed a rapid spurt in prestige. Six of the twelve Armenian delegates in the first Turkish parliament of 1908 were to be Tashnag party members.[6] Rallies in Washington, New York, Boston, and Fresno paid tribute to the Tashnags.[7]

At the same time, the most powerful revolutionary leaders in exile in the New World immediately took ship for Constantinople. By the fall Sabah Culian (Old Hnchag), Souren Bartevian (Reformed Hnchag), and Arshag Vramian (Tashnag) were editing or writing for journals in Constantinople, Smyrna, or Alexandria.[8]

The third and most important development in Armenian politics stemming from the Young Turk coup was the emergence of the Hai Sahmanatragan Ramgavar Gusagtsutiun (Armenian Democratic Constitutional Party), commonly known as the Ramgavars.

Ramgavar Party Founded. The Ramgavar party was born in Alexandria in October 1908 as a fusion of three disparate groups: the moderate Reformed Hnchags who had split from their party in 1907 and had founded *Azk* (in Boston), the tiny Ideological Union (an offshoot of the old Armenagan party), and more generally moderate business and professional groups affiliated with the Armenian Apostolic Church and the Armenian General Benevolent Union. *Azk* served as the first Ramgavar journal in the United States.[9]

The platform of the Ramgavar party differed sharply from that of Tashnagtsutiun. To be sure, the party applauded the return of constitutional government in Turkey and endorsed the principle of reform — not revolution — in the empire. "We accept the principle that the minority groups who constitute the Ottoman Empire, both as communities of citizens and as individual or historical entities must keep firm, in its entirety, the integrity of the Ottoman Empire."[10] However, the Ramgavars were much more cautious about the Young Turks, fearing that the nationalist movement would press for the .amalgamation and eventual obliteration of the empire's "potentially disloyal" minorities into a Pan Turan or Pan Ottoman state. (The deep-seated apprehension of the Ramgavars that Young Turk rule imperiled the autonomy of Armenians qua Armenians in the empire was spelled out in a lengthy interview in September 1908 between Souren Bartevian, a Ramgavar chieftain, and Ahmed Riza, a Young Turk leader.) The fact that Tashnagtsutiun swooned at the Young Turk entente and that its socialist credo seemed to negate ethnic loyalties heightened Ramgavar anxiety at the Young Turk connection.[11]

The church-backed, middle-class Ramgavars also clashed with the Tashnags' socialist position (adopted in 1907) on the Armenian Question. To the Ramgavars, western socialism was irrelevant to Turkey because, said Azk, quoting the eminent socialist Arthur Johnson, the Ottoman Empire was "one thousand years behind Europe and America."[12] Moreover, socialism sowed discord and distrust of the church and middle classes, the traditional pillars of the nation.

While the Ramgavars criticized Tashnagtsutiun and the Young Turk-Tashnag entente in 1908–1909, the Old Hnchag party of Nazarbeg, which maintained a doctrinaire attachment to the armed socialist revolution, was also attacking the Tashnags and their entente with the Young Turks. First, men like Sabah Culian, touring the Turkish provinces on his party's behalf and corresponding with Eridasart Hayastan in the New World, labeled the new alliance "despicable, immoral and unjust." Surely the Turks, with the blood of 1894–1896 and 1904 fresh on their hands, remained the mortal enemies of the Armenians — whatever the Turks' political designation. To emphasize their point, issues of Hnchag and Eridasart Hayastan, circulating through the interior, warned of the Young Turk "snare," and special issues were devoted to the horrors of the Sasun massacres to remind Armenians of the Turks' "true character." Further, the alliance with the Young Turks, according to the Old Hnchags, signified a sellout of the Tashnags' historic advocacy of the socialist proletarian revolution. To the Hnchags, victory for the Armenian cause in Turkey lay in alliance not with the perfidious Young Turks but with the socialist revolutionary parties of eastern Europe, especially Russia.[13] (Thus the Tashnags were denounced by the Ramgavars for a surfeit of socialism and by the Hnchags for a repudiation of their socialist past.)

Repatriation Urged. Despite the political infighting, national leaders sought to rebuild Turkish Armenia in this "honeymoon period" with the Young Turks, and in so doing, many looked to Armenian Americans as a fertile source of manpower, finance, and technical expertise. The first call to Armenian Americans for a massive repatriation to Armenia in the early Young Turk period came from the American wing of Tashnagtsutiun in the summer of 1908. On August 5, the central committee of the party exulted: "A New Year opens before us. For Armenia, as for all Turkey, the dawn of happiness and peace is upon us." On September 15 a central committee circular, which emphasized the new freedoms to travel and engage in political activity, urged all comrades to return to Turkey for the sake of "the party and the race." On November 10 another circular summoned *all* Armenian Americans, including chezoks (neutrals), to repatriate before being "consumed on foreign soil."[14]

Tashnagtsutiun's call for repatriation was not unexpected. Since the mid-1890s, the party intellectuals had exhorted partisans to regard America not as a permanent home but rather as a temporary resting place. "Our homeland is not here, but in Armenia," exhorted *Hairenik* in 1899. "We are pilgrims in America, not colonists."[15] Then the establishment of constitutional government in July 1908 seemed to provide the political conditions for exiles to return.

The Ramgavars were equally active. On January 30, 1909, *Azk* in Boston called upon "talented Armenian immigrants" to return to regenerate Armenia. The vastly underdeveloped country, it noted, required railroads, improved farming methods, and cadres of "civil, mining, and mechanical engineers, draftsmen, patternmakers, moulders, machinists, plumbers and agricultural and horticultural experts, and architects."[16] At about the same time, in response to the Young Turk consul's speech to the Boston Commercial Club calling for American products to rebuild Turkey, *Azk* expressed grave fears that Turkey's lack of technical experts would require the importation of American, English, German, French, and other European engineers, and "we shall occupy under them the place of workmen." Accordingly, *Azk* insisted: "Our greatest need is . . . technical schools. . . . Students in these schools will obtain scientific knowledge with less expense and will examine on the spot the goods and needs of their country and will successfully compete with foreigners." On March 6 *Azk*, buoyed by Young Turk rule, noted with obvious pleasure that "The opening of Turkey in 1908 and the promising political future" was attracting young Armenians.[17]

At the same time the politically conservative Armenian General Benevolent Union also summoned all Armenians to shoulder responsibilities in rebuilding Armenia. Dr. Nazareth Dagavarian, a founding father and first secretary of the AGBU's general board, left for Turkey to supervise the AGBU's enormous plans to build schools and hospitals and assist the country's agriculture and industry.[18]

The response to the heady events of mid-summer 1908 was indeed overwhelming.

Counterreaction: The Adana Massacre of 1909

Tensions Build. After early 1909, harsh realities intruded into Armeno-Turkish relations. Politically, the new regime was continuously beset by foreign embroilments which reverberated throughout Turkey. Simultaneously, the enormous social, political, and ideological forces unleashed by the Young Turk revolt produced a severe backlash in internal affairs.

The first problem in Muslim-Christian relations in the early Young Turk period stemmed from the voracious European incursions into Ottoman territory. As early as October 1908 Bulgaria declared its full independence from Ottoman rule, the Austro-Hungarians announced their annexation of Bosnia and Herzgovina, and Crete declared its intention to unite with Greece. Now, as later, each European attack exacerbated Armeno-Turkish relations.

At the same time the new freedoms of the Young Turk government gave impetus to revolutionary and nationalist Armenians, who appeared to throw caution to the winds in politicizing and arming Armenian youth. "At Kessab, Adana and other places, the Armenian revolutionists gradually became irritatingly overbearing and arrogant. At Adana, they might be heard at night singing their national war songs, and foolishly shouting threats and exultation at their ancient enemies."[19] The bishop of Adana, Musheg Seropian, was especially active in arousing jealousies and age old animosities.[20] Meanwhile, conservative Turks, threatened by the Young Turk regime and the freedoms of the hitherto subservient Christian nationalities, girded themselves for counterrevolution. In early 1909 these religious and political counterrevolutionary forces coalesced into the Society of Mohammed, a group dedicated to the restoration of traditional rule under Sultan Abdul Hamid.[21]

Rising tensions were not masked from foreign observers. In late 1908 the American ambassador in Constantinople warned that uneducated Turks were troubled that "Armenians were usurping too much authority and that if these new reforms came about, . . . in a short time the Armenians would far outstrip the Turks in the acquisition of money, and then the Armenians would be in authority, so in order to prevent this state of affiars, it was decided to inaugurate another massacre."[22]

Attack and Reactions. And the massacres soon exploded. In early 1909 savage anti-Armenian pogroms ripped through the Cilician Plain and northern Syria. The first killings, initiated by conservative anti-Armenian backers of Abdul Hamid, erupted in Adana, a populous, Europeanized city on the Cilician Plain. There pitched battles raged in the city's streets between armed Turkish irregulars in connivance with Young Turk authorities and the almost defenseless Armenian populace. Stern remonstrances from the European powers in Constantinople abruptly halted the killings. Soon after, however, the carnage recurred when Turkish troops from Macedonia, dispatched to Adana purportedly to "prevent further slaughter," abetted the irregulars in looting and mutilating and killing Adana's Armenian population. By mid-April the death toll in Adana province rose to 30,000 Armenians, mostly males. At the same time pro-Hamidean forces seized the capital of Constantinople.[23]

The outraged European powers promptly dispatched warships to the Eastern Mediterranean, and President Taft, on the news of the killing of two American missionaries, ordered the battleships *Montana* and *North Carolina* to join the six European men of war at the Turkish port of Mersin.[24] Meanwhile, Turkish troops from Aleppo joined irregulars in bloodying the Armenian communities in northern Syria, especially Antioch, Aleppo, and Kessab. In all over 35,000 Armenians were slain, and over 40 towns and villages and more than 10,000 homes and shops were destroyed. The arrival of European battleships, the crushing of the counterrevolution in Constantinople by the Action Army, and the deposition of Abdul Hamid in late April finally ended the bloodletting.[25]

To "soothe the raging passions," the Young Turk government promised swift punishment for the guilty and appropriate reparations, establishing a military tribunal at Adana for such purposes.[26] This step and the deposition of "Abdul the Damned" apparently mollified the infuriated American Congress. In early May 1909 a joint resolution sponsored by Representative Wanger of Pennsylvania tendered to the new Sultan Mohammed V "the friendly regard of the government and people of the United States, for him, his government and people and our earnest hope and firm confidence that among the earliest achievements of his reign will be the complete restoration of order . . . and elimination of the appalling atrocities upon Christian missionaries and other non-Moslems."[27] The American colossus moved no further. Some weeks later, when the Armenian Evangelical Alliance petitioned the president to employ the influence of the country to improve the condition of the Armenians in Turkey, the State Department reiterated platitudes, "convinced that, in the obvious impossibility of intervention, it is powerless."[28]

In 1909, as in 1894–1896 and 1904, care for the wounded, homeless, and orphaned survivors of the massacres sprang from many humanitarian and philanthropic sources. The International Red Cross, the Armenian General Benevolent Union, and the Armenian patriarchate in Constantinople were joined in January 1910 by the newly established Armenian Relief Society of New York to assist in the staggering task. The first such efforts were funneled through the Red Cross to American missionaries in Cilicia and northern Syria. Not long after, orphanages, which by now had become the doleful symbol of the nation's suffering, were founded at Mersin, Adana, Hadjin, Dort Yol, Hasanbeylin, Aintab, and Marash. The AGBU provided tents, food, clothing, and medicine to an estimated 50,000 to 75,000 homeless and hungry Armenians, and they assisted in founding orphanages and rebuilding schools.

Unlike the sultan's government in earlier tragedies, the new Turkish government contributed to the rebuilding of villages by voting a grant of 100,000 liras, a five-year annual allocation of 10,000 liras for the care of women and orphans, and a credit of 50,000 liras to Armenian businessmen. Djemal Bey, the newly installed governor general of Adana, took pride in establishing an orphanage for the children orphaned in the Adana massacre. The Turkish government also assisted in the rehabilitation and economic recovery of the Armenian communities of Antioch and Kessab which had been hard hit by the massacres.[29]

Political Repercussions. The humanitarian efforts to aid the suffering victims and rebuild their homes and industries united Armenians on both sides of the Atlantic, but the issues of the responsibility for 35,000 slain Armenians and the future of Armeno-Turkish amity produced more violent and permanent political divisions in the Armenian American colonies. The crucial issue was Tashnagtsutiun's pro-Young Turk policy. The party, though staggered and stunned by the frightful pogroms, ascribed the massacres not to the Young Turk party but to the last, embittered impulses of Hamidean reactionaries. The Tashnag central committee early underscored this point (*Hairenik*, May 11, 1909): "The Armenians of Cilicia have become victims of the remaining base and plotting intriguers of the old regime; the Mohammedan rabble has once again put its hand in Armenian blood. . . . This extensive crime in Cilicia is not the first but it is perhaps the last." And even with the abdication and exile of Sultan Hamid in late April, the central committee warned of more

reactionary uprisings, since "our neighbors' most primitive bloodthirsty instincts have been awakened."[30]

In view of this position, Tashnagtsutiun resolved to cooperate
with Young Turk elements in an "armed peace" to defend the Turkish constitution from its reactionary enemies. On May 2, the executive committee of the newly organized Armenian Volunteers in New
York City posed the most critical question: "Who is going to guarantee the defense of our nation, ... who is going to explain the
meaning of our common human rights to the raving and bloodthirsty
mobs, and defend us from those uncertain storms which are so preg-
nant in the anarchic Turkish future? Who? ... Who?" To this the
volunteers replied: "No one but we the Armenians are able to save
us, if we wish, if we recognize our responsibility." The time had thus
arrived for "Armenian American youth, both neutralist and pro revolutionary, to cease its talk and join a volunteer army," so that few
would say that "ARMENIANS KNOW ONLY HOW TO BE MAS-
SACRED." In Boston, the Tashnag central committee recommended
that all comrades departing America for Turkey carry at least one
Mauser revolver on their persons.[31]

Fighting against Turkish reactionaries and an Armenian backlash against the Young Turks which might "spell new massacres,"
Tashnagtsutiun also campaigned on a pro-Young Turk self-defense
platform. "The Adana massacres," said a prominent Tashnag in later
years, "were an unfortunate occurrence but we were cooperating
with the Ittihadists [Young Turks] ... in order to eliminate all such
future events." In late summer 1909, despite evidence of Young Turk
involvement in the massacres, a Young Turk-Tashnag accord affirmed
their principles of cooperation.[32]

To the Ramgavars, Tashnagtsutiun's policy in 1909 was crimi-
nally naive. For them, the Young Turk-Tashnag entente had paved
the way for Adana. *Azk*, May 22, 1909: "The Young Turk Tashnag
bloc [was responsible] for the irresponsible high hopes, the alluring
words and solemn promises of justice, liberty and equality." "Let
Armenians everywhere understand," rued the journal, that "despite
so many vows, embraces and oaths, the Turk can thus massacre and
exterminate us. ... They shout of liberty, equality and fraternity and
then 40,000 Armenians are cut to pieces." Similarly, as Turkish
tribunals made official inquiries into the massacres in mid-1909, *Azk*
mocked the fact that high-ranking Young Turks in Adana implicated
in the bloodletting not only escaped punishment but also remained
in power, whereas five innocent Armenians were executed for "complicity." And the Tashnags, charged *Azk*, by pandering to the Young
Turks, were embracing principles of the "COMPLETE AMALGAM-
ATION" of Armenians and Turks — an act of "national assassination

and betrayal." In summation, Adana was the first "definitive indication that the 'freedom' brought by the Young Turks was the gift of a counterfeit revolution, and that the nation could expect even greater ordeals in the future."[33]

After Adana, few non-Tashnags espoused hopes for reform in Turkey. In the May 1910 English-language *Armenia*, Diana Apcar, a highly respected social scientist, warned that the Turks' deep-seated economic jealousy of the Armenians and their religious fanaticism spelled continuing oppression. "No Mohammedan race or dynasty has ever shown itself able to govern well even subjects of its own religion, while to extend equal rights to subjects of a different creed is forbidden by the very law of its being." Notwithstanding the efforts of a "few Turks of liberal ideas" the Turkish race would not change from its history of "Massacre and Oppression."[34]

On the other hand, official American opinion was less pessimistic. In addition to the congressional resolution of confidence in Abdul Hamid's successor and the constitutional government, the American consul in Beirut in mid-1909 expressed hope of progress in Turkey if Armenians worked at the new constitution instead of emigrating to the United States, and in 1911 a distinguished political scientist at Columbia ventured high praise for the Young Turks' achievements. Perhaps Adana *was* the last of the Armenian massacres.[35]

The Fatherland Calls: 1910–1911

Adana weakened but did not destroy Tashnagtsutiun's faith in the Young Turks. The challenge remained to build a new Turkey. How was a renascent Armenia to be created? Where were the funds and manpower to build the roads, schools, and factories, till the fields and defend the nation from its manifold enemies? How could the backward, stagnant economy be transformed to keep Armenians in the empire?

As in the past, Tashnagtsutiun turned to the expanding Armenian American community as the wellspring of assistance. In 1910 the party chose as its delegate to enlist the immigrants' support, the enormously influential Turkish Armenian E. Agnooni. A charismatic leader, Agnooni had represented Tashnagtsutiun at the 1902 Paris Congress of Ottoman Liberals; in 1907, along with the Turkish liberals Ahmed Riza and Prince Sabhaddein, he had presided over the second assembly of that prestigious group. A poet, distinguished orator, and the ranking Armenian in the Turkish parliament, his immense popularity ranked him just below the party's founding triumvirate of Christopher Mikaelian, Stepan Zorian, and Simon Zavarian.[36]

Agnooni arrived in the United States in September 1910. Soon he visited and addressed Armenians in Lynn, Brockton, Worcester, Whitinsville, Lawrence, Lowell, Newburyport, Haverhill, Portland, Troy, New York, New Britain, New Haven, West Hoboken, Philadelphia, Richmond, Granite City, East St. Louis, Cleveland, and Detroit. By mid-1911 he had spoken to 50,000 Armenians in 50 cities and made contacts with Greek, Bulgarian, Turkish, and Kurdish colonies in the United States.[37] And everywhere he traveled, he was enthusiastically received. In Providence everyone from 6 to 60 turned out to greet the handsome, renown orator; according to the *Providence Journal*, virtually the entire colony of 2000 Armenians greeted him with "enthusiasm unknown to the group." In Fresno, where he arrived after 11 P.M. one November night, he found over 100 Armenians crowded into the tiny train station shouting *gettzas* (hurrahs) as he descended from the car. There, as elsewhere, a few days later he spoke for nearly 2 hours, preceded by impassioned welcoming speeches and violin solos.[38]

To the New World Agnooni preached the sermon of repatriation; Turkey's salvation lay in the return of scattered Armenians (and Greeks, Turks, Kurds, and Bulgarians) who with their wealth, talent, education, and American spirit could revitalize the "sick man of Europe." Today, however, lamented Agnooni, Turkey was being drained by the emigration. "Whole villages are vacated. Numerous vilayets are without male inhabitants and in the 'dying villages' only the old and women had remained." Repatriation was therefore absolutely indispensable. To dramatize his theme, Agnooni recited his famous hymn, "Tebi Yergir" (To the Homeland):

> Tarnank, paghstagan hayer
> Tarnank, bantukhd hayer
> Tarnank, Tebi Yergir
>
> (Let us return, refugee Armenians
> Let us return, émigré Armenians
> Let us return to the Homeland.)

What specific steps would facilitate the repatriation? First, Agnooni urged the Turkish government to hasten economic reform so that "those who return will not go hungry and will not be compelled to flee once again to the other side of the ocean but remain in their own country, cultivate the soil, form families and elevate the country." Second, all proconstitutional elements in the diaspora needed to form bureaus of emigration "to help those who wish to go back to their country, but have no means, and to provide work for them when they arrive there." Third, all Ottoman émigré groups in the United States and Canada should foster mutual cooperation in the "name of that beautiful future . . . which leads, undeviatingly, [to] the solidarity and harmonious co-operation of the immigrants of all nations and religions." Agnooni concluded, "The 400,000 Ottoman immigrants in America have a great role to play. . . . They, being educated in the atmosphere of the New World, can more easily come out of the pale of racial and religious antagonism which has been the cause of so many ruins."[39]

Agnooni's tumultuous speaking tour triggered a steady stream of Tashnag appeals, broadsides, editorials, and propaganda directed to Armenian Americans. The 16th Annual Representative Assembly of the party in Providence in late December 1910 resolved to educate all gomides to the solemn task of repatriation by — flooding *Hairenik* and *Asbarez* with articles and editorials about the emigration; forming "repatriation committees" in the major cities; assisting needy Armenians to book passage; informing new or prospective immigrants that America was no "fountain of happiness and money," and that the Armenian young men in the United States "endured extremely harsh and punishing conditions" as immigrant laborers. A central committee circular letter of May 1911, calling attention to the "astonishing proportions" of the emigration streaming out of Turkey to America, urged Tashnags in the United States to warn Old World relatives that migration had its dire perils — no jobs and heartbreaks for those newly arrived who "do not know the English language and have no craft." At the same time Tashnags sought to dissuade young Armenian males from fleeing the Turkish draft and instead to enlist to defend constitutional Turkey and the Armenians.[40]

The repatriation campaign continued after 1911. In May 1912, for example, *Hairenik* proposed that Armenians in the United States raise $500,000 to develop the "apparel, shoe and linen" industries in Turkey to help attract Armenians from the diaspora to the homeland.[41] And the subject of repatriation was regularly enunciated in all public forums.[42] However, statistics from the United States Commissioner General of Immigration revealed that relatively few Armenians actually repatriated. (The chart below shows the numbers of Armenians who annually, from 1908 to 1914, entered the United States, and who returned to Turkey).

	Entering U.S.	Leaving U.S.
1908	3,299	165
1909	3,108	464
1910	5,508	447
1911	3,092	902
1912	5,222	670
1913	9,353	625
1914	7,785	1,117

Moreover, the return movement included large numbers of laborers and old people, but few of the doctors, engineers, and planners summoned by Tashnagtsutiun.[43]

The Tashnag call for repatriation was a failure, for obvious reasons — growing adaptation to America, the fear of political instability, the stagnant economic situation, and the failure of Young Turk reforms.

Crisis and Unity: 1912–1914

As Tashnagtsutiun struggled with the repatriation campaign, a new drama, spurred by European developments, was unfolding in Turkey. In September 1911 Italy seized the Turkish territories in Tripoli. Then in October 1912 Greece, Serbia, and Bulgaria began an attack on Western Turkey; a second Balkan War erupted in June 1913. As before, these conflicts had dire repercussions for the Armenian population in Turkey. In Anatolia, the depredations of the marauding Kurds, which had not been curbed by and perhaps were abetted by the government, grew more frequent. Armenians were murdered near Bitlis at the rate of twenty-seven a month and cattle stealing, rape and murder reported from places as far apart as Van and Adana, Bitlis and Hadjin showed a general condition of terror such that no Armenian dared travel alone.[44] The military conscription of able bodied young men for service in the Balkan Wars intensified the situation.[45] There were ugly incidents in Constantinople where even the Armenian patriarch received ominously threatening letters.[46] A report from Kharpert in April 1913 summed up the dire situation: "The Adana massacring chauvinists are at work; who knows what horrible drama is underway to throttle the Armenian Question. We find ourselves before a real fight. This . . . threatens a great storm for the Armenians."[47]

Throughout the world Armenian communities promptly responded to the new crisis. In Russia, Armenian writers, journalists, and lay and religious leaders penned protests to St. Petersburg. In Echmiadzin, Catholicos Kevork V petitioned the Russian government for action against Turkey and urged all Armenian colonies to send representatives to the upcoming Balkan peace conference in London to plead the Armenian cause before the European concert.[48] In America on October 18, 1912, a newly organized Worcester International Committee issued a circular letter — signed by the clergy of the Worcester Armenian Apostolic and Armenian Evangelical churches and by ten distinguished Armenian leaders representing all political factions — calling on all Armenian political parties, religious bodies, cultural groups, newspapers, and interested individuals in the United States and Canada to convene in Worcester to "discuss, consult and draw up a clear proposal" to assist the powers in the resolution of the Armenian Question. Surely the sacrifices of the Armenians for the Constitution of 1908, and the 30,000 massacre victims in Adana in 1909, compelled the world to listen to the plea.[49]

At the conference, over 100 men of "liberal education, professional men, educators, physicians, lawyers, journalists, religious teachers" met for 4 days of "feverish activity." The conference elected Dr. M. Smpad Kaprielian as the Armenian American community's representative to the delegation of the Catholicos to the London conference in early 1913. It sent a series of resolutions to Washington condemning the Young Turk government's continued inactivity and "neglect of the Armenians." And it formed a permanent committee representing the Armenians in the United States and Canada to prosecute the Armenian Question in the United States.[50]

Simultaneously, Armenian political organizations in the United States, agitated by the anarchy in Turkey, laid aside mutual recriminations to work in unity. In August 1913 in Providence, for example, the four political groups — the Tashnags, Ramgavars, Old Hnchags, and Reformed Hnchags — convened to "secure some measure of cooperation between the parties." Then in November 1913, on the basis of successful meetings between their organizations, the Tashnags, Old Hnchags, and Reformed Hnchags (the Ramgavars failed to join) proposed a joint organizational structure of the parties, composed of three members from each organization, to issue joint circulars, form similar unity committees throughout the colonies, and form closer links between the political press.[51]

The international outcry, in which Armenians from as far away as Japan and Burma participated, did not fall on deaf ears. The czar's government especially — struck by the anguished outcry of Russian Armenians, the desire to keep ethnic peace in the Caucasus, and the wish to ward off German plans to take over the Armenian Plateau by championing the cause of their brother Christians in Turkey — was receptive to the Armenian cause. Meanwhile, in Turkey in May 1913, the Armenian National Assembly, the governing body of the Apostolic Armenians of the empire, was encouraged by Russia's quickened interest in the nation's pleas. Calling attention to the "disquieting symptoms, precursors of a massacre, or a catastrophe capable of overshadowing, in its horror, the most fearful tragedies of the past," the National Assembly proposed a comprehensive set of reforms for the beleaguered Turkish Armenian provinces.[52]

The main provisions of the plan, subsequently incorporated into a Russian-backed program, included selection of an European or Ottoman Christian administrator for the Armenian provinces, which would be reorganized into a single political unit; dissolution of the former Kurdish Hamidié regiments; restitution of Armenian losses of property usurped during the massacres; and the obligation of the European powers to guarantee enactment of the reforms. Championed by the czar's regime, the proposed reforms became the basis for Great Power deliberations in Constantinople in mid-1913.

European diplomatic rivalries, again intruding into the Armenian Question, succeeded in emasculating the proposed reforms; as the Powers deliberated through 1913 and early 1914, the dreams of the Armenians were compromised bit by bit. By early 1914 the tortuous negotiations between the Great Powers produced a watered down scheme in which the proposed territorial arrangement for administration was weakened; there was no mention of restitution for Armenian losses; and, most important, Europe failed to guarantee execution of the reforms.

In the United States the Tashnag central committee, feeling deeply embittered and betrayed, called for a boycott by Armenians of the general Turkish parliamentary elections and a plan of armed self-defense on the part of the Armenians in Turkey.[53] Nevertheless, many Armenians greeted the European reform scheme of February 1914 with joy. For, after a quarter century of strife, bloodshed, and unfulfilled promises, Europe was intervening — at least by dispatching trained administrators to the new political subdivisions of the Armenian provinces. By May 1914 two men, Westenenk, the chief provincial administrator in the Dutch East Indies, and Major Hoff of the Norwegian Army, were in Turkey en route to their respective posts in Van and Erzerum to commence the Great Power reforms. A moment of triumph had arrived.

But the conclusion of this chapter of the Armenian Question was bitterly ironic. For the Armenians in mid-1914, on the verge of seeing the Great Power reforms, were soon to endure the onslaught of World War I and their greatest tribulation: the holocaust of 1915 which annihilated the Armenian nation in Turkey.

PART FIVE

Acculturation

15.

Becoming Armenian Americans

In time the Armenians grew accustomed to the New Country and became Armenian Americans. Even though all Armenians remained fervently attached to the Old Country and wished to educate their children as "good Armenians"; even though their political parties, newspapers, churches, and village compatriotic societies constantly reminded them of the Old Country and their responsibilities to it; at the same time the newcomer learned American ways.

Part of the acculturation process came from the physical and economic adjustments and the familiarity induced by time. The "greener" just off the boat yesterday was becoming an "American" today. However, it was the American educational system which systematically transformed the community. The children of the immigrants rapidly adjusted to American ways through public schools, while many immigrants themselves attended night schools. (Parents, while encouraging public education, at the same time required the children to learn the old language.) Some were exposed to the immigrant-sponsored lectures and lyceums. And many hastened the learning process by attaining citizenship and participating in American politics. All of these factors molded the ideas and values of the new individuals — the Armenian Americans.

Public Education

Grade Schools. The most potent influence on the Armenian immigrant community was the requirement of public schooling for all minors to the age of fourteen. By law every native or foreign-born Armenian American child of school age was required to attend a public school whose classroom language was English and whose curriculum and teachers inculcated Anglo-Saxon values.

In its 1907–1910 survey of the public schools in 37 cities (including Boston, Lynn, New York, Philadelphia, Providence, and Worcester), the United States Immigration Commission counted 1,031 children of "Armenian-born fathers." In practically all of the cities investigated, the overwhelming majority of the Armenian students were in the "elementary grades" (from kindergarten to the ninth grade), and of these the largest numbers were in grades 1 through 3. In New York, for example, 83 percent of the children of immigrants were found in the elementary grades and most numerously in grades 1 through 4. In Worcester, 78 percent were in the elementary grades.[1]

What explained the preponderance of Armenian children in the elementary grades? Why were so few in high school? According to the Immigration Commission, the "Mexicans, Italians, Portuguese, and German Russians [of Fresno] are apt to leave school early in order to begin work or because of deficiencies due to irregular attendance. This was less true of the Armenians."[2] And the California State Immigration Commission testified that the Armenians "take full advantage of the public school and keep their children there as long as possible."[3] Certainly Armenians prized education for their children, making every sacrifice to educate them. The Armenians, heirs to the nineteenth-century awakening in Turkey, boasted the highest literacy rate of all the "new" immigrants streaming to America between 1880 and World War I; for them education and advancement were natural corollaries. *Tbrots kna vor mart ellas* (go to school to be a man) was a common immigrant injunction.

However, older children were often forced to sacrifice schooling to assist their struggling parents or to permit younger siblings to earn the prized high school diploma. Moreover, many children who were old enough to attend high school knew no English and were accordingly placed in classes with much younger children. These were the so-called overage students, for whom American education was often painful. For example, Hagop Kuyumjian arrived in the United States at the age of eighteen. Fully grown with a beard and mustache but unable to speak a word of English, he was placed in a sixth-grade class. When the students half his size and age began to laugh at him, he was mortified. "If the floor had had a hole in it at that moment, I would have thrown myself into it . . . to cover my shame." Kuyumjian left school that day.[4] Other children of foreign-born parents who were unable to speak English were placed in "special and ungraded classes — either 'steamer classes' " for foreign-born students only, or "with the special class of backward and subnormal children."[5]

Some sympathetic teachers notwithstanding, for the "foreigners" the atmosphere of the schools was neither cordial nor friendly. In Fresno, where the anti-Armenian prejudice was most virulent, one teacher recalled that the children of natives "think that it is smart to ape their elders and often fight or annoy Armenians just because it seems clever. . . ."[6] Remembered one Armenian, "Even while I was in high school, I felt the prejudice towards me as an Armenian so strongly that I made little effort to force myself into non-Armenian groups."[7] William Saroyan's educational odyssey illustrates the foreigner's plight. Saroyan, who was born in Fresno in 1906, entered the Emerson School in 1914, and recalled that

the immigrants are quickly made aware of a number of attitudes held by others about them, mainly that they are not the equal of Americans. . . . First there was a nickname for each group that amounted to an insult, not so much because of the nickname itself, but for the contempt with which it was frequently flung at a member of the group not only by angered members of other groups, but also by adults and teachers themselves. It was so bad that simply to refer to a boy by his nationality, as an Armenian, for instance, became the equivalent of an expression of contempt and of course an insult.[8]

And the obloquy had direct results:

It was soon so undesirable to be what you were that many boys and girls wished to God they were something else, and even tried to pretend that they were actually not Armenian, for instance, but Persian. Or they couldn't wait to get out of school, and out of town, so that they could forget what an unfortunate thing it was to be who they were.[9]

If the insults made many children seek new identities, or anonymity outside Fresno, it would also make them seek recognition through excellence and superiority in school life.

Night Schools.   While children attended public schools, Armenian adults learned English and the rudiments of American history through the publicly financed, supplementary night school system. The American night school system was a response to the waves of southern and eastern European and Middle Eastern immigrants entering the United States after 1880, and by World War I each state had adopted increasingly strict educational requirements for its immigrant population. In Massachusetts an 1886 statute compelled all minors in cities with populations in excess of 10,000 to learn to read and write in English. In 1913 the Bay State mandated that every minor from 16 to 21 years of age — whether employed or not, married or single — who could not pass fourth grade requirements in reading, writing, and spelling in English attend a night school.[10] In California, night schools were the option of local communities. For example, in Fresno in 1910, the public schools conducted a night school but it continued for only one year from lack of funds. By 1916, however, special evening classes for English instruction were regularly held in that city's elementary schools.[11]

The Armenian-language press in the United States heartily endorsed night schools as a boon to the immigrants. In 1901 *Gotchnag*, noting that mastery of English was the "key to success and leaving the factory," urged readers to learn English through night school classes, by speaking with "Americans, by reading papers and copying words." "Every advanced nation," it later trumpeted, "was a nation of readers." *Azk*, which commented in 1911 that schooling was one of the "primary factors in a nation's progress," listed night school offerings whenever possible. Shahan Natalie, a Boston University graduate and editor of *Hairenik*, in 1913 informed Armenians in Boston that night schools were "no more than ten minutes away," were a great economic benefit to newcomers to "get on in the world," and provided "free books, free ink and paper, and a free, warm room." Finally, in response to the belief that English was unnecessary for Armenians intending to repatriate to the old country, one patriot argued that the homeland desperately needed "vigorous, enlightened, regenerated and civilized citizens" — night school products.[12]

Despite the promptings, attendance at night school involved many sacrifices. In the first place, the young factory laborers found it especially taxing to spend two hours each night of the week in class after putting in at least ten hours during the day in a mill or foundry, and many naturally preferred to rest and relax in a coffeehouse. In Worcester, night schools began at 7 p.m. Because of this the Worcester School Department lamented in 1897 that "as most of them are employed until six o'clock, they find it wearing if not positively dangerous to their health to hurry to their homes, which may be one or two miles from the building, eat the evening meal, and reach the school at seven o'clock."[13] The teachers involved in the night school programs also added to their problems. To be sure, in municipalities with a large Armenian community, Armenian teachers were occasionally hired; Worcester had two Armenian teachers as early as 1900, and Azniv Beshgetourian, a 1902 graduate of Bridgewater State Normal School, taught at the Franklin Evening School in Boston.[14] However, observers were skeptical of the value of special language teachers who might be useful as assistants in large classes, but who usually had no teaching experience and a poor command of English themselves.[15]

The vast majority of night school teachers, of Anglo-Saxon and Irish stock, were drawn from the day school faculties. Like the students, night school for them was also a "great physical strain," and they were grossly underpaid (one Bay State town paid its night school teachers 75 cents a day, thereby attracting the "lower calibre teachers" to the job).[16] Such conditions for these teachers made their assignments an unattractive chore. Hagop Kuyumjian, who had a catastrophic introduction to Philadelphia's elementary schools (at the age of 18), noted of one such evening school class: "The class was overcrowded, with elderly male and female immigrants from every conceivable background, and with no knowledge of English;

and it was noisy."[17] Kuyumjian's night school stay was no more successful than his sixth-grade experience.

It was perhaps for these reasons that municipal school officials found it impossible to obtain regular attendance from the foreign born. In Worcester officials encountered difficulty in locating Armenians and Swedes, and others confessed that they were "not looking for trouble" by compelling immigrants to attend. Indeed, the Massachusetts Immigration Commission bluntly conceded that "48 percent of those whom the law required to attend regularly had never been in an evening class." The best estimates placed the percentage of the Armenian adult population which attended night schools at 20 percent.[18]

Notwithstanding all these problems, the night schools performed important functions for the immigrants. For those who worked and lived among fellow Armenians and thereby lacked contacts for learning English in their daily routine, the schools provided an opportunity to attain a rudimentary knowledge of the new language. There, too, they learned about their world and especially about the United States. Mixed in with other nationalities, they were also spared the painful effects of the daytime public schools. And their demeanor reflected their deep interest in the venture:

The serious application of the pupils and their excellent conduct are invariably the cause of immediate comment on the part of visitors . . . and it could not be otherwise, since the very great majority of the pupils are foreigners, who are not posted in the ways that are dark [the outside world], as is the boy who has served his apprenticeship before he entered an evening school.[19]

The classrooms and halls of the night schools were important educational arenas for ambitious newcomers from abroad.

Armenian Schools and Lyceums

As foreign-born Armenians enrolled in the public schools and night schools, the Armenian community sought with considerable sacrifice to retain its cultural identity by establishing Armenian-language schools and lyceums, especially for the second generation. The injunction *Hayeren Khose* (Speak Armenian) which young people heard daily in the household and at church and family gatherings, was institutionalized in the ubiquitous *Hai Tbrots* (Armenian School).

Armenian schools were founded as soon as colonies formed in the New World, for parents feared that children would forget the ancestral language and become lost to the nation. The first Armenian-language school started in New York in the late 1880s; by World War

I, the schools, as adjuncts of the Apostolic or Protestant churches, appeared in every Armenian community in the United States.

The Armenian school was a wholly immigrant institution. Meeting daily in the later afternoon hours or on Saturday mornings, it was usually staffed by immigrant parents, a poorly paid tutor, or occasionally a priest. There the youngsters were instructed in the Armenian ABCs while the older students, in the same room, learned more about the language, the rudiments of Armenian history, geography, and folk tales. Most textbooks came from abroad.

The immigrant women were the backbone of the Armenian-language schools. For example, the Armenian Women's School Union of Arlington, Massachusetts, engaged the language teacher, rented rooms from the local public school, and provided the moral and financial support for the effort. Support came from fees of fifty cents to a dollar a month, and from community donations.[20]

Immigrants conceded that children attended the Armenian schools "mostly because of parental insistence."[21] For, in contrast to the modern municipal school, the Armenian schools were often held in poorly lit and poorly equipped basement rooms, desks were undersized or too few in number, and the classes were held when the students' friends were playing out of doors.

On Saturdays we were herded to the one-room Armenian school where a . . . new immigrant tried to teach us grammar. But the texts were as musty as her pedagogy, and we resisted fiercely, longing to be playing baseball or to be watching "Tarzan and the Apes". . . . As children we experienced an immense frustration when we had to answer a call to the sandlot with the apology, "Sorry I got to go to Armenian School."[22]

The school year invariably ended with a hantes and performance by the star pupils reciting lengthy Armenian poems as their parents looked on proudly. Medals and toy banks, which were often the sum total of their acquisitions from the year-long courses, were distributed to those present.

To what degree did the schools perpetuate the language? The ability to read and write the language with fluency was limited to a very few children who graduated from the schools. Because Armenian was the language at home, most children acquired a smattering of the language there, particularly when they had to converse with elders. However, the language as a living instrument was not transmitted whole to the second generation.

The quest to preserve the language and instill the history of Armenia led other groups to organize reading rooms and lyceums, usually in a church, library, or office building. There Armenian- and

English-language periodicals and books were made available, and college students and visiting intellectuals spoke to reading room members in Armenian on matters of current political and literary interest. In 1875 the Aramian Society of New York set the pattern by seeking to found a library and museum "where our members can have access to Armenian and foreign language newspapers and books" and where at a weekly forum "the members can assemble and wage discussions on questions which concern the best interests of the nation as well as to deliver instructive lectures for the edification of the members."[23] The Armenian Academy, which was inspired by the visit of Mgerdich Portukalian to Worcester in 1889 (Chapter 11), within a decade had raised over $2,000 and boasted a library of 700 volumes. The desire for a reading room was so ardent that even the tiny Armenian community in Kenosha, Wisconsin, raised funds at an Armenian wedding in 1905 for an "Armenian reading room."[24]

The lecture topics of the reading room-lyceums ranged from contemporary affairs to history. In 1898 the active Boston Lyceum sponsored a talk entitled "Will the Armenians of the Diaspora be more helpful to Armenia by preparing with arms or knowledge?" The Armenian Lyceum in New York, founded in 1890, drew 400 Armenians to a talk in 1898 on "The Cuban Crisis," and the inaugural lecture of the Fresno Lyceum, delivered by Dr. B. Tufenkjian in 1906, was on "The Armenians and the Hittites."[25]

The lectures were often rough and ready debates. One critic, writing in *Yeprad* in 1898, accused the speakers of "monotonous, unsophisticated" speeches which unleashed "curses and reproaches like thunderbolts" against the Turks.[26] The typical long-winded, newly minted, Armenian intellectual was often forced to endure interruptions from political rivals or infants' cries. Nonetheless, the Armenian lyceum like the Armenian reading room reflected and appealed to the eagerness of the young Armenians to learn, listen, and debate. These "national" institutions also enabled many immigrants who could not pursue high school or college educations to earn "unsigned diplomas" in relevant topics.

If some of the Armenian educational institutions were wedded to the old language and culture, others proposed to mediate between the immigrants and the new environment, assisting the acculturation of the newcomers. The Armenian Colonial Association, founded in New York City in 1901, helped bewildered immigrants with jobs, transportation, and medical and legal problems (Chapter 5). In 1910 that organization, assuming that "all classes of Armenians" required instruction in American "customs and habits," sponsored Wednesday evening lectures on current topics ("The Balkan War," "Greece"), and in 1914 added Sunday evening meetings on religion and learning English. A program for the social and educational progress of women, instituted in 1910, included the following topics:

The Armenian Woman and the Armenian Home in America
Children's Health
The Woman as Family Doctor
The Good and Evil Facets of American Family Life and Lessons for Armenian
    Women
Armenian Women's Difficulties in America and How to Conquer Them
Care of the Teeth and the Mouth
What To Do with Sickness until the Doctor Arrives
Mother and Child[27]

In October 1911 the West Hoboken Educational Society emulated the ACA's efforts in its own community.[28] In addition, the Armenian Progressive Association, though founded in 1909 for the political and cultural advancement of the Armenian nation in Turkey, nonetheless sponsored lectures, slide demonstrations, and debates by prominent Armenian and American authorities in New York to facilitate the newcomers' entry into the United States.[29]

Immigrants seeking to learn English were also assisted by such textbooks as the Pictured Conversationalist and English Self Taught, both in Armenian and English. Like the Armenian American Conversationalist for Turkish speaking Armenians and Professor H. H. Chakmakjian's Armeno-American Letter Writer, which contained in English and Armenian a large variety of "model letters adapted to all occasions," these works espoused a strong self-help ethic in learning the language of the new country.[30]

The adoption by the Armenian immigrant of the mores of the New World and the shedding of inherited customs and values were also accelerated by outside forces, namely the bigotry prevalent in the many communities, especially on the West Coast. In Fresno, Armenians were held in "derision and execration," and a streetcorner story went that Fresno needed 300 Turks to massacre half the city's Armenian population while the Americans would "take care of the rest."[31] Frequently, such hostility intensified the Armenian's national pride and reaffirmed his identity as a son of Hayastan. Said William Saroyan: "If you were an Armenian in Fresno, this was an enormous fact about you, of special importance, and you had no choice but to carry the fact in one of two ways: proudly or even arrogantly, or shyly (if not secretly) and with embarrassment," Saroyan himself was not reticent: "I was not prepared to be belittled at the very beginning of my life, and so it was necessary for me to meet contempt with contempt."[32] A similar response came from Bagdasar Baghdigian, who

walked up to the registration desk of a Kansas City night school and struggled through an application. The teacher glanced at the Armenian name and snapped: "Oh, give that up and change your name to Smith, Jones or a name like that and become Americanized. Give up everything you brought with you from the Old Country. You did not bring anything worthwhile anyway." Baghdigian froze into group consciousness. "The Turkish sword," he told himself, "did not succeed in making me a Turk, and now this hare-brained woman is trying to make an American out of me. I defy her to do it." After that, Baghdigian recalled later, "I was more of an Armenian patriot than I had ever thought of being."[33]

On the other hand, many immigrants sought to disguise their foreign birth. In Fresno, for example, one first-generation Armenian physician reported: "In general I have not been treated well here in Fresno. I was forced to change my name before I could get any non-Armenian clients and even now I get mostly the poorer ones."[34] A second-generation Armenian growing up in a Yankee town in the East, who was taunted for his dark skin, felt compelled as a second grader to tell his tormenters that his name was "Smith" and not an Armenian name. According to one study, about 5 percent of Fresno Armenians changed their family names, although the research probably overlooked wholly anglicized names which gave no clue as to the Armenian roots.[35]

In fact, name changing became a hotly debated issue between the ethnic "patriots" and the "realists." According to the zealot Papken, writing in *Hairenik* in 1901, parents who called a son "Albert" were extirpating race feeling from the child. In fifteen years, he warned, the son would be an odar (non-Armenian) and would ignore his family and nation, whereas a "Raffi" would pursue his cultural background, speak Armenian, and become a patriot. On the other hand, *Gotchnag*, organ of the more assimilationist Protestant Armenian community, suggested the compromise solution that Armenians shorten their names to facilitate communication with the Americans. "Changing clothes and names doesn't make an Armenian into a Saxon, Swede or Irishman," wrote *Gotchnag* in 1906. "Why is it reckoned racial betrayal if a father gives an ordinary name to his son, and if that name is Lincoln instead of Kevork or Sarkis, and Flora instead of Khatoon or Altoon?"[36] One ingenious compromise was the name given to the Armenian American child born in 1908: William Howard Taft Kazarian.[37]

The anti-foreign pressures on the immigrants were also reflected in more sophisticated circles. Dr. Mihran Kassabian was a distinguished x-ray physicist in Pennsylvania. At a talk to the Wisconsin

Historical Society in 1911, he stressed to his audience that the Armenians "are the quickest people to adopt and comply with their surroundings. . . . Armenians are very readily assimilated by a higher type of civilization." Kassabian also facilely reported that Armenian children born in the United States spoke poor Armenian as proof of their ability to be "completely Americanized."[38]

Naturalization

In addition to adjusting to American culture, many immigrants went on to become full-fledged citizens of the United States through the process of naturalization. To some Armenians, becoming an American citizen was an unrivaled blessing. "You who have been born in America," wrote George Mardikian, "I wish I could make you understand what it is like not to be an American — not to have been an American all your life — and then suddenly, with the words of a man in flowing robes, to be one, for that moment, and forever after. Think of it . . . One moment, you belong with your fathers to a million dead yesterdays. The next, you belong with America to a million unborn tomorrows."[39]

On the other hand, there were several obstacles to citizenship for the immigrants, such as age and lengthy residency requirements and an examination in English about the American constitution and system of government. Then, too, Armenians held back from citizenship for fear of losing their property in Turkey or because they had families in the Old Country and wished eventually to return.

Nonetheless, there were many inducements for the foreign-born to become citizens. In 1889 for example, Armenians in Fresno founded the Armenian Foreigners' Club to "prepare Armenians for citizenship and provide books for their use." (In 1892 the society changed its name to the Fresno Armenian Library Union to "avoid the undesirable connotation of the word foreigner.")[40] The Armenian Republican Club of Boston urged fellow Armenians to adopt American citizenship to avoid discrimination, since Armenians in Rutland, Vermont, had been refused admission to a tuberculosis sanitorium because "preference is given to citizens."[41] According to Gotchnag in 1901, Armenians without first papers had trouble opening businesses and were disadvantaged in the courts, "as many Armenians know by experience." In 1911 Dr. Bedros Torosian of West Hoboken published a thick tome on American Citizenship to assist the newcomers. "Do not hire a lawyer, it isn't necessary," he added.[42]

Much of the impetus of the public night school movement was directed toward teaching English and civics to the foreign born, and these efforts were supplemented by the North American Civic League for Immigrants, founded in Boston in 1908, to "push the teaching of English and Primary Civics to the immigrants." By 1909 the league was giving lectures in Armenian on "The United States, Its People and Its Laws," "The Need to Learn English," "Abraham Lincoln (The Great Citizen)," "Naturalization," and "A Primer for Aliens Desirous of Becoming a Citizen." By the eve of World War I, naturalization lectures in Armenian reached the immigrants in Chelsea, Lawrence, Haverhill, Lowell, Manchester, and Bridgeport.[43]

Urged to adopt citizenship, the immigrants were also sternly warned not to do so fraudulently. Evidence from the State Department and consular officials in Turkey (Chapter 11) reveals that Armenians returning to Turkey easily acquired American citizenship papers, and *Gotchnag*, among others, labeled this a "grave crime" which damaged the community's reputation in the United States. Moreover, officials of the United States Naturalization Service used the practice to blacken the immigrants' name before receptive audiences. Thus Commissioner Fritz Braun said to the House of Representatives:

Once in possession of these naturalization papers (gotten legitimately or illegitimately) their owners embark upon different kinds of trade and engage in various lines of business prohibited by the Turkish laws . . . with impunity and defiance, relying on the protection their American citizenship affords them. As . . . American citizens, . . . they are not subject to taxation, and . . . many of the gambling houses, houses of ill repute are being conducted by these "made-to-order American citizens."[44]

How many immigrants became citizens? According to the Immigration Commission's sample survey (1907–1910) of 171 foreign-born males who had been in the United States for over 5 years and who were 21 years of age or over at the time of immigrating, 28 percent were fully naturalized and an additional 21 percent had received their first papers. After World War I naturalization proceeded rapidly, because Armenians had been in the country longer, their educational levels had risen, and they harbored little hope of returning to the Old Country, shattered by the genocide of 1915 and the collapse of the Armenian Republic in 1920. The census of 1920 revealed, for example, that of the *entire foreign-born stock* of Armenian immigrants, males and females of all ages, fully 29 percent were naturalized and in addition 13 percent had received their first papers.[45]

Although many spokesmen urged the immigrants to become citizens, there were those who were hostile to the practice. In 1909, in

the midst of rising nativist fears, the United States Bureau of Naturalization sharply challenged the right of Armenians to become naturalized American citizens. Richard Campbell, chief of the
Naturalization Division, ordered federal district attorneys to oppose
naturalization petitions of Armenians on the grounds that Armenians
were Asiatics and not "white persons," and thus were excluded from
citizenship. "Without being able to define a white person," stated
Campbell, "the average man in the street understands distinctly what
it means, and would find no difficulty in assigning to the yellow race
a Turk [Armenian] or Syrian with as much ease as he would bestow
that designation on a Chinaman or a Korean." Campbell also charged
that Armenians were polygamists![46]

The governmental action seriously threatened the immigrants.
"If the Armenians lost their rights as citizens or potential citizens,"
warned Asbarez, "the entire colony [in California] and its 10-20 years
of labor would be nothing. Men had come, had undertaken large
mortgages as farmers to become landowners; and they would be
wiped out. . . . Naked we came and naked would we leave."[47]

Then in December 1909 in the United States Circuit Court of
Massachusetts the legal rights of Armenians as petitioners for naturalization were determined. In a twelve-page decision, Judge Francis
Cabot Lowell, with the Brahmin Friend of the Armenians Moorfield
Storey as an amicus curiae, demolished the government's case. Lowell ruled that the Armenians belonged to the "white or Caucasian
race" because the petitioners before him were "white people in
appearance, not darker in complexion than some persons of north
European descent traceable for generations"; historically, the Armenians had been "always classified in the white or Caucasian race,
and not in the yellow or Mongolian," a fact attested to by their Indo-
European language and the testimony of all books on ethnology; their
"ideas, standards, and aspirations" were chiefly Caucasian, and their
religion and history had been European in orientation; furthermore,
they had become "westernized and readily adaptable to European
standards." If they originated from Asiatic Turkey, that did not mean
that they were "Asiatics," for Europe's arts, letters, and its great
religion of Christianity had also been born in Asia. Lowell found for
all the petitioners against the government, and in so doing effectively
slammed the door shut on such nativist moves until 1924. In that
year, in United States vs. Cartozian, the issue of the eligibility of
Armenians to become American citizens was again raised, only to be
roundly quashed for a second and final time.[48]

But while the Naturalization Bureau in Washington sought to
deny citizenship to the Armenian immigrants, various other nativists
in California moved to abridge the landowning and leasing rights of

aliens in that state. In January 1909 Assemblyman A. M. Drew of Fresno introduced the "Alien Land Bill" which stipulated that an alien acquiring title to lands was given five years to become a citizen. If he failed to do so, he was required to sell his holdings to a citizen or the county district attorney would do it for him. Further, as a devastating challenge to the foreign born, no alien could lease land for longer than one year.

The bill, which would have wiped out all alien landholding in California, was chiefly directed at the Japanese. Because President Theodore Roosevelt and California Governor James Gillett lobbied hard against it, the bill was defeated, causing jubilation in the Armenian community.[49] In 1913, however, rising fears of the "Yellow Peril" and of other aliens in California revivified the issue in more vociferous form. Assemblyman Cary, also of Fresno, proposed again that all aliens be restricted from landowning or leasing (for more than one year). Nativist arguments were heated: "When a foreigner comes to the United States," said one assemblyman, "pledged to remain subject to his king, he cannot become a good American citizen." Thundered assemblyman W. F. Chandler of Fresno, "This is a question of race. It is a question of whether you are to permit the cheap labor of Southern Europe to take possession of our soils and drive out the American people." The California assembly (House) passed the bill, 60 to 15. Meanwhile, however, Canadian and European economic interests lobbied strenuously to safeguard their "alien" investments in California. Their efforts were successful: the final bill legislated only against those "excluded from citizenship" — the Orientals. But the Armenians of California had had a second ominous threat mounted against their interests. To avoid this anti-foreign animus in the future, counseled community leaders, the Armenians should immediately become citizens and voters.[50]

Politics and Parades

Educated through a variety of institutions and experiences from schoolyards to the streets, many immigrants became voters and participants in American symbolic ceremonies. In doing so they identified themselves as Armenians and Americans.

First-generation Armenians were too few in number, too poor, and too inexperienced in American politics to constitute a legitimate ethnic bloc on state or national levels. Moreover, many were preoccupied with Old World issues. Nonetheless, to ethnic spokesmen, it was critical that the immigrant Armenians mobilize as voters, for their participation in elections would prove that Armenians were "interested and eager" to provide their "force and aid to the government," and were not merely a "neutral and mercenary parasitic group seeking to live off the nation's wealth." By shouldering their responsibilities, wrote another, Armenians would not be classified as "useless citizens, like the Chinese" who were barred from citizenship. Moreover, voting would help the allies of the Armenians both in the United States and on the international scene when the Armenian Question was raised.[51]

To educate newly minted voters in political issues, the Armenian-language papers devoted considerable attention to national issues. And every four years, the immigrant press backed its favorite presidential candidates. The conservative papers — Gotchnag and Azk — resolutely supported the campaigns of Theodore Roosevelt and William Howard Taft. On the other hand, Tashnagtsutiun's Hairenik steadily backed the American Socialist Party and William Debs as its candidate in 1912. The West Coast pro-Tashnag Asbarez steered an independent course. In 1908 the young editors championed the cause of the Republican party and Taft, because the candidate had "ability and knowledge of trusts," and because the party would continue its course of prosperity and "domestic vigor." In 1912, however, the paper favored Theodore Roosevelt's American Progressive party for its "progressive principles . . . its socialist leanings, and its positive good."[52] No immigrant journal espoused the Democratic party cause after Grover Cleveland studiously avoided involvement during the massacres of 1894–1896.

The Armenian American vote had most impact on the local level. In the Boston mayorality campaign of 1905, for example, candidate Otis Frothingham purchased a half page advertisement in Hairenik.[53] In Fowler, California, it was observed that during civic elections, "those natives who used to turn their faces on seeing Armenians now greet them from as far as fifty paces, never losing an opportunity to shake their hands for love of a few votes."[54] In Fresno, as early as 1906 there were an estimated 300 registered Armenian voters. Remaining aloof from the Republican or Democratic organizations, they succeeded by their "collective force" in "electing candidates friendly to their group." Confirming this, Chester Rowell of the Fresno Daily Republican, a lonely paladin of the San Joaquin Valley Armenians, was always assured of the Armenian vote in his successful mayoral campaigns before World War I.[55]

By involving themselves in the American political process to defend their group interests, the immigrants were displaying dual identities and dual commitments. Once newcomers, they had now become Armenian Americans with loyalties and roots in both the Old World and the New.

Another reflection of their new identity came from their participation in national celebrations such as Independence Day parades.
In Springfield, Massachusetts, in July 1908 a young Armenian "king"
and his "son," dressed in handsome Armenian garb, proudly rode a
carriage decorated with oriental rugs in an Independence Day celebration. In another such fete in Fresno, "no float attracted more
attention or favorable criticism than the Armenian float. . . . Two
Russian Armenians in exact costume rode at the head. . . . Noah's
Ark capped the summit of Mount Ararat . . .; around the base were
strewn wrecks of Armenian cities. . . ." The focal point of the float
was "Miss Markarian [who] sat a free Armenian woman on American
free soil as the idealization of the motto blazened boldly forth: 'When
shall Armenia Celebrate Her Fourth of July?' "[56]

Armenian and American symbols also fused in the personal lives
of the immigrants, as can be seen in this description of a first-generation home:

On one wall hung an etching of George Washington. Not far from it was a
picture of Khrimian Hayrig, an Armenian Catholicos, head of the church and
patriot. . . . On another wall was a lithography of the Grand Canyon and
close to it a desert oasis scene of Arabs and camels, a reminder that Krikor's
wife was from Syria. An ornate handwrought Damascus floor lamp in brass
was in one corner whereas . . . a small table . . . [held] several volumes of the
Book of Knowledge. The largest wall, facing the sofa, was reserved for the
Declaration of Independence, in a heavy mahogany frame.[57]

There were some, to be sure, who clung to the Old Country,
often in a noble commitment to a free Armenia. "We had had the
belief," recalled one immigrant, "that to take over America as our
native land was a sin, to be shunned by all loyal Armenians. Most of
us have simply vegetated here in America; our minds and souls have
never severed from the fatherland and we have been constantly
preoccupied with her minor and major problems."[58] Others urged
Armenians on just the opposite course — to adopt American culture
at the expense of the old ways. "For many years," wrote one prominent Armenian, "I have urged them to become naturalized citizens;
to learn the language; attend American churches; and take part in all
community interests. For I have realized that as a nation there is no
longer an Armenia and for personal salvation for themselves and
their children, uniting with other Christian nations is their only
hope."[59]

Yet to many a third way remained, a fusion of the Old World
and the New, a commitment to the tenacity and Christian faith of
historic Armenia and a belief in the vast political freedoms and
opportunities of the United States. It was with such values and such

heady aspirations that many Armenians began a new life in a new land.

In Conclusion

The Armenian American experience, which spanned the quarter century from 1890 to World War I, was not unique. All the "new immigrants" who accompanied them — the Italians, Greeks, Syrians, Poles, Russians, and Eastern European Jews — endured poverty, slum living, derision as "foreigners," and the alienation of the second generation. Yet, the adjustment of the Armenians differed from that of their contemporaries in two significant respects. First, Armenian economic advancement was more rapid than that of most newcomers. Evidence from contemporaries, the press, and the Immigration Commission testified to their ability to adapt to the new environment — to flee the factories for small businesses or farms in California. And a few became singularly successful in the oriental rug business.

A second distinguishing characteristic was the intensity of their inner political life. To be sure, no ethnic group from the Greek nationalists to the Zionists forgot their Old World struggles, but the Armenians inherited a bitter, cataclysmic irredentist struggle which generated intensely passionate battles in the community. The conflicts among the Tashnags, Ramgavars, and Hnchags left deep cleavages in their lives, and these cleavages would continue to disrupt community life for decades. The political parties created a host of ancillary institutions of critical importance to the community, especially the immigrant press, and they kept alive the dream of a free Armenia. But they also brought division and violence into the midst of the community.

In 1914 few Armenians were aware of the magnitude of the tragedy confronting them and their nation. But having struggled to gain a foothold in the New World, they were now better prepared to assist their brethren in the ordeal to come. And when the gates to America opened again, in 1919–1924, and after 1964, they became a haven for their oppressed and uprooted kinsmen from the Middle East. In time, too, a second and third generation arose. And although they turned their backs on their Armenian background because of the harsh nativist pressures of the 1920s and 1930s, after World War II these generations rediscovered their heritage and the strength of their ancestry. Some of the children and grandchildren, if they listened, also learned of the struggles and sacrifices of the "old timers" on their behalf. It is hoped that this work recaptures some of that enduring contribution.

Appendix

Armenian Immigration to the United States, 1834–1914:
A Statistical Analysis

In this appendix I try to set forth as accurately as possible the total volume of Armenian immigration to the United States prior to 1915. The attempt bears two-fold significance. First, a precisely accurate total will never be known, as annual data by ethnic categories were not collected by any of the various United States governmental agencies until 1899. Nevertheless, reasoned estimates from the earlier periods can be derived from the limited, often overlapping, series of geographical breakdowns published originally by the United States Treasury Department and later by the United States Commissioner General of Immigration. Second, the earliest and traditionally accepted immigration figure source still cited by modern writers, M. Vartan Malcom's *The Armenians in America* (Boston, 1919), failed to utilize all the relevant data available at that time. As a result, Malcom grossly exaggerated the volume of Armenian emigration in periods when estimates only were possible and, further, effected a portrait of the character of the migration which was misleading. Of the data previously not considered, most pertinent for inclusion are, from 1869 to 1895, the "Armenia" series of the United States Treasury Department, the United States Customs passenger lists, and the federal census materials, of which the latter two provide valuable crosschecks for the reliability of estimates. Employing these additional sources permits considerable refinement of estimates yielding a more reliable and realistic statistical profile of the immigration.

The earliest annual data are presented in U.S., Treasury Department, *Arrivals of Alien Passengers and Immigrants in the United States from 1820 to 1892* (Washington, 1893). After 1892, this publication ceases, but the pertinent geographic series are continued for three years (1893–1895) in a similar Treasury Department publication, *Immigration and Passenger Movements at Ports of the United States* (Washington, 1894–1896). (The designation therein, "Asiatic Turkey," is assumed to be approximately identical to the earlier "Turkey in Asia" category). After 1895 this publication too lapses, and henceforth, from 1895 through World War I, the U.S. Commissioner General of Immigration, *Annual Reports*, provide the fullest data, although the geographic series "Armenia" is dropped, and no alternative is substituted until 1899 when ethnic categories become standard. Additionally, the U.S. "Records of the Bureau of Customs, Passenger Lists from Vessels Arriving in New York Harbor, 1820–1914," National Archives Microfilm Publication, and the U.S. Department of Labor, Bureau of the Census, *Thirteenth Census 1910* and *Fourteenth Census 1920* provide supportive crosschecks for estimates.

1834–1890: Origins. Between 1834, the accepted arrival year of the first Armenian immigrant in any sequential migration, and 1868, the single printed source, the U.S. Treasury Department, *Arrivals . . . 1820 to 1892,* used only one geographic category "Turkey in Europe" to classify all immigrants entering the United States from the Ottoman Empire. This all-encompassing designation clearly included Syrians, Greeks, Bulgarians, and Jews as well as Armenians. The total number of immigrants for the entire period 1834–1868 was 253, with a peak of 26 immigrants in 1867 and one or more every year from 1839. Collectively, scattered references to individual Armenian immigrants in early works suggest that perhaps 100 of the above total, or 40 percent, were Armenians.

In 1869, reflecting the rise in emigration from the Turkish interior, the Treasury Department added to "Turkey in Europe" two new and distinct categories: "Turkey in Asia" and "Armenia" (Appendix Table I). For the period 1869–1890 all immigrants in the "Armenia" category (981) are counted as Armenians. Further, 400 of those 2,289 designating "Turkey in Asia" as place of origin are reasoned to be Armenians as well. This gives a combined total of 1,381 Armenians, which constitutes over 40 percent of the total immigration into the United States from Armenia and Turkey in Asia. The use of the 40 percent plus, here and later, as the valid proportion for Armenians in the total is explained and based on data and analysis in the 1890–1898 period (below). An additional 20 Armenians, 1 percent of the total of 1,923 immigrants from "Turkey in Europe," brings the total for the 1869–1890 period to 1,401, and for the entire period 1834–1890 to approximately 1,500. (A note on the 1 percent from "Turkey in Europe" in this period: from 1869–1898 dramatically reduced consideration must be given to the "Turkey in Europe" series as it comprises now less than one-seventh of the immigration totals from *all* of Turkey through 1898, and the establishment of the categories "Armenia" and "Turkey in Asia" means the movement now from "Turkey in Europe" is comprised almost entirely of Jews, Greeks, and other non-Armenians. Corroborating this assumption, the United States Census of 1910 shows that about 1 percent of Armenians then living in the United States listed "Turkey in Europe" as their place of origin. Hence, 1 percent of "Turkey in Europe" totals will be used as the standard for the proportion of Armenians from this category through 1898.)

1891–1898: Flight.   Here, for the years 1891–1895, as before all "Armenia" is assumed to be Armenians, subtotalling 2,909 (Appendix Table II). In addition, it is reasoned that 2,668 of the more than 11,000 immigrants from "Turkey in Asia" were Armenians as well, on the assumption that Armenians comprised 40 percent of the combined totals for Turkey in Asia and Armenia). The total yields a figure of over 5,500 for 1891–1895.

The years 1896–1898 present the most difficulty, since only one category "Turkey in Asia" is employed, apparently now incorporating the "Armenia" figures — see Appendix Table II where overlapping statistics suggest the new Commissioner General of Immigration, *Annual Reports*, incorporated the 1895 "Armenia" annual figure into a newly inclusive "Turkey in Asia" total. The problem now is to establish for these important massacre and post-massacre years (1896, 1897, and 1898), the number of Armenians included within the new "Turkey in Asia" series.

Invaluable here were the complete United States Customs Bureau passenger lists for vessels arriving in New York Harbor. A complete name check from July 1, 1896, to June 30, 1897, yielded a conservative count of 1,818 Armenians (those clearly identifiable by Armenian surname or given name). This number may be realistically expanded to 2,500 persons for each of the upheaval years 1896 and 1897 — many Armenians were not clearly identifiable on the New York passenger lists (often purposely), and Armenians entered through other American ports and by way of Canada. The figure of 2,500 Armenians would comprise a little over 50 percent of the "Turkey in Asia" figure for 1896 and 1897 respectively. This is reasonable if we accept a 40-43 percent Armenian proportion for normal periods on two bases. First, the 1910 United States Census figures show 37 percent of the total immigrants living in the United States from "Turkey in Asia" listed Armenia as their mother language or native tongue in the old country (a conservative figure since clearly some Armenians listed Turkish or Arabic as their native tongue). Second, after 1899 the new ethnic designations show that the category "Turkey in Asia" is composed of Syrians as well as Armenians, and there is little reason to assume this not to have been the pattern in the years immediately preceding. (Prior to 1904 immigration to the United States of ethnic Turks was negligible, therefore no allowance is made for them in the "Turkey in Asia" figures for these years). In fact, ethnic totals for Armenians and Syrians in each year from

1899 to 1904 (Appendix Table III), give figures well approximating "Turkey in Asia" totals for the same years.

Consider a post-massacre year, 1910, for which data are available and derive the proportion of Armenians to the total (Armenians plus Syrians) to apply to the 1896–1897 similar massacre period. The proportion (5,508 Armenians to a total of 11,825 Armenians and Syrians) is approximately 47 percent. Finally, the return to more stable times in 1898 suggests the 40-43 percent proportion or a figure of 1,900 Armenians. With an additional 100 Armenians (2.5 percent of "Turkey in Europe") for the entire period 1891–1898, the complete figure for the period 1891–1898 is approximately 12,500:

1891–1895	5,500
1896–1897	5,000
1898	1,900
Turkey in Europe	100
Total	12,500

1899–1914: Mass Migration. With the adoption in 1899 of ethnic categories, annual totals for Armenian immigration are derived solely from the "Armenian" category. The period 1899–1914 totals 51,950 Armenians entering the United States.

Total volume of Armenian immigration to the United States prior to 1915 is estimated to be about 66,000:

1834–1890	1,500
1891–1898	12,500
1899–1914	51,950
Total	65,950

Appendix Tables I – IV detail year-by-year immigration figures and the destinations of the newly arrived Armenians.

Appendix Table I. Immigration from Turkey and Armenia, 1869–1890

Year [a]	Armenia	Turkey in Asia	Turkey in Europe
1869	—	2	18
1870	—	—	6
1871	—	4	23
1872	—	—	20
1873	—	3	53
1874	2	6	62
1875	1	1	27
1876	3	8	38
1877	1	3	32
1878	1	7	29
1879	—	31	29
1880	1	4	24
1881	15	5	72
1882	11	—	69
1883	19	—	86
1884	15	—	150
1885	39	—	138
1886	19	15	176
1887	121	208	206
1888	39	273	207
1889	96	593	252
1890	598	1126	206
Total	981	2289	1923

Source: U.S., Treasury Department, *Arrivals of Alien Passengers and Immigrants in the United States from 1820 to 1892* (Washington, 1893).
[a] Calculated for fiscal year ending June 30.

Appendix Table II. Immigration From Turkey and Armenia, 1891–1898

Year ending June 30	Turkey in Asia		Armenia	Turkey in Europe
1891	2,488[a]		812[a]	265[a]
1892	3,172		1,069	1,331
1893	1,829[b]		552[b]	625[c]
1894	1,219		243	298
1895	2,326	2,766[c]	233	245
1896		4,139		169
1897		4,732		152
1898		4,275		176

Sources: (a) U.S., Treasury Department, *Arrivals of Alien Passengers and Immigrants in the United States from 1820 to 1892* (Washington, 1893); (b) U.S., Treasury Department, *Immigration and Passenger Movements, 1892–1895* (Washington, 1893–1896); (c) U.S., Commissioner General of Immigration, *Annual Reports,* 1893–1898.

Appendix Table III. Armenian Immigration, 1899–1914

Year ending June 30	Geographic and ethnic categories		
	Turkey in Asia	Armenians	Syrians
1899	4,436	674	3,708
1900	3,962	982	2,920
1901	5,782	1,855	4,064
1902	6,223	1,151	4,982
1903	7,118	1,759	5,551
1904	5,235	1,745	3,653
1905	6,157	1,878	4,822
1906	6,354	1,895	5,824
1907	8,053	2,644	5,880
1908	9,753	3,299	5,520
1909	7,794	3,108	3,668
1910	15,399	5,508	6,317
1911	10,311	3,092	5,444
1912	12,963	5,222	5,525
1913	24,220	9,355	9,210
1914	21,982	7,785	9,023

Source: U.S., Commissioner General of Immigration, *Annual Reports,* 1899–1914.

**Appendix Table IV. Destinations of Armenian Immigrants
Arrived in the United States, 1899–1914**

	Number	%		Number	%
California	2,443	5	New Jersey	1,990	4
Connecticut	1,467	3	New York	15,943	31
Illinois	3,220	6	Pennsylvania	1,851	4
Massachusetts	14,674	28	Rhode Island	4,740	9
Michigan	1,213	2	Other	4,409	8
	Total	51,950	100%		

Source: U.S., Commissioner General of Immigration, *Annual Reports,*
1899–1914.

NOTES
BIBLIOGRAPHY
INDEX

Notes

Notes to Chapter 1

1. Hovannisian, *Armenia on the Road to Independence*, 2. A very distinguished work.

2. Der Nersessian, *Armenia and the Byzantine Empire*, 4.

3. *Missionary Herald*, February 1859.

4. Information on the natural resources of Armenia is most detailed in Karajian, *Mineral Resources of Armenia and Anatolia*.

5. A useful work on the early history of the Armenians is Manantian, *Knnagan Desutiun hai zhoghovrti badmutian*, vol. 1. The most comprehensive history in English of the Armenians is Lang's *Armenia, Cradle of Civilization*.

6. *The Treatment of the Armenians in the Ottoman Empire 1915–1916* (London, 1916), 601. This Parliamentary Blue Book, a compilation of first-hand accounts of the atrocities during World War I, also contains an excellent brief account of Armenian history by Arnold Toynbee.

7. *Ibid.*

8. *Ibid.*, 604.

9. Arpee, *The Armenian Awakening*, 8.

10. *Ibid.*, 9.

11. The history of the Armenian diaspora in this period is in Abrahamian, *Hamarod urvakidz hai kaghtavaireri badmutian*, and Alboyajian, *Badmutiun hai kaghtaganutiun*, vol. 2, treats the period from the 11th to the 15th centuries.

12. *Treatment of the Armenians*, 604.

13. Sanjian, *Armenian Communities in Syria*, 32. An important scholarly treatment.

14. *Ibid.*, 33. A trailblazing study of the Armenian millet is Gibb and Bowen, *Islamic Society* vol. 1, pts. 1 and 2, especially vol. 1, pt. 2, 207–261.

15. Abdolonyme Ubicini, *Letters on Turkey*, vol. 2, 9. See also Gibb and Bowen, *Islamic Society* vol. 1, pt. 2, especially 212–213, 220–222.

16. G. C. Knapp to Judson Clark, Bitlis, December 17, 1888, American Board of Commissioners for Foreign Missions, MSS, 16.9.7 vol. 8, hereafter cited as ABCFM. The phrase was taken from an 18th century document, which continued: "To the wearer of satan's crown, and of tar-black clothes [an Armenian bishop] — a castaway from the gate of heaven. Thou Infidel Teacher: One of your nation has died. You have asked permission to bury him. According to the requirements of the Koran, it is not necessary to bury the body in the earth; but to avoid the stench of putrifaction on the earth's surface, dig the grave deep, fill the earth upon the body, and stamp it down well."

17. Ubicini, *Letters on Turkey*, vol. 2, 6, 12. See also Roderic Davison, *Reform in the Ottoman Empire*, 115–116.

18. Ubicini, *Letters on Turkey*, vol. 2, 252–253.

Notes to Chapter 2

1. Yale, *The Near East*, 119.

2. Statistics are from Ubicini, *Letters on Turkey*, vol. 1, 24. A modern history of this very important community is lacking. A guide to references on the community is in Sanjian, *Armenian Communities in Syria*, 327–328, and a useful work is Johnson, *Constantinople Today*, especially 32–46.

3. Ubicini, *Letters on Turkey*, vol. 2, 311–313.

4. Smith, *Researches* . . . vol. 1, 58. See also Arpee, *Armenian Awakening*, 173.

5. *Missionary Herald*, November 1855. See also the comments in Davison, *Reform in the Ottoman Empire*, 118.

6. Smith, *Researches* . . . *in Armenia*, vol. 1, 212.

7. *Missionary Herald*, March 1833.

8. Arpee, *Armenian Awakening*, 52.

9. This paragraph is based on Davison, *Reform in the Ottoman Empire*, 134, 284, and Johnson, *Constantinople Today*, 41.

10. Smith, *Researches* . . . *in Armenia*, vol. 1, 213.

11. Lewis, *Emergence of Modern Turkey*, 448. A very important work for an understanding of 19th century Turkey and the breakdown of Armeno-Turkish relations. For other comments on the general economic role of the Armenians in the empire, see Mears, *Modern Turkey*, especially 40, and Pears, *Turkey and Its People*, 270–275.

12. Lewis, *Emergence of Modern Turkey*, 35.

13. Johnson, *Constantinople Today*, 36.

14. Ubicini, *Letters from Turkey*, vol. 1, 24, and Lynch, *Armenia, Travels and Studies*, vol. 2, 427, one of the classic travel works of the period.

15. *Missionary Herald*, February 1871. For this phenomenon consult also Hodgetts, *Round About Armenia*, 40, and Young, *Constantinople*, 225.

16. Population estimates for the permanent Armenian population of the city are from the *Missionary Herald*, July 1872, and Leart, *La question arménienne*, 17.

17. *Missionary Herald*, July 1872.

18. *Gotchnag*, March 8, 1902. *Missionary Herald*, 1833; Totomiantz, *L'Armenie économique*, 53–54.

19. Ubicini, *Letters on Turkey*, vol. 1, 19.

20. Mesrob, *L'Arménie au point du vue*, 70.

21. *Treatment of the Armenians*, 610, and Gibb and Bowen, *Islamic Society*, vol. 1, pt. 2, 227, discuss the Kurdish problem. Regarding the matter of population, in the province of Sivas, once the historic center of Lesser Armenia, the ethnic mixture was 38 percent Turkish, 33 percent Armenian, 10 percent Kurdish. In Mamuret-ul-Aziz, the Armenian population outnumbered the Turkish population by 37 percent to 23 percent, but the Armenians

still remained a religious minority when the Muslim Kurds, Lazes, and Circassians are taken into account. In Van, the easternmost of the provinces, it was agreed that the Armenians constituted a clear majority — 53 percent. But over all, the patriarchal census of 1882 calculated that the Armenians made up 39 percent of the total population of the "Armenian" provinces. For documentation, see Atamian, *Armenian Community*, chart following 52, and Mesrob, *L'Arménie au point de vue*, 79, both derived from the 1912 patriarchal census, itself detailed in Williams, *Armenia: Past and Present*, 22.

22. Mesrob, *L'Arménie au point de vue*, 87–88; Haig, *Kharpert*, 638–640.

23. *Missionary Herald*, September 1855. For this topic as well as the history of Arabgir generally, see Poladian, *Badmutiun Hayots Arabgiri*.

24. Kazemzadeh, *The Struggle for Transcaucasia*, 8. Kazemzadeh's figures are derived from Mesrob, *L'Armenie au point de vue*, 85.

25. Haig, *Kharpert*, 640ff; American Carpet . . . Journal, October, 1911.

26. Barsumian, *Stowaway to Heaven*, 20; Great Britain, . . . Turkey No. 3 (1896), 1; Pears, *Turkey and Its People*, 55.

27. Krikorian, *Armenians in the Service of the Ottoman Empire*, an extremely valuable and pioneering work.

28. *Ibid.*, 23.

29. Karpat, *Turkey's Politics*, 79 claims that the crafts in Anatolia passed into non-Muslim hands after the 17th century.

30. Haig, *Kharpert*, 307–310, 661; Kalousdian, *Marash* [in Armenian], 284ff.

31. Smith, *Researches . . . in Armenia*, vol. 1, 130.

32. Lynch, *Armenia, Travels and Studies*, vol. 2, 89.

33. *Missionary Herald*, June 1851.

34. *Ibid.*, February 1876. See also Hamlin, *My Life and Times*, 212; *Hairenik*, May 7, 1912. According to Bailey, *British Policy*, 86, in 1855 one ninth of the total British production of cotton goods was exported to Turkey. Additional details on the Turkish policy and its deleterious impact on the native industries are in Azhderian, *The Turk*, 315, and Tozer, *Turkish Armenia*, 91. Western consular officials were also aware of the situation. See U. S., State, *Commercial Relations*, 1042; U.S., Commerce and Labor, *Consular Reports*, February 1903.

35. Norman, *Armenia and the Campaign of 1877*, 31.

36. Hepworth, *Through Armenia on Horseback*, 120–121.

37. Hodgetts, *Round About Armenia*, 43.

38. Mesrob, *L'Arménie au point de vue*, 85.

39. Quoted in Atamian, *Armenian Community*, 44.

40. U. S. Commerce and Labor, *Consular Reports*, February 1881. Ubicini, *Letters on Turkey*, vol. 2, 317.

41. Mears, *Modern Turkey*, 280, called Turkey a land of "marvelous richness." The quotation is from U.S., Commerce and Labor, *Consular Reports*, February 1910.

42. For transportation, see Mears, *Modern Turkey*, chap. 9, 201–237, also *Missionary Herald*, October 1888; Great Britain, Commercial, (Trade), Turkey, 1894, 88, 7.

43. Langer, *Diplomacy of Imperialism*, 147–148. See also Gibb and Bowen, *Islamic Society*, vol. 1, pt. 2, 227; Yale, *The Near East*, 116; and *Treatment of the Armenians*, 613.

44. *Missionary Herald*, April 1853.

45. Bryce, *Transcaucasia and Ararat*, 402. Also consult Lynch, *Armenia, Travels and Studies*, vol. 2, 85; *Missionary Herald*, April 1853, September 1877; and Atamian, *Armenian Community*, 48–49.

46. Atamian, *The Armenian Community*, 48–49.

47. Buxton and Buxton, *Travels and Politics*, 46.

48. Davison, *Reform in the Ottoman Empire*, 118.

49. Hepworth, *Through Armenia on Horseback*, 257–258.

50. Greene, *Armenian Crisis* 61. Abuses of the military exemption tax are detailed in W. A. Chambers to Judson Smith, Erzerum, January 25, 1890, ABCFM 16.9.7. Other taxes are detailed in Norman, *Armenia and the Campaign of 1877*, 317–319, and Hodgetts, *Round about Armenia*, 130–132.

51. Yerevanian, *Badmutiun Charsanjaki Hayots*, 265. See also Nazarbek, *Through the Storm*, 68, 91; and *Gotchnag*, July 2 and November 5, 1910.

52. Smith, *Researches . . . in Armenia*, vol. 2, 49.

53. *Missionary Herald*, September 1860.

54. *Ibid.*, August 1874; see also Tozer, *Turkish Armenia*, 89.

55. ABCFM, *Annual Reports, 1890, 1891, 1892, 1893*.

56. Bitlis Field Report, 1888, ABCFM Ms. 16.9.7. vol. 6.

57. The pattern of seasonal or annual migration is recorded in Lynch, *Armenia, Travels and Studies*, vol. 2, 91, and U.S., *Consular Reports*, January 1884.

58. The estimates of remittances are in U.S., Commerce and Labor, *Consular Reports*, March 1902. The quotation is from Lynch, *Armenia, Travels and Studies*, vol. 1, 143.

59. Quoted in A. O. Sarkissian, "Concert Diplomacy and the Armenians," in Sarkissian, *Studies in Diplomatic History*, 52.

60. Raffi, *Dajgahaik*, 65–67.

61. Quoted in *Armenia*, October 1904, frontispiece.

62. Smith, *Researches . . . in Armenia*, vol. 2, 334.

63. Ormanian, *The Church of Armenia*, xvi.

64. Totomiantz, *L'Arménie économique*, 84.

65. Surmelian, *I Ask You*, 23, 29.

66. Excellent descriptions of provincial religious practice are in the regional Armenian language studies such as Kalousdian, *Marash*, 331ff.; Haig, *Kharpert*, 315ff.; Yerevanian, *Charsanjak*, 310ff.; and Alboyajian, *Badmutiun Hai Gesario*, vol. 2, 1305, 1743ff.

67. Hartunian, *Neither to Laugh*, 114.

68. Sanjian, *Armenian Communities in Syria*, 204.

Notes to Chapter 3

1. A modern account of the Protestant missionary movement to the Armenians is much needed. The most important primary sources for the

movement are the voluminous documents of the American Board of Commissioners for Foreign Missions, such as the correspondence of individual missionaries, the Annual Reports of the missions, and the *Missionary Herald* cited above in this work. The most useful secondary accounts are Arpee's *Armenian Awakening*, and *History of Armenian Christianity*, as well as Chopourian, *Armenian Evangelical Reformation*. Also consult Strong, *Story of the American Board*, and Richter, *History of Protestant Missions*.

2. Quoted in Chopourian, *Armenian Evangelical Reformation*, 26.

3. *Missionary Herald*, March 1868.

4. *Ibid.*, January 1839. See also Smith, *Researches . . . in Armenia*, vol. 2, 330–331, and Barton, *Daybreak in Turkey*, 158.

5. Hamlin, *My Life and Times*, 183–195; Chopourian, *Armenian Evangelical Reformation*, 65–71.

6. Arpee, *Armenian Awakening*, 108, 145–146.

7. Quoted in *ibid.*, 119–120; *Missionary Herald*, June 1846.

8. Quoted in Arpee, *Armenian Awakening*, 125.

9. *Ibid.*, 139.

10. Statistics drawn from ABCFM Annual Report, *1908*, in Arpee, *Armenian Awakening*, 148 note.

11. *Ibid.*, 143, note.

12. U.S., State, *Foreign Relations, 1883*, 828.

13. *Missionary Herald*, August 1853. Occasionally Turkish officials sided with the beleaguered Protestants. One pasha, in Aintab, in 1851 rebuked the local Armenian vartabed for his persecution of the Protestants. *Ibid.*, January 1851.

14. N. Gulesarian, Mezerah, May 28, 1881, ABCFM 16.9.7 vol. 6.

15. Arpee, *Armenian Christianity*, 153.

16. The history of the founding of the colleges is in *ibid.*, 275, and in Daniel, *American Philanthropy*, 53. The correspondence of the missionaries is rife with examples of the powerful educational influence of their schools on the Armenians. See C. W. Wheeler to Judson Clark, Kharpert, February 22, 1887, ABCFM, 16.8.9, vol. 8, and anonymous to N. G. Clark, Aintab, November 18, 1880, ABCFM, 16.9.7 vol. 6. The medical advances of the missionaries should not be minimized. Consult Barton, *Daybreak in Turkey*, 207–208.

17. *Missionary Herald*, May 1840.

18. *Ibid.*, April 1837.

19. Kharpert Station Report 1866, ABCFM 16.9.7. vol. 1.

20. ABCFM, Annual Report, *1890*; Lynch, *Armenia, Travels and Studies*, vol. 1, 95.

21. Cook, "The United States and the Armenian Question," 37.

22. Wheeler to Rev. J. Smith, Kharpert, July 22, 1889, ABCFM, 16.9.7., vol. 8.

23. Van Station Report 1891, ABCFM 16.9.7.

24. Sarkissian, "Concert Diplomacy," in *Studies in Diplomatic History*, 54. It should be pointed out that German and French missionaries were also active among the Armenians.

25. Lewis, *Emergence of Modern Turkey*, 62.

26. A useful treatment of the founder of the important order is Torosian, *Vark Mkhitara Appayi Sepasdatsio.*

27. Davison, *Reform in the Ottoman Empire,* 121, is the source of this paragraph.

28. An English translation of the Constitution is in Lynch, *Armenia, Travels and Studies,* vol. 2, 448–467. See also Sanjian, *Armenian Communities in Syria,* 37–44.

29. Davison, *Reform in the Ottoman Empire,* 132.

30. *Ibid.;* Sanjian, *Armenian Communities in Syria,* 44,76. Also consult Sarkissian, *History of the Armenian Question to 1885,* 129. An excellent work.

31. Mesrob, *L'Arménie au point de vue,* 91–93, for a statistical treatment of educational developments.

32. Bryce, *Transcaucasia and Ararat,* 109, note. According to the Russian census of 1897, there were 1,218,463 Apostolic and Catholic Armenians in the empire, of whom 1,161,909 lived in the Caucasus. Mesrob, *L'Arménie au point de vue,* 74–75.

33. Sarkissian, *History of the Armenian Question,* 123, and Langer, *Diplomacy of Imperialism,* 154–155.

34. Norman, *Armenia and the Campaign of 1877,* is the classic account of the military aspects of the war, and its devastating impact on the Armenian minority in Turkey. The source of the quotation is Hovannisian, *Armenia on the Road,* 26.

35. The background to the political developments of the 1890s is best told in Sarkissian, *History of the Armenian Question to 1885,* 57–115. See Missakian, *Searchlight* 7–24. Langer's *Diplomacy of Imperialism* contains an excellent encyclopedic analysis of the political movements which has been sharply criticized for its anti-revolutionary bias. See especially Atamian, *Armenian Community,* 142–144, notes 22–24, 147–148, for this criticism.

36. A useful introduction to the Armenian political parties is Nalbandian, *Armenian Revolutionary Movement.* For the Armenian Revolutionary Federation, the official history is Varandian, *H. H. Tashnagtsutian Badmutiun.* The Tashnag aim was autonomy, *not* political independence.

37. Nalbandian, *Armenian Revolutionary Movement,* chap. 5. The best sources for the Hnchag movement are Khan Azad, "Hai Heghapoghagani husherits," *Hairenik Amsakir,* vols. 5–7 (June 1927–May 1929).

38. For a fascinating description of Hnchag activities in this period, see Consul Milo A. Jewell to Edwin H. Uhl, Assistant Secretary of State, Sivas, February 26, 1895, in U.S., Department of State, "Dispatches from United States Consuls in Sivas, 1886–1906," Record Group 59, National Archives Microfilm Publication, T681, roll 1, hereafter cited as RG 59, NA, T 691.

Notes to Chapter 4

1. Malcom, *Armenians in America.* Other English language works on the history of the community are Tashjian, *Armenians of the United States;* Minasian, "They Came from Ararat"; "Armenians in America," *Ararat* (Winter 1977); and Avakian, *Armenians in America.* I have been unable to obtain,

Hagop Nazarentz, *History of the Armenian Communities in Foreign Lands, I: The Armenians in America* (New York, 1970). Bibliographical and other information is in Kulhanjian, *Guide on Armenian Immigrants*. For comments regarding the writing of the history of the Armenian diaspora, especially that of the United States, see Mirak, "Outside the Homeland."

2. Account of Martin in Malcom, *Armenians in America*, 51–55; quoted passage, 52.

3. *Ibid.*, 52–55.

4. Paragraph derived from *ibid.*, 55–56. The 173 line poem is in Peter Force, ed., *Tracts and Other Papers*, vol. 3, no. 53, 31–35. See also Minasian, "The First Armenians in America," *Ararat* (Spring 1968).

5. Hamlin, *Among the Turks*, chaps. 13 and 14. See also, Malcom, *Armenians in America*, 58.

6. *Missionary Herald*, September 1840.

7. *Ibid.*, March 1842.

8. G. C. Knapp to N. G. Clark, Bitlis, April 3, 1882, ABCFM, 16.9.7., vol. 8.

9. *Ibid.* See also C. W. Wheeler to Clark, Kharpert, June 22, 1886, ABCFM 16.9.7., vol. 8, and Arpee, *History of Armenian Christianity*, 282–285, for missionary-native "tensions."

10. Seropian, *Amerigahai 1912*, 23. Wallis, *Fresno Armenians*, 32–33. Haig, *Kharpert*, 375–378.

11. Derived from Malcom, *Armenians in America*, 57–60.

12. For details on Osganian (also known as Christopher Oscanyan) see Seropian, *Amerigahai . . . 1912*, 16–21; Ashjian, *Vijagatuits ev Badmutiun*, 159; Minasian, "They Came from Ararat," 44–49. The citation from the *Cincinnati Inquirer* is in Wittke, *We Who Built America*, 110. Osganian became the first Armenian American to be embroiled in the thorny question of naturalized Americans' citizenship rights in Turkey. See Daniel Webster to David Porter, August 26, 1842; James Buchanan to C. Dalvey, December 7, 1848, and February 17, 1849, Washington, in U.S., Department of State, *Diplomatic Instructions of the Department of State, 1801–1906*, Record Group 59, National Archives Microfilm Publication M77, Roll 162, hereafter cited as RG 59, NA, M77.

13. Malcom, *Armenians in America*, 58.

14. *Gotchnag*, December 10, 1904. For Vartanian (also Vartanyan), personal correspondence to author from Vartanian's granddaughter, Mrs. Kay Herbekian, Los Angeles, California.

15. Bogigian, *In Quest of the Soul*, 20–43. For his quarrel with the missionaries, see Bogigian to Clark, August, 1881, ABCFM 16.9.7, vol. 6.

16. For Arakelyan, see U.S., State, *Foreign Relations*, 1885, 861ff. Also, Bogigian, *In Quest of the Soul*, 118.

17. For Pushman, *Gotchnag*, February 4, 1905; March 27 and August 21, 1909; Isganian, Kalousdian, *Marash*, 872–873; Donchian, *Gotchnag*, October 6, 1906, September 24, 1910.

18. Alboyajian, *Badmutiun Hai Gesario*, vol. 2, 2147ff.

19. *Gotchnag*, April 16, 1910.

20. *Ibid.*, October 7, 1914. Garabedian sparked a diplomatic incident when, upon his return to Turkey in 1899 to visit his sister, he was incarcerated by Turkish officials in Smyrna. According to them, his membership in the Salvation Army and his street preaching to Muslims might lead to bloodshed. The American Consul secured his release from the Turkish jail on the condition that he depart immediately from the empire. Account in the Salvation Army journal, *The War Cry*, enclosure, Oscar Straus to Secretary of State, Constantinople, November 20, 1899. See also letter of Rufus W. Lane, Consul, to Straus, November 14, 1899, also enclosure, in U.S., Department of State, "Diplomatic Dispatches from the United States Ministers to the Ottoman Empire to the Department of State, 1818–1906," Record Group 59, National Archives Microfilm Publication M46, Roll 50, hereafter cited as RG 59, NA, M46.

21. Barton, *Daybreak in Turkey* 131, quoting the impressions of Rev. Dunmore as he first toured the plain in the early 1850s.

22. *Ibid.*

23. Haig, *Kharpert*, 338. ABCFM, Annual Report, *1880*.

24. Kharpert Field Station, Report, 1889, ABCFM 16.9.7., vol. 6.

25. *Ibid.*, 1885. See also Barton to Clark, Kharpert, August 31, 1886, ABCFM 16.9.7, vol. 7.

26. *Armenians in Massachusetts*, 26–27.

27. Barton to Clark, Kharpert, August 31, 1886, ABCFM 16.9.7, vol. 7.

28. Kharpert Field Station, Report, 1885, ABCFM 16.9.7, vol. 6.

29. Barton to Straus, Kharpert, August 4, 1888, enclosure, Pendleton King, Chargé d'Affaires, Constantinople, to Secretary of State Bayard, September 25, 1888, RG 59, NA, M46, Roll 49, If Barton's figures accurately reflect the volume of emigration, they only serve to heighten emphasis on the difficulties encountered in gaining leave from Turkey or en route or upon entry to the United States. The Appendix, "Armenian Immigration to the United States, 1834–1914: A Statistical Analysis," carries only minimal figures for Armenians entering the United States in the late 1880s, clearly indicating that only a small proportion of the emigrants projected by Barton succeeded in entering the country.

30. King to Bayard, September 25, 1888, *ibid.*

31. G. L. Rives, Acting Secretary of State, to Straus, Washington, October 23, 1888, RG 59, NA, M77, Roll 166.

32. Norman, *Armenia and the Campaign of 1877*, 330. Seropian, *Amerigahai . . . 1912*, 57.

33. Arpee, *Armenian Christianity*, 282.

34. Bitlis Field Report, 1887, ABCFM 16.9.7., vol. 6.

35. Papazian, *M. Smpad Kaprielian* [in Armenian], *passim*.

36. Jewett to Rives, Sivas, May 9, 1888, RG 59, NA, T 681; Alvey A. Adee, Acting Secretary of State to Straus, Washington, June 9, 1888, RG 59, NA, M77, Roll 165.

37. Frank Calvert to D. Lynch Pringle, Constantinople, September 8, 1888, enclosure in King to Bayard, September 25, 1888, RG 59, NA, M46, Roll 49.

38. James G. Blaine to Mavroyeni Bey, Washington, June 7, 19, 21, 1889; W. F. Wharton, Acting Secretary of State, to Bey, Washington, August 16, 20, 1889, in U.S., Department of State, *Notes to Foreign Legations in the United States from the Department of State, 1834–1906*, Record Group 59, National Archives Microfilm Publication, M99, Roll 96.

39. *Worcester Daily Telegram*, January 12, 1889.

40. U.S., House. "Report of the Select Committee on Immigration and Naturalization."

41. U.S., Commerce and Labor, *Special Consular Reports*, II (1890–1891), 235.

42. U.S., Treasury, *Arrivals . . . 1820 to 1892*.

43. Consult Appendix for basis of statistics.

44. Barton to Straus, Kharpert, January 26, 1888, in U.S. State, *Foreign Relations . . . 1888*, 1116.

45. U.S., Treasury, *Arrivals . . . 1820 to 1892*.

46. An important eyewitness account of the Erzerum episode is in Erzerum Station Annual Report, 1890, ABCFM 16.9.7. Accounts of the Armenian nationalist movement are numerous. See above, Chapter 3, notes 35 and 36.

47. Great Britain, *Turkey No. 8* (1896), Report of Consul Graves, Erzerum, October 8, 1892; also, May 28, 1892. See also *Correspondence relating to the Asiatic Provinces of Turkey, 1894–1895. Turkey No. 6* (1896), Vice Consul Hallward to Consul Graves, Van, July 31, 1894, and Lynch, *Armenia, Travels and Studies*, vol. 2, 219ff.

48. Great Britain . . . *Turkey No. 1* (1892), Diarbekir, April 13, 1891. Most observers considered the conditions less severe on the Kharpert Plain. See Great Britain . . . *Turkey No. 3* (1896), Vice Consul Boyajian to Sir Clare Ford, Diarbekir, April 18, 1893. Also, Kharpert Field Station, Annual Report, 1894, ABCFM 16.9.7.

49. Report of Boyajian, Diarbekir, April 18, 1893, cited above, note 48.

50. *Missionary Herald*, September 1892.

51. Great Britain . . . *Turkey No. 1* (1892), Erzerum, May 2, 1891. Lynch, *Armenia, Travels and Studies*, vol. 2, 219; Great Britain . . . *Turkey No. 3* (1896), Erzerum, March 9, 1894.

52. Great Britain . . . *Turkey No. 6* (1896), Erzerum, March 9, 1894.

53. ABCFM, Annual Reports *1890, 1891*; Great Britain . . . *Turkey No. 3* (1896), Diarbekir, Boyajian to Ford, April 18, 1893.

54. Turkish restrictions were reimposed on Armenian emigration in June 1892. See Great Britain . . . *Turkey No. 3* (1896), Longworth to Ford, Trebizond, January 10, 1893; also Boyajian to Ford, cited above, note 53. Numerical figues in U.S., Treasury, *Immigration and Passenger Movements*.

55. The literature on the massacres, much of it first hand, is voluminous. Important contemporaneous works include Greene, *Armenian Crisis*; Bliss, *Turkey and the Armenian Atrocities*; Harris and Harris, *Letters from . . . Armenia*. Important analyses of the massacres are in Pears, *Turkey and its People*, and Lewis, *Emergence of Modern Turkey*. For further citations consult Sanjian, *Armenian Communities in Syria*, 366–367. The ensuing diplomacy of the Armenian Question is in Langer, *Diplomacy of Imperialism*.

56. The Four Power investigation of the Sasun massacre is in Great Britain . . . *Turkey No. 1* (1895).

57. Dwight to Smith, Constantinople, October 17, 1895, ABCFM 16.9.3.

58. For Constantinople, see Dwight to Smith, Constantinople, October 2,5, 1895, ABCFM 16.9.3; Langer, *Diplomacy of Imperialism*, Chapter 10. The sequence is in Arpee, *Armenian Christianity*, 297, and Gaidzakian, *Illustrated Armenia and the Armenians*, 256. Contemporary estimates in American circles of loss of life varied widely — from 37,085 in Terrell to Olney, Constantinople, February 4, 1896 (a figure derived from missionary estimates admittedly before the last of the massacres were over) to 120,000 in Terrell to Olney, Constantinople, July 21, 1896, culled from estimates by agents of the American Red Cross in Turkey with Clara Barton, RG 59, NA, M46, Roll 61. See also Nalbandian, *Armenian Revolutionary Movement*, 206 note 54, for other estimates.

59. Arpee, *Armenian Christianity*, 297.

60. Great Britain . . . *Turkey No. 8* (1896), Erzerum, February 22, 1896.

61. ABCFM, Report, *1896*. Flight from Constantinople described in *London Times*, October 18, 24, November 16, 1895; September 7, 8, 10, 12, 17, 18, 21, 28, 1896. For statistics see Appendix.

62. A. G. Fuller to Bryce, Aintab, March 15, 1896, ABCFM 16.9.5. Also, Fuller, July 4, 1896, in Harris and Harris, *Letters from . . . Armenia*, 136.

63. Harris and Harris, *Letters from . . . Armenia*, 102, 18–19, 51.

64. Olney to Terrell, Washington, January 20, 23, 25, 1896, RG 59, NA, M77, Roll 167.

65. Terrell to Olney, Constantinople, February 15, 18, 1897, RG 59, NA, M46, Roll 62. Olney to Terrell, Washington, February 4, June 6, 18, 19, 1896, RG 59, NA, M77, Roll 167.

66. U.S., State, *Foreign Relations . . . 1896*, 925.

67. Consult Appendix for basis of estimates of volume of emigrants.

68. U.S., Commerce and Labor, *Monthly Consular Reports*, March, 1902. Missionaries perceived a diminution in the volume of emigration from Kharpert after 1902. See ABCFM, Report, *1902*. Bitlis reported heavy migration from 1903, *ibid., 1903*.

69. ABCFM, Report, *1897*.

70. *Ibid., 1898*.

71. *Ibid., 1904*.

72. Jewett to State Department, Sivas, Enclosure, April 6, 1900, RG 59, NA, T 681, Roll 2.

73. Norton to State Department, Kharpert, January 22, 1901, U.S., Department of State, "Dispatches from United States Consuls in Harput, 1895–1906," Record Group 59, National Archives Microfilm Publication T 579, Roll 1, hereafter cited as RG 59, NA, T 579.

74. U.S., State, *Commercial Relations, 1898, 1899*. U.S., Commerce and Labor, *Consular Reports*, February 1903.

75. U.S., State, *Commercial Relations*, 1903, II. Consul Sullivan to Secretary of State Loomis, Trebizond, February 4, 1904, U.S., Department of State, "Dispatches from United States Consuls in Erzerum, 1895–1906," Record Group 59, National Archives Microfilm Publication T 568, Roll 2.

76. Norton to David Hill, Assistant Secretary of State, Kharpert, March 14, 1901, RG 59, NA, T 579, Roll 1.

77. *Ibid.* ABCFM, *Report*, 1900.

78. Interview with Stephen P. Mugar, May 30, 1972, Boston, Massachusetts. Broadcast, Station WBUR (Boston University), Boston, Mass., June 29, 1972.

79. ABCFM, *Report*, 1900.

80. Norton to Loomis, Kharpert, September 2, 1903, RG 59, NA, T 579, Roll 1.

81. *Ibid.*, to State Department, Kharpert, January 22, 1901.

82. *Ibid.*

83. U.S., Commissioner General of Immigration, *Annual Reports*, 1899–1914.

84. U.S., State, *Reports of Diplomatic and Consular Officers.*

85. See, for example, *Hairenik*, October 13, 1906.

86. *Hairenik*, 1913, listed as follows: Constantinople to New York, $24; to Providence, $26.44.

87. Kharpert Annual Report, 1908, ABCFM 16.9.7.

88. Lamentations in *Hairenik*, October 23, 1908, June 10, 1913, January 8, 1914. Emigration rose each year; conceivably "good news" would have further swollen the flow.

89. Useful general English language works on the Young Turk period are Ramsaur, *Young Turks*, Ahmad, *Young Turks.*

90. Consul Masterson, to Asst. Secretary of State, Kharpert, May 18, 1909, U.S., Department of State, Record Group 59, National Archives, Numerical File 1358.16 [file 161] Washington, D.C. Hereafter cited as RG 59, NA, NF.

91. See the optimism of the eyewitness Barton, *Daybreak in Turkey.* For a general view of the historical context of the Adana massacre, see Lewis, *Emergence of Modern Turkey*, 210ff, Sanjian, *Armenian Communities in Syria*, 279–282. Further bibliographical citations in *ibid.*, 367, note 3.

92. S. Trowbridge to C. Mugee, Secretary, American Red Cross, Beirut, July 26, 1909, RG 59, NA, NF 19240/124–125 [file 1059].

93. "Report of Dr. Dorman of Beirut," enclosure, Straus to Secretary of State, October 11, 1908, RG 59, NA, NF, 19240/140–141.

94. Estimates of numbers of victims in Hovannisian, *Armenia on the Road*, 30.

95. Trowbridge to G. Bie Ravndal, Aintab, June 15, 1909; Ravndal to Trowbridge, Beirut, July 10, 1909, RG 59, NA, NF 19274/39–41 [file 1060].

96. W. C. Carr, for the Secretary of State, to Ravndal, Washington, August 5, 1909, *ibid.*

97. Rev. F. W. Macallum to Beirut Relief Committee, Marash, n. d., enclosure in Ravndal to Assistant Secretary of State, Beirut, June 12, 1909, RG 59, NA, NF 19274/30–31 [file 1060].

98. Masterson to Assistant Secretary of State, Kharpert, May 18, 1909, "Report on Armenian Emigration," RG 59, NA, NF 1358/16 [file 161]. See also Masterson to Leishman, Kharpert, June 11, 1909, RG 59, NA, NF 10044/

321-322 [file 718]. Also, *Hairenik*, July 26, August 10, October 19, 1909; ABCFM, Report, 1909.

99. Lewis, *Emergence of Modern Turkey*, 114, 214, 331–332.

100. Consul J. Jackson to Secretary of State, Aleppo, October 3, 1912, U.S., Department of State, Record Group 59, National Archives, Decimal File 867.00/413, Washington D.C. Hereafter cited as RG 59, NA, DF.

101. *Hairenik*, December 21, 1909, May 14, 1912. Jackson to Secretary of State, citation in note 113 above.

102. *Asbarez*, April 12, 1912.

103. For detailed report, see Ambassador Rockwell to Secretary of State, Constantinople, January 21, 1913, RG 59, NA, DF, 876.00/465.

104. Rockwell to Secretary of State, Constantinople, May 15, 1913, RG 59, NA, NF 876.00/543. For further reports, consult *Hairenik*, January 23, September 24, 1912, April 18, 1914, and *Asbarez*, January 3, 1912.

105. *Hairenik*, February 25, 1913; *Asbarez*, February 6, 1914.

106. *Gotchnag*, August 30, 1913; December 9, 1911.

107. *Asbarez*, June 20, 1913.

108. *Ibid.*

109. *Ibid.*, June 27, 1913.

110. A history of the Molokans is needed. A description of their settlements is in Young, *Pilgrims of Russian-Town*. See also Wright, *Slava Bohu*. A brief but useful work on the Russian Armenian community in the United States is Siragan Kaloian, *Shiragi Hayutiun Kaghte tebi Ameriga*. See also *Asbarez*, June 27, July 4, 1913.

111. U.S., Commissioner General of Immigration, *Annual Report*, 1911.

112. *Asbarez*, June 27, 1913.

Notes to Chapter 5

1. Caraman, *Daughter of the Euphrates*, xvii. *Asbarez*, June 27, 1913.

2. Interview with Stephen P. Mugar, May 30, 1972.

3. *Hairenik*, September 5, 1903.

4. Masterson to Leishman, Kharpert, April 30, 1909, RG 59, NA, NF 10044/ 234–235 [file 718].

5. Ottoman regulations were extremely complex. Briefly, until 1896 emigration was permitted only with the sultan's special permission. In October 1896, a new law regarding nationality was promulgated which permitted Armenian emigration only if the emigrant signed a document and posted a negotiable guarantee, confirmed by the patriarchate, that he would not return to Turkey. (Terrell to Olney, Constantinople, October 10, 1896, U.S., State. *Foreign Relations*, 1896.) Abdul Hamid himself expressed the view (1899) that "he had no objection to all Armenians going to America, and in fact if they had not money to pay their passage he would pay the passage for them, but on the condition never to return to Turkey; . . . [for] he regarded their going to America and returning here, claiming American protection, as a fraud upon his country, and if any of his ministers were weak enough to yield this point he would dismiss them all." (Straus to Hay,

Constantinople, September 23, 1899, U.S., State. *Foreign Relations*, 1899.) The overriding purpose of the regulations was to keep Armenians from returning to Turkey as revolutionaries with the protection of American citizenship. The issue became an embroiled one. For greater detail see Chapter 11.

6. Norton to David S. Hill, Assistant Secretary of State, Kharpert, February 28, 1901, RG 59, NA, T 579, Roll 1.

7. For the cost of the teskeres, see *ibid.*, January 22, and February 28, 1901.

8. William Saroyan, "The Bicycle Rider in Beverly Hills," in *Saroyan Reader*, 469. For an "underground railroad" to the Russian frontier used by Armenian emigrants, see Norton to Loomis, Kharpert, September 2, 1903, RG 59, NA, T 579, Roll 1, Other smuggling out of the country is noted in U.S., Commerce and Labor, *Monthly Consular Report*, December, 1907.

9. G. C. Stephopoulo, Consular Agent, to Jewett, Samson, April 16, 1906, enclosure in Jewett to Assistant Secretary of State, Sivas, April 21, 1906, RG 59, NA, T 681, Roll 1. See also Mirak, "Outside the Homeland," 122–123.

10. *Hairenik*, February 21, 1903.

11. *Ibid.*, July 25, 1905, November 24, 1906; *Azk*, September 22, 1909, February 9, 1910, September 11, 1912. *Tzain Haireneats*, February 22, 1905.

12. Jewett to Assistant Secretary of State, Sivas, April 21, 1906, enclosure no. 2. (labeled enclosure no. 1, "Consul Norton's notice regarding expenses,"), RG 59, NA, T 681, Roll 1; Norton to Loomis, Kharpert, May 18, 1904, RG 59, NA, T 579, Roll 1.

13. Consul Alphonse Gaulin to Secretary of State, Marseilles, December 22, 1913, RG 59, NA, DF 867.5611/48.

14. U.S., Commissioner General of Immigration, *Report*, 1905; U.S., Immigration Commission, *Reports*, vol. IV, 70; Norton to Loomis, Kharpert, May 17, 1904, RG 59, NA, T 579, Roll, 1; *Azk*, November 7, 1908; Brandenburg, *Imported Americans*, 200.

15. U.S., Commissioner General of Immigration, *Report*, 1901; Norton to Loomis, cited in note 14 above.

16. Unnamed newspaper, December 18, 1906, in Ward, *Newspaper Clippings*; *Azk*, February 9, 1910; *Gotchnag*, March 12, 1910; *Hairenik*, July 30, 1914; U.S., Commissioner General of Immigration, *Report*, 1905.

17. *Asbarez*, October 28, 1910.

18. Norton to Loomis, Kharpert, May 17, 1904, RG 59, NA, T 579, Roll 1; U.S., Commissioner General of Immigration, *Report*, 1901.

19. Consul General H. Diederich to A. A. Adee, Acting Secretary of State, Antwerp, September 8, October 22, 1909, RG 59, NA, NF 21372 [file 1110].

20. *Hairenik*, March 24, 1906, November 16, 1907.

21. U.S., Commissioner General of Immigration, *Reports*, 1899–1914.

22. *Hairenik*, January 10, 1911, June 13, 1914.

23. *Asbarez*, September 19, 1913, quoted an Armenian from Kharpert that "no Armenian village now . . . has sufficient men to defend itself. . . . The fatherland is emptied."

24. *Hairenik*, October 19, 1909; January 10, February 11, October 31, 1911; March 26, May 14, 1912; June 17, 1913.

25. *Asbarez*, August 8, 1913.

26. For Ferrahian, see *Asbarez*, July 30, 1909; for the other Tashnag views, *Hairenik*, January 19, 1909, July 31, 1913.

27. *Hairenik*, July 26, 1913.

28. *Ibid.*, September 6, August 9, 1913.

29. Quoted in *Literary Digest*, December 13, 1913.

30. *London Times*, September 23, 1896; *Worcester Daily Telegram*, November 9, 1896.

31. *Worcester Daily Telegram*, November 9, 1896.

32. *Ibid.*; *Boston Evening Transcript*, October 28, 1896.

33. *Boston Evening Transcript*, October 12, 1896; *Worcester Daily Telegram*, October 20, 1896.

34. *Boston Globe*, October 23, 1895 [sic] in Hall, *Immigration*, vol. 2.

35. Burnham *Not by Accident*, 106; *Boston Evening Transcript*, October 24, 30, 1896; Bogigian, *In Quest of the Soul*, 118.

36. *Boston Evening Transcript*, October 3, 19, November 14, 18, 1896; Burnham, *Not by Accident*, 107ff; *Gotchnag*, May 14, 1904.

37. *Gotchnag*, March 30, December 21, 1901; *Hairenik*, December 21, 1901. The story of the four orphans is in *Hairenik*, October 14, December 9, 1899.

38. *Hairenik*, December 7, 1901; *Gotchnag*, December 14, 1901.

39. *Gotchnag*, January 1, 1910, January 6, 1912, March 1, April 19, 1913. See also *Hairenik*, April 5, 1910, for notice of another immigrant protective society and its journal *Kavazan* (The Staff).

40. *Hairenik*, August 9, 1910, April 2, 1912, August 2, 1913.

41. U.S., Commissioner General of Immigration, *Reports*, 1899–1914.

42. U.S., Immigration Commission, *Reports*, vol. I, 214; vol. V, 16–17.

43. Statistics for Armenians in U.S., Commissioner General of Immigration, *Reports*, 1899–1914. Comparative figures in U.S., Immigration Commission, *Reports*, vol. I, 97.

44. U.S., Commissioner General of Immigration, *Reports*, 1899–1914.

45. U.S., Records of the Bureau of Customs, Record Group 36, Passenger Lists, 1820–1897, New York, National Archives Publication M 237, Rolls 667–675, Passenger Lists, 1897–1914, National Archives Microfilm Publication T 715, Roll 1. U.S., Commissioner General of Immigration, *Reports*, 1899–1914.

46. U.S. Immigration Commission, *Reports*, vol. I, 101.

47. Great Britain . . . *Turkey No. 8* (1896), Angora, May 28, 1896.

48. U.S., Commissioner General of Immigration, *Reports*, 1899–1914.

49. *Ibid.*, for comparative statistics see U.S., Immigration Commission, *Reports*, vol. I, 99.

Notes to Chapter 6

1. U.S., Immigration Commission, *Reports*, vol. III, 350; U.S., Commissioner General of Immigration, *Reports*, 1912.

2. Washburn, *Industrial Worcester* (Worcester, 1917), 244–245. See also U.S., Industrial Commission, *Reports*, vol. VII, 359, XIV, 498ff.

3. Massachusetts, Bureau of Statistics, *Decennial Census, 1915,* 312, 536, 631.

4. U.S., Labor, *Thirteenth Census, 1910,* vol. I, 982, 1005; *Fourteenth Census, 1920,* vol. II, 984–985, 993–1005. Fuller details are in chapter 8.

5. U.S., Immigration Commission, *Reports,* vol. XX, 55.

6. Story of Garo in *Armenians in Massachusetts,* 26–27. Role of Washburn and Moen in Jizmejian, *Badmutiun,* 3. See also Washburn, *Industrial Worcester,* 160, 166, 261.

7. A. A. Glidden, "Hood Rubber Company History 1896–1929," Hood Rubber Company Archives, Watertown, Mass., Report of the Employment Department of April 1, 1919, placed the figure at 425 Armenians employed at the plant. Mason, *Silk Industry,* 42ff; U.S., Immigration Commission, *Reports,* vol. XI, 19ff.

8. *Hairenik,* July 8, 1905; *Gotchnag,* August 24, 1901, April 5, 1913.

9. *Gotchnag,* January 1, 1910.

10. See Bogigian, *In Quest of the Soul; Hairenik,* April 14, 1900; *Yeprad,* November 27, 1897. Other "advertisements" or notices of jobs are in *Hairenik,* May 11, 1901, May 18, 1907, August 3, 1909, April 12, 1910. *Azk* carried a report on placing refugees of the Adana massacres in jobs, September 22, 1909.

11. Berthoff, *British Immigrants,* 34, 66–67; Massachusetts, Bureau of Statistics of Labor, *Report,* 1881; U.S., Industrial Commission, *Reports* vol. V, 50.

12. *Hairenik,* September 10, 1912, July 4, 1908.

13. Roberts, *New Immigration,* 61.

14. Young, *American Cotton Industry,* 5.

15. Lesley, *Portland Cement Industry,* 101–104; California, Bureau of Labor Statistics, *Reports, 1913–1914,* 161–168; *Hairenik,* August 28, 1908; *Azk,* February 23, 1910.

16. *Hairenik,* August 10, December 21, 1907, March 30, 1909, June 24, 1913; Keljik, *Amerigahai Badgerner,* 20.

17. *Worcester Daily Telegram,* February 16, 1890, April 7, 1892; *Asbarez,* March 7, 1913; *Hairenik,* May 20, 1899, April 19, 1912, October 23, 1913, December 5, 1914; Worcester, *City Documents, 1908.*

18. U.S., Immigration Commission, *Reports,* vol. I, 385; Massachusetts, Bureau of Statistics of Labor, *Report, 1904.*

19. U.S., Immigration Commission, *Reports,* vol. I, 385–386.

20. Derived from *ibid.*

21. Malcom, *Armenians in America,* 85–86.

22. Roberts, *New Immigration,* 292–293.

23. U.S., Immigration Commission, *Reports,* vol. I, 412–414.

24. U.S., Department of Labor, *Bulletin,* no. 4 (May, 1896); U.S., Industrial Commission, *Reports,* vol. VII, 185; U.S., Immigration Commission, *Reports,* vol. XI, 693–694; *Gotchnag,* October 19, 1907, December 16, 1911.

25. *Worcester Daily Telegram,* July 29, 1893, January 15, 1894; Seropian, *Amerigahai . . . 1913,* 99ff.

26. *Boston Herald,* January 17, 1897, in Hall, *Immigration,* "Clippings," vol. 2, 23.

27. *Gotchnag*, January 11, April 25, May 23, 1908, July 24, 1909; *Hairenik*, March 28, 1908.

28. *Azk*, December 4, 1912; *Hairenik*, September 16, 1913, February 12, July 21, 25, September 10, 26, October 3, 24, 1914.

29. *Yeprad*, February 17, 1898; *Hairenik*, February 14, 1914; *Boston Directory*, 1915.

30. Consul at Kharpert to Assistant Secretary of State, May 18, 1909, quoted in Cook, "The United States and the Armenian Question," 105.

31. *Azk*, May 2, 1908.

32. U.S., Treasury Department, Immigration Service, *Report of the Immigration Investigating Commission to the . . . Secretary of the Treasury*, 1895, 63; *Hairenik*, August 3, 1907.

33. U.S., Immigration Commission, *Reports*, vol. XI, 19; *Hairenik*, August 10, 1907, August 17, September 14, November 2, November 16, 1909; Jizmejian, *Badmutiun*, 3–4; U.S., Industrial Commission, *Reports*, vol. XV, 445–446. For other evidence see notes 45 and 47 below.

34. *Hairenik*, February 21, March 7, 1903.

35. *Ibid.*, May 19, 1906.

36. *Social Work*, January, 1969.

37. Bagdikian, "Us Yankees," 263.

38. Great Britain, *Burnett Report*, 294.

39. *Hairenik*, October 26, 1909; blacklists in *ibid.*, July 6, 1906, August 17, September 7, 1907, November 2, 1909.

40. U.S., Treasury, *Report of the Immigration Investigating Commission*, 70–71; *Worcester Daily Telegram*, August 21, 1894.

41. U.S., Treasury, *Report of the Immigration Investigating Commission*, 103–104.

42. U.S., Industrial Commission, *Reports*, vol. XV, 8.

43. *Worcester Daily Telegram*, August 14, 1887.

44. *Hairenik*, June 17, 1899.

45. *Ibid.*, December 20, 1902, July 22, October 28, 1913. Occasionally Armenians took bribes and failed to produce jobs, Seropian, *Amerigahai . . . 1913*, 76; *Hairenik*, November 12, 1914.

46. *Hairenik*, June 17, 1899.

47. *Hairenik*, October 28, 1913; *Worcester Daily Telegram*, February 12, 21, 1889; Seropian, *Amerigahai . . . 1913*, 77.

48. *Azk*, January 29, 1913; *Hairenik*, July 2, October 29, 1912; *Gotchnag*, September 23, 1911, November 2, 1912.

49. *Azk*, November 7, 1908; *Hairenik*, October 28, 1899, May 7, 1912; New Jersey, Commission of Immigration, *Report*, 1914.

50. For a general, city wide portrait of the immigrants and the Lawrence strike, see Cole, *Immigrant City*. Also, *Gotchnag*, March 16, 1912; *Hairenik*, February 6, 13, 20, March 5, 12, 19, September 17, 1912.

51. *Hairenik*, August 5, October 28, 1899, September 29, 1900, April 25, 1911, August 16, 1913; exhortations and examples of collaboration in *ibid.*, November 5, 19, 1912.

52. Navin, *Whitin Machine Works*, 162; *Hairenik*, September 28, 1909.

53. Roberts, *New Immigration*, 61; U.S., Immigration Commission, *Reports*, vol. XXIV, 633–634.

54. *Gotchnag*, February 27, 1904.

55. *Hairenik*, October 6, 1906. For other espousals of the middle-class work ethic, see *Asbarez*, August 21, 1908; *Hairenik*, July 14, 1906; *Tzain Haireneats*, June 1, 1901; *Gotchnag*, January 23, March 13, 1909, July 26, 1913; Seropian, *Amerigahai . . . 1913*, 209ff.

56. U.S., Immigration Commission, *Reports*, vol. XXIV, 634; *Gotchnag*, July 8, 1901.

57. *Boston Herald*, December 27, 1897, in Hall, *Immigration*, "Clippings," vol. I, 169.

58. Examples: A. B. Keljikian, & Co. (Providence); S. K. Sarajian (Worcester); B. K. Janjigian (Boston); S. M. Azarigian (New York).

59. Hagopian, *Faraway the Spring*, 34–35.

60. Malcom, *Armenians in America*, 94.

61. Narrative in *Armenian Review*, vol. 9, 2 (1956); *Gotchnag*, April 6, 1912.

62. *New York Directory, 1915*. The estimate by Malcom, *Armenians in America*, 93, that there were "over 500 repairing and tailor shops, about an equal number of shoe-repairing stores . . ., and over 500 grocers" in New York City alone is absurdly high. *Boston Directory, 1915*.

63. U.S., Immigration Commission, *Reports*, vol. XVII 231, 295–296; Warner and Srole, *Social Systems*, 62. By 1933 Armenians in this community had reached the "native" level of economic class and ranked second only to the Jews. (*Ibid.*) See also, Navin, *Whitin Machine Works*, 162; "Being able businessmen, second-generation Armenians rose to a middle-class status in the village. Exercising their seemingly innate urge to own property they came to possess a large portion of the privately owned (as against company-owned) real estate in Whitinsville. As small shopkeepers, they also gained prominence beyond the proportion of their numbers." Censuses in the immigrant press confirmed the pattern of rapid penetration in these fields: *Gotchnag*, November 9, 1907, February 29, 1908, December 28, 1912; *Hairenik*, October 12, 1907, March 5, 1912, August 4, September 1, 10, 1914.

64. *Azk*, September 5, 1908; *Gotchnag*, July 15, 1911; *Armenian Review*, vol. 13, 4 (1961).

65. Haig, *Haireni Dzkhan*, vol. 3, 209. See also *Hairenik*, May 7, 1912.

66. Massachusetts, Commission on Immigration, *Problem of Immigration*, 99.

67. LaPiere, "Armenian Colony in Fresno County," appendix, 130–131.

68. See Bogigian, *In Quest of the Soul*, 118; *Gotchnag*, July 19, 1913.

69. Interview with Stephen P. Mugar, May 30, 1972.

70. *Armenians in Massachusetts*, 37.

71. See the biography of Gulesian, Burnham's *Not by Accident*, especially 17, 19–27, 80, and 143ff.

72. Massachusetts, *Decennial Census, 1915*.

73. Gaidzakian, *Illustrated Armenia and the Armenians*.

74. Filian, *Armenia and Her People*, xivff.

75. Sona Shiragian, "A Trip to Armenia," *New Yorker*, April 27, 1963.

76. Gilbert and Bridgeman, *Foreigners or Friends*, 156–157.

77. Malcom, *Armenians in America*, 110. *Gotchnag*, November 8, 1913, estimated the total number to be 300. See *Gotchnag*, July 16, 1910, for list of the students' backgrounds and academic preferences.

78. *Gotchnag*, April 13, 1907, June 8, 1912; Malcom, *Armenians in America*, 115.

79. *Gotchnag*, July 12, 1913. For criticism of same see *Hairenik*, October 23, 30, 1913. Earlier organizational steps are cited in *Hairenik*, January 19, 1901, February 14, 1903, and *Tzain Haireneats*, October 24, 1903.

80. The estimate is from Malcom, *Armenians in America*, 96.

81. Kalousdian, *Marash*, 874–875.

82. The lengthy account and quotations about Kazanjian are from Hagop Martin Deranian, "With a Passion for Humanity," *Ararat*, Autumn, 1972. See also *Armenian Review*, vol. I (1948), and Wittke, *We Who Built America*, 450.

83. *Armenia*, August, 1910; *Hairenik*, July 19, 1910. Interview, Prof. H. H. Chakmakjian, Boston, April 14, 1961. Alboyajian, *Badmutiun Hai Gesario*, vol. 2, 2006–2011. The first Armenian to graduate from West Point was Haig Shekerjian (1911); he later attained the rank of general.

84. *Who's Who in America, 1926–1927*, 1255–1256.

85. *Hairenik*, July 26, 1902; *Tzain Haireneats*, October 18, 1902.

86. *Armenians in Massachusetts*, 117.

87. *Azk*, June 29, 1907; *Armenia*, July, 1906; *Hairenik*, June 11, 1912; Malcom, *Armenians in America*, 98; Haig, *Kharpert*, 1162, 1233.

88. *Hairenik Amsakir*, 1924; Eaton, *Immigrant Gifts*, 136.

89. *Gotchnag*, December 16, 1911, June 8, 1912.

90. Saroyan, "The Fire," in *Bicycle Rider* 100–101. Ivan Galamian's distinguished career in teaching at the Juilliard School of Music should not be overlooked. Interview with Judith Patterson Schultz, January 5, 1983.

Notes to Chapter 7

1. Prior to the 1880s Yankee tastes were attuned to more sedate English or Pennsylvania and New England carpetings, which were manufactured in the long roll, not the specific sized rug. By the Civil War annual production was valued at $27,432,000. To be sure, the firms of John H. Pray, John Wild and Sloane's of New York imported orientals in the 1870s, but as late as 1883 the authoritative *American Carpet and Upholstery Journal* noted that "the number of firms actually importing Oriental rugs from Turkey and Persia into New York City could almost be counted on one hand." Total value of imports of all Orientals and other "foreign" rugs in 1890 was only $135,000. See Cole, *American Carpet Manufacture*, 21–22, 42, 250; Ewing and Norton, *Broadlooms and Businessmen*, 93; *American Carpet and Upholstery Journal*, February 1908; and U.S., Industrial Commission, *Reports*, vol. XIV, 712.

2. Lynes, *Tastemakers*, 99, 141, 170, 213, 215, is the source of this paragraph.

3. Cole, *American Carpet Manufacture*, 103.

4. Lynes, *Tastemakers*, 170, 213. U.S., Industrial Commission, *Reports*, vol. XIV, 712; Ewing and Norton, *Broadlooms and Businessmen*, 171. Interview with G. B. Harper, April 22, 1982.

5. *American Carpet . . . Journal*, March 1909, February 1910, February 1913.

6. *New York Directory, 1915*.

7. See Bogigian's autobiography, *In Quest of the Soul*.

8. Alboyajian, *Badmutiun Hai Gesario*, vol 2, 2147ff; *American Carpet . . . Journal, passim*.

9. For Karagheusian, *Gotchnag*, December 10, 1904, and *American Carpet . . . Journal*, May 1908. For Costikyan, *California Courier*, June 18, 1964.

10. For Telfeyan, Alboyajian, *Badmutiun Hai Gesario*, vol. 2, 2200ff; for Pushman (ian), Haig, *Kharpert*, 380; and *Gotchnag*, February 4, 1905, March 27, August 21, 1909; Isganian, Kr. H. Kaloustian, *Marash*, 872–873. Also for Dicran Donchian's career, see *Gotchnag*, October 6, 1906. The largest rug importers in New York joined a "Turkish American Chamber of Commerce for the promotion of commercial relations between the United States and the Ottoman Empire," *Gotchnag*, November 5, 1910.

11. Interview, Dr. Parsegh Kanlian, August 12, 1962. Malcom, *Armenians in America*, 94–95. See also *Literary Digest*, January 4, 1919.

12. Ewing and Norton, *Broadlooms and Businessmen*, 171; interview, Dr. Kanlian, August 9, 1962.

13. *American Carpet . . . Journal*, February, May 1908, March 1909.

14. Mumford, *Oriental Rugs*, 3.

15. Bogigian, *In Quest of the Soul*, 78.

16. Mumford, *Oriental Rugs*, 9.

17. Interview, Dr. Kanlian, August 9, 1962; *Armenia*, November 1910.

18. Ewing and Norton, *Broadlooms and Businessmen*, 170.

19. Cole, *American Carpet Manufacture*, 119.

20. One of its productions — the Ispahan No.. 621 — came with a "key from which purchasers could learn the meaning of the many Eastern symbols which adorned it." Ewing and Norton, *Broadlooms and Businessmen*, 181, 195, 211–212, 242.

21. See Cole, *American Carpet Manufacture*, 164, note; *American Carpet . . . Journal*, May 1908; and *Gotchnag*, November 8, 1913.

22. Barsumian, *Stowaway to Heaven*, 62–64.

23. *New York Directory, 1915*.

24. The quoted passage is from U.S., Immigration Commission, *Reports*, vol. XXIV, 568–569. Other useful information on the topography, soil and climate of Fresno County is in California, Bureau of Labor Statistics, *1st Biennial Report*, 1883–1884; Agricultural Experiment Station, *Report*, 1889, and Eisen, *Raisin Industry*, 45.

25. *Memorial and Biographical History of the Counties of Fresno*, 81–82. See also Walker, *Fresno County Blue Book*, 42ff; and Vandor, *History of Fresno County*, vol. 1, 359. The biographical sketches, including many of first generation Armenian Americans, are extremely useful. Quotation from M. Theo Kearney, "Fresno County . . . the Center of the Raisin and Dried Fruit Industries, 1893," in *Pamphlets on California*, 27.

26. Walker, *Fresno County Blue Book*, 102ff; *Fresno Morning Republican*, January 1, 1896.

27. Quotation from *California Courier*, June 22, 1972; *Asbarez, Joghovadzu Dasnamiagi 1908–1918*, 298; *Fresno Morning Republican*, March 26, 1905; Mahakian, "History of the Armenians in California," 14.

28. Wallis, *Fresno Armenians*, 39–40.

29. Statistics in U.S., Immigration Commission, *Reports*, vol. XXIV, 566ff.

30. For the specific impact of the 1893 depression, see below, note 54.

31. *Gotchnag*, July 1, 1901.

32. *Gotchnag*, July 12, 1912. Other examples of such promotions are *ibid.*, December 22, 1900; *Yeprad*, July, 1898. Easterners who went to Fresno often stated their reasons in the press. See for example, *Hairenik*, April 25, July 11, November 7, 1903; July 16, September 3, 17, 1912; May 20, June 17, 1913.

33. LaPiere, "The Armenian Colony in Fresno," appendix, 124.

34. *Ibid.*

35. U.S., Immigration Commission, *Reports*, vol. XXIV, 633–634.

36. Documentation in Chapter 8.

37. California, Immigration Commission, *Fresno's Immigration Problem*, 19.

38. U.S., Immigration Commission, *Reports*, vol. XXIV, 633.

39. *Ibid.*, 634, 984–987.

40. *Ibid.*, 984–1001; 1003.

41. *Ibid.*, 634. The University of California, Division of Vocational Education, *A Study of Vocational Conditions in the City of Fresno* (1926), noted that the qualities essential for successful farming were "recognition of farming as a business and ability to handle capital wisely, . . . ability to attend to details, . . . good soil."

42. U.S., Immigration Commission, *Reports*, vol. XXIV, 634–635; 1002.

43. *Ibid.*, 634, 986–987.

44. *Ibid.*, 573–583.

45. *Ibid.*, 575.

46. California Fruit Growers' 33rd Convention, *Report*, 1907. See also *California Fruit Grower*, February 2, 1889; and U.S., Immigration Commission, *Reports*, vol. XXIV, 566, 592–593.

47. U.S., Immigration Commission, *Reports*, vol. XXIV, 584–585; Eisen, *Raisin Industry*, 156.

48. U.S., Immigration Commission, *Reports*, vol. XXIV, 602, 612–613; Eisen, *Raisin Industry*, 188.

49. California Immigration Commission, *Fresno's Immigration Problem*, 26.

50. U.S., Immigration Commission, *Reports*, vol. XXIV, 614. Nativists quickly seized on this. "Now the American women are leaving because of the low moral tone that prevails in the working force by reason of the coming in of foreigners with lax notions of propriety." Ross, *The Old World in the New*, 303.

51. U.S., Immigration Commission, *Reports*, vol. XXIV, 602–605.

52. *Asbarez*, October 3, 1913.

53. U.S., Immigration Commission, *Reports*, vol. XXIV, 646.

54. The *California Fruit Grower*, December 25, 1915, provides figures for the annual California raisin crop for the period 1893–1914. See also California Fruit Growers' 24th Convention *Report*, 1899, and 25th Convention *Report*, 1900. Growers' costs are in *California Fruit Grower*, July 22, 1897. Other pertinent data on costs are in Vandor, *History of Fresno County*, vol. 1, 193–194.

55. *California Fruit Grower*, April 21, 1894, July 22, 1897. For the cooperative and its founder, see Ben Walker, "M. Theo Kearney," typescript, address to Fresno County Historical Society, February 7, 1949, and his *Fresno County Blue Book*, 152. Also useful is Vandor, *History of Fresno County*, vol. 1, 218–223. For the problems of cooperatives in California agriculture see U.S., Industrial Commission, *Reports*, vol. VI, 430ff; and Walker, *Fresno County Blue Book*, 104.

56. California Fruit Growers' 25th Convention, *Report*, 1900; *Fresno Morning Republican*, January 1, March 9, April 2, 1901. *California Fruit Grower*, July 22, 1897, remarked that "growers should receive 2½ to 3 cents in the sweatbox in order to be able to meet their expenses and pay interest on their mortgages." This seems a trifle high. The estimate of costs of Armenians in normal times is in *Asbarez*, September 17, 1909, and *Gotchnag*, October 2, 1909.

57. For the events of the cooperative, see *California Fruit Grower*, June 16, 1900, and *Fresno Morning Republican*, March 9, 1901, February 20, 24, 1906. Market conditions are in *California Fruit Grower*, August 6, 13, 19, November 19, 1904; December 9, 1905; September 8, October 27, December 22, 1906, December 14, 1907. Also, *Fresno Morning Republican* August 31, October 22, November 1, 1906; *Gotchnag*, October 13, 1906; *Hairenik*, November 17, 1906.

58. *California Fruit Grower*, December 17, 1908; September 4, December 11, 1909; *Asbarez*, February 26, 1909.

59. *Gotchnag*, March 27, 1909. Other bitter criticism of the packers is in *ibid.*, October 29, 1910. The suicide is in *Azk*, February 6, 1909. The *Fresno Daily Republican*, January 14, 1909, ascribed it to the fact that the farmer "could not return at once to his native land." Perhaps both motives were involved.

60. *Fresno Bee*, October 27, 1960, relates the origins of the Raisin Day celebration.

61. The new cooperative, the California Raisin Exchange, received considerable attention in the Armenian press. See *Gotchnag*, February 19, 1910, April 19, 1913; *Asbarez*, July 19, October 4, 1912; *Hairenik*, June 10, 1913. Other useful data in California, Department of Agriculture, *Monthly Bulletin*, November–December, 1919; and LaPiere, "The Armenian Colony in Fresno," 152ff.

62. *Asbarez*, February 26, September 17, 1909; *Gotchnag*, July 27, 1912; *Hairenik*, February 1, 1902; California Fruit Growers' 38th Convention, *Report*, 1910.

63. *Fresno Morning Republican*, April 7, October 20, 1907.

64. *Gotchnag*, November 6, 1909. The November 9, 1912, issue reported that relatively few Armenian farmers had joined the cooperative. *Fresno Morning Republican*, October 28, 1909.

65. *Fresno Morning Republican*, September 5, 8, 13, 18, October 12, 1907, March 13, 1908.

66. U.S., Immigration Commission, *Reports*, vol. XXIV, 635.

67. *Ibid.*, 626–627; 634–635.

68. *Ibid.*, 566.

69. *Ibid.*, 577, 579, 634.

70. For a general statement of the trials of raisin growing, see Eisen, *Raisin Industry*, 62–65. *Hairenik*, August 1, 1903, is also useful. See also *Fresno Morning Republican*, February 8, 1908; *Asbarez*, April 21, October 13, 1911, and *Gotchnag*, November 21, 1908, for examples of problems encountered by Armenian growers.

71. *Gotchnag*, October 22, 1904. In all this there was always optimism. Even in bad times, the Armenians held that the "soil is a blessing and with patience and hard work, better times will come," *Asbarez*, September 17, 1909.

72. Roeding, *Smyrna Fig*, 39–43. See also, Mahakian, "History of the Armenians in California," 22–24; Wallis, *Fresno Armenians*, 40–41; California, State Agricultural Society, *Transactions*, 1894; and Vandor, *History of Fresno County*, vol. 1, 210–216, on the Markarians.

73. Winchell, *History of Fresno County*, 291–292; Wallis, *Fresno Armenians*, 41.

74. *Fresno Morning Republican*, July 6, 1919; *Asbarez*, April 26, 1912.

75. LaPiere, "Armenian Colony of Fresno," appendix, 33; *Asbarez*, September 2, 1910, November 24, 1911; *Gotchnag*, July 2, 1910.

76. *Asbarez*, October 27, 1911; see also *ibid.*, September 10, 1909.

Notes to Chapter 8

1. The general pattern of immigrant settlement is ably discussed in Carpenter, *Immigrants and their Children*, 23, 139–149. For Worcester, see *Worcester City Documents*, 1908; for Paterson, U.S., Immigration Commission, *Reports*, vol. XI, 19.

2. Ashjian, *Vijagatuits ev Badmutiun*, is useful on the Old World backgrounds of the various Armenian colonies in the United States.

3. *Ibid.*, 188–189; *Gotchnag*, March 26, 1910.

4. *Hairenik*, June 4, 1912; *Gotchnag*, August 23, 1913.

5. *Azk*, February 5, 1913.

6. Keljik, *Amerigahai Badgerner*, 47; interview, Vahan Topalian, January 15, 1973.

7. *Hairenik*, May 20, 1913 (Yonkers), June 10, 1913 (Los Angeles); *Gotchnag*, July 4, 1914 (Riverside).

8. *Boston Directory*, 1905, 1910, 1915.

9. Woods, *City Wilderness*, 30–34, 61–65.

10. *Ibid.*, 61, note; Wolfe, *Lodging House Problem*, 119–120; *Boston Directory*, 1900, 1905, 1910.

11. *New York City Directory, 1900.*

12. *Ibid.*, 1915.

13. *Gotchnag*, February 22, 1902.

14. Mann, *Yankee Reformers*, 4.

15. This discussion is derived almost exclusively from Cole, *Immigrant City.*

16. Todd and Sanborn, *Lawrence Survey*, 250.

17. *Ibid.*

18. Cole, *Immigrant City*, 25, 72; *Gotchnag*, May 17, 1913; U.S., Immigration Commission, *Reports*, vol. X, 748ff.

19. *Lawrence Directory*, 1913.

20. Cole, *Immigrant City*, 72, and note, 72.

21. *Lawrence Directory*, 1913.

22. U.S., Immigration Commission, *Reports*, vol. X, 470.

23. *Gotchnag*, May 17, 1913.

24. U.S., Senate, *Report on Strike*, 146. The peril of fire needs elaboration, since like Lawrence most communities in which the immigrants dwelled were composed of closely packed fire traps (94 percent of Lowell's immigrant dwellings were of wood). When a building caught fire, it signaled a disaster. In 1914, when an Armenian restaurant-boardinghouse in Milford, Massachusetts, was destroyed by fire (the building lacked any "fire fighting devices"), 9 Armenians were killed and 22 were injured; the average age of the victims was 27. Similarly, 8 Armenians were hospitalized when an Armenian boardinghouse in Salem was gutted by flames in 1910. Most extensive was the 1908 Chelsea fire; high winds swept through Chelsea's tinderboxes, and left homeless and destitute 250 of the community's 300 Armenian families. For data, see Kenngott, *Record of a City* (Lowell), 49ff; *Hairenik*, June 20, 1914 (Milford); *Azk*, February 9, 1910 (Salem), and *Gotchnag*, May 2, 1908 (Chelsea).

When a native American booster in Worcester was asked about the life of the immigrants in his city, that they were "crowded in," he replied, "the emigrants from the old world do not mind it one bit. They are always ready to take potluck, and taking potluck, they prosper." The victims of the Chelsea fire were probably somewhat less sanguine. Quote from *Worcester Magazine*, August 1915.

25. Quoted in U.S., Senate, *Report on Strike*, 148.

26. Todd and Sanford, *Lawrence Survey*, 218–220.

27. U.S., *Fourteenth Census*, 1920, vol. II, 1008–1009 gives figures for 1910 and 1920. U.S., *Fifteenth Census*, 1930, vol. II, 375–387.

28. *Gotchnag*, April 12, 1902.

29. *Ibid.*, May 3, 1913.

30. Washburn, *Industrial Worcester*, 163.

31. *Hairenik*, November 24, 1906.

32. *Ibid.*

33. *Gotchnag*, July 11, 1914.

34. *Azk*, January 4, 1908.

35. For the Canadian settlements, see Ashjian, *Vijagatuits ev Badmutiun*, 145–146, 228–233, 243–244; *Hairenik*, August 12, 1899; *Yeprad*, June 18, 1898.

36. *Michigan*, 111, 234; Roberts, *New Immigration*, 132.

37. U.S., Immigration Commission, *Reports*, vol. IX, 50–51.

38. *Ibid.*, 81–82.

39. *Gotchnag*, October 1, 1910.

40. U.S., *Fourteenth Census*, 1920, vol. II, 984–985; 993–1005.

41. LaPiere, "The Armenian Colony of Fresno," 263. *Fresno Morning Republican*, March 26, 1905, describes the very first Armenian settlements in Fresno.

42. California, Commission on Immigration and Housing, *1st Annual Report*, 1915, 86–88; *2nd Annual Report*, 1916, 210.

43. *Fresno Morning Republican*, September 13, 15, 1906; June 11, 1907.

44. U.S., Immigration Commission, *Reports*, vol. XXIV, 643.

45. *Ibid.*, 646.

46. *Worcester City Documents*, 1910, 1920.

47. *Worcester City Documents*, 1905, 1910, 1915; LaPiere, "The Armenian Colony of Fresno," Tables 46, 50 appendix.

48. Massachusetts, Immigration Commission, *Report*, 1914, chap. 9.

49. *Asbarez*, January 1, 1909.

50. Cole, *Immigrant City*, 75–76; Massachusetts, Bureau of Statistics, *Labor Bulletin*, No. 65, July, 1909.

51. *Gotchnag*, May 17, 24, 1913.

52. *Ibid.*, April 23, 1904.

53. See Chapter 8.

54. California, Bureau of Labor Statistics, *Report*, 1913–1914. See also report of Dr. George E. Tucker, Public Health officer in Riverside, California, regarding the male laborers' living habits, in *Asbarez*, June 26, 1914.

55. *Gotchnag*, November 1, 1902, May 13, 1911. Other examples of exhortations to better health are in *Hairenik*, May 13, 1899, August 20, 1912, and December 25, 1913.

56. LaPiere, "The Armenian Colony of Fresno," appendix 69.

57. *Hairenik*, May 3, 1902, December 1, 1906; *Tzain Haireneats*, June 8, 1904; *Asbarez, Joghovadzu*, 6–7.

58. Worcester, Overseers of the Poor, *Annual Report*, 1898; Worcester, Associated Charities, *Annual Reports*, 1896–1900.

59. California, Immigration Commission, *Fresno's Immigration Problem*, 24; LaPiere, "The Armenian Colony of Fresno," appendix, 75.

60. *Boston Evening Transcript*, September 13, 1895. Deer Island and Long Island had public hospitals for the poverty stricken and ill.

61. *Armenia*, June 1912.

62. *Ibid.*

63. *Asbarez*, April 15, 1910; *Armenia*, June 1912. See also *Boston Evening Transcript*, October 21, 1896, for report of "BOGUS ARMENIANS."

64. *Gotchnag*, December 5, 12, 1914.

65. The reference to the Irish is in *Gotchnag*, February 16, 1901. For the feminist campaign against drink, see *Asbarez*, April 16, 1909.

66. Woods, *City Wilderness*, 163.

67. U.S., Industrial Commission, *Reports*, vol. XIV, 124.

68. For the background, Walker, *Fresno County Blue Book*, 80ff. See also *Fresno Morning Republican*, February 24, 1904, May 6, June 20, July 31, September 4, 1906.

69. *Asbarez*, August 7, 1914. Torosian, *Serayin Aroghchabahutiun*, 199–204, estimated that 25 percent of his patients had contracted venereal diseases. In time some anti-American Old World writers stereotyped repatriates as boors who brought back "syphilis, gold teeth and corrupted accents." Totovents, *Scenes from an Armenian Childhood*, 125. See also in this vein *Gotchnag*, August 8, 1914.

70. *Asbarez*, September 13, 1912. The same theme is treated by a writer from Niagara Falls, in *ibid.*, November 14, 1913.

71. U.S., Immigration Commission, *Reports*, vol. XXIV, 662; Fresno County Jail Register, 1910, MS, Fresno County Court House, Fresno; Fresno City Police Records in LaPiere, "The Armenian Colony of Fresno," appendix, 80.

72. The Tavshanjian murder is discussed in Chapter 12. For the other episodes, see Mavroyeni Bey to William Olney, Washington, March 31, 1896, in U.S., Department of State, "Notes from the Turkish Legation to the Department of State, 1867–1906," Record Group 59, National Archives Microfilm Publication T815, hereafter cited as RG 59, NA, T815.

73. *Asbarez*, July 2, 1909.

74. *Hairenik*, June 10, 24, August 12, 1899, September 29, November 10, 1900. The story about the tavloo players is in interview, Vahan Topalian, January 15, 1973.

75. Worcester, *City Documents*, 1892, *Worcester Daily Telegram*, December 2, 1889, September 8, 1890; Seropian, *Amerigahai ... 1913*, 45–46.

76. *Worcester Daily Telegram*, September 5, 7, 1891.

77. *Hairenik*, December 29, 1914; E. Agnooni to Turkish Ambassador in Washington, "Open Letter," May, 1911, Archives of the Armenian Revolutionary Federation, Boston, Massachusetts, hereafter cited as ARF archives.

78. Mavroyeni Bey to William Olney, Washington, March 31, 1896, RG 59, T815.

79. *Hairenik*, June 4, 1914.

80. *Ibid.*, September 26, 1914.

81. *Ibid.*, September 12, 1911, September 24, 1912, July 25, 27, August 6, 1914.

82. *Ibid.*, June 14, September 24, 1914.

83. *Ibid.*, September 10, 1912.

84. *Ibid.*, August 2, 1913.

85. *Ibid.*, July 13, 1907.

86. See *Common Ground*, Spring 1944, and Autumn 1945; and *Gotchnag*, June 28, 1913. The quotation is from Armen Don Minasian, "Settlement Geography of Armenians in Fresno," Part II, *Armenian Review* (Winter 1972), 64.

87. Hovsepian was fined $10 for assaulting the real estate broker in his office, but nothing for the second beating on the street (*Asbarez*, November 28, 1913).

88. Minasian, "Settlement Geography," 58.

89. For this episode, see Chapter 5.

90. LaPiere, "The Armenian Colony of Fresno," 337–342.

91. U.S., Immigration Commission, *Reports*, vol. XXIV, 668; *Asbarez*, October 1, 1909, concurred.

92. *Fresno Morning Republican*, September 26, 1909; LaPiere, "The Armenian Colony in Fresno," 346.

93. U.S., Immigration Commission, *Reports*, vol. XXIV, 665.

94. Dr. Chester Rowell (1844–1912) settled in Fresno in 1875 and founded the *Fresno Morning Republican*. He was an unfailing champion of the Armenians, publicly defended them against the "locals" and went out of his way to assist the fledgling editors of *Asbarez*. In 1913 Haig Patigian, the noted Armenian sculptor, was commissioned to cast a statue for Rowell. *Gotchnag*, July 26, 1913. A brief biography is in Vandor, *History of Fresno County*, vol. 1, 238. Se also LaPiere, "The Armenian Colony of Fresno," 323 note.

95. *Asbarez*, June 23, 1911.

96. *Boston Directory, 1915*; U.S., Labor, *Fourteenth Census, 1920*, vol. II, 762–763.

97. U.S., Labor, *Fourteenth Census, 1920*, vol. II, 1008–1009.

98. LaPiere, "The Armenian Colony of Fresno," 263ff.

99. *Ibid.*, 165–168.

100. *Asbarez*, June 23, 1911.

101. *Gotchnag*, November 1, 1913; *Asbarez*, August 15, 1913.

102. See Chapter 6, note 63.

103. *Asbarez*, June 19, 1914.

Notes to Chapter 9

1. U.S., Immigration Commission, *Reports*, vol. I, 447, 451.

2. See, for example, story in *Hairenik*, September 14, 1907.

3. U.S., Commissioner General of Immigration, *Reports*, 1908–1914.

4. Lynch, *Armenia, Travels and Studies*, vol. 1, 92.

5. *Armenians in Massachusetts*, 31.

6. See Norton to Hay, Kharpert, May 31, 1902, and Leishman to Norton, Constantinople, March 26, 1903, RG 59, NA, T579, Roll 1. The episode received national attention. *The Outlook*, vol. 74 (1903).

7. Adee to Sarkis Babayian, Washington, April 3, 1907, RG 59, NA, NF 458/1-4 [file 66].

8. Hovannes K. Assadourian to Department of State, Batum, October 13/25, 1906, RG 59, NA, NF 739/1-2 [file 101].

9. These statistics, derived from the annual reports of the Commissioner General of Immigration, are in Drachsler, "Intermarriage in New York City."

10. *Hairenik*, January 12, 1900.

11. *Fresno Morning Republican*, March 23, 1907; *Hairenik*, April 14, 1906, June 22, 1907.

12. William Smith-Lyte to Peter Jay, Constantinople, April 13, 1906, U.S., Department of State, "Dispatches from United States Consuls in Con-

stantinople, 1886–1906," Record Group 59, National Archives Microfilm Publication T 194, Roll 24.

13. See Chapter 4. One Armenian had no trouble whatsoever in returning prior to 1908 because his name had been anglicized to "Paul." See story of B. F. Paul in *Fresno Morning Republican*, August 29, 1907.

14. Hamasdegh, "Vartan," *Hairenik Amsakir*, December 1922, January, February, 1923.

15. Epilents, *Ash-Kar*, is based on the theme of mismatched marriages and their tragic results. See also the story in Kuyumjian, *Aha Kezi Ameriga*, 246–250.

16. *Hairenik*, April 14, 1914.

17. *Asbarez*, December 15, 1911; *Worcester Daily Telegram*, March 9, 1891.

18. *Hairenik*, September 12, 1911.

19. Drachsler, "Intermarriage in New York City," 43–45.

20. For Woonsocket, see Wessel, *Ethnic Survey of Woonsocket*, 105. For Boston, Treudley, "Ethnic Group's View," 717, a very suggestive article; for Fresno, U.S., Immigration Commission, *Reports*, vol. XXIV, 667.

21. Housepian, *Houseful of Love*, 145. The theme of eventual cultural extinction is powerfully rendered in Saroyan, "Seventy Thousand Assyrians," in *Daring Young Man*.

22. U.S., Immigration Commission, *Reports*, vol. XXIV, 667.

23. Nelson, "Armenian Family," 60–61.

24. Shiragian, "Trip to Armenia."

25. Housepian, *Houseful of Love*, 17.

26. U.S., Immigration Commission, *Reports*, vol. I, 431.

27. *Gotchnag*, July 12, 1902, March 27, 1909; *Azk*, March 15, 1909.

28. Housepian, *Houseful of Love*, 18.

29. Warner and Srole, *Social Systems*, 111.

30. Nelson, "Armenian Family," 35.

31. *Ibid.*, 19.

32. *Gotchnag*, March 15, 19, 1902.

33. *Ibid*, August 23, 1902.

34. Nelson, "Armenian Family," 244, note, 250.

35. See Chapter 10.

36. Hagopian, "Well, my father," 31.

37. LaPiere, "Armenian Colony of Fresno," 337.

38. *Ibid.*, appendix, 158–159.

39. *Ibid.*, 339.

40. *Ibid.*, appendix, 159.

41. *Ibid.*, appendix, 163.

42. LaPiere, "Armenian Colony of Fresno," 387; Nelson, "Armenian Family," 42, 157.

43. Nelson, "Armenian Family," 42–43.

44. William Saroyan, "Myself upon the Earth," in *Daring Young Man*, 206.

45. Shiragian, "Trip to Armenia."

46. U.S., Immigration Commission, *Reports*, vol. XXIV, 667.

47. Hagopian, "Well, my father," *Ararat*, Summer, 1961, 32.

48. Treudley, "Ethnic Group's View," 717.

49. Keljik, *Amerighai Badgerner*, 9.

50. Treudley, "Ethnic Group's View," 717.

51. U.S., Immigration Commission, *Reports*, vol. XXIV, 662.

52. Shiragian, "Trip to Armenia," Native Fresnans objected to Armenian social gatherings. "Of course, people do not want them for neighbors. Suppose one moves in next door to you. Every Sunday all their friends come to visit them and sprawl all over the yard making the neighborhood a bedlam." LaPiere, "Armenian Colony of Fresno," appendix, 108.

53. *Hairenik*, August 19, 1899.

54. *Ibid.*

55. Atamian, *Armenian Community*, 357.

56. *Hairenik*, June 17, 1899.

57. *Ibid.*, August 19, 1899.

58. Kuyumjian, *Aha Kezi Amerigan*, chap. 27.

59. *Gotchnag*, July 11, 1908, September 1, 1906.

60. Fictionalized in Housepian, *Houseful of Love*, chap. 9.

61. *Gotchnag*, August 30, September 13, 1902.

62. See Chapter 7.

63. William Saroyan, *Fresno County Centennial Almanac* (Fresno, 1956), 161.

64. *Asbarez*, May 15, 1914.

65. Kuyumjian, *Aha Kezi Amerigan*, 482–490, contains an excellent description of a hantes.

66. *Worcester Daily Telegram*, January 31, 1890.

67. For Eastern Theatre group, see *Hairenik*, October 9, 1913. Also, *Yeprad*, March 19, 1898; and *Azk*, January 9, 1909.

68. *Hairenik*, March 11, 1913.

69. *Hairenik Amsakir*, December, 1923.

70. *Azk*, November 3, 1909.

71. *Ibid.*, February 1, 1908.

72. *Fresno Morning Republican*, January 16, 1906; *Azk*, November 7, 1908. *Hairenik*, April 28, 1900, urged young readers to attend the performances of Baronian's "The Gamblers" for the "helpful lessons."

73. *Azk*, February 1, 1908.

74. *Fresno Morning Republican*, February 17, 1906.

75. *Asbarez*, May 8, 1914.

76. *Fresno Morning Republican*, January 30, 1904. See also *Gotchnag*, February 4, 1911.

77. *Hairenik*, June 10, 1899; *Gotchnag*, July 26, 1913.

78. *Armenians in Massachusetts*, 43–44.

79. See *Worcester Daily Telegram*, May 5, 1896, May 1, 1897; *Yeprad*, June 11, 1898.

80. *Armenian Review*, vol. 7, 3 (1954), 31; *Hairenik*, July 22, 1899.

81. *Azk*, March 29, 1911.

82. *Tzain Haireneats*, January 3, 1905.

83. *Asbarez*, October 11, 1912; January 23, 1914.

84. *Armenians in Massachusetts*, 44–45.

85. Massachusetts, Commission on Immigration, *Report*, 1914, 67–68.

86. Barsumian, *Stowaway to Heaven*, 47.

87. See Chapter 8.

88. Epilents, *Ash-Kar*, 53.

89. *Yeprad*, August 13, 1898.

90. *Hairenik*, January 15, 1914.

91. *Ibid.*, November 21, 1914.

92. *Ibid.*, November 19, 1912.

93. *Gotchnag*, February 8, 15, 1913.

94. Kuyumjian, *Aha Kezi Amerigan*, 93, 97. Kuyumjian's uncle amplified this by stating that "coffeehouse customers are friendlier and more honest than many fervent churchgoers."

95. For the Kharpert Union see *Hairenik*, April 21, 1900, July 21, 1901.

96. U.S., Commerce, *Religious Bodies*, 1906, Part II, 39.

97. *Azk*, January 25, 1911; *Gotchnag*, January 28, 1911.

98. U.S., Commerce, *Religious Bodies*, 1906, Part II, 39.

99. Alboyadjian, *Badmutiun Hai Gesario*, vol. 2, 1964.

100. Interview, John Millian, Watertown, Massachusetts, July 14, 1969.

101. *Gotchnag*, January 11, 1902.

102. U.S., Commerce, *Religious Bodies*, 1906, Part II, 39.

103. *Ibid.*, February 1, 1902; *Hairenik*, December 8, 1906.

104. *Yeprad*, January 22, 1898.

105. *Charities Review*, July, 1900; *Hairenik*, July 23, 1914.

106. Norehad, *Armenian General Benevolent Union*, 5. A useful history of the AGBU is *Vosgemadean*.

107. Norehad, *Armenian General Benevolent Union*, 5–15, is the source for the quotation and the statistics in the next paragraph.

108. *Ibid.*, 13–15; Armenian General Benevolent Union, *Historic Outline*, 77.

109. *Azk*, January 30, 1909.

110. *Ibid.*

111. *Hairenik*, July 23, 1912. See, for example, M. Dickranian, *Why Do We Criticize?* (Los Angeles, 1961), for a contemporary critique of the organization.

112. The only important source on the Armenian Relief Society is *Hushamadean Hai Oknutean Miutean*.

113. *Ibid.*, 17–26.

Notes to Chapter 10

1. The Armenian Apostolic Church is also referred to as the Armenian Orthodox Church, and the Armenian Gregorian Church, after its patron saint, Gregory. The date of the conversion of Armenia to Christianity is controversial. The long-accepted date is 301; however, recent scholarship is more inclined to set it at 314. The Armenian Church broke with the great churches of Byzantium and Rome in 451 but remained in communion with the Syriac

churches of Antioch and Persia, the Church of Alexandria, the Caucasian Albanians and the Georgians (until the sixth century). The official schism occurred at the Council of Dvin (506).

The most reliable general history of the Armenian Church in English in Ormanian, *Church of Armenia*. Indispensable is his *Azkabadum*. A critical source on the final schism is Sarkissian, *The Council of Chalcedon*. A brief, useful description of the church-state under the Ottomans is in Sanjian, *Armenian Communities*, 31–45.

2. The organizational structure of the church is in Ormanian, *Church of Armenia*, 111–118, 125–128.

3. The early history of the church is in *ibid.*, 3–62.

4. Arpee, *Armenian Christianity*, 288.

5. Ormanian, *Church of Armenia*, 177–178.

6. The story of the first church in Worcester is in Seropian, *Amerigahai . . . 1913*, 49ff; and Ashjian, *Vijagatuits ev Badmutiun*, 18–20, 277–282. A recent thoroughly researched study is Minassian, "A History of the Armenian Holy Apostolic Church in the United States." The story regarding the Baptist preacher is in Minasian, "They Came from Ararat," 67.

7. See Chapter 7.

8. Ashjian, *Vijagatuits ev Badmutiun*, 277–278.

9. *Ibid.*, 278–279; Seropian, *Amerigahai . . . 1913*, 60–62.

10. Seropian, *Amerigaihai . . . 1913*, 60–62; *Dedication of the Armenian Church of Our Saviour Cultural Center* (N.p., n.d.), passim; *Worcester Daily Telegram*, July 29, 1889. Description of Sarajian in *ibid.*, August 22, 1893.

11. Ashjian, *Vijagatsuits ev Badmutiun*, 278, translated in *Dedication of the Armenian Church*.

12. Consecration described in *Worcester Daily Telegram*, January 19, 1891.

13. U.S., Commerce, *Religious Bodies, 1906*, 37.

14. The political struggles of the Armenians in the Old World and the New comprise Part IV of this study.

15. Jizmejian, *Badmutiun*, 19–20; Seropian, *Amerigahai . . . 1913*, 83ff.

16. *Worcester Daily Telegram*, March 27, 1893.

17. *Ibid.*

18. Jizmejian, *Badmutiun*, 19–20; *Worcester Daily Telegram*, March 27, 1893.

19. *Worcester Daily Telegram*, March 27, April 3, 1893.

20. *Ibid.*, April 3, 1893.

21. *Ibid.*, August 22, 1893.

22. Seropian, *Amerigahai . . . 1913*, 74–75.

23. *Worcester Daily Telegram*, March 29, 1894.

24. *Ibid.*, March 30, 1894.

25. *Yeprad*, February 19, 1898; Seropian, *Amerigahai . . . 1913*, 105.

26. *Yeprad*, December 18, 1897, January 1, August 20, 1898.

27. The control of the Armenian American church community was transferred from the patriarch in Constantinople to the Catholicos in Echmiadzin in 1898 owing to the political chaos ensuing from the 1894–1896 massacres. See Ormanian, *Azkabadum*, vol. 3, 5102–5105, and Ashjian,

Vijagatuits ev Badmutiun, 281. The reputed comment by the Catholicos was related by the Rev. Papken Maksoudian, interview, Cambridge, Mass., August 18, 1971.

28. Ashjian, *Vijagatuits ev Badmutiun*, 21–23, related the story of Sarajian's episcopacy. A separate chapter in this work is devoted to each American parish of the Armenian Apostolic Church. See also U.S., Commerce, *Religious Bodies, 1906*, vol. II, 39, which lists 73 "organizations" as of 1906, but no other source corroborates this figure.

29. U.S., Commerce, *Religious Bodies, 1916*, vol. II, 37; *Sahmanatrutiun Hayastaniatz Surp Egheghetzo . . . Amerigayi*, 11–12; Ashjian, *Vijagatuits ev Badmutiun*, 21–23.

30. Seropian, *Amerigahai . . . 1913*, 123–124.

31. *Hairenik*, December 2, 1899, November 3, 1900; see also *ibid.*, March 31, 1900.

32. *Tzain Haireneats*, February 7, 1906.

33. *Ibid.*, March 14, April 11, 25, 1906.

34. *Gotchnag*, September 22, 1906, March 2, 1907; *Hairenik*, September 15, 1906. *Hairenik*, June 22, 1907, grudgingly acknowledged some of Sarajian's many achievements.

35. Quoted in Atamian, *Armenian Community*, 175.

36. *Hairenik*, September 20, 1913.

37. *Azk*, November 30, 1910, January 18, February 15, 1911.

38. The earliest move to "draft" Seropian is in *Azk*, January 18, 1911, and *Hairenik*, February 12, 22, 1911. Election accounts are in *Hairenik*, March 7, 1911; *Gotchnag*, April 1, 1911.

39. *Hairenik*, April 4, July 18, October 31, 1911; February 27, 1912.

40. *Gotchnag*, July 19, 1911; *Hairenik*, July 18, August 22, 1911. The background to the dispute is in *Asbarez*, May 24, 1912; and *Gotchnag*, May 18, 1912.

41. *Hairenik*, January 14, 1913, chronicles his return to the Old World.

42. See *Gotchnag*, October 4, 1913, for a description of the problems confronting Vehooni. On his accomplishments to the outbreak of World War I, consult Ashjian, *Vijagatuits ev Badmutiun*, 27–29.

43. The dire conclusions were drawn by Vahan Kurkjian, founder of the Armenian General Benevolent Union in the United States, in *Gotchnag*, August 3, 1912.

44. U.S., Commerce, *Religious Bodies, 1906*, vol. II, 39.

45. *Ibid.*, *1916*, vol. II, 37ff.

46. *Azk*, November 10, 1909.

47. Hovanesian, "Armenian Community," 100.

48. Quoted in *People of the Eastern Orthodox Churches*, 92.

49. Malcom, *Armenians in America*, 103.

50. Ashjian, *Vijagatuits ev Badmutiun*, 211, 288. The comment on the lack of qualifications of the Providence clergy is in *Azk*, February 23, 1910.

51. The scandal was widely reported: *Fresno Morning Republican*, July 12, 1906; *Gotchnag*, August 4, 1906; *Hairenik*, July 28, 1906. See also *Asbarez*, February 10, 1911.

52. The episode is fully detailed in Chapter 12, but see also Ashjian, *Vijagatuits ev Badmutiun*, 24, and *Hairenik*, August 10, 1907. Even before the episode, Martoogesian had an odious reputation: *Hairenik*, March 22, April 26, 1902, January 17, 1903.

53. Malcom, *Armenians in America*, 1903. The comments are familiar to most second generation Armenian Americans.

54. *Hairenik*, April 14, 1900; *Asbarez, Joghovadzu*, 2ff.

55. *Gotchnag*, March 1, 1902, June 14, 1913; *Hairenik*, April 5, 1902, March 23, 1907, September 13, 1913.

56. Interview, Rev. Maksoudian, August 18, 1971.

57. *Ibid.*

58. Ormanian, *Church of Armenia*, 156.

59. U.S., Commerce, *Religious Bodies, 1916*, vol. II, 38.

60. *Gotchnag*, August 12, 1906. Women sought the right to speak in church as early as 1899. See the lively debate in *Hairenik*, July 15, 29, 1899.

61. Ormanian, *Church of Armenia*, 143.

62. *Ibid.* In Worcester women were still segregated and required to sit in the balcony as late as 1911. *Hairenik*, September 26, 1911.

63. Contemporary estimates of the percentage of Protestant Armenians in the community were: 25 percent, "Armenians of Worcester," *Worcester Magazine*, August 1902, and 15 percent, *Fresno Morning Republican*, July 13, 1919. A brief account of the Armeno-Catholics is in Mirak, "Armenians."

64. Starratt, *Astounding Persecution* contains extracts from contemporary newspaper accounts of the episode. See also the Meserve, *Extracts from a letter*. Also, see Seropian, *Amerigahai . . . 1912*, 63ff.

65. Seropian, *Amerigahai . . . 1913*, 373–374; Walker, *Fresno County Blue Book*, 233. See *Fresno Morning Republican*, March 25, 1907; and Seropian, *Amerigahai . . . 1913*, 374ff.

66. The history of the Armenian Protestant Churches outside Fresno is in Seropian, *Amerigahai . . . 1913*, 375ff; and Mahakian, "History of the Armenians in California," Chap. 3.

67. Seropian, *Amerigahai . . . 1913*, 357–358.

68. *Worcester Daily Telegram*, January 12, 1891. See also Worcester, City Missionary Society, *Reports*, 1893–1897.

69. *Gotchnag*, July 13, 20, 1901.

70. Account of the politics is in Chapter 11.

71. *Gotchnag*, January 19, February 2, 1907; correspondence from Armenian Evangelical Church of New York to author, February 3, 1983.

72. *Ibid.*, May 26, 1906; *Hairenik*, March 28, 1908.

73. Barsumian, *Stowaway to Heaven*, 208. The note about the itinerant preachers in East St. Louis, etc., is in *Gotchnag*, July 14, 1906.

74. Barsumian, *Stowaway to Heaven*, 194; also *Gotchnag*, April 5, 1913. It should also be pointed out, however, that segments of the Protestant clergy espoused the adoption of the United States as the new homeland. Some ministers, such as the Rev. Santigian, especially, were quoted (correctly or not) as follows: "Love of Armenianism and nation is a stupidity. Now we are here, this is our fatherland, our land. . . . These children should not be raised as Armenians but as Americans and they should learn enough Arme-

nian only to understand their mother's words." *Tzain Haireneats*, April 25, 1906. See also *Hairenik*, November 6, 1913.

75. Interview, Reverend Vartan Hartunian, Belmont, Massachusetts, August 20, 1971.

76. Saroyan, "Sunday Is a Hell," in *I Used to Believe*, 18.

77. Interview, Rev. Vartan Hartunian, August 20, 1971. See also Kuyumjian, *Aha Kezi Amerigan*, 496–504.

78. As quoted in *Hairenik*, May 6, 1906.

79. William Saroyan, "The First Armenian Presbyterian Church, Fresno, 1914," in *Places Where I've Done Time*, 171.

80. Greater detail about the ACA is in Chapter 5.

81. Worcester, City Missionary Society, *Reports*, 1897.

82. In addition to citations in Chapter 9, see *Gotchnag*, May 27, 1911, March 29, 1913, also interview Reverend Vartan Hartunian, August 20, 1971.

83. *Asbarez*, March 22, 1912.

84. Interview, Reverend Vartan Hartunian, August 20, 1971.

85. *Gotchnag*, July 5, 12, 1902.

86. Interview, Reverend Vartan Hartunian, August 20, 1971.

Notes to Chapter 11

1. For these early revolutionary groups see Nalbandian, *Armenian Revolutionary Movement*, chap. 4.

2. Details of Portukalian's trip and the formation of the Armenian Academy are in Seropian, *Amerigahai . . . 1913*, 51ff; and Jizmejian, *Badmutiun*, 7–9. Alice Stone Blackwell publicized Portukalian and his writings in her *Armenian Poems* (Boston, 1896).

3. Jizmejian, *Badmutiun*, 7–9.

4. *Ibid.*; Nalbandian, *Armenian Revolutionary Movement*, 94, 95, 99.

5. The Social Democratic Hnchagian Party was first known as the Hnchagian Revolutionary Party. The history of the organization is in Leo, *Tiurkahai Heghapohutean Kaghaparapanutiune*, especially vol. 1, 145ff. Also important is *Hisnameag Eridasart Hayasdani, 1903-1953* [Fifty Year Memorial of Eridasart Hayastan, 1903–1953] (New York, 1950). Nalbandian, *Armenian Revolutionary Movement*, devotes Chapter 5 to the party to 1896. For extremely critical comments on Nazarbeg, see Langer, *Diplomacy of Imperialism*, 156.

6. Generally consult sources above. For the Hnchags' economic policy, Ohanian, *Arevelahai Dndesakidagan Mdki*, 152.

7. Langer, *Diplomacy of Imperialism*, 156.

8. An excellent primary source is Jewell to Uhl, Sivas, February 26, 1895, RG 59, NA, T 681, Roll 1.

9. Jizmejian, *Badmutiun*, 10. The *Worcester Daily Telegram*, July 16, 1894, reported that the Hnchags' first annual national convention in the United States included delegates from New York, Chicago, Philadelphia, Lawrence, Haverhill, Fitchburg, Lynn, Providence, Lowell, Salem, Fall River, Whitinsville, Woonsocket, and "one or two other small New England towns."

10. For Chitjian's Old World career, consult Haig, *Kharpert*, 1113; Jizmejian, *Badmutiun*, 10–11, and Seropian, *Amerigahai . . . 1913*, 378–379. The clash with the missionaries is detailed in the *Worcester Daily Telegram*, January 4, 22, 1894.

11. The anonymous pamphlet, *The Armenian Troubles and Where the Responsibility Lies*, probably written by Mavroyeni Bey, Turkish minister to the United States, pinpointed Garabedian as the party's chieftain in the United States. Khrimian's warning is in Langer, *Diplomacy of Imperialism*, 157. Garabedian's memoirs, Khan Azad, "Hai heghapoghagani husherits," are extremely valuable for the early years of the party.

12. *Worcester Daily Telegram*, July 31, 1893.

13. *Ibid.*, August 14, 1893.

14. *Ibid.*, July 31, 1893.

15. Langer, *Diplomacy of Imperialism*, 158.

16. Jizmejian, *Badmutiun*, 21–24; *Worcester Daily Telegram*, June 14, 1894.

17. *Worcester Daily Telegram*, July 16, 1894.

18. Jizmejian, *Badmutiun*, 25ff.

19. *Worcester Daily Telegram*, April 2, 1894.

20. For details of this prominent early Armenian American, see Papazian, *Kaprielian, passim*. Quotations from *Haik* are in U.S., State, *Foreign Relations . . . 1893*, 712.

21. Jewett to Hess, Marsovan, February 15, 1893, U.S., State, *Foreign Relations . . . 1893*, 605. See also Edward Riggs, "Memorandum Concerning the Present Attitude of the Imperial Ottoman Government Toward the American Missionary Institutions at Marsovan," Constantinople, August 28, 1893, *ibid.*, 673–675.

22. Hamlin's letter originally appeared in the December 23, 1893, *Congregationalist* and was reproduced in U.S., State, *Foreign Relations . . . 1895*, 1415–1416. A vigorous denunciation of Hamlin's charges is in *Worcester Daily Telegram*, February 15, 1894.

23. Jizmejian, *Badmutiun*, 17–18.

24. A useful overview of Turkish American relations in the nineteenth century is in Cook, "United States and the Armenian Question." The diplomatic correspondence is Bey to Gresham, Washington, August 28, 1893, U.S., State, *Foreign Relations . . . 1893*, 711, and Bey to Gresham, Washington, May 24, 1894, *ibid.*, *1894*, 729.

25. Bey to Gresham, Washington, January 16, 1894, U.S., State, *Foreign Relations . . . 1894*, 72; Bey to Secretary of State, Washington, June 18, 1894, U.S., Department of State, "Notes from the Turkish Legation to the Department of State, 1867–1906," Record Group 59, National Archives Microfilm Publication T 815, Bey to Secretary of State, Washington, July 29, 1894, *ibid.*

26. To expand on the conflict between the American and Turkish positions. The Law Concerning Ottoman Nationality of January, 1869 (Article 5) read: "The Ottoman subject who has acquired a foreign nationality with the authorization of the Imperial Government is considered and treated as a foreign subject; if, on the contrary, he is naturalized as a foreigner without the previous authorization of the Imperial Government, his naturalization

shall be considered as null and of no effect, and he will continue to be considered and treated in all respects as an Ottoman subject.

No Ottoman subject can, in any case, naturalize himself as a foreigner except after having obtained a certificate of authorization issued in virtue of an Imperial *irade.*" Quoted in U.S., State, *Foreign Relations . . . 1893,* 714.

On the other hand, the Treaty of 1830 between the United States and Turkey (Article 4) read: "Citizens of the United States of America quietly pursuing their commerce, and not being charged or convicted of any crime or offense, shall not be molested, and even when they may have committed some offense they shall not be arrested and put in prison by the local authorities, but they shall be tried by their minister or consul and punished according to their offense, following in this respect the usage observed toward the Franks." U.S., State, *Foreign Relations . . . 1890,* 917.

To reiterate the point: were Armenian Americans naturalized in the United States without Turkish permission after the Law of 1869 bona fide American citizens with the rights stipulated above? Since the American and Turkish governments could not resolve the issue through a Treaty of Naturalization, the dispute raged on.

27. Said Pasha to Soloman Hirsh, Constantinople, January 9, 1892, U.S., State, *Foreign Relations . . . 1892,* 533; Bey to Secretary of State, Washington, August 20, 1893, U.S., State, *Foreign Relations . . . 1893,* 709; Boston Herald (n.d.), enclosure, Bey to Secretary of State, Washington, February 14, 1894, RG 59, NA, T 815.

28. The concession of 1893 is stated in Grover Cleveland's message to Congress, in December: "There being no naturalization treaty between the United States and Turkey, our minister at Constantinople has been instructed that, against naturalized Americans, he is expected to protect them from unnecessary harshness of treatment." It was agreed, however, that the Turkish government had the right to exclude "undesirable foreigners" after 10 days' stay in Turkey. Cleveland's message in Cook, "United States and the Armenian Question," 20. See also U.S., State, *Foreign Relations . . . 1893,* 704.

29. The background to Sasun is in Varandian, *H. H. Tashnagtsutian,* vol. 1, 143ff. See Lynch, *Armenia, Travels and Studies,* vol. 1, 159, for comments about Mihran Damadian, the first Hnchag organizer in Sasun. The phrase, a "grand coup" is from Langer, *Diplomacy of Imperialism,* 160.

30. Nazarbek, *Through the Storm,* describes Hnchag organizational techniques. See also Langer, *Diplomacy of Imperialism,* 161.

31. The details of the Sasun uprising and the Ottoman response are in Greene, *Armenian Crisis.* See also note 49 below, and Chapter 4, note 55.

32. *New York Daily Tribune,* November 20, 1894.

33. *Worcester Daily Telegram,* November 26, 30, 1894.

34. Jizmejian, *Badmutiun,* 48–49; *Worcester Daily Telegram,* December 26, 1894, January 21, February 7, 1895.

35. The background to American attitudes towards the Turks is in Moore, "America Looks at Turkey." Also consult the brief, but suggestive account in May, *Imperial Democracy,* 27–29.

36. *Worcester Daily Telegram,* December 8, 1894.

37. U.S., *Congressional Record*, Senate, January 12, February 1, 7, 1895.

38. In 1893, Isabel Barrows, wife of the influential editor of the *Christian Register*, met a young Russian Armenian student in Leipzig, Hachadoor Hatchumiantz, who kindled her interest in Armenian history and literature. In the United States the following year as a delegate of the Armenian Apostolic Church to the Parliament of Religion at the Chicago World's Fair, Hatchumiantz also met Alice Stone Blackwell. The three became the nucleus of the Friends of Armenia which, after Sasun, joined forces with the Boston Philarmenian Society to become the United Friends of Armenia, the most powerful pro-Armenian lobby in the nation in the period to World War I. The Brahmin society publicized the Armenian cause throughout the United States, particularly through Alice Stone Blackwell's *Armenian Poems*. The United Friends also assisted refugees and gave useful legal advice to them.. The most detailed, though somewhat factually careless account of the United Friends, is Burnham, *Not by Accident*, 89ff. See also Jizmejian, *Badmutiun*, 29–34; the *Worcester Daily Telegram*, May 23, 1896; and *Yeprad*, July 2, 1898, for details of Hatchumiantz's career.

39. Said Pasha to Bey, Washington, November 11, 1894, U.S., State, *Foreign Relations . . . 1894*, 718; Terrell to Gresham, Pera, November 28, 1894, *ibid.*, 718–719.

40. Quoted in Message of the President, *ibid.*, 715.

41. The Turkish government at first requested the United States government to dispatch an American consul to accompany the inquiry commission, but Cleveland's ineptitude resulted in the United States losing an excellent opportunity for first hand involvement in the crisis. See Cook, "United States and the Armenian Question," 49ff.

42. U.S., *Congressional Record*, Senate, December 3, 1894.

43. Message from Cleveland in *ibid.*, December 18, 1894; *Worcester Daily Telegram*, March 14, 1895. The reference is to ex-Secretary of State James G. Blaine, who had staunchly defended the rights of naturalized Armenian Americans returning to Turkey in an earlier period.

44. *New York Herald*, November 19, 20, 1894.

45. *Worcester Daily Telegram*, January 4, 5, 24, 1895.

46. *The Armenian Troubles and Where the Responsibility Lies*.

47. Dillon was called the *Daily Telegraph's* "Special Commissioner to Armenia." See Greene, *Armenian Crisis*, *passim*.

48. Langer, *Diplomacy of Imperialism*, 161–162.

49. Quoted in Nalbandian, *Armenian Revolutionary Movement*, 122.

50. *Worcester Daily Telegram*, April 16, 1895.

51. Jizmejian, *Badmutiun*, 27ff; *Worcester Daily Telegram*, February 11, August 19, 26, 1895, emphasis added. See also *ibid.*, May 31, August 12, 1895 for similar attitudes.

52. Nalbandian, *Armenian Revolutionary Movement*, 125.

53. Terrell to Olney, Constantinople, October 24, 1895, U.S., States, *Foreign Relations . . . 1895*, 1326–1327.

54. See Chapter 4, note 55 for a list of the voluminous literature on the massacres.

55. Great Britain, Parliamentary Papers, Commercial (Trade), Turkey, 1898, XCIV, 10.

56. Gaidzakian, *Illustrated Armenia*, 256ff.

57. For typical stories, see *Worcester Daily Telegram*, March 14, 1895.

58. Cook, "United States and the Armenian Question," 52ff.

59. The Turkish attacks on missionary property are described in U.S., State, *Foreign Relations . . . 1895*, 1257ff.

60. May, *Imperial Democracy*, 28–29, lists four of these important journals as taking an active role.

61. *Ibid.*, 29.

62. *Boston Evening Transcript*, September 30, 1895.

63. U.S., *Congressional Record*, Senate, February 12, 1896.

64. *Ibid.*, House, January 27, 1896.

65. *Ibid.*

66. *Ibid.*, Senate, January 24, 1896.

67. *Ibid.*

68. For the debate, see *ibid.* The resolution was introduced on December 10, 1895.

69. U.S., State, *Foreign Relations . . . 1895*, 1407ff.

70. *Ibid.*, 1247.

71. Terrell to Dwight, Constantinople, December 27, 1895, in *ibid.*, 1341–1343.

72. Bayard to Cleveland, London, January 29, 1896, in Nevins, *Letters of Grover Cleveland*, 428.

73. *Worcester Daily Telegram*, January 1, 1896; Hamlin, in *The Outlook*, December 7, 1895.

74. Edward G. Porter, *The Independent*, March 5, 1896, Armenian Relief Committee, *Circular Letter*, no. 1 (September 23, 1895), no. 2 (December 28, 1895); Mooradian, "Red Cross in Armenia."

75. Curti, *American Philanthropy Abroad*, 123.

76. *Ibid.*, 124.

77. *Ibid.*; *Worcester Daily Telegram*, January 14, 1896.

78. Mooradian, "Red Cross in Armenia." No statistics are available for the amounts sent by Armenians, but it was said that in 1901 about $200,000 was sent from America, so that perhaps $300,000 was sent by Armenians during the massacre years. See U.S., Commerce and Labor, *Consular Reports*, March 1902.

79. Curti, *American Philanthropy Abroad*, 125.

80. The most complete account of the expedition is Clara Barton et al., *America's Relief Expedition*. Most American newspapers closely watched the expedition. See, for example, *Worcester Daily Telegram*, January 1, 3, 6, 11, 15, 21, 23, 25, February 18, and March 26, 1896. The patriotic response is in *ibid.*, January 1, 1896.

81. Terrell quoted in Cook, "United States and the Armenian Question;" see also Barton et al., *America's Relief Expedition*.

82. Details in *Worcester Daily Telegram*, August 21, 1896, and Barton et al., *America's Relief Expedition*.

83. Langer, *Diplomacy of Imperialism*, 321.

84. The official history of the party is Varandian, *H. H. Tashnagtsutian.* See also Nalbandian, *Armenian Revolutionary Movement,* chap. 7, for the early history of the party. Throughout, the Tashnag aim was autonomy, not statehood.

85. Account is in Nalbandian, *Armenian Revolutionary Movement,* 176–178; and Langer, *Diplomacy of Imperialism,* 322–325.

86. Quoted in Cook, "United States and the Armenian Question," 94.

87. *Boston Evening Transcript,* October 24, 1896.

88. May, *Imperial Democracy,* 61; "Message of the President," U.S., State, *Foreign Relations . . . 1896,* xxviii.

89. Langer, *Diplomacy of Imperialism,* 355.

Notes to Chapter 12

1. Langer, *Diplomacy of Imperialism,* 349–350.

2. J. B. Angell to Hay, Constantinople, July 25, 1898, RG 59, NA, M46, Roll 65.

3. Jizmejian, *Badmutiun,* 52ff; *Worcester Daily Telegram,* January 4, 1897.

4. M. Smpad Kaprielian, *Haigagan Jknajamn ev Veradznutiun,* 79, 82; Langer, *Diplomacy of Imperialism,* 158ff; 203. After the Constantinople massacre of 1895, Father Deroonian of the Worcester parish responded as follows to the charge that the Hnchags had stirred uprisings to incite massacres: "While he deplores the action of the Hunchagists, he does not think that they are guilty of the charges made against them." *Worcester Daily Telegram,* October 22, 1895.

5. The development of the Reformed Hnchag party is discussed in Jizmejian, *Badmutiun,* 66ff.

6. *Tzain Haireneats,* September 9, 1899.

7. *Ibid.,* September 9, 1899; September 29, December 29, 1900; Jizmejian, *Badmutiun,* 69–71.

8. *Tzain Haireneats,* June 3, 1901. Tashnag opposition to the union is discussed in *ibid.,* December 12, 14, 1901. See also *Hairenik,* September 14, 21, October 19, 1901, and Rosdom to American gomides, February 18, 1897, archives, Armenian Revolutionary Federation, hereafter cited as ARF archives.

9. *Hairenik,* January 25, February 8, 1902, April 11, 1903; *Tzain Haireneats,* February 8, 1902.

10. *Tzain Haireneats,* May 3, 17, 24, 1902; Jizmejian, *Badmutiun,* 75–76.

11. Jizmejian, *Badmutiun,* 81ff.

12. *Tzain Haireneats,* May 23, 1903; Jizmejian, *Badmutiun,* 85.

13. *Tzain Haireneats,* July 25, 1903.

14. *Ibid.* Chitjian's son later discussed the assassination, *Gotchnag,* May 11, 1907.

15. *Tzain Haireneats,* July 25, 1903.

16. *Eridasart Hayastan,* November 7, 1903.

17. The bloodletting drew considerable coverage. See *ibid.,* July 11, November 11, 1903; and *Hairenik,* July 11, 18, October 31, December 3, 1903.

18. *New York World*, November 9, 1903.

19. Circular Letter, ARF American Central Committee, Boston, 1903, ARF archives.

20. Leishman to Hay, Constantinople, August 15, 1903, U.S., State, *Foreign Relations . . . 1903*, 763.

21. Leishman to Hay, Constantinople, April 28, 1904, in *ibid.*, *1904*, 836.

22. Leishman to Hay, Constantinople, September 3, 1904, *ibid.*, 838. Note the statement of Varandian, the party's official historian, regarding its objectives: "To wage war against Ottoman persecution, to create a perpetual revolutionary condition in the country, always having in mind the intervention of a third factor . . . European power." (*H. H. Tashnagtsutian*, vol. 1, 302–303). The "old" Hnchag party enthusiastically endorsed the Macedonian uprising. *Eridasart Hayastan*, January 16, 1904.

23. Leishman to Hay, Constantinople, August 28, 1904, U.S., State, *Foreign Relations . . . 1904*, 837.

24. Quoted in *Tzain Haireneats*, February 1, 1905.

25. Leishman to Hay, American Legation, Pera, June 11, 1904, U.S., State, *Foreign Relations . . . 1904*, 836–837; Ramsaur, *Young Turks*, 62.

26. *Gotchnag*, July 2, 1904; *Tzain Haireneats*, February 1, 1905; *Armenia*, January, March 1905. A congressional resolution in December 1903 urged President Roosevelt to convene the signatories of the Congress of Berlin to effect reforms. U.S., *Congressional Record*, 58th Congress, 2nd Session, Senate, December 18, 1903.

27. Atamian, *Armenian Community*, 139.

28. *Tzain Haireneats*, June 1, July 13, 1904, February 2, 1905.

29. Leishman to Norton, Constantinople, June 15, 1903, U.S., State, *Foreign Relations . . . 1903*, 655.

30. The background to the Russian seizure of the Armenian church properties is in Varandian, *H. H. Tashnagtsutian*, vol. 1, 332ff.; and Hovannisian, *Armenia on the Road*, 17–21.

31. *Eridasart Hayastan*, January 9, 1904; *Tzain Haireneats*, May 11, 18, 1904; *Hairenik*, October 10, November 7, 1903; and *Hairenik Amsakir*, May 1923; *Fresno Morning Republican*, February 21, 1904.

32. Sarajian's call is in *Tzain Haireneats*, September 19, 1903. See also *ibid.*, October 7, 1903; and *Eridasart Hayastan*, October 10, 1903. With respect to the Friends of Armenia, consult *Eridasart Hayastan*, October 10, 31, 1903, February 13, April 9, March 26, 1904; *Tzain Haireneats*, May 14, October 12, 1904.

33. Hovannisian, *Armenia on the Road*, 18.

34. As quoted in *Tzain Haireneats*, December 6, 1905.

35. Roosevelt to G. O. Trevelyan, Washington, May 13, 1905, in Morison, *Letters of Theodore Roosevelt*, vol. 4, 1175; Roosevelt to Straus, Washington, September 28, 1904, *ibid.*, 958. The Reformed Hnchags especially regarded the Hague Tribunal as the only possible means of U.S. involvement. *Tzain Haireneats*, January 31, 1906. Influential non-Armenians concurred. See Reform initiative to Roosevelt, U.S., State, *Foreign Relations . . . 1906*, 1417–1419.

36. See *Armenia*, April 1906, and "Address of American Friends of Armenia," n.d. ARF Archives. The petition is cited in 35 above.

37. For examples of Roosevelt's attitudes, see Roosevelt to J. H. Schiff, Washington, December 14, 1905, 112–113; to Straus, Washington, April 10, 1906, 207, to Schiff, Oyster Bay, July 26, 1906, 336–337; to A. Carnegie, Oyster Bay, August 6, 1906, 345, in Morison *Letters of Theodore Roosevelt*, vol. 5.

38. Leishman to Secretary of State, Constantinople, February 15, 1906, U.S., State, *Foreign Relations . . . 1906*, 1418–1419.

39. *Armenia*, April 1906, May, June, 1907.

40. Deghegakir, shrchanagan joghov [Report, regional conference] Chicago, October 5, 1905, ARF archives.

41. The European background of the 1907 movement is in Varandian, *H. H. Tashnagtsutian*, vol. 1, 120–121, 477–481.

42. See report in *Azk*, June 20, 1908.

43. *Ibid.*, August 3, November 16, 1907.

44. Details in Chapter 13.

45. A general description of the schism is in Jizmejian, *Badmutiun*, 117–120. See also *Azk*, May 11, 25, June 22, July 6, 1907.

46. See Chapter 13.

47. The assassination was widely reported. *Hairenik*, July 27, August 3, 10, 1907; *Gotchnag*, July 27, August 3, 10, 1907; *Azk*, July 27, August 3, 1907. The assassin, Hampartzumian, died in the electric chair at Sing Sing Prison on December 6, 1909. *American Carpet and Upholsters' Journal*, December, 1909.

48. Quoted in *Gotchnag* and *Hairenik*, August 3, 1907. Efforts of the Friend of the Armenians are discussed in *Azk*, August 3 and 31, 1907, and *Gotchnag*, August 17, 1907. Tavshanjian's killing was followed by that of the distinguished Reformed Hnchag journalist, Arpiar Arpiarian, in Cairo, in March 1908. *Azk*, April 11, 1908.

Notes to Chapter 13

1. For the growth of Tashnagtsutiun in the United States, see *Voroshumner, H. H. T. Ameriga Shrchani, 9th Badkm. Joghovin* [Resolutions, A (Armenian) R. (Revolutionary) F. (Federation), 9th Rep. (Representative) Assembly], Providence, December 24–28, 1903; *Voroshumner, . . . 13th Badkm. Joghovin*, Boston, December 25–29, 1907; and *Shrchaperagan, H. H. T. Amerigai Getronagan Gomide* [Circular Letter, A. R. F. American Central Committee], Boston, June 14, 1914, all in ARF archives.

2. Enclosure, Report of Consul General Dickinson, Constantinople, to Leishman, September 21, 1905, in RG 59, NA, M46, Roll 76. Figures for the Old Hnchag and Ramgavar party membership are my estimates.

3. *Ibid.*

4. The inclusion of women in the gomides is in *Voroshumner, 9th Badkm. Joghovin* (1903); the recruiting of Kurds and Turks is in *Hairenik*, January 10, 1911.

5. For the Turkish request that the American government put the revolutionary societies under Secret Service surveillance, see Chekib Bey, Turkish Minister, Washington, to Adee, September 29, 1905, RG 59, NA, T815. A further note to Adee of October 2, 1905, enclosed in this correspondence, stated: "I think we may properly ask the secret service to place the parties named under surveillance." The first full report of the investigation is summarized in Robert Bacon, Acting Secretary of State, Washington to Chekib Bey, March 9, 1906, RG 59, NA, M99, Roll 97. The eruption of widespread terrorist activity in 1907 prompted further investigations. See U.S., State, *Foreign Relations*, . . . *1907*, 1070. Also, Arthur Woods, Deputy Commissioner, New York City Police Department to Robert Woods, Acting Secretary, Department of State, Washington, August 14, 1907, RG 59, NA, NF 676/1-10/file 528: and American Consul General and Agent, Lewis Iddings, Cairo to Assistant Secretary of State, Washington, December 10, 1907, *ibid.*, 10758/117 [file 743] and 11990/1-9, March 7, 1908.

6. *New York Times*, August 1, 2, 6, 1907; also Mandalian, *Armenian Freedom Fighters*, 49.

7. Mandalian, *Armenian Freedom Fighters*, 51. Also, *New York Times*, August 1, 2, 1907.

8. Consult, for example, *Tzain Haireneats*, October 25, 1904. *Troshag's* circulation was estimated at 1,500 per week in 1904 but dropped to 400 by 1914. See *Shrchaperagan* . . . *Amerigai Getronagan Gomide*, February 1, 1904, and August 1, 1914, ARF archives.

9. The functions of the kordzich are described in Mandalian, *Armenian Freedom Fighters*, 41–42. There is a voluminous correspondence in the ARF archives on the American Central Committee's requests for more effective field agents. See Amerigai Getronagan Gomide Arevmdean Biroin [American Central Committee to Western Bureau], May 5, 1905, and April 8, 1908, and Amerigai Getronagan Gomide Arevelean Biroin [American Central Committee to Eastern Bureau], December 9, 1907.

10. Langer, *Diplomacy of Imperialism*, 158; Amerigai Getronagan Gomide Arevmedean Biroin, April 8, 1908.

11. Enclosure, Report of Dickinson to Leishman, September 21, 1905, RG 59, NA, M46, Roll 76.

12. Mandalian, *Armenian Freedom Fighters*, 44.

13. Bacon to Chekib Bey, Washington, March 9, 1906, RG 59, NA, M99, Roll 97.

14. *Ibid.*

15. *Ibid; Voroshumner, 12th Badkm. Joghovin*, November 29–December 2, 1906, ARF archives. Also, Wm Wilsohn, G. D., to Consul-General of Turkish Government, at New York City, July 8, 1908, ARF archives.

16. *Tzain Haireneats*, October 25, 1904.

17. *New York Times*, August 1, 1907.

18. The quotation is from Jizmejian, *Badmutiun*, 130–131. See also *Azk*, February 15, 29, 1908; and *Hairenik*, February 1, 1908, for details of Murad's tour.

19. The issues surrounding the strife are in Chapter 10.

20. Jizmejian, *Badmutiun*, 81ff. Also consult *Tzain Haireneats*, May 23, July 25, 1903; *Gotchnag*, May 11, 1907; *Hairenik*, July 11, December 5, 1903; and *Eridasart Hayastan*, July 11, November 7, 14, 1903.

21. *New York Times*, August 1, 1907. See also *Azk* and *Hairenik*, July 27, 1907.

22. Oundjian, a "rich Armenian," had been singled out for refusing to donate to the revolutionary organization. See Leishman to Secretary of State, Constantinople, October 3, 1907, U.S., State, *Foreign Relations . . . 1907*, 1070. The affidavit is the Enclosure, report of Dickinson to Leishman, Constantinople, September 21, 1905, RG 59, NA, M46, roll 76.

23. The release of Vartanian and Afarian is in Leishman to Root, Constantinople, September 9, 1908, RG 59, NA, NF 15795 [file 937]. The first instance of extortion and assassination appearing in State Department archives involved the Armenian Revolutionary Federation. See R. Lane to Leishman, Smyrna, March 16, 1903, RG 59, NA, M46.

24. Information about Eginian's life is in *Fresno Morning Republican*, July 6, 1919; Vandor, *History of Fresno County*, vol. 1, 547; and Jizmejian, *Badmutiun*, 6–7.

25. Kaprielian's career is detailed in Papazian, *Kaprielian*.

26. *Armenians in Massachusetts*, 73–74. The May 6, 1899 issue of *Hairenik* noted that there was also a handwritten, Armenian-language paper in Boston called *Grag* (The Flame).

27. *Tzain Haireneats* is discussed in *Armenians in Massachusetts*, 74–75. The history of *Hairenik* is in *Hairenik Amsakir*, November 1922, May 1923.

28. A few typical diatribes of the immigrant writers are in *Azk*, June 9, 1909, April 6, 1910; *Tzain Haireneats*, September 28, 1904. Transations of classic English and French language works are in *Azk*, which serialized Victor Hugo in mid-1909; *Hairenik*, November 18, 1913 (Edgar Allen Poe), February 5, 1914 (Galsworthy), and April 9, 1914 (Jack London).

29. See *Gotchnag's* first issue, December 15, 1900. The biography of its first editor is in Haig, *Kharpert*, 364. Armenians succeeded Allen as editor after 1902. The only other "religious" journal of the period was *Pem* (The Pulpit) which appeared in Fresno from 1912 to 1914 as a single sheet weekly. *Fresno Morning Republican*, July 13, 1919.

30. For beginnings of this journal, see *Fresno Morning Republican*, August 15, 1908. A very useful history of the journal is *Asbarez, Joghovadzu*, especially 9–27.

31. *Ibid.*; *Hairenik*, April 18, 1903 is one example of the staunch nationalism of this journal.

32. The history of the Hnchag journal is in the important collection, Sotsialisdagan . . . Gusagtsuiun, *Hisnameag Eridasart Hayasdani*. The Hnchag press also published a large number of important socialist tracts, detailed in *ibid.*, 197–200.

33. *Asbarez*, September 20, 1912.

34. *Armenians in Massachusetts*, 82. *Hai Usanogh* is noted in *Hairenik*, February 20, 1912. Another student monthly was the shortlived *Hai Tbrots* (Armenian School), as noted in *Hairenik*, July 30, 1914.

35. *Armenians in Massachusetts*, 81.

36. See *Armenia's* first volume, October 1904, which carried at its mast-head Gladstone's famous saying, "To serve Armenia is to serve Civilization." *Armenia*, November 1906 noted its list of subscriptions. A brief biography of its editor is in Haig, *Kharpert*, 1181.

37. See these fascinating reminiscences in *Hairenik Amsakir*, January 1924.

38. Interview, Dr. E. Chrakian, Watertown, Massachusetts, January 5, 1972.

39. *Hisnameag Eridasart Hayasdani*, 182–183.

40. *Hairenik*, May 19, 1900, October 19, 1901. *Voroshumner*, 13th *Badkm. Joghovin*.

41. *Armenians in Massachusetts*, 73.

42. George Mardikian, *Song of America* (New York, 1956), 147.

Notes to Chapter 14

1. A useful treatment of the Young Turk movement is Ramsaur, *Young Turks*.

2. Lewis, *Emergence of Modern Turkey*, 200ff.

3. Barton, *Daybreak in Turkey*.

4. *Hairenik*, August 22, 1908. Perhaps the earliest espousal in the United States of a Young Turk-Tashnag entente was made by Ferrahian, an outspoken, maverick party member, who argued, as quoted in *Tzain Haireneats*, February 10, 1900: "We can do nothing since whatever we could do or tried to do spilled blood. We waited for Europe to save us, but we saw that we received no assistance from them. Therefore, there is no hope. Our only opportunity will be to join with the Young Turks, because they, like us, are discontent with the present regime and wish to reform the country."

5. *Asbarez*, October 16, 1908.

6. Atamian, *Armenian Community*, 159.

7. *Hairenik*, August 22, 25, 28, 1908.

8. *Azk*, December 12, 1908.

9. A history of the Ramgavar party is badly needed. The best source in Armenian is Jizmejian, *Badmutiun*. Papazian, *Patriotism Perverted*, is a vituperative Ramgavar attack on the Tashnags. With its December 12, 1908, issue, *Azk* officially became the organ of the new organization.

10. Quoted in Atamian, *Armenian Community*, 167.

11. The conservatives who joined the Ramgavar party in late 1908 were attacking the entente as early as February of that year. See *Azk*, February 15, 29, November 28, 1908.

12. The Ramgavar attack on the Tashnags for their socialist platform was unending. See *Azk*, May 1, August 4, 1909, August 10, 1910 for typical examples. The ideological struggle against the Tashnags was later recounted in Papazian, *Patriotism Perverted*, 35. The quotation is from Arthur Johnson, editor of the socialist monthly, *Evolution*, and is in *Azk*, January 5, 1910.

13. Jizmejian, *Badmutiun*, 130ff; *Hisnameag Eridasart Hayasdani*, 145ff.

14. *Shrchaperagan . . . Amerigai Getronagan Gomide*, August 5, September 15, November 10, 1908.

15. *Hairenik*, July 8, 1899.

16. *Azk*, January 30, 1909.

17. Quoted in RG 59, NA, NF 14933/6-7 [file 905]. See also *Azk*, March 6, 1909, and the earlier September 19, 1908, issue.

18. Norehad, *Armenian General Benevolent Union*, 12.

19. Ravndal to Assistant Secretary of State, Beirut, May 7, 1909, RG 59, NA, NF 10044/234-235 [file 718].

20. *Ibid*. See also Atamian, *Armenian Community*, 175.

21. Lewis, *Emergence of Modern Turkey*, 210ff.

22. Masterson to Leishman, Harput, December 23, 1908, RG 59, NA, NF 10045/123 [file 717].

23. For contemporary reports, see *Hairenik*, *Azk*, and *Gotchnag*, from April 27, 1909.

24. Cook, "United States and the Armenian Question," 110.

25. Hovannisian, *Armenia on the Road*, 29–30.

26. Hovannisian, *Armenia on the Road*, 30.

27. U.S., *Congressional Record*, 61st Congress, 1st Session, House, May 3, 1909.

28. See Huntington Wilson, Acting Secretary of State, to Hon. W. S. Bennet, Washington, June 28, 1909, in U.S., State, *Foreign Relations . . . 1909*, 557.

29. For the Armenian and American relief efforts, see *Armenia*, May, 1910; *Gotchnag*, February 12, 1910; *Asbarez*, June 25, 1909. The relief efforts of the Turkish government are detailed in Sanjian, *Armenian Communities in Syria*, 282.

30. *Hairenik*, May 11, 1909.

31. *The Fatherland's Call to Armenian Americans*, Executive Committee of the Armenian Volunteers, New York, May 2, 1909; *Shrchaperagan . . . Amerigai Getronagan Gomide*, June 11, 1909, ARF archives.

32. Comments of Reuben Darpinian, later Minister of Justice of the Armenian Republic (1918–1920), and then editor of *Hairenik*, in Boston, quoted in Atamian, *Armenian Community*, 175.

33. *Azk*, May 22, October 6, 1909; Norehad, *Armenian General Benevolent Union*, 13. See also *Azk*, March 2, 1910.

34. *Armenia*, May 1910.

35. Ravndal to Trowbridge, Beirut, July 10, 1909, RG 59, NA, NF 19274/39-41 [file 1060]; Professor Richard Gotthiel in *Armenia*, February 1911.

36. *Armenia*, October 1910.

37. *Hairenik*, September 20, 27, 1910, gave details of his travels; see also E. Agnooni, "Open Letter" to the Turkish Ambassador in the United States, New York, May, 1911, in ARF archives.

38. *Hairenik*, September 27, 1910; *Asbarez*, November 11, 1910.

39. Agnooni, "Open Letter."

40. *Voroshumner, 16th Badkm. Joghovi*, Boston, 1911; *Shrchaperagan Namag . . . Amerigai Getronagan Gomide*, May 17, 1911, both in ARF

archives. The Tashnag press carried many appeals in this regard. For documentation, see Chapter 5, notes 22–25.

41. *Hairenik*, May 7, 1912. See also *ibid.*, September 3, 1912.

42. For example, *Armenia*, July 1911; *Hairenik*, June 11, 1914.

43. Between 1904 and 1914, about 3 percent of the Armenians entering the United States were 45 years of age or older, whereas in the same period about 15 percent of the repatriates were in that age category. U.S., Commissioner General of Immigration, *Reports*, 1904–1914. There were a number of impressive individuals among the repatriates; especially striking was the career of Donabed G. Livlejian, whose writings are collected in his *Hasgakagh*. Like so many of the repatriates, he was killed in the holocaust of World War I.

44. Davison, "The Armenian Crisis," 499; *Hairenik*, May 6, 13, October 23, 1913.

45. Hovannisian, *Armenia on the Road*, 30.

46. *Asbarez*, December 26, 1913. See also *Gotchnag*, May 17, 1913.

47. *Gotchnag*, April 5, 1913.

48. Unless otherwise cited, this paragraph and the following are derived from Hovannisian, *Armenia on the Road*, 30–34, 38–39. Conditions were so unsettled during the 1st Balkan War that the United States government dispatched the cruisers *Tennessee* and *Montana* to Turkish waters to protect American citizens in the Ottoman Empire.

49. Worcester International Committee, *Srchaperagan Goch* [Circular Letter-Appeal], Worcester, Mass., October 18, 1912, in ARF archives.

50. *Armenia*, June 1913; *Gotchnag*, November 2, 1912; Jizmejian, *Badmutiun*, 190.

51. *Hairenik*, August 14, 1913, January 1, 1914; *Shrchaperagan 9, . . . Amerigai Getronagan Gomide*, November 6, 1913.

52. Quoted in Cook, "United States and the Armenian Question," 113.

53. See *Shrchaperagan 2, . . . Amerigai Getronagan Gomide*, March 15, 1914; *Amerigai Getronagan Gomide Arevmdean Biroin*, March 14, 1914, ARF archives.

Notes to Chapter 15.

1. U.S., Immigration Commission, *Reports*, vol. XXIX, 8–13; XXXII, 624; XXXIII, 570.

2. *Ibid.*, vol. XXIV, 660.

3. California, Immigration Commission, *Fresno's Immigration Problem*, 7–8. The report added, "Last year 50 percent of the High School orchestra was Armenian, and there were a number of girls enrolled at the Normal School."

4. Kuyumjian, *Aha Kezi Amerigan*, 215–220.

5. Massachusetts, Immigration Commission, *Report*, 1914, 115–116.

6. LaPiere, "Armenian Colony in Fresno," 402.

7. *Ibid.*, 403.

8. William Saroyan, "Miss Carmichael, Miss Thompson," in *Letters from 74 rue Taitbout* (New York, 1969), 84.

9. *Ibid.*, 84–85.

10. Massachusetts, Immigration Commission, *Report*, 1914, 117–125.

11. Fresno, School Department, *Annual Reports*, 1910, 1916.

12. *Gotchnag*, March 16, 1901, March 6, 1909; *Azk*, May 11, 1911. See also *Azk*, September 22, 1909, for its promotions of the Cambridge, Mass., Prospect Union School. *Hairenik*, September 18, 1913, also October 14, 1899.

13. Worcester, *City Documents*, 1897.

14. *Ibid.*, 1900; Massachusetts, Immigration Commission, *Report*, 1914; *Gotchnag*, October 8, 1914.

15. Worcester, *City Documents*, 1898.

16. Massachusetts, Immigration, *Report*, 1914, 130–131.

17. See Chapter 17 of Kuyumjian's autobiography, *Aha Kezi Amerigan* for details of this episode.

18. Worcester, *City Documents*, 1891–1894; Massachusetts, Immigration Commission, *Report*, 1914, 122,132; *Gotchnag*, November 18, 1911.

19. Worcester, *City Documents*, 1893.

20. *Armenians in Massachusetts*, 71.

21. *Ibid.*

22. Hagopian, "Well, my father."

23. *Armenian Review*, vol. 7, 3 (1954).

24. *Hairenik*, July 3, 1899; *Tzain Haireneats*, October 25, 1905.

25. *Yeprad*, February 5, May 7, 1898; *Fresno Morning Republican*, November 27, 1906.

26. *Yeprad*, February 12, 1898.

27. For the Armenian Colonial Association, see *Gotchnag*, November 26, 1910, July 15, November 2, 1912, October 10, 1914.

28. *Ibid.*, October 21, 1911.

29. Various activities of the Armenian Progressive Association are described in *Gotchnag*, January 8, 1910, March 25, November 4, 1911; *Hairenik*, December 23, 1913; and *Armenian Review*, vol. 8, 3 (1954), 31.

30. Chakmakjian, *Amerigahai Namagani*. On December 2, 1913, *Hairenik* advertised Bedros Torosian's *Inknusutsich Anklieren Lezvi* [English Self-Taught]. The 768 page tome carried drawings showing the disappointed immigrant who was unemployed because he didn't know English, but who, when he learned the language, obtained a position in a bank, married, and lived in a comfortable home. An illustrated English language conversationalist was also prepared for Turkish-speaking Armenian immigrants. *Hairenik*, March 19, 1914.

31. *Asbarez*, March 24, 1911. The phrase "execration and derision" is in the *Fresno Morning Republican*, May 19, 1907.

32. Saroyan, "The Typewriter," in *Bicycle Rider*, 55.

33. As quoted in Goldman, *Rendezvous with Destiny*, 230.

34. LaPiere, "Armenian Colony in Fresno," 398.

35. *Ibid.*, 27, appendix.

36. *Hairenik*, February 9, 1901; *Gotchnag*, June 2, 1906.

37. *Fresno Morning Republican*, December 4, 1908.

38. Kassabian, "Armenians . . . in Grand Rapids," 113–114.

39. Mardikian, *Song of America*, 117.

40. Mahakian, "History of the Armenians in California," 80–81.

41. *Gotchnag*, November 2, 1907.

42. Ibid., October 26, 1901; Torosian, *Amerigain Kaghakatsi*, xiv.

43. North American Civic League for Immigrants, *Annual Reports*, 1909–1910, 1912–1913, 1913–1914, 1914–1915. By World War I Armenians were actively assisting the League in Chelsea, Massachusetts, and Bridgeport, Connecticut. For a view of the League in the context of the Americanization movement of the period, see Hartmann, *Movement to Americanize the Immigrant*, chap. 2.

44. *Gotchnag*, February 9, 1901; U.S., House, 59th Cong., 1st Sess., "Certain Reports of Immigrant Inspector Marcus Braun."

45. U.S., Immigration Commission, *Reports*, vol. I, 484. For 1920, see Carpenter, *Immigrants and their Children*, 263.

46. The problem of naturalization and citizenship is ably dealt with in the entry, "Naturalization and Citizenship," in Thernstrom et al., eds., *Harvard Encyclopedia of American Ethnic Groups* (Cambridge, Mass., 1980), with specific references to the Armenians on 741–742. The first mention in the press was *Fresno Morning Republican*, September 21, 1909. See also *Asbarez*, September 24, 1909; *Azk*, December 8, 1909; *Gotchnag*, December 25, 1909; and *Hairenik*, October 26, 1909.

47. *Asbarez*, November 12, 1909.

48. *In Re Halladjian* (1909), 174 *Federal Reporter*, 834 (Circuit Court of Massachusetts); *United States vs. Cartozian* (1925), 6 *Federal Reporter*, 2nd Series, 919 (District Court of Oregon).

49. *Asbarez*, February 5, 1909.

50. Hichborn, *California Legislature of 1913*, 239–240. For the Armenian reaction to the issue, see *Asbarez*, May 1, 9, 23, 1913.

51. Gotchnag, September 3, October 15, 1904, November 17, 1906; *Hairenik*, June 9, 1900.

52. See *Gotchnag*, October 31, 1908; *Azk*, November 14, 1908; *Hairenik*, October 30, 1908, March 30, 1909, January 10, 1911 (an important statement of its socialist position), March 12, July 2, 9, October 29, 1912.

53. *Hairenik*, December 9, 1905.

54. *Gotchnag*, October 29, 1910.

55. *Hairenik*, November 24, 1906; U.S., Immigration Commission, *Reports*, vol. XXIV, 658ff.

56. *Azk*, July 18, 1908; *Fresno Morning Republican*, July 5, 1895. See also *Gotchnag*, July 26, 1913.

57. David Ollan, "The Father of an American," *Common Ground* (Autumn 1945).

58. *Asbarez*, June 20, 1922, as quoted in LaPiere, "Armenian Colony in Fresno," 406–407.

59. Bogigian, *In Quest of the Soul*, 254.

Bibliography

Primary Sources

A. Manuscripts

American Board of Commissioners for Foreign Missions, MSS. Correspondence and Annual Reports: Western Turkey Mission, 1890–1899, vols. 1–4, ABCFM 16.9.3; Cental Turkey Mission, 1880–1889, vols. 1–4; 1890–1899, ABCFM 16.9.5; Eastern Turkey Mission, 1880–1889, vols. 1–4; 1890–1899, ABCFM 16.9.7. Houghton Library, Harvard University, Cambridge.

Armenian Revolutionary Federation, Archives, 1897–1914, Boston, Massachusetts.

Avakian, Anne. Collection . . . relating . . . to Armenians. 2 vols. Berkeley, University of California Library.

Fresno County, California, Jail Register, 1910.

Hall, Prescott F. Collection. *Immigration* (newspaper). "Clippings," 11 vols. "Magazine Articles," 7 vols. Harvard College Library, Cambridge.

U.S. General Records of the Department of State. Record Group 59. 1834–1906, National Archives Microfilm Resources. 1906–1914, National Archives, Washington, D. C.

U.S. Records of the Bureau of Customs. Record Group 36. National Archives Microfilm Resources.

Ward, Robert DeCourcy. *Immigration*. "Newspaper Clippings, 1901–1907." Harvard College Library, Cambridge.

B. Official Documents

American Board of Commissioners for Foreign Missions. *Reports*. Cambridge, 1870–1914.

Barton, Clara, et al. *Report America's Relief Expedition to Asia Minor under the Red Cross*. Washington, 1896.

Boston Directory. Boston, 1900.

Boston Directory. Boston, 1915.

California. Bureau of Labor Statistics. *Biennial Reports*. Sacramento, 1883–1917.

California. Commission of Immigration and Housing. *Annual Reports*. Sacramento, 1915–1916, 1919.

California. Commission of Immigration and Housing. *Americanization of Foreign-Born Women* (1917); *Bulletin of Information for Immigrants* (1920); *Camp Sanitation and Housing* (1914); *Fresno's Immigration Problem* (1918); *Report on Unemployment* (1914).

California. Department of Agriculture. *Monthly Bulletin*. Sacramento, 1919–1920.

California. Fruit Growers' Convention. *Official Reports*. Sacramento 1888–1890, 1903–1910.

California. State Agricultural Society. *Transactions and Reports*. Sacramento, 1892–1895, 1899–1901, 1904–1910.

California, University of. Agricultural Experiment Station. *Bulletin*. Berkeley, 1890–1914.

California, University of. General Vocation Education Series. *A Study of Vocational Conditions in the City of Fresno*. Berkeley, 1926.

Force, Peter, Ed. *Tracts and Other Papers Relating Principally to the Origin . . . of the Colonies in North America . . . to the Year 1776*. 4 Vols. New York, 1947.

Fresno. Public School Department. *Annual Reports*. 1898–1909, 1910.

Fresno City and County Directory. 1900. n.p., 1915.

Fresno City and County Directory. 1915. Sacramento, 1915.

Great Britain. Parliamentary Papers. Accounts and Papers. Turkey. *Further correspondence respecting the Conditions of the Population in Asiatic Turkey. Turkey No. 1* (1892).

Correspondence relating to the Asiatic Provinces of Turkey. Turkey No. 1 (1895).

Correspondence relative to the introduction of Reforms in the Armenian Provinces of Asiatic Turkey. Turkey No. 1 (1896).

Correspondence relative to the Armenian Question and Reports from her Majesty's Consular Offices in Asiatic Turkey. Turkey No. 2 (1896).

Correspondence relative to the Asiatic Provinces of Turkey. 1892–1893. Turkey No. 3 (1896).

Correspondence relating to the Asiatic Provinces of Turkey. Turkey No. 5 (1896).

Correspondence relating to the Asiatic Provinces of Turkey. 1894–1895. Turkey No. 6 (1896).

Correspondence relating to the Asiatic Provinces of Turkey. Turkey No. 8 (1896).

Correspondence respecting the Disturbances at Constantinople in August 1896. Turkey No. 1 (1897).

Great Britain. Parliamentary Papers. Commercial (Trade), Turkey, 1898, XCIV.

Great Britain. Parliamentary Papers. Vol. 22 (LXXI) Reports to the Board of Trade on Alien Immigration. *Burnett Report*. 1893.

Lawrence Directory. Boston, 1911.

Massachusetts. Bureau of Statistics of Labor. *Annual Reports*. 1880–1914.

Massachusetts. Bureau of Statistics. *Decennial Census*. 1905, 1915.

Massachusetts. Bureau of Statistics. *Labor Bulletin*. 1897–1912.

Massachusetts. Commission on Immigration. *The Problem of Immigration in Massachusetts*. Boston, 1914.

New Jersey. Commission of Immigration of the State of New Jersey. *Report*. Trenton, 1914.

New York Directory. New York, 1900.

New York Directory. New York, 1915.

North American Civic League for Immigrants. *Annual Reports.* Boston, 1908–1919.

Rhode Island. Commissioner of Industrial Statistics. *Annual Reports.* Providence, 1888–1895.

U.S. Commissioner General of Immigration. *Annual Reports.* Washington, 1899–1915.

U.S. Commissioner of Labor. *Annual Reports.* Washington, 1886–1910.

U.S. *Congressional Record.* 53th Cong., 3rd sess., 1894–1895; 54th Cong., 1st sess. 1895–1896.

U.S. Department of Commerce. Bureau of the Census. *Religious Bodies, 1906, 1916.* Washington, 1910, 1919.

U.S. Department of Commerce and Labor. *Monthly Consular Reports.* Washington, 1881–1910.

U.S. Department of Labor. Bureau of the Census. *Twelfth Census . . . 1900.* Washington, 1901; *Thirteenth Census . . . 1910.* Washington, 1913; *Fourteenth Census . . . 1920.* Washington, 1923; *Fifteenth Census . . . 1930.* Washington, 1933.

U.S. Department of State. Bureau of Foreign Commerce. *Commercial Relations of the United States with Foreign Countries.* Washington, 1885–1904.

U.S. Department of State. *Reports of Diplomatic and Consular Officers Concerning Emigration from Europe to the United States.* Washington, 1889.

U.S. Department of State. *Foreign Relations of the United States.* Washington, 1890–1914.

U.S. House. *The Importation of Contract Laborers, Paupers, Convicts, and Other Classes.* 50th Cong. 1st Sess. Washington, 1888.

U.S. House. *Report of the Select Committee on Immigration and Naturalization* (Owen Report). 51st Cong., 2nd Sess. Washington, 1891.

U.S. House. *Certain Reports of Immigrant Inspector Marcus Braun.* (Braun Report). 59th Cong., 1st Sess. Washington, 1906.

U.S. Immigration Commission. *Reports.* 41 vols. Washington, 1907–1910.

U.S. Industrial Commission. *Reports.* 19 vols. Washington, 1900–1902.

U.S. Senate. *Report on the Strike of Textile Workers in Lawrence, Mass. in 1912.* 62nd Cong., 2nd Sess. Washington, 1912.

U.S. Treasury Department. *Arrivals of Alien Passengers and Immigrants in the United States from 1820 to 1892.* Washington, 1893.

U.S. Treasury Department. *Immigration and Passenger Movement at Ports of the United States.* Washington, 1892–1895.

U.S. Treasury Department. *Report of the Immigration Investigating Commission to the . . . Secretary of the Treasury.* Washington, 1895.

Worcester. The Associated Charities. *Annual Reports.* 1891–1898, 1910–1915.

Worcester. Board of Trade. *Reports.* 1896–1899.

Worcester. *City Documents.* 1890–1914.

Worcester. City Missionary Society. *Annual Reports.* 1893–1895, 1897.

Worcester. Overseers of the Poor. *Annual Reports.* 1880–1902.

Worcester Directory. Worcester, 1915.

C. Newspapers, Periodicals, and Pamphlets: Armenian-Language

Amsakir [The Monthly]. Fresno, 1913–1914. Avakian Collection. Berkeley, University of California Library.

Asbarez [The Arena]. Fresno, 1908–1914. Library, *Asbarez* Publishing Company, Los Angeles.

Azk [The Nation]. Boston, 1907–1911. Library, Baikar Publishing Company, Watertown, Mass.

Eridasart Hayastan [Young Armenia]. Boston, 1904. Library, Armenian Revolutionary Federation, Boston.

Gotchnag [The Church Bell]. Boston and New York, 1899–1914. Library, Armenian Holy Trinity Church, Cambridge.

Hairenik [The Fatherland]. New York and Boston. 1899–1914. Library, Armenian Revolutionary Federation, Boston.

Hairenik Amsakir [Hairenik Monthly]. Boston, 1918–1920. Harvard College Library, Cambridge.

Sahmanatrutiun Hayastaniatz Surp Egheghetzo . . . Amerigayi [Constitution of the Armenian Church . . . of America]. Venice, 1903.

Tzain Haireneats [Voice of the Homeland]. New York, Worcester, and Boston, 1899–1906. Armenian Cultural Foundation, Arlington, Mass.

Yeprad [Euphrates]. Worcester, 1897–1898. Library, Massachusetts State House, Boston.

D. Newspapers, Periodicals, and Pamphlets: English-Language

American Board of Commissioners for Foreign Missions. *Historical Sketch of the Missions in Eastern Turkey, Asia Minor and Armenia.* New York, 1861.

The American Carpet and Upholstery Journal. Philadelphia, 1906–1914.

An American Story; A Brief History of the House of Karagheusian. N.p., n.d.

Ararat. 1965–1980.

Armenia. Boston, 1904–1913. Became *Oriental World*, Boston, 1913–1914, and *The New Armenia*, Boston, 1915–1929.

Armenian Relief Committee. "Circular Letter." No. 1. Boston, September 23, 1895. No. 2. Boston, December 28, 1895. Library, Massachusetts State House, Boston.

Armenian Review. Boston, 1948–1979.

The Armenian Troubles and Where the Responsibility Lies. New York, 1895. Library, Massachusetts State House, Boston.

Boston Evening Transcript. 1895–1896.

California Fruit Grower. 1888–1914.

Common Ground. New York, 1940–1949.

Dedication of the Armenian Church of Our Saviour Cultural Center. N.p., n.d.

Dickranian, M. *Why Do We Criticize?* Los Angeles, 1961.

Fresno Morning Republican. 1889–1901; 1904–1911.

London Times. 1895–1896.

Meserve, William N. *Extracts from a Letter of a Former Pastor of the Fresno Church.* N.p., 1894 ? Library, Massachusetts State House, Boston.

Missionary Herald. Boston, 1840–1895.

New York Times. 1907.

Starratt, William, et al. *Astonishing Persecution of Armenian Christians in Central California.* N.p., n.d. Library, Massachusetts State House, Boston.

Worcester Daily Telegram. 1886–1904.

Secondary Sources

A. ARMENIAN-LANGUAGE WORKS

Abrahamian, A. G. *Hamarod urvakidz hai kaghtavaireri badmutian* [Concise outline of the history of the Armenian colonies]. Erevan, 1964.

Alboyajian, Arshag. *Badmutiun Hai Gesario* [History of the Armenians of Caesaria]. 2 vols. Cairo, 1937.

———. *Badmutiun hai kaghtaganutian* [History of Armenian emigration]. vol. 2. Cairo, 1955.

Asbarez, Joghovadzu Dasnamiagi 1908–1918 [Asbarez decennial collections, 1908–1918]. Fresno, n.d.

Ashjian, Arten. *Vijagatuits ev Badmutiun Arhachnortagan Themin Hayots Amerigayi* [Resume and history of the Armenian American prelatical diocese]. New York, 1949.

Chakmakjian, H. H. *Amerigahai Namagani* [Armenian American letter writer]. Boston, 1914.

Epilents. *Ash-Kar* [Spring-fall]. Boston, 1930.

Haig, Vahe. *Haireni Dzkhan* [Ancestral hearth]. 3 vols. Fresno, 1941–1947.

———. *Kharpert ev anor Vosgeten Tashde* [Kharpert and her golden plain]. New York, 1959.

Hushamadean Hai Oknutean Miutean 1910–1970 [Commemorative volume of the Armenian Relief Society 1910–1970]. Boston, 1970.

Jizmejian, Manug. *Badmutiun Amerigahai Kaghakagan Gusagtsuteants 1890–1925* [History of the Armenian American political parties 1890–1925]. Fresno, 1930.

Kaloian, Siragan. *Shiragi Hayutiun Kaghte tebi Ameriga* [The emigration of Armenians of Shirag to America]. Los Angeles, 1950.

Kalusdian, Krikor H. *Marash.* New York, 1934.

Kaprielian, M. Smpad. *Haigagan Jknajamn ev Veradznutiun* [The Armenian crisis and recovery]. Boston, 1905.

Keljik, Bedros. *Amerighai Badgerner* [Armenian American portraits]. New York, 1944.

Khan Azad [Nishan Garabedian]. "Hai Heghapoghagani husherits" [From the memoirs of an Armenian revolutionary], *Hairenik Amsakir* 5–8 (June 1927–May 1929).

Kosian, Hagop H. *Haik i Zmirnia ev i Schrchagais* [The Armenians of Smyrna and its environs]. Vienna, 1899.

Kuyumjian, Hagop. *Aha Kezi Amerigan* [This is America]. Boston, 1949.

Leo [A. Babakhanian]. *Tiurkahai Heghapohutean Kaghaparapanutiune* [Ideology of the Turkish Armenian revolution]. Paris, 1934.

Livlejian, Donabed G. *Hasgakagh* [Gleanings]. Fresno, 1955.

Manantian, Hagop H. *Knnagan Desutiun hai zhoghovrti badmutiun* [Critical history of the Armenian people]. Erevan, 1944.

Ohanian, Aram. *Arevelahai Dndesakidagan Mdki Badmutiunits* [History of the economic mind of Eastern Armenia]. Erevan, 1960.

Ormanian, Malachia. *Azkabadum* [History of the nation]. 3 vols. Constantinople-Jerusalem, 1913–1927.

Papazian, M. G. *M. Smpad Kaprielian.* Los Angeles, 1939.

Poladian, Antranig L. *Badmutiun Hayots Arapgiri* [History of the Armenians of Arapgir]. New York, 1969.

Raffi. *Dajgahaik* [The Turkish Armenians]. Vienna, 1913.

Sarafian, Kevork. *Badmutiun Antebi Hayots* [History of the Armenians of Aintab]. 2 vols. Los Angeles, 1953.

Seropian, Mushegh, ed., *Amerigahai Daretuitse 1912* [Armenian American yearbook 1912] Boston, 1912; *Amerigahai Daretuitse 1913.* Boston, 1913.

Sotsialisdagan Temogradagan Hnchagean Gusagtsutiun. *Hisnameag Eridasart Hayasdani 1903–1953* [Socialist Democratic Hnchagian party, 50th year collections of *Eridasart Hayastan,* 1903–1953]. New York, 1953.

Torosian, Bedros. *Amerigain Kaghakatsi* [American citizen]. West Hoboken, 1912.

——. *Serayin Aroghchabahutiun* [Sexual hygiene]. Boston, 1916.

Torosian, Hovannes. *Vark Mkhitara Appayi Sepasdatsio* [Life of Abbot Mkhitar of Sepastia]. Venice, 1932.

Varandian, Michael. *H. H. Tashnagtsutian Badmutiun* [History of the A. (Armenian) R. (Revolutionary) Federation]. 2 vols. Paris, 1932, and Cairo, 1950.

Vosgemadean, Haigagan Parekordzagan Enthanur Miutian [Golden book of the Armenian General Benevolent Union]. Paris, n.d.

Yerevanian, K. S. *Badmutiun Charsanjaki Hayots* [History of the Armenians of Charsanjak]. Beirut, 1956.

B. ENGLISH-LANGUAGE WORKS: THE BACKGROUND

Ahmad, Feroz. *The Young Turks.* Oxford, 1969.

Armenian General Benevolent Union. *Historic Outline, 1906–1946.* New York, 1948.

Arpee, Leon. *The Armenian Awakening.* Chicago, 1909.

——. *A History of Armenian Christianity.* New York, 1946.

Azhderian, Antranig. *The Turk and the Land of Haig.* New York, 1898.

Bailey, Frank Edgar. *British Policy and the Turkish Reform Movement: A Study in Anglo-Turkish Relations, 1826–1853.* Cambridge, Mass., 1942.

Barkley, Henry C. *A Ride Through Asia Minor and Armenia.* London, 1891.

Barton, James L. *Daybreak in Turkey.* Boston, 1908.

Blackwell, Alice Stone. *Armenian Poems.* Boston, 1896.

Bliss, E. M. *Turkey and the Armenian Atrocities.* Philadelphia, 1896.

Bryce, James. *Transcaucasia and Ararat.* 4th ed., revised. London, 1896.

Buxton, Noel, and Harold Buxton. *Travels and Politics in Armenia.* New York, 1914.

Caraman, Elizabeth. *Daughter of the Euphrates.* New York, 1939.

Chopourian, Giragos H. *The Armenian Evangelical Reformation.* New York, 1972.

Crawford, F. Marion. *Constantinople.* New York, 1895.

Daniel, Robert L. *American Philanthropy in the Near East 1820–1960.* Athens, Ohio, 1970.

Davison, Roderic. "The Armenian Crisis, 1912–1914." *American Historical Review* 53, no. 3 (1948).

———. *Reform in the Ottoman Empire, 1856–1876.* Princeton, 1963.

Der Nersessian, Sirarpie. *Armenia and the Byzantine Empire.* Cambridge, Mass., 1947.

Filian, George H. *Armenia and Her People.* Hartford, 1896.

Gaidzakian, Ohan. *Illustrated Armenia and the Armenians.* Boston, 1898.

Gibb, H. A. R., and Harold Bowen. *Islamic Society and the West.* Vol. 1. London, 1957.

Greene, Frederic Davis. *The Armenian Crisis in Turkey. The Massacre of 1894, Its Antecedents and Significance.* New York, 1895.

Hamlin, Cyrus. *Among the Turks.* New York, 1878.

———. *My Life and Times.* New York, 1893.

Harris, J. Rendell, and Helen B. Harris. *Letters from the Scenes of the Recent Massacres in Armenia.* New York, n.d.

Hartunian, Abraham H. *Neither to Laugh nor to Weep: A Memoir of the Armenian Genocide.* Boston, 1968.

Hepworth, George H. *Through Armenia on Horseback.* New York, 1898.

Hodgetts, E. A. Brayley. *Round About Armenia.* London, 1896.

Hovannisian, Richard. *Armenia on the Road to Independence, 1918.* Berkeley and Los Angeles, 1967.

Johnson, Clarence. *Constantinople Today, or The Pathfinder Survey of Constantinople.* New York, 1922.

Karajian, Hagop A. *Mineral Resources of Armenia and Anatolia.* New York, 1920.

Karpat, Kemal H *Turkey's Politics.* Princeton, 1959.

Kazemzadeh, Firuz. *The Struggle for Transcaucasia, 1917–1921.* New York, 1951.

Krikorian, Mesrob K. *Armenians in the Service of the Ottoman Empire, 1860–1908.* London, 1977.

Lang, David Marshall. *Armenia, Cradle of Civilization.* London, 1970.

Langer, William L. *The Diplomacy of Imperialism, 1890–1902.* 2nd ed. New York, 1956.

Leart, Marcel. *La question arménienne — à la lumière des documents.* Paris, 1913.

Lewis, Bernard. *The Emergence of Modern Turkey.* New York, 1961.

Lynch, H. F. B. *Armenia, Travels and Studies.* 2 vols. London, 1901.

Mandalian, James, ed. *Armenian Freedom Fighters: The Memoirs of Rouben Der Minasian.* Boston, 1956.

Mears, Eliot Grinell, ed. *Modern Turkey*. New York, 1924.

Mesrob, Kevork. *L'Arménie au point du vue géographique, historique, eth-nographique, statistique, et culturel*. Constantinople, 1919.

Missakian, J. *A Searchlight on the Armenian Question*. Boston, 1950.

Nalbandian, Louise. *The Armenian Revolutionary Movement*. Berkeley and Los Angeles, 1963.

Nazarbek, Avedis. *Through the Storm*. London, 1899.

Norehad, Bedros. *The Armenian General Benevolent Union*. N.p., n.d.

Norman, Charles B. *Armenia, and the Campaign of 1877*. London, 1878.

Ormanian, Malachia. *The Church of Armenia*. 2nd ed. Oxford, 1955.

Pears, Edwin. *Turkey and Its People*. 2nd ed. London, 1912.

The People of the Eastern Orthodox Churches. . . . Springfield, Mass., 1913.

Ramsaur, Ernest Edmondson, Jr., *The Young Turks*. Princeton, 1957.

Richter, Julius, *A History of the Protestant Missions in the Near East*. New York, 1910.

Sanjian, Avedis. *The Armenian Communities in Syria under Ottoman Dominion*. Cambridge, Mass., 1965.

Sarkissian, A. O. *History of the Armenian Question to 1885*. Urbana, Illinois, 1938.

Sarkissian, A. O., ed. *Studies in Diplomatic History and Historiography*. London, 1961.

Sarkissian, Karekin. *The Council of Chalcedon and the Armenian Church*, London, 1965.

Smith, Eli. *Researches of the Rev. E. Smith and Rev. H. G. O. Dwight in Armenia*. 2 vols. Boston, 1833.

Strong, William E. *The Story of the American Board*. Boston, 1910.

Totomiantz, Vakhan Fomich. *L'Arménie économique*. Paris, 1920.

Totovents, Vahan. *Scenes from an Armenian Childhood*. London, 1962.

Tozer, Henry Fanshawe. *Turkish Armenia and Eastern Asia Minor*. London, 1881.

The Treatment of Armenians in the Ottoman Empire, 1915–1916. London, 1916.

Ubicini, Abdolonyme. *Letters on Turkey*. 2 vols. London, 1856.

Williams, W. Llew. *Armenia: Past and Present*. London, 1916.

Yale, William. *The Near East: A Modern History*. Ann Arbor, 1958.

Young, George. *Constantinople*. London, 1926.

C. ENGLISH-LANGUAGE WORKS: THE NEW WORLD

Adamic, Louis. *A Nation of Nations*. New York, 1945.

American Men of Science. 3rd ed. New York, 1921.

The Armenians in Massachusetts. Boston, 1937.

Atamian, Sarkis. *The Armenian Community: The Historical Development of a Social and Ideological Conflict*. New York, 1955.

Avakian, Arra. *The Armenians in America*. Minneapolis, 1977.

Bagdikian, Ben. "Us Yankees." in Jack Antreassian, ed., *Ararat: A Decade of Armenian American Writing*. New York, 1969.

Barger, Harold, and Hans. H. Landsberg. *American Agriculture, 1899–1939.* New York, 1942.

Barsumian, Nazareth. *Stowaway to Heaven.* Wilmette, Illinois, 1960.

Berthoff, Rowland T. *British Immigrants in Industrial America, 1790–1950.* Cambridge, Mass., 1953.

Bogigian, Hagop. *In Quest of the Soul of Civilization.* Richmond, Virginia, 1925.

Brandenburg, Broughton. *Imported Americans.* New York, 1904.

Burnham, Irene H. *Not by Accident.* Boston, 1938.

Carpenter, Niles. *Immigrants and Their Children, 1920.* Washington, 1927.

Cole, Arthur H. *The American Carpet Manufacture.* Cambridge, Mass., 1941.
———. *The American Wool Manufacture.* 2 vols. Cambridge, 1926.

Cole, Donald B. *Immigrant City: Lawrence, Massachusetts, 1845–1921.* Chapel Hill, 1963.

Cook, Ralph Elliott. "The United States and the Armenian Question, 1894–1924." Ph.D. diss., Fletcher School of Law and Diplomacy, 1957.

Curti, Merle. *American Philanthropy Abroad.* New Brunswick, New Jersey, 1963.

Drachsler, Julius. "Intermarriage in New York City: A Statistical Study of the Amalgamation of European Peoples," *Studies in History, Economics and Public Law,* 94, no 2 (1921).

Eaton, Allen H. *Immigrant Gifts to American Life.* New York, 1932.

Eisen, Gustav. *The Raisin Industry.* San Francisco, 1890.

Ewing, John S., and Nancy P. Norton. *Broadlooms and Businessmen.* Cambridge, Mass., 1955.

Fresno County Centennial Almanac. Fresno, 1956.

Gilbert, Charles K., and Charles T. Bridgeman. *Foreigners or Friends.* New York, 1921.

Glidden, A. A. "Hood Rubber Company History 1896–1929." Typescript, n.d.

Goldman, Eric. *Rendezvous with Destiny.* New York, 1956.

Hagopian, John V. "Well, my father was an Armenian, yes," *Ararat* 2 (Summer 1961).

Hagopian, Richard. *Faraway the Spring.* New York, 1952.

Hall, Prescott F. *Immigration and its Effects upon the United States.* New York, 1906.

Hartmann, George Edward. *The Movement to Americanize the Immigrant.* New York, 1948.

Hichborn, Franklin. *Story of the Session of the California Legislature of 1909.* San Francisco, 1909.

Housepian, Marjorie. *A Houseful of Love.* New York, 1957.

Hovanesian, Archibald, Jr. "The Armenian Community: A Study in Social Change." B.A. thesis, Princeton University, 1962.

Kassabian, Nishan H. "Armenians and their Colony in Grand Rapids and Western Michigan," *Publications of the Historical Society of Grand Rapids.* Vol. I, no. 7 p. 7. Grand Rapids, 1912.

Kearney, M. T. "Fresno County . . . the center of the raisin and dried fruit industries, 1893" *Pamphlets on California,* 27, n.p., n.d.

Kenngott, George F. *The Record of a City.* New York, 1912.

Kulhanjian, Gary. *A Guide on Armenian Immigrants, Studies, and Institutions.* Ann Arbor, 1977.

LaPiere, Richard Tracy. "The Armenian Colony in Fresno County, California: A Study in Social Psychology." Ph.D. diss., Stanford University, 1930.

Lesley, Robert W. *History of the Portland Cement Industry in the United States.* Chicago, 1924.

Lynes, Russell. *The Tastemakers.* London, 1954.

Mahakian, Charles. "History of the Armenians in California." M.A. thesis, University of California, Berkeley, 1935.

Malcom, M. Vartan. *The Armenians in America.* Boston, 1919.

Mann, Arthur. *Yankee Reformers in the Urban Age.* Cambridge, 1954.

Mardikian, George. *Song of America.* New York, 1956.

Mason, Frank R. *The American Silk Industry and the Tariff.* Cambridge, Mass., 1910.

May, Ernest R. *Imperial Democracy.* New York, 1961.

Memorial and Biographical History of the Counties of Fresno, Tulare, and Kern, California. Chicago, 1892.

Michigan, A Guide to the Wolverine State. New York, 1941.

Minasian, Edward. "They Came from Ararat: The Exodus of the Armenian People to the United States." M.A. thesis, University of California, Berkeley, 1961.

Minassian, Oshagan. "A History of the Armenian Holy Apostolic Church in the United States (1888–1944)." Ph.D. diss., Boston University School of Theology, 1974.

Mirak, Robert. "Armenians." In *Harvard Encyclopedia of American Ethnic Groups,* edited by Stephan Thernstrom et al. Cambridge, Mass., 1980.

———. "Outside the Homeland: Writing the History of the Armenian Diaspora," *Recent Studies in Modern Armenian History.* Cambridge, Mass., 1972.

Mooradian, Moorad. "The Red Cross in Armenian: 1895." *Armenian Digest* (July-August 1973).

Moore, John Hammond. "America Looks at Turkey, 1876–1909." Ph.D. diss., University of Virginia, 1961.

Morison, Elting E., ed. *The Letters of Theodore Roosevelt* 8 vols. Cambridge, Mass., 1951–1954.

Mumford, John Kimberly. *Oriental Rugs.* 4th ed. New York, 1915.

Navin, Thomas R. *The Whitin Machine Works Since 1831.* Cambridge, Mass., 1950.

Nelson, Harold. "The Armenian Family: Changing Patterns of Family Life in a California Community." Ph.D. diss. University of California, Berkeley, 1954.

Nevins, Allan, ed., *Letters of Grover Cleveland.* New York, 1933.

Papazian, K. S. *Patriotism Perverted.* Boston, 1934.

Porter, Edward G. "Armenian Relief Measures." *The Independent.* March 5, 1896.

Richards, Laura E., and Maud Howe Elliott. *Julia Ward Howe 1819–1910.* 2 vols. Boston, 1916.

Roberts, Peter. *The New Immigration*. New York, 1912.

Roeding, George C. *The Smyrna Fig at Home and Abroad*. Fresno, 1903.

Ross, Edward A. *The Old World in the New*. New York, 1914.

Saroyan, William. *The Bicycle Rider in Beverly Hills*. New York, 1952.

———. *The Daring Young Man on the Flying Trapeze*. London, 1948.

———. *I Used to Believe I Had Forever, Now I'm Not So Sure*. New York, 1968.

———. *Places Where I've Done Time*. New York, 1972.

———. *The William Saroyan Reader*. New York, 1959.

Shiragian, Sona. "A Trip to Armenia." *The New Yorker* (April 27, 1963).

Surmelian, Leon Z. *I Ask You, Ladies and Gentlemen*. New York, 1945.

Tashjian, James H. *The Armenians of the United States and Canada*. Boston, 1947.

Todd, Robert E., and Frank B. Sanborn. *The Report of the Lawrence Survey*. Lawrence, Mass., 1912.

Treudley, Mary Bosworth. "An Ethnic Group's View of the American Middle Class." *American Sociological Review* 11 (1946).

Vandor, Paul E. *History of Fresno County California with Biographical Sketches*. 2 vols. Los Angeles, 1919.

Walker, Ben Randal, ed. *Fresno Community Book*. Fresno, 1946.

———. *The Fresno County Blue Book*. Fresno, 1941.

Wallis, Wilson D. *Fresno Armenians (to 1919)*. Lawrence, Kansas, 1965.

Warner, W. Lloyd, and Leo Srole. *The Social Systems of American Ethnic Groups*. New Haven, 1945.

Washburn, Charles G. *Industrial Worcester*. Worcester, 1917.

Wessel, Bessie Bloom. *An Ethnic Survey of Woonsocket, Rhode Island*. Chicago, 1931.

Who's Who in America. Vol. 14 (1926–1927). Chicago, 1926.

Winchell, Lilbourne A. *History of Fresno County*. Fresno, 1933.

Wittke, Carl. *We Who Built America*. New York, 1939.

Wolfe, Albert Benedict. *The Lodging House Problem in Boston*. Boston, 1906.

Woods, Robert A., ed. *The City Wilderness*. Boston 1898.

The Worcester Magazine, 1901–1917.

Wright, J. F. C. *Slava Bohu: The Story of the Dukhobors*. New York, 1940.

Young, Pauline V. *The Pilgrims of Russian-Town*. Chicago, 1932.

Young, T. M. *The American Cotton Industry*. London, 1902.

Index

355